Native Americans and Their Land

The Schoharie River Valley
New York

Mary Druke Becker

HERITAGE BOOKS
2006

HERITAGE BOOKS
AN IMPRINT OF HERITAGE BOOKS, INC.

Books, CDs, and more—Worldwide

For our listing of thousands of titles see our website
at
www.HeritageBooks.com

Published 2006 by
HERITAGE BOOKS, INC.
Publishing Division
65 East Main Street
Westminster, Maryland 21157-5026

Copyright © 2006 Mary Druke Becker

All rights reserved. No part of this book may be reproduced or transmitted in any form or by any means, electronic or mechanical, including photocopying, recording or by any information storage and retrieval system without written permission from the author, except for the inclusion of brief quotations in a review.

International Standard Book Number: 978-0-7884-3596-5

DEDICATED TO

The Iroquois Indian Museum

TABLE OF CONTENTS

NATIVE AMERICANS OF THE SCHOHARIE RIVER VALLEY vii
    Preface vii
    1700s Schoharie ix
    Native American Presence in the Schoharie Region x
    Who Were the Native Americans of Schoharie? xiii
    Eighteenth Century Native American Life in the Schoharie Region xv
    Eighteenth Century Chronology xxi
    Conclusion xxvii
SOURCES OF DOCUMENTS xxix
    Published Sources xxix
    Archives xxx
    Helpful Guides and Catalogues xxx
KEY TO CALENDAR OF DOCUMENTS xxxi
CALENDAR OF DOCUMENTS 1

NATIVE AMERICANS OF THE SCHOHARIE RIVER VALLEY AND THEIR LAND

Preface

In 1987, the Iroquois Indian Museum (at that time called the Schoharie Museum of the Iroquois Indian) sponsored a project to document Native American occupation of the Schoharie River Valley. I was hired to head that project. With the aid of superb volunteers, over five hundred documents pertaining to the Schoharie River Valley, many specifically relating to Native Americans, were located. The goal was to search for sources in order to present an historical perspective on Native Americans in the Schoharie River Valley, an important route of travel and settlement in what is now New York State. Research and analysis has continued. I present my interpretation of information gathered, with references to specific data, in this essay. A calendar of documents follows. The evidence of Native American occupation of the Schoharie River Valley is rich enough to provide an excellent, focused example of Native American life, the process of Euro-American settlement, and the alienation of Native American land.

I could not have completed my work successfully without the expert volunteer assistance of Sylvia Van Houten, a genealogist. She proceeded systematically through the Calendar of Indorsed Land Papers in the New York State Archives for citations to manuscripts pertaining to Schoharie; provided me with access to her files of personal names culled from church records; and made herself available for frequent consultation on the topography and history of the Schoharie River Valley.[1] Stephanie Shultes, an anthropologist who has been both an employee and a volunteer at the Iroquois Indian Museum, was another valuable associate on this project. She searched through the Indian treaties at the New York State Archives for information pertaining to Schoharie and scanned other manuscript sources. Also, discussions, friendly arguments, and continued intellectual stimulation through the years from John Ferguson, an anthropologist who is one of the founders of the Iroquois Indian Museum and was Chair of the Board of the Museum, have helped me in enhancing and refining my perspectives. I am grateful as well to the late Dr. Gunther Michelson, a scholar who did significant work in Iroquoian linguistics. He provided useful comments on a working draft of this essay.

I was well prepared to undertake the Iroquois Indian Museum project by my experience as Associate Editor of *Iroquois Indians: A Documentary History of the Diplomacy of the Six Nations and Their League*, a microfilm publication of documents pertaining to Iroquois treaties done through the Newberry Library in Chicago. The calendar that my colleagues Francis Jennings, William N. Fenton, David R. Miller, and I compiled for that project provided a model for the one presented here.[2]

---

[1] *Calendar of N.Y. Colonial Manuscripts Indorsed Land Papers in the Office of the Secretary of State of New York 1643-1803*, compiled by E. B. O'Callaghan, (Harrison, NY: Harbor Hill Books, 1987, Revised Reprint. Originally published Albany, NY: Weed, Parsons, and Co., 1864) and Calendar of Council Minutes 1668-1783, compiled by Berthold Fernow (Harrison, NY: Harbor Hill Books, 1987, Reprint; originally published New York State Library Bulletin 58, (History 6), Albany, 1902) were useful guides in the course of this project.

[2] *Iroquois Indians: A Documentary History of the Diplomacy of the Six Nations and Their League*, ed. by Francis Jennings, William N. Fenton, Mary A. Druke, and David R. Miller (Woodbridge, Ct: Research Publications, Inc., 1985).

I am grateful to staff members of all of the libraries and archives listed as sources of documents cited. They have been most gracious in answering questions, finding manuscripts, and providing information. A debt of gratitude is due especially to the staff of the New York State Archives, particularly to James D. Folts, William Gorman, and former archivist William Evans, and that of the New York State Library, most notably former archivist James Corsaro.

Last, but far from least, I am indebted to my husband, Charles A. Becker, and my son, Adrian B. D. Becker. Charles provided hours of patient toil in computer programming to format the original database on which this calendar was based. I could not have accomplished the project without his assistance, his advice, and listening ear. Adrian filed and sorted copies of manuscripts, proofed text, and rescued me from computer snafus. I thank all of the people who aided me in seeing this project to fruition. I accept, of course, full responsibility for the final product.

1700s Schoharie

The name "Schoharie" by itself refers to many things: an eighteenth century Native American settlement known as Schoharie, the Euro-American village of Schoharie, a county, a river, an area of land bordering the Schoharie River in what is now Upstate New York. During the time period of most data for this project (the eighteenth century), it was used most often to refer generically to an *area*. This encompassed the region from the confluence of the Schoharie and Mohawk rivers (Tienonderoga/Fort Hunter) to the source of the Schoharie River (south of Gilboa), including the drainage areas east and west of the river, an area also commonly known as the Schoharie River Valley.[3] One document specifically describes Schoharie as having these limits (1754,10,25).[4] Manuscripts from the eighteenth century note that the Schoharie River was also called the Tienonderoga River, Tienonderoga being the name of a Mohawk village on the south side of the Mohawk River where it meets the Schoharie (1720,06,03; 1725,10,04; 1733,10,16; 1737,10,17; 1754,11,01).

Particular locations are usually indicated in documents by specific phrases such as "where the Indians lived", "the Schoharie Patent" or "the village of Schoharie". Likewise, when the subject is the river or the county, the reference usually is unambiguous. If not obviously so, contextual remarks, sometimes including landmarks or boundary lines, most often clear up confusion.

Because the term "Schoharie", with its many variant spellings, was used in the past in both general and specific ways, the scope of the project for the Iroquois Indian Museum was defined as including the whole region.[5] It was important that this was done. Otherwise, crucial information might have been missed. For example, it has become clear that the eastern border of Mohawk country extended considerably east of the Schoharie River. Although Mohawk settlements were west of the Schoharie, Mohawks controlled land east of

---

[3] Tienonderoga is but one of several spellings found throughout historic documents. Others include Tiononderoge, Tionnondoroge, Tiononderoga, Tienonderoge, and Tiondorogue. The last version may be in some ways the most linguistically accurate. Linguistic evidence indicates that the first "n" that appears commonly in renderings of this name may be extraneous (Foster, Michael, personal communication, March 30, 2003; pp.51-51 in Lounsbury, Floyd *Iroquois Place-Names in the Champlain Valley*, Report of the New York-Vermont Interstate Commission on the Lake Champlain Basin, 1960, Legislative Document (1960), No. 9, pp. 23-66, Reprinted by The University of the State of New York, the State Education Departmant, Albany, 2000). I have chosen Tienonderoga because it appears frequently, and is similar to other orthographic renderings that also do, in the historic record. The rendering Tiondorogue is less common.

[4] Citations used here and throughout this essay refer to listings in the Calendar of Documents Pertaining to Native American Occupation of the Schoharie River Valley that follows this essay. Manuscripts from the eighteenth century note that the Schoharie River was also called the Tienonderoga River, Tienonderoga being the name of a Mohawk village on the south side of the Mohawk River where it meets the Schoharie (1720,06,03; 1725,10,04; 1733,10,16; 1737,10,17; 1754,11,01).

[5] Spelling of the name varies in historical documents. The following is at least a partial list: Schoharee, Schohoree, Schohary, Scohare, Schohere, Scohere, Skohare, Skoery, Schoharry, Schoharey, Shohary, Schohire, Scoharee, Schohara, Schowherre, Schory, Scokery, Schorie, Scohwee, Shorie, Scohare, Schoherry, Schokery, Skohaare, Eskahare, Schohang. One commonly accepted gloss of the name Schoharie is 'driftwood' or 'floodwood', from an analysis presented by William M. Beauchamp in 1907 (*Aboriginal Place Names of New York*, New York State Museum Bulletin 108, [Albany: N.Y. State Education Department, 1907], p. 126, 202). Gunther Michelson, working with the Iroquois Indian Museum on place names and personal names, suggests, however, that 'a natural bridge', a meaning attributed to the name by Franklin B. Hough in 1853, may be more accurate. Michelson identifies the term as being based on the noun root –(a)hsk(w)- 'bridge' and the verb root –ohar- 'suspend'. The phonemic spelling that he provides is *yohskohare?* (from unpublished List of Place Names provided to John Ferguson, Chair, Board of Trustees of the Iroquois Indian Museum, and to Mary Druke Becker, Research Associate, Iroquois Indian Museum, May/ June 1997; see also *A History of St. Lawrence and Franklin Counties, New York, from the Earliest Period to the Present Time*, by Franklin B. Hough [Albany, N.Y.: Little and Company, 1853], p. 180). See John P. Ferguson, *The Search for the Schoharie Mohawk*, May 2000 Edition, available on CD from the Department of Archaeology, Iroquois Indian Museum for a description of archaeological evidence linked to glosses of the name (p. 42).

that river as well. Mohawks, and interestingly enough, Oneidas, were ceding land twenty miles or so east of the Schoharie River and south of the Mohawk through the 1760s (1716,02,10; 1722,02,06; 1723,03,07; 1729,11,00; 1735,10,07; 1739,01,04; 1750,11,29; 1752,11,13; 1769,03,21 (2)). These cessions went undisputed. Mohawk and Oneida control, or assertion of control, over lands east of the Schoharie River would not have been clear if focus had only been on references to Schoharie proper.

Native American Presence in the Schoharie Region

Historical data about Native Americans in the Schoharie River Valley goes from rags to riches with the turn of the eighteenth century. They are substantial from the beginning of the century into the 1770s, at which time they again become scarce. In searching for historical documentation, therefore, from before and after the first three-quarters of the eighteenth century, one can have the impression that Native Americans came into the region from nowhere and disappeared as precipitously into thin air. Given that people do not do this, one is naturally led to question what happened. Were they really missing from the Schoharie Valley region, except during this period?[6] If so, where did they come from and where did they go?

The Schoharie region was obviously Native American land for hundreds, if not thousands, of years. Archaeological work in the Schoharie River Valley provides evidence of this. The Haviland site, near Cobleskill, excavated by the Iroquois Indian Museum and the State University of New York at Cobleskill, appears to be an Early Archaic workshop for manufacturing lithics, and has been preliminarily dated from 8,400 B.P.[7] The Chance site, studied by Kenneth Brate and William Ritchie in 1949, is on the east side of the Schoharie River, near its conjunction with Fox Creek. This site is dated mainly to the first half of the fifteenth century. However, it contained artifacts from the Late Archaic, Terminal Archaic, and Middle Woodland periods. As Dean Snow writes, "the site was a popular camp for many centuries prior to its use by fifteenth-century Mohawks."[8]

In 1973, William Ritchie and Robert Funk published an analysis of their excavation of the Narwold Site, an Owasco village.[9] Archaeologists Daniel F. Cassedy, Paul A. Webb, and James Bradley found archaeological evidence of protohistoric Iroquois occupation (c. A.D. 1575-1600) of the Vanderwerken Site on the Schoharie River, near the present town of Esperance, south of the Mohawk River in 1991. More archaeological work needs to be done to determine whether this was the site of a "seasonal hamlet" or of a permanent village. The evidence, however, points to intensive occupation, in either case.[10] The Bohringer site, on the west side of the

---

[6] It should be remembered, of course, that there is not necessarily a correspondence between the amount of documentary evidence about something and whether or not it exists or existed.

[7] John P. Ferguson, "The Haviland Site: The Early Archaic in Schoharie County", *The Bulletin: Journal of the New York State Historical Association*, Fall 1995, No. 110, pp. 1-15.

[8] Dean R. Snow, *Mohawk Valley Archaeology: The Sites*, Occasional Papers in Anthropology, No. 23, (University Park, PA: Matson Museum of Anthropology, The Pennsylvania State University, 1995), pp. 91-93. See also, William Ritchie, *The Chance Horizon: An Early Stage of Mohawk Iroquois Cultural Development*, New York State Museum Circular 29, (Albany: University of the State of New York, The State Education Department, 1952).

[9] William Ritchie and Robert Funk, *Aboriginal Settlement Patterns in the Northeast*, New York State Museum and Science Service Memoir 20, (Albany: University of the State of New York, the State Education Department, 1973).

[10] Cassedy, Daniel F., Webb, Paul A., and James Bradley, "The Vanderwerken Site: A Protohistoric Iroquois Occupation on Schoharie Creek", *The Bulletin: Journal of the New York State Archaeological Association*, Spring/Fall 1996, Nos. 111-112, pp. 21-34.

Schoharie River in the town of Fulton, New York, excavated by John Ferguson and James Osterhout through the Iroquois Indian Museum, provides evidence of an eighteenth century village.[11]

It is clear that Native American presence in the Schoharie River Valley has been long. The particulars of it, however, are often difficult to determine. More excavation of archaeological sites in the Schoharie River Valley is needed, and in some cases is being done. The region is rich with locations that merit careful archaeological study.[12] Since there is no documentary evidence before the sixteenth century, it remains for archaeologists to fill in the picture on the nature of Native American land use before that time.

Although there is historical documentation from the seventeenth century, it is scarce and does not provide much information pertaining to Native Americans in the Schoharie River Valley. In 1686, for example, one manuscript testifies that an individual named Andrew Brown applied for permission to purchase land at Schoharie from the Indians (1686,00,00); and in 1694, another records that Nicholas Bayard bought land at Schoharie from Native Americans (1694,05,16). These documents do not provide other data pertaining to the people from whom the purchases were made, however. They offer little, if any, evidence of the nature of the use or occupation of the land involved. We may be fairly sure only that land on the Schoharie River being purchased by Euro-Americans was considered to be Indian land. It is not known if it was used by the Native Americans as hunting or fishing, or other types of seasonal camps, or for stopping places along the river (which was undoubtedly an important route of travel), or if permanently occupied. There must have been, however, some reason for Euro-Americans who were not accustomed to making concessions to recognize Native American control over the land.

When one moves into the eighteenth century, the amount of documentation mushrooms. This is due no doubt in great part to the fact that Euro-Americans began settling in the Schoharie River Valley and hence began to make and leave records as they sought to acquire title to the land.[13] There is definite data from 1710 that the area was occupied. In August of that year, a Mohawk leader Hendrick specified that Native American land at Schoharie be reserved on the west side of the river. Hendrick, speaking for the Mohawk, claimed the land, and ceded and surrendered it to the Queen of England "for christian settlements", while reserving: 1) the area near the hill called Onistagrawa where the Indians "now" plant and 2) enough woodland to provide firewood for them (1710,08,22).[14] In 1713, we get even more direct evidence of Native American occupation in the form of a mission report from the Society for the Propagation of the Gospel (SPG) missionary William Andrews who listed Mohawk settlements. He mentioned two in the Mohawk River Valley: Tienonderoga (Fort Hunter) and Canajoharie. He said that there was also a third, small settlement called "Eskare", about twenty-four miles from Fort Hunter at the confluence of the Schoharie and Mohawk rivers (1713,09,07).

---

[11] Dean R. Snow, *op.cit.*, pp. 481-483; James A. Osterhout and John P. Ferguson, Schoharie Museum of the Iroquois Indian, Department of Archeology, Field Work Reports for 1985 and 1986, unpublished, on file at the Iroquois Indian Museum, Howes Cave, NY; and the detailed account of archaeological work undertaken by the Iroquois Indian Museum, by John P. Ferguson, *The Search for the Schoharie Mohawk, op.cit.*

[12] See Dean R. Snow, *op.cit.*, p. 15-18.

[13] A recent publication by Barbara J. Sivertsen contains a brief history of Schoharie during the first half of the eighteenth century and presents a chart listing the children of Karighondontee, a Mohawk leader living in Schoharie, and his wife Marie (*Turtles, Wolves, and Bears: A Mohawk History* [Bowie, MD: Heritage Books, Inc., 1996], pp. 72-79, 184-194).

[14] The meaning of the Mohawk "surrender" or "cession" is unclear. Native American deeds for land encompassed in this "cession" were sought and/or acquired by Euro-Americans well into the 1760s. Apparently, even for Euro-Americans, there was some acknowledgement of a retention of Native American rights to at least some of this land. The Native Americans who were involved most likely understood "cession" to mean an agreement that put the land under the protection of the Queen of England for use for "christian settlements", but did not entail the complete surrender of control over the land that is implied by the use of the English terms "surrender" or "cession" (See 1710,08,07-21).

Where was this settlement and what was it like? Andrews does not leave any details other than its distance from Fort Hunter and its population, which he lists as about forty. It is not clear that he ever visited Schoharie, but he tells us some interesting things about the villages in the Mohawk River Valley some of which might likely have applied as well to the settlement in the Schoharie River valley. He says that Tienonderoga "Stands by the ffort [i.e. Fort Hunter], consisting of 40 or 50 wigwams or houses, pallizadoed [sic] Round. another of their Chief Towns between 20 & 30 houses is 3 0r 4 and 20 miles distant from this. They have several other little Towns 7 or 8 houses in a Town, and single houses up and Down pretty near their Castle next to the ffort."[15] This settlement pattern of a main village with surrounding hamlets and a few single houses characterized Iroquois settlements in the first half of the eighteenth century.[16]

Data that I have gathered for this project give a broader picture of what life was like in the Schoharie Valley region. It seems clear from evidence from the 1700s that there was definitely at least one village, most probably on the west side of the river (1713,09,07; 1714,05,03; [1758,00,00]; [1763,11,18]). At one point at least, in the mid-eighteenth century, it was at what is known as the Bohringer site in the present day village of Middleburgh.[17] Whether it was always at this site, and/or only at this site, is unclear. It is known from studies of Iroquois settlement patterns that the Iroquois often tended to move villages every ten years or so because of firewood depletion, soil infertility, insect and worm infestation and/or for ritual reasons.[18] We should also remember Andrews comment about the dispersed nature of the settlements that he observed in the Mohawk River Valley. We are, of course, confined by archaeological exploration, by the limits of historical documentation, and oral tradition. We may never have the full picture.

There may also have been a seasonal settlement pattern as a map showing land reserved by the Indians in 1753 on the east side of the Schoharie "Being where they Live in winter" (1753,05,06) suggests. There are also data that indicate that, in ceding land to Euro-Americans throughout the 1700s, some was reserved by Indians on the east side of the river (1734,00,00; 1768,00,00). Apparently, they used land there for hunting, planting, gathering of wood, if not other things. Whether this was land of a main settlement or for winter camps as suggested by the 1753 map is not known. A document dated, [1734,00,00], refers to "Schoharie castles", in the plural. It is a distinct possibility that there were more than one. However, supporting evidence of specific multiple settlements, whether on the east or west side of the river, or both, is difficult to find. What is clear from documentary evidence--both in terms of maps and citations in deeds, surveys of land, etc.--is that Indians

---

[15] *The Faithful Mohawks*, by John Wolfe Lydekker, (Reprinted Port Washington, Long Island, N.Y.: Ira J. Friedman, Inc., 1968. Originally published in 1938), p. 37.

[16] See a 1755 map of the settlement of Onaquaga (Oquaga), a primarily Iroquois settlement southwest of Schoharie (*Onaquaga: Hub of the Border Wars of the American Revolution in New York State* by Marjory Barnum Hinman, [Copyright, Marjory Barnum Hinman, 1975. Printed in the United States of America by Valley Offset, Inc., 1975], p.2. Original map is in the Congregational Library in Boston.) For a discussion of the scattered nature of eighteenth century settlements, see "Otsiningo, an Example of an Eighteenth Century Settlement Pattern", by Dolores Elliott, In *Current Perspectives in Northeastern Archeology: Essays in Honor of William A. Ritchie*, ed. by Robert E. Funk and Charles F. Hayes III, *Researches and Transactions of the New York State Archeological Association* 17(1): 100-101; see also Dean R. Snow, *The Iroquois*, (Cambridge, MA & Oxford: Blackwell Publishers), p. 133; and Dean R. Snow, *Mohawk Valley Archaeology: The Sites*, *op.cit.*, p. 471.

[17] Dean R. Snow, *op.cit.*, p. 471, 481-483.

[18] For information about village removal, see *Aboriginal Settlement Patterns in the Northeast*, by William A. Ritchie and Robert E. Funk, New York State Education Department Memoir 20, February 1973, especially pp. 361-369; "Northern Iroquoian Horticulture and Insect Infestation: a Cause for Village Removal," by William A. Starna, George R. Hamell, and William L. Butts, *Ethnohistory* 31(3): 197-204 (1984); David Guldenzopf, "Frontier Demography and Settlement Patterns of the Mohawk Iroquois, *Man in the Northeast*, Spring 1984, 27: 88-90; William N. Fenton, *The Great Law and the Longhouse: A Political History of the Iroquois Confederacy*, (Norman: University of Oklahoma Press, 1998), p. 23.

at Schoharie did have at least one settlement on the west side of the river, and made use of land on the east side of the river.[19]

There are many references to cessions of land on the east and west sides of the Schoharie. Attention to the nature of the cession is important not only for understanding of the culture of the Indian inhabitants, but also of the differences between Native American and Euro-American views toward land. Use of wide expanses of land was a fundamental part of Iroquois lifestyle, particularly on river systems like the Schoharie. Travel was widespread up and down these river systems--for hunting, fishing, trading, counseling, visiting. Andrews wrote in 1713 "there are seldom above half the Indians at home together, but always coming and going." It was upon use of the land that the Indians based, and Euro-Americans recognized, their claim to it.[20]

Evidence from a variety of sources throughout the 1700s indicates that the size of Native American settlement at Schoharie was relatively small (probably with no more than about 100 inhabitants at any one time). In 1760, for example, Conrad Weiser, a prominent negotiator with Native Americans for the colonial government of Pennsylvania, identified the Schoharie Indian settlement as a "small Indian Mohocks [Mohawks] Town" about 36 miles from Albany. Weiser lived about two miles from the village while growing up from 1714-1729 (1750,08,25-10,13). Granted, population figures are often open to interpretation. The sources from William Andrews (1713,09,07), to Conrad Weiser (1750,08,25-10,13), to William Johnson, English Superintendent of Indian Affairs, (1758,11,18-12,04; 1770,09,04), to returns at Niagara in 1783 (1783,09,25) are consistent, however, in categorizing it as small. Also, related data such as attendance figures for councils, numbers of warriors involved in certain expeditions, all indicate that numbers from Schoharie were proportionately small, compared to numbers of Indians from Canajoharie and the Lower Mohawk Village (1760,09,13; 1760,10,00; 1764,07,00; 1768,09,15-10,30). Nonetheless, Schoharie was a vibrant community, linked intricately to the rest of Iroquoia, to other Indian people, and to Euro-Americans.

---

[19] See also John P. Ferguson, *The Search for the Schoharie Mohawk, op.cit.*, pp. 72. Barbara J. Sivertsen in *Turtles, Wolves, and Bears: A Mohawk Family History* writes as follows about villages at Schoharie: "In the Schoharie River Valley in 1712 there were several Indian settlements. The main settlement, called Eskahare, was about twenty-four miles south of Ticonderoge and had about forty people in seven or eight houses. It was probably above Central Bridge on both sides of the creek and was later abandoned or moved several miles up the valley to the site of the old Schoharie railroad depot. The latter place was occupied by the Mohawks nearly to the time of the Revolution and contained a burying ground. Eight miles south of Eskahare was another Indian settlement called the Wilder Hook on about four hundred acres of land on the west bank of Schoharie Creek near Middleburgh. . . By 1712 there were also Mohegans living along Schoharie Creek in a small settlement on the east bank in present day Middleburgh." This information, with the exception of the reference to Eskahare (which comes from William Andrews account), however, is speculative based primarily on early nineteenth century Euro-American traditions written down by Jeptha R. Simms, *History of Schoharie County and the Border Wars of the Revolution* (Albany, NY: Munsell & Tanner, 1845 and John M. Brown, *Brief Sketch of the First Settlement of the County of Schoharie by the Germans*, (Schoharie, NY: Printed for the Author, by L. Cuthbert, 1823). Although it is likely that there was more than one settlement, hard data are difficult to find.

[20] For a discussion of Iroquois concepts of property rights, see Mary Druke Becker, "'We are an Independent Nation", *Buffalo Law Review* 46(3): 987-989; Daniel K. Richter, *The Ordeal of the Longhouse: The Peoples of the Iroquois League in the Era of European Colonialization* (Chapel Hill and London: Published for the Institute of Early American History and Culture, Williamsburg, Virginia, by the University of North Carolina Press, 1992), pp. 21-24; and William A. Starna, "Aboriginal Title and Traditional Iroquois Land Use An Anthropological Perspective," In *Iroquois Land Claims*, ed by Christopher Vecsey and William A. Starna, pp. 31-48.

Who were the Native Americans of Schoharie?

Schoharie was considered (certainly by Euro-Americans and most probably by Indians as well) primarily as a Mohawk village (1750,08,25-10,13; 1758,05,17; 1794,07,31 (2)). Mohawks clearly predominated. The association of Mohawks with Schoharie, however, can mask the ethnic diversity of Indian settlement of the region. Schoharie was referred to by William Johnson in the mid-eighteenth century as an emigrant village ([1763,11,18]; [1763,11.18] (2)). As such, it most likely spun off of the Mohawk village of Tienonderoga (Lower Mohawk Village) in the Mohawk River Valley. Links with this village, and another founded in the Mohawk River Valley in the late 1740s, Canajoharie, were strong throughout the eighteenth century. Indians of both of these Mohawk settlements, for example, sometimes ceded land at Schoharie both alone and in conjunction with Indians of Schoharie. There is no evidence disputing these cessions on the grounds that the Indians were from these two settlements rather than from Schoharie. Moreover, Indians of Schoharie often acted in concert with Indians of Canajoharie and the Lower Mohawk Village (1757,12,27). The links between individuals of these settlements were most likely based primarily on kinship and affinity, and occasionally on ritual friendships.[21] Schoharie was also the residence of other people of different Indian groupings, in addition to Mohawks, who were interrelated through such ties, including refugees moving from other locations.[22]

In the late 1750s Mahicans were moving to Schoharie and one subsequently finds several references to Mahicans of Schoharie (1757,09,15-20; 1757,09,16; 1760,09,13; 1761,12,23; 1764,03,05-23). Oneidas were also at Schoharie, hunting, if not living there (1758,12,05-09). William Johnson identified Schoharie in 1757 as a small settlement of Six Nations people (1757,09,28). After Seth a prominent chief of Schoharie died in 1756, warriors of Schoharie went out to secure a prisoner or scalp with which to condole his death (1757,05,24). I do not know which they brought back, but if it was a prisoner, he or she might very likely have been incorporated into the family of the deceased in the Iroquois pattern. During the mid-1700s warfare with the Flatheads (Catawbas) also was going on. Warfare was another source of prisoners. As Warren Johnson, William Johnson's brother, wrote in 1760-61, "When the Indians lose a man in Action, & chance to take an Enemy prisoner [sic], he belongs to the family of the Deceased, who take great Care of him, & look on him in the Same light as the Person lost, & even leave him the same fortune." (1760,06,29-1761,07,03 [p. 191]). Some of the presence of people other than Mohawks came through these channels. In writing about a visit to Schoharie in 1753, the missionary Gideon Hawley explained that the mother of his friend Jonah alias T'hanhanagwanageas at Schoharie "was a very old person, and of French extract, and full blooded, being captured from Canada when very young" (1794,07,31 (2)). Jonah's wife was Tuscarora.

As for links between the Native American settlement at Schoharie and the Six Nations confederate council at Onondaga, the Indian village at Schoharie in being largely occupied by Mohawks was primarily an Iroquois settlement; and village leaders participated in Six Nations affairs. For example, thirty-six Indians of Schoharie attended the treaty at Fort Stanwix in 1768 (1768,09,15-10,30). They frequently joined in conferences involving all of the Six Nations of the Iroquois Confederacy (Mohawk, Oneida, Onondaga, Cayuga, Seneca, and Tuscarora) and participated in war parties composed of Six Nations Indians. Nonetheless, they apparently did not hesitate to distinguish themselves from the Onondaga council, the central confederate

---

[21] Warren Johnson wrote in a journal from 1760-61, when visiting his brother William in Mohawk country, "If an Indian takes you for a Mate, or friend, he will doe any thing for you, & Expects the same from you; but must have the greatest opinion of you before they commence such a friendship." (1760,06,29-1761,07,03 [p. 206].) See Barbara J. Sivertsen, *op.cit.*, pp. 72-79, 184-194 for information about kinship ties involving individuals living at Schoharie.

[22] Dean Snow, *op.cit.*, p. 472; Laurence M. Hauptman, "Refugee Havens: The Iroquois Villages of the Eighteenth Century," In *American Indian Environments: Ecological Issues in Native American History*, (Syracuse, NY: Syracuse University Press, 1980), pp. 128-139.

council, when it was to their advantage. In 1757, a Schoharie leader, David, and two others of Schoharie complained to William Johnson, "Our Young Men are not so well pleased as they ought to be, they think the Six Nations have been taken more notice of than they, altho not so deserving, which makes them discontented." (1757,02,20-04,01).[23]

There is no evidence of confederate chiefs at Schoharie. It should be noted, however, that there is little evidence of individual confederate chiefs for any of the Six Nations during the eighteenth century. Whether lack of evidence represents absence of these positions in the eighteenth century or the failure of Euro-Americans to hear, recognize, and/or record the names is not known. Interestingly enough, however, the manuscript for the *Iroquois Book of Rites*, presenting the Roll Call of Chiefs (the names of the founders of the Iroquois confederacy which, according to oral tradition, have been passed down through time to the chiefs of the confederacy), was reportedly written by a man named David of Schoharie.[24] If this is correct, the link of Schoharie with the confederate council may have been stronger than other evidence indicates.

In addition to interrelations with other Native Americans, Indians at Schoharie interacted with Euro-Americans as well. As Euro-American settlement began and increased in the Schoharie River Valley, Euro-Americans were accepted by the Indians of Schoharie in most cases as neighbors, sometimes as friends, other times as intruders. Intermarriage was not uncommon, as church records show.[25]

Eighteenth Century Native American Life in the Schoharie Region

Native Americans in the Schoharie River Valley lived in bark houses, at least for the first half of the eighteenth century. William Andrews described ones in the Mohawk River Valley in 1713 as "made of Mats & bark of Trees together with poles about 3 or 4 yards high".[26] A map of the area around the village of Schoharie, drawn in 1734, is illustrated with what is called an Indian "Wigwam" (1734,00,00). These were probably longhouses made of bark, as Andrews indicated. As the century wore on, most homes probably shifted gradually to single-family dwellings built in Euro-American styles, as they did in the Mohawk River Valley.[27] I have not found direct evidence of this at Schoharie, however.

Andrews described beds for sleeping as being "a Mat or a skin".[28] Warren Johnson, William Johnson's brother, writing in a journal from 1760-1761 noted from his experiences among Native Americans in the Mohawk River Valley that they sleep on bear and deer skins. He also gives additional information about their homes, stating, "Indians keep their Corn, over their fires, or on Lofts" (1760,06,29-1761,07,03 [p. 191]).

Iroquoians of Schoharie, like their brethren in the Mohawk River valley, were agriculturalists. (1710,08,22; 1722,09,26). William Andrews reported in 1713 that the women "hoe the Ground, plant ye Corne

---

[23] This may reflect more of an attempt by David and his associates to manipulate William Johnson for more attention to them and their affairs, however, than dissatisfaction with the Six Nations council. Note the reference to "Young Men". The Six Nations council, being associated with elders and peace, was commonly juxtaposed with the Young Men, the warriors.

[24] *The Iroquois Book of Rites*, ed. by Horatio Hale. (Reprinted with an introduction by William N. Fenton, Toronto: University of Toronto Press, 1963. First published by D. G. Brinton, Philadelphia, 1883), p. 42.

[25] Baptism Records, St. Paul's Lutheran Church, Schoharie, N.Y., 1728-1899; Genealogical Records of Schoharie County, Schoharie County Historical Society, Schoharie, N.Y., Cady Records; Schoharie Reformed Church, 1732-1892.

[26] *The Faithful Mohawks*, by John Wolfe Lydekker, (Reprinted Port Washington, Long Island, N.Y.: Ira J. Friedman, Inc., 1968. First Published in 1938), p. 37.

[27] Dean R. Snow, *The Iroquois*, op.cit., p. 131, 141; Dean R. Snow, *Mohawk Valley Archaeology: The Sites*, op.cit., p. 471.

[28] Ibid.

[sic]"²⁹ In 1755, William Johnson noted in his accounts, "To David of Schoharee [sic] who come wth. 6 young Men to go to War, Cash to send home to pay for Cutting his Grain, &c." (1755,03,00-1756,10,00 [Sept. 14, 1756]). When Mahicans of Schoharie visited William Johnson in 1757, he admonished them to plant corn (1757,05,04-12). They were just moving among the Indian people already settled at Schoharie. The agriculture was apparently slash and burn, or a modification thereof. Warren Johnson stated, "When clearing Land, the[y] Set fire to the Timber & burn it to ashes, which they Scatter about on the ground; . . . they never clear more Land than Serves for their Own Use." (1760,06,29-1761,07,03 [p. 195]).

Foodstuffs for the Native Americans of Schoharie were varied. Like Mohawks in the Mohawk River Valley, they most likely ate agricultural products and deer, bear, and small game, roots, nuts, and fruits hunted and gathered in fields and forest, and fish from streams and rivers.³⁰ Apparently the Indians of Schoharie also ate domesticated pork as well, at least occasionally by the mid-1700s (1758,12,05-09).³¹ Warren Johnson reported in 1760-61: "Indians chiefly live on boiled Indian Corn." (1760,06,29-1761,07,03 [p. 196]); Indians feast greatly upon Dogs; both white People & Indians eat bears' Flesh."; "They put Lice on Broth to make it rich."; and he mentions fishing for salmon (1760,06,29-1761,07,03 [pp. 196, 186, 197]). He notes, "The Indians are great Eaters, yet can fast ten, or twelve Days on Water" (1760,06,29-1761,07,03 [p. 199]).

Hunting was an occupation of the men in spring, summer, and fall. Women helped in carrying venison out of the woods (1760,06,29-1761,07,03 [p. 199]).³² Warren Johnson had several things to say about hunting, "The Indians have particular Hunting Ground for Each Tribe, & never intrude upon One another's Places"; ". . .the Indians have a Method of calling Deer to them, by immitating [sic] a Fawn. There is Plenty of Game at the Ohio & Virginia, Indians, good Archers, can kill any thing with Bows & Arrows."; "April the 15th [1761] many Indians going out on their Spring Hunt. take Snow Shoes with them, as the Snow is Still 4 foot Deep in many places backwards in the Woods." (1760,06,29-1761,07,03 [pp 197, 205, 210]). A threat used by Indians of Schoharie against the Esopus or Delawares if they attempted to sell any land west of the Catskill hills was that they would be hunted up "like Deer' (1756,05,17). Hunting was very much a part of their lives.

There were other activities in addition to agriculture, hunting, and fishing that provided for the livelihood of the Native Americans of Schoharie, as well. The missionary Gideon Hawley, writing about a trip to Schoharie in 1753, referred to some Indians at Schoharie "who the summer passed had been gathering, with their wives and children genseng [sic] root for the European market." (1794,07,31 (2)). Payment for such items was often made in terms of trade goods. There was some participation in the cash market, too, however, at least by the mid-eighteenth century. William Johnson noted in his accounts from 1758 through 1759 that Seth of Schoharie requested cash "in lieu of his laced Cloaths [clothes]" (1758,11,00-1759,12,00 [May 13, 1759]). Native American residents of Schoharie were given cash quite often by William Johnson (1758,11,00-1759,12,00; 1755,03,00-1756,10,00--Aug 6,1756 [Sept. 14, 1756]). Johnson's brother Warren reported in 1760, "An Indian makes 40 L & upwards yearly by hunting Winter, Spring & Fall. The Indian Women make up their

---

²⁹Lydekker, op.cit., p. 38.

³⁰ James A. Osterhout and John P. Ferguson in Schoharie Museum of the Iroquois Indian, Department of Archaeology, Field Work Reports for 1985-1986 note that they found evidence of a diet of "mainly deer, with occasional bear and pig, some fish, in addition to corn, beans, butternuts, hazel and hickory nuts" (p. 3, unpublished, available at the Iroquois Indian Museum, Howes Cave, NY). See also John P. Ferguson, *The Search for the Schoharie Mohawk, op.cit.*, pp. 20,29, 60, 67-68. For information about the Mohawk River Valley, see Dean R. Snow, *Mohawk Valley Archaeology: The Sites, op.cit.*, pp. 478, 492, 493, 495.

³¹ Dean R. Snow notes that cow, pig, sheep/goat, and chicken remains have been found in archaeological work at the Indian Castle (Canajoharie) Site Assemblage, dating from 1755-1776, in the Mohawk River Valley, see *Mohawk Valley Archaeology: The Sites, op.cit.*, p. 493.

³²See also, Lydekker, *op.cit.*, p. 38.

Corn & there is 8s-6d Currency for making A Shirt." (1760,06,29-1761,07,03 [p. 188]). European manufactured products such as rifles, ammunition, knives, ribbons, clothes, pipes, scissors, razors, and needles all found their way to Native Americans of Schoharie (1746,12,13-1747,11,07 [Apr. 29, 1747]; 1755,03,00-1756,10,00 [Apr. 24, 1756]; 1758,11,00-1759,12,00 [Nov. 16, 1758, May 13, 1759]; 1760,06,29-1761,07,03 [p. 193]).[33]

The Native Americans of Schoharie relied heavily on wood stores from the forests around them (primarily for firewood), with women usually being the ones to gather it (1710,08,22; 1760,06,29-1761,07,03 [pp. 187-188].)[34] Warren Johnson reported that the bark of trees was sometimes used for tobacco, and he noted that the Indians "make Charcoal of Wood" (1760,06,29-1761,07,03 [pp. 211; 195]). They also, according to Johnson, "know all Medicinal herbs". He reported, "They are Excellent at curing Disorders by herbs gathered in the woods, they cure the french Disease [i.e., venereal disease] well, by herbs; they have got it, & other Disorders very much among them" (1760,06,29-1761,07,03 [p. 200, 195]).

William Andrews wrote in 1713, of the Mohawks of the Mohawk River Valley, "Their Cloathing is a Match [?] Coat like a Mantle either a blankett or a bear's skin... They paint & grease themselves much with bears' fat clarified, cut their hair off from one side of their heads and some of that on the other they tie up in Knots upon the Crown with ffeathers [sic], Tufts of ffur [sic] upon their Ears and some of them wear a Bead fastened to their Noses with a Thread hanging down to their Lips, Bead and Wampum about their Hocks and wrists." (Lydekker, p. 37). It is likely that Indians of Schoharie dressed similarly. Later, in 1760-61, Warren Johnson's journal indicates that not much had changed by way of personal adornment. He noted, ". . .most Indians have their Ears cut, & Trinkets in them, & their Noses, which they think a great Ornament: . . ." (1760,06,29-1761,07,03 [p. 201]). Johnson reported that most of the men went bare-headed and plucked their beards (1760,06,29-1761,07,03 [p. 200, 205]). This is probably what they did on a daily basis. Other evidence indicates that they wore headdress for warfare (1747,04,29). Johnson witnessed tattooing, as well (1760,06,29-1761,07,03 [p. 194]). "Indian shoes", most probably moccasins, are referred to by Johnson. He also noted, however, that the Indians "are accustomed to keep in their Toes to avoid stump's in the woods", suggesting that in some instances at least they went bare-footed (1760,06,29-1761,07,03 [p. 204, 190)].

There is evidence, too, however, that the Native Americans of Schoharie and the Mohawk River Valley were wearing some products of European manufacture (1758,11,00-1759,12,00--25 Nov 1758 [p. 151]; 1764,01,02-31; 1758,11,18-12,04; 1755,03,00-1759,10,00 [p. 611]). A French blanket given to an Indian of Schoharie by William Johnson in 1758-59 may very well have been used in a traditional manner as a mantle mentioned by Andrews (1758,11,00-1759,12,00--May 1, 1759, p. 166). Other times, however, European items were worn in a Euro-American manner.[35]

---

[33] See John P. Ferguson, *The Search for the Schoharie Mohawk, op.cit.*, pp. 67-71 for a discussion of use of artifacts of Euro-American manufacture by native inhabitants of Schoharie. Pp. 54-61 of this work contain an inventory of artifacts found in excavations by the Iroquois Indian Museum. Comparing the documentary and archaeological evidence can be enlightening.

[34] See also, Lydekker, *op.cit.*, p. 38.

[35] Matchcoats and shirts, for example, were popular. The Mohawk leader Joseph Brant's response to a request that he have his portrait painted in 1816, however, may shed some light on attitudes toward such clothing. As Isabel Thompson Kelsey explains in her biography of Joseph Brant, "Joseph protested he had brought no Indian regalia, for of course he must be painted as an Indian. The lady of the house thought that deficiency was easily remedied. She went out and bought some figured calico, and an Indian shirt was quickly stitched together. With the addition of a few beads and an earring, Joseph was able to look as he ought, and he sat for his portrait." (*Joseph Brant 1743-1807 Man of Two Worlds* [Syracuse, NY: Syracuse University Press, 1884], p. 645). Euro-American clothing might be fine for day-to-day wear. It did not symbolize Indianness, however. Although Brant certainly wore Euro-American clothing as the anecdote indicates that he did at the time, I am not aware of any portrait of him in clothing that was strictly Euro-

Both William Andrews and Warren Johnson reported the existence of cradleboards. Andrews stated that women "carry the Children about at their backs".[36] Johnson described them more specifically, "An Indian Cradle (which they mostly all use) is a flat Board with a Top over the Childs face, on which hangs a Curtain. & the Child bound round to keep it Straight; They have a belt fixed to the Cradle, which they put round them, & carry it in that Manner." (1760,06,29-1761,07,03 [p. 192]).

The Indians of Schoharie traveled along well-worn paths to hunting grounds, other Indian villages, councils, and warfare (1728,04,25; 1751,05,06; [1751,00,00]; 1773,02,15). They were very familiar with the woods. Warren Johnson noted, "They know in the Woods, whether People passed by, lately by the impression of the Leaves, & their Numbers, by the Paths they make." He mentioned that the women sometimes go as many as thirty miles into the forests after deer that the men have killed simply by following broken twigs that the men have left every three or four miles (1760,06,29-1761,07,03, [p. 199]). Horses were available, although I do not know to what extent they were used (1760,06,29-1761,07,03 [p. 197]). Long-distance journeys and fishing were undertaken by canoe (1760,06,29-1761,07,03 [p. 190, 197]). Indians traveled by snow shoes in winter. Warren Johnson also observed that most had sleighs for winter travel, as well (1759,02,10; 1760,06,29-1761,07,03 [p. 199, 190]).

Christianity was practiced by Native Americans of Schoharie, many of whom were baptized.[37] The missionary Gideon Hawley conducted services at Schoharie in 1753. From his description, it is clear that not everyone attended, however. He wrote, "Those who are in meeting behave devoutly in time of service. But without, they are at play. I have been at their meetings, when the boys through the service, and even at the celebration of the Lords'-supper, have been playing bat and ball the whole term [sic] around the house of God. Coming out of meetings, we observed the lower orders at all sorts of recreation. To us, who had been used to the strictures of a New-England Sabbath, it appeared very profane. But custom will make any thing familiar." (1794,07,31 (2)) Life was obviously not all drudgery! One of Gideon Hawley's friends Jonah, whom he visited at Schoharie, and who was apparently a very devout Christian, commonly spent the winters at the missionary Indian settlement at Stockbridge (1794,07,31 (2)).

Evidence that traditional beliefs were very much a part of the lives of many of the Indians can also be found. Hawley described the Indian guide who led him from Fort Hunter to Schoharie, stopping near Schoharie to look for a stone, which he then threw on a heap of stones. When asked why he did this, he informed Hawley that ". . .his father practiced it, and enjoined it on him." He was reluctant to discuss it further with Hawley (1794,07,31 (2)). Warren Johnson noted several times in his journal that burial was done with much solemnity, often involving traditional condolence practices. He further noted, "Indians greatly reverence their forefathers, whom they look upon to have been the wisest of Men, & are themselves obliged to such persons as keep up to their Laws, Ceremonies, & Customs. . ." (1760,06,29-1761,07,03 [pp. 189, 197, 204, 191]).

The Native Americans of the Schoharie River Valley had several traditional ways of communicating messages via lasting symbols. Warriors sometimes marked trees, for example, to give an account of numbers of the enemy killed or captured on an expedition. Such a tree was listed as a boundary marker in a land deed in the Schoharie region, "Beginning at a certain large tree formerly marked & painted by the Indians standing near the

---

American. Euro-American and Indian dress was apparently distinct to contemporaries. The distinction was subtle, however. Often the items classified as "Indian dress" were of Euro-American manufacture, as in the case of the "Indian shirt" stitched together by Mrs. Ames. The way they were worn, however, classified them as Indian or not.

[36]Lydekker, op. cit., p. 37.

[37]Baptism Records, St. Paul's Lutheran Church, Schoharie, N.Y., 1728-1899; Genealogical Records of Schoharie County, Schoharie County Historical Society, Schoharie, N.Y., Cady Records; Schoharie Reformed Church, 1732-1892.

fort path from Fort Hunter to Scohary" (1737,10,12). William Johnson reported in 1771 that "in things of much Consequence they usually delineate a steel [originally flint]. . . they call Canniah. . . & themselves Canniungaes ['People of the Flint', Mohawks]." Clan totems signified the affiliation of signers of deeds (1723,02,06; 1734,00,00; 1736,08,13; 1742,08,30; 1751,05,23 (2); 1752,11,09; 1766,10,03 (3); 1768,06,10; 1769,02,08; 1771,02,28). Wampum, beads made from quahog clam shells and grouped into strings or belts, provided a record of important negotiations (1771,02,28).[38] Speeches and/or messages were associated with these strings or belts of wampum. Warren Johnson wrote in 1760-61, "An Indian letter or message is A String of Wampum." (1760,06,29-1761,07,03 [p. 195]).

As contact with Euro-Americans increased in the eighteenth century, knowledge of English increased as well, particularly among Christianized Indians (1771,02,28). Some became literate in English. Instead of clan totems or X's, they began signing their Christian names or initials to deeds (1753,05,19; 1766,10,03).

There seem to have been some significant groupings of Indians at Schoharie. Among the data on personal names that I have, certain names appear in specific contexts more than others. For example, David ("Otkoghraro") and Joseph ("Attrewaghti", "T'hrewaghty") are most frequently found in context of warfare, while Seth is rarely, if ever, referred to as a warrior.[39] Moreover, names that appear on Indian deeds, and the groupings of them are pretty uniform through time. This leads to the hypothesis that distinctions were made between warriors and sachems (peace chiefs). There are also some data that indicate that the distinction between young and old, and the association of warriors with the former and sachems with the latter may be appropriate (1755,03,00-1756,10,00, [Sept. 14, 1756, Oct. 3, 1756]). This is consistent with other data that we have on the Iroquois. For example, Warren Johnson wrote of the Mohawks in 1760-61, "Indian Warriours unacquainted with managing affairs, Sachems doe all & seldom goe out to fight . . ." (1760,06,29-1761,07,03 [p. 189]; see also, 1757,02,20-04,01; 1758,06,21-07,01).

Warriors and sachems do not appear to be groupings that are totally exclusive, however. For example, Hance Ury, who is commonly found as a signer of deeds, a function appropriate to sachems, is in one instance, in 1751, said to be away fighting Flathead (1751,05,23). This does not lead me to throw away the hypothesis, for I am reminded of a speech of the Oneida, Skaroyady, in December 1754, "What I am now going to say is in the Character of a Warrior. I lay down the Counsellor, and take up the Warrior."[40] Moreover, in the Constitution of the League of the Iroquois, provisions are made for a peace chief to lay up his horns to go to war.[41]

Warfare was highly ritualized (1755,03,00-1756,10,00 [Aug. 6, 1756; Oct. 3, 1756]; 1757, 05,27-06,07). Warren Johnson reported, "When going [to war] all Sing the War song, & get a Charge from the Old Women, particularly to behave well, & not to be a Discredit to themselves or their forefathers. " (1760,06,29-1761,07,03 [p. 192]; see also [pp. 189,192, 194, 206]). On at least one occasion, women and children accompanied men

---

[38]See also, Lydekker, op. cit., p. 45. For a discussion of the role of wampum, see William N. Fenton, *The Great Law and the Longhouse: A Political History of the Iroquois Confederacy, op.cit.*, pp. 224-239. Mary A. Druke, "Iroquois Treaties: Common Forms, Varying Interpretations," pp. 85-98, in *The History and Culture of Iroquois Diplomacy: An Interdisciplinary Guide to the Treaties of the Six Nations and Their League*, ed. by Francis Jennings, William N. Fenton, Mary A. Druke, and David R. Miller (Syracuse, N.Y.: Syracuse University Press, 1985), pp. 88-90.

[39] First names alone are commonly used in documents to identify Native Americans in the Schoharie River Valley. Careful study allows one to identify individuals in some cases. The Seth referred to here was a prominent leader during the 1730s into the 1750s. He died in 1756.

[40]Historical Society of Pennsylvania, Philadelphia, Indian and Military Affairs of Pennsylvania, 1737-1775, MS, P. 249.

[41]"The Constitution of the Five Nations, in *Parker on the Iroquois*, ed. by William N. Fenton, (Syracuse, N.Y.: Syracuse University Press, 1968), p. 54.

preparing for the warpath (1759, 02,11-23). There are also data on the size of war parties (1757,05,24; 1758,05,30; 1758,06,21-07,01; 1760,09,13; 1760,10,00).

Leaders, both war chiefs and peace chiefs, were judicious, seldom, if ever, holding themselves above their followers. William Johnson writing about the disposition of a leader, in 1771, phrased it as follows: ". . . his authority is scarcely discernible, he seldom assuming any power before his people. And indeed this humility is judged the best policy." (1771,02,28).

I have not found evidence of ritual specialists at Schoharie, but Warren Johnson wrote about Iroquois in 1760-61, that they "are themselves obliged to such persons as keep up to their Laws, Ceremonies, & Customs. . ." (1760,06,29-1761,07,03 [p. 191]). There is much evidence that rituals were performed, especially those associated with condolence, replacing chiefs, and warfare (1755,09,24; 1757,01,15-25; 1757,05,24; 1757,05,27-06,07; 1757,05,24; 1757,02,20-04,01; 1758,11,00-1759,12,00 [Dec. 13, 1758]; 1764,01,02-31; 1768,11,14). Warren Johnson reported on these:

> "The Indians goe in Mourning for their Relations, the white people condole with them, by clearing their throats to make them Speak, they wipe Away the Tears from their Eyes, & the Blood of the Deceased from their Bed. & out of their sight that their Hearts may be chearful [sic]: this is done by giving them Strings of Wampum, & black Strouds, & by Covering the Grave of the Deceased that they may morn noe more over it." (1760,06,29-1761,07,03, [p. 189]).

Despite the richness of Johnson's presentation of the Requickening of condolence just given, there is no detailed outline of any of these rituals from the eighteenth century, however. The possible exception is the account of the condolence ceremony presented in the *Iroquois Book of Rites*, if this does indeed date back to David of Schoharie.[42]

Indian women were apparently quite active at Schoharie. In addition to mundane, fundamental, tasks like raising children, planting and cultivating corn, and gathering wood, they often signed deeds, attended councils, advised young warriors, and on occasion bought land (1733,09,18; 1734,12,11; 1738,10,20; 1744, 04,14; 1744,09,02; 1752,11,09; 1752,11,09; 1754,06,06; 1756,03,05-05,26; 1760,06,29-1761,07,03 [pp. 192, 193]; 1766,05,24-27; 1771,03,15; 1772,05,08).

Marriage was most likely monogamous, as reported among Mohawks in the Mohawk River Valley.[43] Matrilineality was in evidence. In 1766, for example, at Johnson Hall, William Johnson was given a gift by "Old Laurence, chief of Schohare [sic] aged 78 Years". Laurence (Lawrence) was accompanied by his "Wife and Nephew named Nicolas [Nicholas] son of Catherine chief Women of Schoharie" (1766,05,24-27). The Mother's Brother/Sister's Son (MoBr/SiSo) relationship is a classic link in matrilineal kinship systems.

It is very clear from deeds and notes appended to them that kinship affiliation was significant (1710,08,22; 1723,02,12; 1732,05,09; 1733,09,18; 1744,04,14; 1751,08,24; 1757,05,27-06,07; 1766,10,03 (3); 1771,02,28). Three clans are associated with Schoharie, Bear, Wolf and Turtle. It appears to have been necessary for a cession of land that members of a particular clan, if not all three clans (Wolf, Turtle, Bear) sign the deed (1710,08,22; 1723,01,12; 1733,09,18). The distinction between whether it was an individual clan or all three may have been tied to the extent of the purchase, i.e., if it was matrilineally held then one clan was enough, if larger, than all three were necessary. Warren Johnson mentioned "both Houses" at councils, in his

---

[42]Horatio Hale, ed., *op. cit.*
[43]Lydekker, op. cit., p. 38. Note also, the missionary Gideon Hawley's reference to his friend Jonah of Schoharie's wife as being Tuscarora (1794,07,31 (2)).

journal of 1760-61 (1760,06,29-1761,07,03 [p. 193]). This may indicate that a moiety system was in place, as well. (In the twentieth century, the Turtle and Wolf form one moiety among the Mohawk, the Bear the other.)[44]

Leadership was in some cases, at least, hereditary, most likely, matrilineally. As William Johnson expressed it, when writing about the Iroquois in general, "The sachems of each tribe are usually chosen in a public assembly of the chiefs and warriors, whenever a vacancy happens by death or otherwise. . .There are however several exceptions; for some families have a kind of inheritance in the office." (1771,02,28). During the nineteenth and twentieth centuries sachemships were passed down in matrilineages. Andrews latter statement most likely refers to the same, or similar practice.

Euro-Americans began settling among the native people of Schoharie at the beginning of the eighteenth century. These newcomers would increase in numbers as the century passed, and whether friend or foe have a devastating effect on the Native American population of the region.

Eighteenth Century Chronology

As the eighteenth century began, the first definite historical documentation of Native American presence in the Schoharie River Valley appears, although undoubtedly the area was used, if not occupied by Native Americans prior to 1700. Euro-Americans certainly seemed to recognize Indian control over the region, and continued to do so well past mid-century.

Land cessions, at least according to Euro-Americans, began in the late 1600s (1686,00,00; 1694,00,00; 1694,05,14; 1694,05,16;1695,09,28;1695,12,12). Significant Euro-American settlement did not start, however, until the first decade of the seventeenth century. How were these cessions viewed by Native Americans? It is not clear that they were considered to be the giving up of land in the same sense in which Euro-Americans interpreted them. It is more likely that they were considered to be transfers of right to use land. As time went on, however, Indians became aware of the construction being put on the negotiations by Euro-Americans.[45]

The earliest complaint by Native Americans concerning land at Schoharie came in 1698, against a large cession, made to Nicholas Bayard. Two Indians of the Mohawk nation, Henry and Joseph, complained that "about three years agoe [sic] when they were out fighting against the French Six Idle drunken People of their nation took upon themselves to sell a vast Tract of Land belonging to his Excellcys Complainants called Ikohere (Skohere) of so large an Extent that a Young man has enough to doe [sic] to runn [sic] over it in a day's time, . . . which Land Arent Schuyler bought for Coll Nicolas Bayard of New-York: . . ." The objection was considered valid, and Bayard's patent was rescinded (1698,10,19; 1699,05,19). All was not well, however. In 1710, surveyors came to chart the land encompassed in Bayard's grant. The Indians would not allow land at Schoharie to be surveyed, until Hendrick (Theyanoguin), one of their leaders, returned from Great Britain (1710,07,13).[46] They maintained that the land, which was encompassed in Bayard's grant had been returned to them (1710,07,20; 1710,07,24; 1710,10,03). N.Y. Provincial Governor Robert Hunter agreed "and they had a new consultation where they resolved to make a present of those Lands to her Majesty . . .[Hunter] ordered them a suitable present which they have not yet called for . . ." (1710,10,03). I have found no record of their ever having come for the present. The persistence of the Native Americans in fighting what they considered to be the fraudulent claim of Nicholas Bayard, however, had taught Euro-Americans that they were not pawns, and would

---

[44] Observation from personal, unpublished field notes of Mary Druke Becker, Akwesasne, Winter 1976-1977.
[45] See footnotes 12 and 18, above.
[46] See Barbara J. Sivertsen, *op.cit.*, pp. 136-137. She was the first to point out the distinction between the two Hendricks who were/are commonly confused by historians.

not tolerate inequities. Exorbitant grants of land were forbidden and in 1736 a committee of the N.Y. Provincial Council passed an act requiring "an actual survey in the presence of the Indians" (1785,09,20).

In 1714, Myndert Schuyler and others requested a patent for 10,000 acres of land, formerly Nicholas Bayard's Grant (1714,05,08; 1714,06,03; 1722,07,09). This patent (thereafter referred to as the Myndert Schuyler Patent or the Schoharie Patent) was granted, and the Euro-American town of Schoharie was settled there.

Other land was also involved in negotiations at Schoharie in 1710 (1710,08,22). Interestingly enough, these "cessions" and virtually all others between Native Americans and Euro-Americans in the Schoharie River valley were deeds of land to the sovereign of Great Britain for the use of a particular individual or individuals. There were not direct "cessions" between Indians and individuals. This was accepted as policy by Euro-Americans because it placed control over land negotiations in colonial offices. It was most likely accepted by Native Americans because it fit their picture of negotiations with leaders for use of land by individuals.[47]

In 1712, settlement increased rapidly with the arrival of Palatine Germans in the Schoharie Valley region. These refugees from Germany were brought to America from Europe under the auspices of the Queen of England to provide naval stores. Land had been secured for them near the Hudson River. However, a number of these people (at least fifty families) insisted on settling in the Schoharie region rather than on lands provided for them by the colonial government of New York (1711,05,30; 1712,10,31; 1713,07,18; 1718,07,07; 1720,08,02). They did this with the approbation of Indian inhabitants of the Schoharie River Valley, but much against the wishes of officials in the colony of New York.

Meanwhile in 1711 and 1714, Adam Vrooman, a Euro-American of Dutch descent, secured deeds to a great deal of land near Onistagrawa from the Indians (1711,08,22; 1714,04,09; 1714,04,10; 1714,04,30; 1714,07,12; 1714,08,01; 1714,08,06; 1714,08,26). Two hundred-sixty acres of this land was from that reserved by the Indians from their "surrender" to the Queen of England in August 1710. A map of this land indicates that it encompassed the area where the Indian village was located (1711,08,22). However, the village was apparently assigned a reserved status because it remained at that location until at least 1771 (1768,10,10; 1771,03,07; 1771,03,15; 1771,09,28). Other deeds were also secured in the early eighteenth century from the Native Americans.[48]

The Palatines did not get along well with other Euro-American settlers of the region (1715,02,28; 1718,07,07; 1721,08,29), although their relations with Native Americans were quite cordial (1715,02,25; 1715,06,09; 1720,08,02). One, Conrad Weiser, residing in a Palatine German settlement not far from the Indian village, was learning the Mohawk language well and would one day come to be a prominent interpreter (1715,07,09). The Palatines purchased Indian land in the Mohawk River Valley during the 1720s and eventually moved there (1721,10,16 (2); 1722,07,09).

As Native Americans and Euro-Americans interacted, accommodations were quickly made. From the beginning, in most negotiations Euro-Americans took up many Indian usages, such as wampum and condolence; and Native Americans were faced with accepting reliance on a written piece of paper, rather than ongoing relations, and face-to-face renewal of agreements as a record of negotiations (1760,06,29-1761,07,03 [p.189]; 1757,08,01-21; 1757,05,04-12; 1698,05,31).[49]

---

[47] It is quite clear that the concept of control of land use rather than alienation through fee simple was at the basis of Iroquois understandings of these cessions. See Mary Druke Becker, "'We are an Independent Nation", *Buffalo Law Review* 46(3): 987-989.
[48] See the attached Calendar of Documents.
[49] See Mary A. Druke, "Iroquois Treaties: Common Forms, Varying Interpretations," *op.cit.*, pp. 86-92..

In the 1720s and 1730s ten or twelve major cessions per year were made. Relations with Esopus Indians to the south ran upon hard times. In 1734, the Indians of Schoharie accused them of deeding land stolen from the Schoharie Indians (1734,00,00). They were given a warning not to do so again. They apparently did not heed this warning. It had no great effect on the Indians of Schoharie, however (1761,12,23; 1769,05,17).

In the 1730s, there were a burgeoning number of land transactions between Native Americans of Schoharie and Euro-Americans, and there began to be more transfers of land between Euro-Americans (1737,05,04; 1737,06,16).[50] This was not new, however, since as early as the 1690s Bayard had purchased land for speculation (1710,10,19).

The 1740s were years of relatively few land transactions between Native Americans and Euro-Americans. Ones during that time tended to be slightly south and southwest of the Schoharie Patent.

In the late 1740s some Indians of Schoharie became involved as English allies in warfare between England and France (1746,07,07; 1746,12,13-1747,11,07; 1747,04,29; 1747,06,16; 1748,07,28). In 1750, with the threat of French attack becoming imminent, the Five Nations were assured that they would be assisted if attacked "and that they may consult with officers of the militia on the Mohawk River and Schoharie" (1750,05,22). During this period of time, few land negotiations between Native Americans and Euro-Americans took place.

Land transactions increased in number again in the 1750s, particularly in the first half of the decade. With them came disputes among Euro-Americans over land (1752,09,18; 1755,09,00). Euro-American acquisitions began to spread along Cobleskill Creek, and south in the area of Breakabeen (1752,11,09; 1753,09,10 (2); 1753,10,26; 1754,06,06).

Indian leaders at Schoharie were concerned with their own problems. In June 1755, for example, Seth "the head Sachem" complained with leaders from Canajoharie and the Lower Mohawk Village to William Johnson about the sale of rum by Euro-Americans to the Indians (1755,06,02). He wished to put a stop to this. It would remain a problem, however (1760,06,29-1761,07,03 [p. 186, 202]; 1764,01,02-31; 1771,02,28). Moreover, if Euro-Americans had questions among themselves about negotiations, the Native Americans involved were often equally confused. In September 1755, Mohawk Indians living in the Schoharie region sent a complaint to Charles Hardy, colonial governor of New York, that Johannes Lawyer was using land that was not his. The Indians maintained that the land was reserved by them for use by Nicholas Matice (Mattys, Mattice) (1755,09,00).

Moreover, in 1756, or shortly before, there was apparently a temporary split among leaders at Schoharie that caused trouble at the time (1756,03,05-05,26 [May 21]). It was reportedly a division "into two parties at the head of which were Seth and David two of their cheif [sic] men". After reporting about the division, David gave a speech on May 21st at a council at William Johnson's residence in the Mohawk River valley, ". . . all former misunderstandings are now removed and an entire end put to every kind of quarrel amongst us." He requested that a fort be built at their village and asked that Johnson "supply the wants of those the River Indians [Mahicans] who have lately come to settle amongst us. . ." David states in his speech, "We are besides in hopes that when we have a Fort it will be the means of drawing many Indians who now live dispersed on the Delaware & Susquehana [sic] Rivers to come and live amongst us which will add to our strength and consequence." (1756,03,05-05,26 [May 21]). Was the split at Schoharie perhaps engendered by the arrival of the River Indians? David explained, ". . . we had a general Meeting of all Women & children belonging to our settlement together with the River Indians who were lately come to live amongst us and all former misunderstandings are

---

[50]Refer to attached Calendar of Documents.

now removed,. . ." Seth died in the summer of 1756. Any animosity that existed between David and Seth had been healed apparently, because in May 1757 David went to William Johnson to explain that Seth had died and that he was going to get a prisoner or scalp to be given in his place (1757,05,24; see also 1757,01,15-25 [Jan. 21]).

All was not always well between the Native Americans and their Euro-American neighbors, either. On 19 November 1758, Seth (son of the Seth who died during the summer of 1756 and Catherine, a matron of Schoharie), a chief of Schoharie, came to Fort Johnson to complain that Germans were settled on lands belonging to the Indians. He explained that the Germans claimed that they were settled there by the Patroon of Albany, Stephen Van Rensselaer, 2nd, but that Hans (Hance) Lawyer of Schoharie showed the Indians a map of Schoharie that indicated that the Patroon "had no right or Title to said Lands." Indians of Schoharie also asked for clothing for their women and children. "[T]wo Horse Loads of Goods" were sent by William Johnson "to cloath [clothe] the Women & Children of that Settlement, being in number 18 Women & 33 Children" on 21 November (1758,11,18-12,04 [Nov. 19, 21]).

The winter of 1758-1759 was to be a hard time. Food was scarce and the Indians were suffering from lack of it. Their Euro-American neighbors in the Schoharie region were often far from willing to help them out (1758,12,05-09; 1758,12,09). Also, sometime during 1758 or 1759, a serious epidemic in the Mohawk River Valley may also have affected the Indians of Schoharie (1760,06,29-1761,07,03 [p. 199]). In January 1759, another complaint was registered against a Euro-American, this time against "one Becker [Nicholas(?)] a German keeping & planting some of their Land" (1759,02,10).

Warfare once more became a reality for residents of the valley, in the late 1750s, as threats of French attacks circulated. At the request of the Native Americans there, a fort was built at their village for protection in case of attack (1756,00,00; 1756,03,05-05,26; 1756,04,03; 1756,04,22; 1756,05,28; 1757,12,27). On 14 March 1758, Johnson warned Schoharie and "Mohickon" (Mahican, Mahickander) Indians of the possibility of attack by the enemy. He admonishes them ". . . to Collect your Scattered people together. . . then your tribes will become once More a respectable body . . . (1758,03,11-14)."

Indians of Schoharie once again joined the English as allies in fighting the French (1755,09,24; 1757,05,27-06,07; 1757,06,26-30; 1758,05,30; 1758,06,21-07,01 [June 24, 29]; 1757,08,01-21; 1759,02,10; 1759,02,11-23; 1760,08,05; 1760,09,13; 1760,10,00). William Johnson wrote to the English Board of Trade, "A number of the six nations who are settled at Aughquaga (Oquaga) on the Susquehanna River, also a small body settled at Schoharie. . . have always, and during this War constantly, shewn themselves firmly attached to our Interest, & no Indians have been more ready on every summons to come and join His Majesty's Arms. They are a flourishing & encreasing [sic] people for many of our friend Indians amongst the Six nations, who are disgusted with the ruling Politics of their people, leave their castles & go and settle at Aughquaga." Johnson wrote, ". . .if measures were fallen upon to satisfy the Indians with regard to their lands, and remove the prevailing Jealousy they have of our views of settling their hunting grounds we might not only releive [sic] our frontiers from calamaties. . . but be able to draw off many Indians from the French Influence. . . " (1757,09,28). As usual during wartime, negotiations concerning land decreased.

As the 1760s began, things hardly looked better. The Native Americans were still concerned about land grievances (1761,01,28), and once again an epidemic was in the Mohawk River Valley, which may also have taken its toll on Indians of Schoharie (1760,06,29-1761,07,03 [p. 199]).

Native Americans were becoming more cautious, more disgusted perhaps, by the continual solicitations for land. In April 1767, William Johnson wrote to Goldbrow Banyar about a division of a tract of land purchased by Johannes Lawyer and others in October 1766. Johnson explained that the Indians were determined to see that the land be divided according to the terms of their cession. They "will not dispose of a foot more of land as they Say, to any Man." (1767,04,08). They were also inquisitive. In a speech of Mohawk and Schoharie Indians about land sold by them last fall to Hannis [Johannes] Lawyer and his associates, they said that they heard that Lawyer and his associates were to have only half of it, and do not understand why this is so" (1767,04,09).

The Schoharie region was again threatened with attack during 1763-64. Delawares and Mingoes of the village of Kanestio in what is now the western New York/Pennsylvania border region had commenced hostilities against the English.[51] At one point, Native Americans of Schoharie feared attacks so much that they discussed with William Johnson the possibility of moving from the Schoharie region. They noted that Barent Vrooman was eager to buy their land. There was enough reality to the threat of attack, that on December 14, 1763, a message was received by Johnson from Euro-American settlers at Schoharie that Delawares had been in the settlement, had behaved badly, and made threats upon leaving. William Johnson assured the Indians then at Johnson Hall that no destruction of Schoharie or any other settlement would be tolerated (1763,12,05-22). English military companies were sent to defend Schoharie; and Schoharie Indians joined war parties against the Delawares and Mingoes (1763,12,07; 1764,01,27; 1764,03,10).

Things quieted down as the decade passed. The Native Americans of Schoharie ceded numerous parcels of land to Euro-Americans in 1766 and 1768. Either their reluctance to do so had passed or the enticements were too great to resist. In August 1766, it was reported that Johannes Lawyer arrived at a conference with three others from "Scohare [Schoharie] to purchase about 3 M Acres of Woodland there from the Mohawks, but could not agree about the Price, and departed." The Indians wanted to be paid more than Lawyer and his associates had expected (1766,08,13-30). In some cases, rum provided an inducement, as can be seen from the high proportion of expenses for rum on a receipt of what Peter and Cornelius Vrooman "have & did and Delivered To the Indians" (1771,09,28).

An enlightening document from this time period is the will of Peter Vrooman which grants to his heirs in the future land that he apparently "purchased" from the Indians, but which was "now in Possession of the Indians. . ." (1768,10,10). This, together with an important document pertaining to the Treaty at Fort Stanwix in 1768, may throw some light on the nature of Native American "cessions" of land. Undoubtedly, some of them were made, and accepted by Euro-Americans, without actually involving at least an immediate transfer of land. A surveyor's map done for the Iroquois Indian Museum graphically shows that land where documentation and archaeological work place an Indian settlement in the mid-eighteenth century was "ceded" in 1711 to Adam Vrooman (1711,00,00; 1711,08,22).[52] Yet, Native Americans continued to maintain a settlement there. In discussion in 1698 of a dispute over a cession of land at Schoharie, two Mohawks insisted that they had been assured that the land "ceded" by them was being put under the protection of the purchasers. They maintained that the purchasers had said that "they would keep their [the Mohawks's] land for them [the Mohawks], that it should not be in the power of any person to make an Infringement upon their Property and as long as any of the Maquase nation lived, the land should be theirs and their Posteritys for ever" (1698,05,31). Peter Vrooman apparently had some implicit agreement with the Native Americans living on the land that he mentions in his

---

[51] 'Mingo' was a name given to Cayugas, Senecas, and other Iroquoians living in the Ohio region at this time (See "Northern Iroquoian Culture Patterns" by William N. Fenton, in *Northeast*, ed. By Bruce G. Trigger, vol. 15 of the *Handbook of North American Indians*, general editor, William C. Sturtevant (Washington, D.C.: Smithsonian Institution, 1978), p. 321. The Ottawa Pontiac and others had inspired the Delawares and Mingoes of Kanestio to join them in taking up arms against the English and their native allies (See *A Spirited Resistance: The North American Indian Struggle for Unity, 1745-1815*, by Gregory Evans Dowd, (Baltimore and London: The Johns Hopkins University Press, 1992), p. 37.

[52] See Map of Patents, based on eighteenth century documentation, prepared by surveyors Joanne Crum and Dennis Weaver for the Iroquois Indian Museum in 1989. The map may be found at the Iroquois Indian Museum, Howes Cave, New York.

will, perhaps one similar to what the Mohawks Henry and Joseph described in 1698, that allowed for their right of use of the land. The Treaty of Fort Stanwix, which set up a boundary between Indians and Euro-Americans, and at which Indians of Schoharie were present, specifically provided for such an arrangement. The deed states, "That the Lands occupied by the Mohocks [Mohawks] around their villages as well as by any other Nation affected by this our Cession may effectually remain to them and to their Posterity and that any engagements regarding Property which they may now be under may be prosecuted and our present Grants deemed valid on our parts with the several other humble requests contained in our said Speech." (1768,11,05).

Smallpox was rampant in 1769 (1769,03,26-10,07). Sometime between 1768 and 1771, a "cession" of land was acquired by Bartholomew and Peter Vrooman from Indians of Schoharie (1771,00,00). Other Indians of the settlement protested the sale (1771,03,15; 1771,03,23; 1772,10,24). I have not been able to find additional data to discover the outcome of the protests. After this point, however, documentation pertaining to Native Americans in the Schoharie region declines precipitously. One is led to ask, "Where did they go?"

There is evidence of Indians associated with Schoharie at a number of locations after this period. They most likely scattered, most probably in response to opposing views on what actions to take in the face of pressure from settlers for their land and differences over where their best interests lay during the American Revolution. Data are lacking so their thoughts can only be surmised. It is likely, however, that they might have echoed those of Indians of the Mohawk River Valley, who exhibited a great deal of turmoil in trying to decide who held the other side of the covenant chain of friendship, now that the English were split in two (British and American).[53]

In 1783, there were reportedly forty-eight Indians of Schoharie, apparently British allies, at the Loyal Village at Niagara (twelve were men, twenty-two were women, and fourteen were children) (1783,09,25). If Horatio Hale's assertion that David of Schoharie was author of the Iroquois Book of Rites is correct, it is likely that he moved to Six Nations Reserve on the Grand River after the American Revolution with others who had been at the Loyal Village at Niagara during the war. Moreover, a silver pipe engraved with reference to the Nine Partner Tract at Schoharie was seen at Six Nations in the nineteenth century, providing another indication of the presence of Indians of Schoharie at Six Nations Reserve (See 1774,01,22)[54].

There was a Schoharie presence at Oneida, as well. In February 1796, Samuel Kirkland, a missionary among Oneidas stayed with a "Schoharry John" who was living at Oneida.[55] There were also Native Americans at Schoharie during the Revolution (1777,02,20). Two "old Indian Women" were so determined to stay in the area in 1771 that they bought land from a Euro-American (1771,05,08). Rufus Grider in 1887-1888 sketched a copy of a warrant issued by an Indian Justice Hawdy in the Schoharie region from 1810 (1810,00,00). That

---

[53] Barbara Graymont, *The Iroquois in the American Revolution*, Syracuse, NY: Syracuse University Press, 1972, pp. 48-85, particularly p. 48; Colin G. Calloway, *The American Revolution in Indian Country: Crisis and Diversity in Native American Communities*, Cambridge: Cambridge University Press, 1995, pp. 26-30;

[54] A twentieth century photograph of chiefs of the confederate council based at Six Nations holding the pipe (ca. 1954) is at the Canadian Museum of Civilization in Ottawa (NMM Neg. No.: 79-2491; NMM Neg. No. 79-2492). The chiefs were apparently in Washington, D.C., participating in a "renewal" council at the time that the photograph was taken. I am indebted to Michael K. Foster for bringing this to my attention. Interestingly enough the pipe was identified in the nineteenth century as being in the hands of George H.M. Johnson, son of John (Smoke) Johnson the man who presented Horatio Hale with the manuscript that Hale published as the *Iroquois of Book of Rites* (Benjamin J. Lossing, *The Pictorial Fieldbook of the War of 1812 by Benjamin Lossing: A Facsimile of the 1869 Edition with a Forward by John T. Cunningham*, Somersworth: New Hampshire Publishing Company, 1976, original published by Harper and Brothers, 1868, p. 422). Hale identifies the original of this document as having come from David of Schoharie. George H.M. Johnson served as translator of the manuscript for Hale (Horatio Hale, ed., *op.cit.*, p. xiv.) See also *The Frontiersmen of New York* by Jeptha Simms, Albany, NY: G. C. Riggs, 1882-1883, 2 vols., vol. 1, pp. 41-43 for information about the pipe.

[55] The Journals of Samuel Kirkland, ed. Walter Pilkington, (Clinton, N.Y.: Hamilton College, 1980), p. 290.

there was some Native American presence after the Revolution is also indicated by a study done by Henry Cady (born 1848, died 1919), a researcher at Schoharie, who compiled a list of "families at Schoharie having Indian blood".[56] It is not known what sources he used for his information. There are also oral traditions circulating in the late twentieth/early twenty-first century that suggest that there remain families at Schoharie that are descended from Native Americans.[57] It is apparent that at least some Indians of Schoharie--most probably those most friendly with, or sympathizing with "Rebels"--remained in the Schoharie River Valley after the American Revolution. In most cases they probably tried to fade as much into the background as possible given largely unjustified anti-Indian feelings generated by British raids on Schoharie during the war.[58]

Conclusion

As I hope the above report has demonstrated, there is a surprising amount of data available about Native Americans in the Schoharie River Valley. Undoubtedly, there is much more to be found, as well. A good deal of information is available on subjects such as the process of land cessions (1785,09,20; 1771,10,12; 1722,09,26; 1751,05,18; 1790,03,02) and the history of particular plots of land. This material merits analyses. Moreover, investigation into the activities of individual Indians whose names appear numerous times in the historical record would personalize the picture of Native American life at Schoharie. There is much more to be learned. I hope that the following will provide a useful tool for further research into the historical record.

---

[56] Records copied from the original collection of Genealogical Records of Schoharie County, New York Families, made by Henry Cady, Schoharie County Historical Society, Schoharie, N.Y.
[57] These are not available in written form.
[58] David Guldenzopf, "Frontier Demography and Settlement Patterns of the Mohawk Iroquois," *op.cit.*, p. 88.

SOURCES OF DOCUMENTS

Published Sources

Amsterdam Evening Recorder, Amsterdam, N.Y., 14 November 1910.

Crown Collection of Photographs of American Maps, selected and edited by Archer Butler Hulbert. Cleveland, Ohio: The Arthur Clark Company, 1907.

Leder, Lawrence H., ed. *The Livingston Indian Records, 1666-1723*. Gettysburg, PA: The Pennsylvania Historical Association, 1956.

Lydekker, John Wolfe, *The Faithful Mohawks*, (Reprinted, Port Washington, Long Island, NY: Ira J. Friedman, Inc., 1968, pp. 34-38. (First Published In 1938).

O'Callaghan, E.B., ed. *The Documentary History of the State of New York.* Albany, NY: Weed, Parsons, and Co., Charles Van Benthuysen, 1849-1851, quarto edition.

O'Callaghan, E.B. and Berthold Fernow, ed. *Documents Relative to the Colonial History of the State of New York.* Albany, N.Y.: Weed, Parsons, and Co., 1856-87.

Pilkington, Walter, ed. *The Journals of Samuel Kirkland.* Clinton, N.Y.: Hamilton College, 1980.

Randall, Lora Vrooman and Florence Vrooman Houghton. *Josiah B. Vrooman: His Ancestors and Descendants.* El Paso, TX: Carol Hertzog, Printer, 1946.

Sauthier, Claude Joseph. *A Chorographical Map of the Province of New-York, in North America, Divided into Counties, Manors, Patents and Townships: Compiled from Actual Surveys Deposited in the Patent Office at New York . . . .* London, England: Engraved and Published by William Faden, January 1, 1779.

Schoharie County Historical Review, (Schoharie, N.Y.: Schoharie Country Historical Society),"Vrooman's Land", May 1950.

Schoharie County Historical Review, Spring-Summer 1087, Vol. 51, No. 1.

Sullivan, James, et al., ed. *The Papers of Sir William Johnson.* 14 vols. Albany: University of the State of New York, 1921-1965.

Archives

Albany County Clerk's Office, Hall of Records, Albany, N.Y.

British Museum, London, England, Manuscripts.

Franklin D. Roosevelt Library, Hyde Park, N.Y. (on indefinite loan from the National Archives and Record Service) Livingston Family Papers, Indian Affairs.

Historical Society of Pennsylvania, Philadelphia.

New-York Historical Society, New York, N.Y.

New York State Archives, Albany, NY. Abbreviations are used in the following calendar for N.Y. Colonial Manuscripts (N.Y.COL.MSS) and N.Y. Council Minutes (N.Y.COUN.MIN.) at the New York State Archives.

New York State Library, Albany, Manuscripts.

Old Stone Church and Fortress, Schoharie, N.Y., Catalogue and Historical Notes, 1933, Deed # 323; Deed #648.

Pennsylvania Historical and Museum Commission, Harrisburg, PA.

Public Archives of Canada, Ottawa, RG 10.

Public Record Office, Kew, England, CO5/1053.

Helpful Guides and Catalogues

Calendar of Council Minutes, 1668-1783, compiled by Berthold Fernow (Harrison, NY: Harbor Hill Books, 1987, Reprint; originally published New York State Library Bulletin 58, (History 6), Albany, 1902).

Calendar of N.Y. Colonial Manuscripts Indorsed Land Papers in the Office of the Secretary of State of New York, 1643-1803, compiled by E. B. O'Callaghan, (Harrison, NY: Harbor Hill Books, 1987, Revised Reprint. Originally published Albany, NY: Weed, Parsons, and Co., 1864).

Catalog of Maps and Surveys in Offices of the Secretary of State, State Engineer and Surveyor and Comptroller and New York State Library by David E. E. Mix. Albany, NY: Charles Van Benthuysen, 1859.

Excelsior: New York State Archives/Library/Museum Catalog. Web-based search tool to the New York State Archives, Library, and Museum Catalog, and to local archives throughout New York State, www.nysl.nysed.gov/xcelsior.htm.

KEY TO CALENDAR OF DOCUMENTS

The following calendar is a list of documents pertaining to Native American occupation of the Schoharie River Valley. It contains references to both manuscript and printed records.

Each entry is set up in the same manner, as the following sample indicates. The first line is the Date in yyyy.mm.dd format. This is followed by a Description of the document, after which is the Source (in capital letters). Comments, if any, are at the end of each entry.

Date: 1710,07,16
Description: Report of the meeting of N.Y. Commissioners for Indian Affairs. Propositions made to Mohawks, at Albany and Schenectady, with their replies.
Source: FRANKLIN D. ROOSEVELT LIBRARY, HYDE PARK, N.Y. (ON INDEFINITE LOAN FROM THE NATIONAL ARCHIVES AND RECORD SERVICE) LIVINGSTON FAMILY PAPERS, INDIAN AFFAIRS.
Comment: Settlement on lands at Schoharie is discussed at the councils.

- Each entry is to a unique document. Therefore, if there is more than one document of a particular date, the first is assigned that date. Subsequent documents are denoted by a "(2)", "(3)", etc., for example 1710,09,01(2).
- In some cases a citation is a cross-reference to a document. In these instances, the date is followed by a "°" (1743,00,00°). The date of the document to which it relates is then listed as the source of the document.
- A date has been assigned to undated documents when additional information has been available to aid in this. Brackets after dates in the calendar indicate undated documents to which I have assigned dates (1728,00,00 [ ]).
- Documents that were not originally dated and to which I am not able to assign a reliable date are listed at the end of the calendar as "n.d."
- For the most part, wording and phraseology from the documents have been incorporated into the descriptions of them that are provided.

In 1582 the means of dating changed in Europe from the Julian Calendar (Old Style) to the Gregorian Calendar (New Style). Although accepted early by several European countries, the change was slow to be accepted by others. England did not adopt the Julian Calendar until 1752. No attempt has been made here to tailor dates to the New Style Calendar. Within the Calendar of Documents presented here the date that is on each document has been used, except in those cases where both Old Style and New Style are noted on the document, for example 3 Mar 1746/7. In those cases, the later date is the one selected. 3 Mar 1746/7, therefore, would become 3 Mar 1747.

Date: 1686,00,00
Description: Petition of Andrew Brown to Thomas Dongan, colonial governor of New York, concerning purchase of about 500 acres of land from the Indians at a place known as Schoharie.
Source: N.Y.STATE ARCHIVES, ALBANY, N.Y.COL.MSS, INDORSED LAND PAPERS, 1643-1803, SERIES NO. A0272, DEPARTMENT OF STATE, APPLICATIONS FOR LAND GRANTS, VOL. 02, P. 164.
Comment:

Date: 1693,07,22
Description: Petition of John Pieterson Mebie (Mebee; Maybe) for confirmation of grant of land on both sides of Trindorogoes (Tionderogoes) creek, known as Kadarode (Kadarrode), by the Mohawk sachem, Roode, of the Lower Mohawk Village.
Source: N.Y. STATE ARCHIVES, ALBANY, N.Y.COL.MSS, INDORSED LAND PAPERS, 1643-1803, SERIES NO. A0272, DEPARTMENT OF STATE, APPLICATIONS FOR LAND GRANTS, VOL. 03, P. 073..
Comment:

Date: 1694,00,00°
Description: Petition of Samuel Bayard concerning land granted to his father after purchase from the Indians in 1694.
Source: SEE 1713,05,27.
Comment:

Date: 1694,05,14°
Description: License issued to Col. Nicholas Bayard for purchase of Indian lands.
Source: SEE 1695,12,12 (3).
Comment: It is unclear whether the date of this license is May 14 or May 16. (SEE 1694,05,16).

Date: 1694,05,16°
Description: Memorial and petition of Nicholas Bayard, dated 19 October 1710, that cites the date of a license issued to Col. Nicholas Bayard for purchase of Indian lands as 16 May 1694.
Source: SEE 1710,10,19
Comment: SEE 1695,09,28; 1695,12,12; 1698,05,31; 1698,10,19; 1699,05,19; 1709,05,27; 1710,07,24 (2); 1714,06,03; 1710,10,19; 1713,05,27; 1713,10,01; 1714,05,08; 1722,09,26. It is unclear whether the correct date of the license is May 14 or May 16, 1694 (SEE 1694,05,14).

Date: 1695,09,28
Description: Petition of Nicholas Bayard to purchase from Indians a tract of land called Schoharie extending from the mouth of the creek at Teaondaroge (Teatontaloga) to its head near a hill called Kanjearegore.
Source: N.Y. STATE ARCHIVES, ALBANY, N.Y.COL.MSS., 1664-1776, VOL. 40, P. 075.
Comment: SEE 1695,12,12; 1695,12,12 (2); 1695,12,12 (3); 1698,05,31; 1698,10,19; 1699,05,19; 1709,05,27; 1710,07,24 (2); 1710,10,19; 1713,05,27; 1713,10,01; 1714,05,08; 1714,06,03; 1722,09,26.

Date: 1695,12,12
Description: N.Y. Colonial Manuscripts. Request by Nicholas Bayard to erect a manor on Skohaare (Schoharie) land.
Source: N.Y. STATE ARCHIVES, ALBANY, N.Y.COL.MSS., 1664-1776, VOL. 40, P. 113.
Comment: SEE 1695,09,28; 1695,12,12 (2); 1695,12,12 (3); 1698,05,31; 1698,10,19; 1699,05,19; 1709,05,27; 1710,07,24 (2); 1710,10,19; 1713,05,27; 1713,10,01; 1714,05,08; 1714,06,03; 1722,09,26.

Date: 1695,12,12 (2)
Description: N.Y. Provincial Council Minutes, about Manor of Kingsfield at Schoharie.
Source: N.Y.STATE ARCHIVES, ALBANY, N.Y.COUN.MIN., SERIES A1895, VOL. 07 (OLD NUMBER)/VOL. 04 (NEW NUMBER), P. 172.
Comment: This document was destroyed by fire, 1911. SEE 1694,05,14; 1694,05,16; 1695,09,28; 1695,12,12; 1695,12,12 (3).

Date: 1695,12,12 (3)
Description: Patent granted to Nicholas Bayard for Manor of Kingsfield.
Source: N.Y.STATE ARCHIVES, ALBANY, N.Y. LETTERS PATENT, 1664-1780, SERIES NO. 12590, BOOK 7, P. 1.
Comment: SEE 1694,05,14; 1694,05,16; 1695,09,28; 1695,12,12; 1695, 12,12 (2).

Date: 1695,12,12°
Description: Memorial and petition of Nicholas Bayard, dated 19 October 1710, that cites the date of his purchase of land from the Indians as 12 December 1695.
Source: SEE 1710,10,19.
Comment: SEE 1695,09,28; 1695,12,12 (2); 1695,12,12 (3); 1698,05,31; 1698,10,19; 1699,05,19; 1709,05,27; 1710,07,24 (2); 1710,10,19; 1713,05,27; 1713,10,01; 1714,05,08; 1714,06,03; 1722,09,26.

Date: 1698,05,31
Description: Deposition of Henry and Joseph of the Mohawk Nation about a fraudulent purchase of land from Mohawk Indians. It is stated in the deposition that "about three years agoe [sic] when they were out fighting against the French Six Idle drunken People of their nation took upon themselves to sell a vast Tract of Land belonging to his Excellcys Complainants called Ikohere (Skohere) of so large an Extent that a Young man has enough to doe [sic] to runn [sic] over it in a day's time, . . . which Land Arent Schuyler bought for Coll Nicolas Bayard of New-York: . . ."
Source: DOCUMENTS RELATIVE TO THE COLONIAL HISTORY OF THE STATE OF NEW YORK, ED. BY E.B. O'CALLAGHAN AND BERTHOLD FERNOW, 15 VOL. (ALBANY, N.Y.: WEED, PARSONS, AND CO., 1856-87), 4: 345-347.
Comment: SEE 1695,09,28; 1695,12,12; 1698,10,19; 1699,05,19; 1709,05,27; 1710,07,24 (2); 1714,06,03; 1710,10,19; 1713,05,27; 1713,10,01; 1714,05,08; 1722,09,26.

Date: 1698,10,19
Description: Report of the Board of Trade on the Affairs of the Province of New York. Refers to Nicholas Bayard's patent.
Source: DOCUMENTS RELATIVE TO THE COLONIAL HISTORY OF THE STATE OF NEW YORK, ED. BY E.B. O'CALLAGHAN AND BERTHOLD FERNOW, 15 VOL. (ALBANY, N.Y.: WEED, PARSONS, AND CO., 1856-87), 4: 385-396.
Comment: Specific reference to Bayard's patent is on p. 391. SEE 1695,09,28; 1695,12,12; 1698,05,31; 1699,05,19; 1709,05,27; 1710,07,24 (2); 1710,10,19; 1713,05,27; 1713,10,01; 1714,05,08; 1714,06,03; 1722,09,26.

Date: 1699,05,19
Description: Instructions to Henrick Hanse and Ryer Schemerhorn in their journey to the Mohawks. Refers to the complaint against the grant of land obtained by Nicholas Bayard. The instructions state that Hanse and Schermerhorn are to tell the Indians that Bayard's grant has been voided, "soe [sic] that the said Indians are possessed of the said land, as if no writing had been, and the said writing fully destroyed as the Indians desired, ..." A grant for land obtained by Domine Dellius and also complained about by the Indians was likewise cancelled.
Source: DOCUMENTS RELATIVE TO THE COLONIAL HISTORY OF THE STATE OF NEW YORK, ED. BY E.B. O'CALLAGHAN AND BERTHOLD FERNOW, 15 VOL. (ALBANY, N.Y.: WEED, PARSONS, AND CO., 1856-87), 4: 565-566.
Comment: SEE 1698, 05,28; 1698,10,19; 1724,07,24 (2). N.B., The document, in stating the grievances of the Indians, refers to complaints filed by the Indians, the other of which of concern was against the minister Domine Dellius: "And at the same time did complain of another injury done them some years ago by Coll Bayard and Arent Schuyler, who in like manner [i.e., like Dellius] had seduced the dispose of another tract of land called Skohire which is alleaged [sic] to be sold by such Indians who had no right to do the same."

Date: 1701,07,19 [ ]
Description: Proceedings of conference at Albany.
Source: PUBLIC RECORD OFFICE, KEW, ENGLAND, C05/1053.
Comment:

Date: 1701,07,19°
Description: Deed in Trust from three of the Five Nations to the King of England. Refers to the deed of 19 July 1701, whereby the Five Nations put their land under the protection of the King of England.
Source: SEE 1726,09,14.
Comment:

Date: 1702,11,20
Description: Petition of John Pieterson Mebie (Mebee; Maybe) for a patent for land on both sides of Tionderogoes Creek.
Source: N.Y. STATE ARCHIVES, ALBANY, N.Y.COL.MSS, INDORSED LAND PAPERS, 1643-1803, SERIES NO. A0272, DEPARTMENT OF STATE, APPLICATIONS FOR LAND GRANTS, VOL. 03, P. 098.
Comment:

Date: 1703,04,28
Description: Patent to John Peterson Mebie (Mebee; Maybe) on Tionderogoes Creek.
Source: N.Y.STATE ARCHIVES, ALBANY, N.Y. LETTERS PATENT, 1664-1780, SERIES NO. 12590, BOOK 11, P. 172.

Date: 1705,06,28
Description: Petition of John Pieterson Mebie (Mebee; Maybe) for a new patent for land called Kadarrode (Kadarode) "downwards of a creeke called Tionderogoes creek".
Source: N.Y. STATE ARCHIVES, ALBANY, N.Y.COL.MSS, INDORSED LAND PAPERS, 1643-1803, SERIES NO. A0272, DEPARTMENT OF STATE, APPLICATIONS FOR LAND GRANTS, VOL. 04, P. 052.
Comment:

Date: 1705,07,20
Description: Patent to John Pieterson Mebie (Maybe; Mebee).
Source: N.Y.STATE ARCHIVES, ALBANY, N.Y. LETTERS PATENT, 1664-1780, SERIES NO. 12590, BOOK 7, P. 280.
Comment:

Date: 1708,05,10
Description: Papers relating to the Palatines and to the First Settlement of Newburgh, Orange County.
Source: THE DOCUMENTARY HISTORY OF THE STATE OF NEW YORK, ED. E.B. O'CALLAGHAN, (ALBANY; WEED, PARSONS, AND CO., CHARLES VAN BENTHUYSEN, 1849-1851), QUARTO ED., 3: 541-542.
Comment:

Date: 1708,08,05
Description: N.Y. Provincial Council Minutes. Order on petition from Adam Vrooman (Vroman).
Source: N.Y.STATE ARCHIVES, ALBANY, N.Y.COUN.MIN., SERIES A1895, VOL. 10, PP. 178-179 (D164/6).
Comment: Document is badly burned.

Date: 1709,05,27°
Description: Petition of Nicholas Bayard concerning land granted to his father after purchase from the Indians in 1694.
Source: SEE 1713,05,27.
Comment: At one time, this document was assigned the date 27 May 1709. SEE 1695,09,28; 1695,12,12; 1698,05,31; 1698,10,19; 1699,05,19; 1710,07,24 (2); 1714,06,03; 1710,10,19; 1713,05,27; 1713,10,01; 1714,05,08; 1722,09,26.

Date: 1709,12,05
Description: Report of the English Board of Trade on the settlement of additional Palatines in New York.
Source: THE DOCUMENTARY HISTORY OF THE STATE OF NEW YORK, ED. E.B. O'CALLAGHAN, (ALBANY; WEED, PARSONS, AND CO., CHARLES VAN BENTHUYSEN, 1849-1851), QUARTO ED., 3: 637-643.
Comment:

Date: 1710,00,00
Description: Peter Wraxall's abridgement of minutes of the N.Y. Commissioners for Indian Affairs, pertaining to councils with the Iroquois in 1710.
Source: AN ABRIDGEMENT OF THE INDIAN AFAIRS CONTAINED IN FOUR FOLIO VOLUMES, TRANSACTED IN THE COLONY OF NEW YORK FROM THE YEAR 1678 TO THE YEAR 1751, BY PETER WRAXALL, ED. BY CHARLES McILWAIN, HARVARD HISTORICAL STUDIES 21, (CAMBRIDGE, MA: HARVARD UNIVERSITY PRESS, 1915), 2 VOLS., 2: 69-80.
Comment:

Date: 1710,00,00 (2)
Description: Information about councils in 1710 involving the Iroquois, from the Livingston Indian Records.
Source: THE LIVINGSTON INDIAN RECORDS 1666-1723, ED. BY LAWRENCE H. LEDER, (GETTYSBURG, PA.: THE PENNSYLVANIA HISTORICAL ASSOCIATION, 1956), PP. 214-217.
Comment:

Date: 1710,07,13
Description: N.Y. Provincial Council Minutes. Indians will not allow land at Schoharie to be surveyed.
Source: N.Y.STATE ARCHIVES, ALBANY, N.Y.COUN.MIN., SERIES A1895, VOL. 10, PP. 528-529 (D164/6).
Comment:

Date: 1710,07,16
Description: Report of the meeting of N.Y. Commissioners for Indian Affairs. Propositions made to Mohawks, at Albany and Schenectady, with their replies.
Source: FRANKLIN D. ROOSEVELT LIBRARY, HYDE PARK, N.Y. (ON INDEFINITE LOAN FROM THE NATIONAL ARCHIVES AND RECORD SERVICE) LIVINGSTON FAMILY PAPERS, INDIAN AFFAIRS.
Comment: Settlement on lands at Schoharie is discussed at the councils.

Date: 1710,07,19°
Description: Indian deed, dated 19 July 1710, to Evert Wendell, Harmanus Wendell, and Abraham Cuyler. Gift of land one mile along west side of Schoharie Creek, beginning at a stone called Keedsienoo, then to Netstograkaarawe Caghsoone creek and one mile from Schoharie creek to the woods. Deed was recorded 28 May 1714.
Source: SEE 1714,05,28.
Comment:

Date: 1710,07,20
Description: N.Y. Provincial Council Minutes. Mohawks consent to have Schoharie land surveyed.
Source: N.Y.STATE ARCHIVES, ALBANY, N.Y.COUN.MIN., SERIES A1895, VOL. 10, PP. 529-530 (D164/6).
Comment:

Date: 1710,07,24
Description: N.Y. Provincial Governor Robert Hunter to the English Board of Trade. Hunter writes, "Soon after my arrival [in the colony of New York] I sent the Surveyor with some skilfull [sic] men to survey the land on the Mohak's [sic] River, particularly the Skohare [Schoharie] to which the Indians had no pretence, being Colonel Bayard's Grant, they however, by the instigation of some ill intentioned men at first refused to suffer it to be surveyed upon pretence of its having return'd to them after the resumption, but have been better advis'd since, so that at this time he is actually surveying it."
Source: THE DOCUMENTARY HISTORY OF THE STATE OF NEW YORK, ED. E.B. O'CALLAGHAN, (ALBANY; WEED, PARSONS, AND CO., CHARLES VAN BENTHUYSEN, 1849-1851), QUARTO ED., 3: 559-560.
Comment:

Date: 1710,07,24 (2)
Description: N.Y. Provincial Governor Robert Hunter to the English Board of Trade. Hunter writes, "Soon after my arrival [in the colony of New York] I sent the Surveyor with some skilfull [sic] men to survey the land on the Mohak's [sic] River, particularly the Skohare [sic] to which the Indians had no pretence, being Colonel Bayard's Grant, they however, by the instigation of some ill intentioned men at first refused to suffer it to be surveyed upon pretence of its having return'd to them after the resumption, but have been better advis'd since, so that at this time he is actually surveying it."
Source: DOCUMENTS RELATIVE TO THE COLONIAL HISTORY OF THE STATE OF NEW YORK, ED. BY E.B. O'CALLAGHAN AND BERTHOLD FERNOW, 15 VOL. (ALBANY, N.Y.: WEED, PARSONS, AND CO., 1856-87), 5:166-168.
Comment: SEE 1695,09,28; 1695,12,12; 1698,05,31; 1698,10,19; 1699,05,19; 1709,05,27; 1710,10,03; 1710,10,19; 1713,05,27; 1713,10,01; 1714,05,08; 1714,06,03; 1722,09,26.

Date: 1710,08,07°
Description: An account of N.Y. Provincial Governor Hunter's conference with Indians. Enclosed in letter, dated 7 May 1711 from Governor Hunter to officials in England.
Source: SEE 1711,05,07.
Comment:

Date: 1710,08,07-21
Description: Minutes of a conference at Albany between N.Y. Provincial Governor Hunter and the Five Nations and River Indians.
Source: DOCUMENTS RELATIVE TO THE COLONIAL HISTORY OF THE STATE OF NEW YORK, ED. BY E.B. O'CALLAGHAN AND BERTHOLD FERNOW, 15 VOL. (ALBANY, N.Y.: WEED, PARSONS, AND CO., 1856-87), 5: 217-229.
Comment:

Date: 1710,08,09-21
Description: An account of a conference between the Five Nations and N.Y. Provincial Governor Hunter.
Source: N.Y.STATE ARCHIVES, ALBANY, N.Y.COL.MSS., VOL. 54, 1664-1776, P. 51.
Comment:

Date: 1710,08,10°
Description: Letter dated September 26, 1710 from the Rev. Thomas Barclay to the Secretary of the Society for the Propagation of the Gospel in Foreign Parts, about the state of the church in Albany, and mentioning meeting of the Five Nations with N.Y. Provincial Governor Hunter, 10 August 1710.
Source: SEE 1710,09,26.
Comment:

Date: 1710,08,15
Description: Copy of propositions made at Albany by N.Y. Provincial Governor Hunter to the Five Nations.
Source: FRANKLIN D. ROOSEVELT LIBRARY, HYDE PARK, N.Y., (ON INDEFINITE LOAN FROM THE NATIONAL ARCHIVES AND RECORDS SERVICE), LIVINGSTON FAMILY PAPERS, INDIAN AFFAIRS.
Comment:

Date: 1710,08,22
Description: Propositions made by the Mohawk Indians to the N.Y. Colonial Governor, Robert Hunter, about cession of land at Schoharie. Hendrick claims the land ceded, and surrenders it to the Queen "for christian settlements", while reserving the area where the Indians "now" plant and enough woodland to provide firewood for the Indians.
Source: N.Y. HISTORICAL SOCIETY, NEW YORK, N.Y., COLLECTION OF MANUSCRIPTS ON INDIAN AFFAIRS.
Comment: N.B. Land near the hill Onitstaehragarawe (Onitstagrawae) where the Indians "now" plant is reserved by them, as well as "woodland Sufficient for fire wood for ye Indians". Also, it is requested that land transactions in the future take place only in public with all three "tribes", i.e. clans (Bear, Wolf, Turtle), of Mohawks being present. Hendrick is speaker.

Date: 1710,09,01
Description: N.Y. Provincial Council Minutes, about Schoharie lands and Indian affairs.
Source: N.Y.STATE ARCHIVES,ALBANY, N.Y.COUN.MIN., SERIES A1895, VOL. 10, P. 534 (D164/6).
Comment:

Date: 1710,09,01 (2)
Description: N.Y. Colonial Manuscripts. Bill for services from Augustin Graham, surveyor of Schoharie for the Palatines.
Source: N.Y. STATE ARCHIVES, ALBANY, N.Y.COL.MSS., 1664-1776, VOL. 54, P. 058.
Comment:

Date: 1710,09,26
Description: Letter from the Rev. Thomas Barclay to the Secretary of the Society for the Propagation of the Gospel in Foreign Parts, about the state of the church in Albany, and mentioning meeting of the Five Nations with N.Y. Provincial Governor Hunter, 10 August 1710.
Source: THE DOCUMENTARY HISTORY OF THE STATE OF NEW YORK, ED. E.B. O'CALLAGHAN, (ALBANY; WEED, PARSONS, AND CO., CHARLES VAN BENTHUYSEN, 1849-1851), QUARTO ED., 03: 540-542.
Comment: N.B., See THE DOCUMENTARY HISTORY OF THE STATE OF NEW YORK, op.cit., 3: 899 for Barclay's opinion of the Mohawk leader, Hendrick.

Date: 1710,10,03
Description: Letter from N.Y. Provincial Governor Hunter to the Board of Trade in London, England, about Palatines settled on Hudson's River.
Source: THE DOCUMENTARY HISTORY OF THE STATE OF NEW YORK, ED. E.B. O'CALLAGHAN, (ALBANY; WEED, PARSONS, AND CO., CHARLES VAN BENTHUYSEN, 1849-1851), QUARTO ED., 3: 560-572.
Comment: Contains an estimate of things necessary for the settlement of the Palatines that provides insight into material culture. Also included is a list of Palatines remaining at New York (1710), names of Palatine children apprenticed by Gov. Hunter (1710-1714), a petition of Peter Willemse Romers, a list of heads of Palatine families and the number of persons in both towns on the west side of Hudson River (Winter 1710), and a list of Palatine volunteers for the expedition against Canada (1711).

Date: 1710,10,03 [ ]
Description: Letter from N.Y. Provincial Governor Hunter to the Board of Trade in London, England. Mentions transactions with "the five Indian Nations". Hunter writes, "They insisted upon their Right to the Lands of Scokery [Schoharie] near the Mohacks Country and refer'd me to Records; I found in Albany Instructions to the Commissioners there to restore them to their Right and Title to these Lands, I owned their Title and they had a new consultation where they resolved to make a present of those Lands to her Majesty...[I] ordered them a suitable present which they have not yet called for..."
Source: DOCUMENTS RELATIVE TO THE COLONIAL HISTORY OF THE STATE OF NEW YORK, ED. BY E.B. O'CALLAGHAN AND BERTHOLD FERNOW, 15 VOL. (ALBANY, N.Y.: WEED, PARSONS, AND CO., 1856-87), 5: 170-172.
Comment: Also mentions purchase of land on the Hudson River for Palatines.

Date: 1710,10,19
Description: Memorial and petition of Nicholas Bayard to have rights of fee simple to land patented to him in 1695 restored, or at least to be reimbursed for costs of acquiring the land.
Source: N.Y. STATE ARCHIVES, ALBANY, N.Y.COL.MSS, INDORSED LAND PAPERS, 1643-1803, SERIES NO. A0272, DEPARTMENT OF STATE, APPLICATIONS FOR LAND GRANTS, VOL. 05, P. 070.
Comment: Bayard writes that he sold a great part of land granted to him in 1695 to three partners. An act to void extravagant purchases of land, however, has since nullified his patent. He has been forced to refund his partners for the money they paid him for the land. SEE 1695,09,28; 1695,12,12; 1698,05,31; 1698,10,19; 1699,05,19; 1709,05,27; 1710,07,24 (2); 1713,05,27; 1713,10,01; 1714,05,08; 1714,06,03; 1722,09,26. N.B. Bayard's articulation of the reasons for nullification of the patent.

Date: 1710,11,10
Description: Letter from J. Bridger, commissioned by the English Board of Admiralty to search for Naval Stores in the American Colonies, to the English Board of Trade. The letter mentions the arrival of the Palatines, and land purchased for them on the Hudson River.
Source: DOCUMENTS RELATIVE TO THE COLONIAL HISTORY OF THE STATE OF NEW YORK, ED. BY E.B. O'CALLAGHAN AND BERTHOLD FERNOW, 15 VOL. (ALBANY, N.Y.: WEED, PARSONS, AND CO., 1856-87), 5: 174-175.
Comment:

Date: 1711,00,00°
Description: Tracing, made in 1731, of a map of a grant of land in 1711 from the Indians to Adam Vrooman (Vroman) and Martinus Van Slyck (Slyke) in 1711.
Source: SEE 1887,00,00-1888,00,00 (41).
Comment: Rufus Grider Collection.

Date: 1711,05,30
Description: Letter from George Clarke to the English Board of Trade. The Palatines insist on settling in Schoharie: ". . .they would have the lands of Schohary [Schoharie] which the Queen had ordered them by their contract." Clarke reports that the N.Y. Provincial Governor told them, "That as to the lands of Scohary [Schoharie] its the malice of those who would have them for their slaves that put them on demanding it, for that those lands the Indians had not yet parted with, nor were they fit for their labour, no Pine being within twenty miles of it, . . ."
Source: THE DOCUMENTARY HISTORY OF THE STATE OF NEW YORK, ED. E.B. O'CALLAGHAN, (ALBANY; WEED, PARSONS, AND CO., CHARLES VAN BENTHUYSEN, 1849-1851), QUARTO ED., 3: 662-666.
Comment: N.B. This document contains much information about material culture.

Date: 1711,05,30 (2)
Description: Letter from George Clarke to the English Board of Trade. The Palatines insist on settling in Schoharie: ". . .they would have the lands of Schohary [Schoharie] which the Queen had ordered them by their contract." Clarke reports that the N.Y. Provincial Governor told them, "That as to the lands of Scohary [Schoharie] its the malice of those who would have them for their slaves that put them on demanding it, for that those lands the Indians had not yet parted with, nor were they fit for their labour, no Pine being within twenty miles of it, . . ."
Source: DOCUMENTS RELATIVE TO THE COLONIAL HISTORY OF THE STATE OF NEW YORK, ED. BY E.B. O'CALLAGHAN AND BERTHOLD FERNOW, 15 VOL. (ALBANY, N.Y.: WEED, PARSONS, AND CO., 1856-87), 5: 238-242.
Comment:

Date: 1711,08,22
Description: Tracing of Indian deed of 1711 for 260 acres in the Schoharie Valley to Adam Vrooman (Vroman) of Schenectady. Signed with totems.
Source: SEE 1887,00,00-1888,00,00 (37).
Comment: Rufus Grider Collection. SEE ALSO 1887,00,00-1888,00,00 (39). Map, 1887,00,00-1888,00,00 (44). According to an article in the Amsterdam Evening Recorder, dated 14 November 1910, the deed was to be sold at auction in New York City by Anderson's the following week. The article printed the text of the deed. With few exceptions (all of which are misreadings of orthography, e.g., "trace" instead of "tract"; "fine wood", instead of "fire wood"), the text is the same in the article and in Grider's copy. SEE 1910,11,14.

Date: 1712,10,31
Description: Letter from N.Y. Provincial Governor Robert Hunter to the English Board of Trade, about the Palatines. ". . .some hundreds of them took a resolution of possessing the lands of Scoharee [Schoharie] & are accordingly march'd thither have been buisy [sic] cutting a road from Schenectedy [sic] to that place, . . ."
Source: DOCUMENTS RELATIVE TO THE COLONIAL HISTORY OF THE STATE OF NEW YORK, ED. BY E.B. O'CALLAGHAN AND BERTHOLD FERNOW, 15 VOL. (ALBANY, N.Y.: WEED, PARSONS, AND CO., 1856-87), 5: 347-349.
Comment:

Date: 1712,11,14-15
Description: Letter from the Rev. Mr. William Andrews, missionary, to the Mohawks.
Source: THE DOCUMENTARY HISTORY OF THE STATE OF NEW YORK, ED. E.B. O'CALLAGHAN, (ALBANY; WEED, PARSONS, AND CO., CHARLES VAN BENTHUYSEN, 1849-1851), QUARTO ED., 3: 542-543.
Comment:

Date: 1713,03,09
Description: Long letter from William Andrews, describing in detail his experiences in beginning his missionary work for the Society for the Propagation of the Gospel among the Mohawks.
Source: THE FAITHFUL MOHAWKS, BY JOHN WOLFE LYDEKKER, (REPRINTED, PORT WASHINGTON, LONG ISLAND, NY: IRA J. FRIEDMAN, INC., 1968, pp. 34-38. (FIRST PUBLISHED IN 1938).
Comment: Provides descriptions of Mohawk life.

Date: 1713,05,11
Description: Letter from N.Y. Governor Robert Hunter to William Popple, Secretary of the English Board of Trade. Hunter reports that many of the Palatines have gone to Schoharie to settle.
Source: DOCUMENTS RELATIVE TO THE COLONIAL HISTORY OF THE STATE OF NEW YORK, ED. BY E.B. O'CALLAGHAN AND BERTHOLD FERNOW, 15 VOL. (ALBANY, N.Y.: WEED, PARSONS, AND CO., 1856-87), 5: 364.
Comment:

Date: 1713,05,27
Description: Petition of Samuel Bayard concerning land granted to his father after purchase from the Indians in 1694.
Source: N.Y. STATE ARCHIVES, ALBANY, N.Y.COL.MSS, INDORSED LAND PAPERS, 1643-1803, SERIES NO. A0272, DEPARTMENT OF STATE, APPLICATIONS FOR LAND GRANTS, VOL. 05, P. 144.
Comment: At one time this document was assigned the date 27 May 1709. SEE 1695,09,28; 1695,12,12; 1698,05,31; 1698,10,19; 1699,05,19; 1709,05,27; 1710,07,24 (2); 1710,10,19; 1713,10,01; 1714,05,08; 1714,06,03; 1722,09,26.

Date: 1713,05,27 (2)
Description: Petition of Samuel Bayard concerning land granted to his father after purchase from the Indians in 1694.
Source: N.Y. STATE ARCHIVES, ALBANY, N.Y.COL.MSS, INDORSED LAND PAPERS, 1643-1803, SERIES NO. A0272, DEPARTMENT OF STATE, APPLICATIONS FOR LAND GRANTS, VOL. 05, P. 173.
Comment: SEE 1695,09,28; 1695,12,12; 1698,05,31; 1698,10,19; 1699,05,19; 1709,05,27; 1710,10,19; 1713,05,27; 1713,10,01; 1714,05,08; 1714,06,03; 1722,09,26.

Date: 1713,07,01
Description: N.Y. Provincial Council Minutes. Petition by Adam Vrooman (Vroman).
Source: N.Y.STATE ARCHIVES, ALBANY, N.Y.COUN.MIN., SERIES A1895, VOL.11, PP. 197-198 (D164/6).
Comment:

Date: 1713,07,18
Description: Letter from N.Y. Provincial Governor Robert Hunter to the English Board of Trade reports, "The Palatines. . .who remain upon the lands on which I planted them, have been by the blessing of God & their own labours able to subsist themselves, those who run to Scohare [Schoharie] have been obliged to the charity of the Province to save them from starving. . ."
Source: DOCUMENTS RELATIVE TO THE COLONIAL HISTORY OF THE STATE OF NEW YORK, ED. BY E.B. O'CALLAGHAN AND BERTHOLD FERNOW, 15 VOL. (ALBANY, N.Y.: WEED, PARSONS, AND CO., 1856-87), 5: 365-367.
Comment:

Date: 1713,09,07
Description: Letter from William Andrews, missionary, to the Society for the Propagation of the Gospel. Andrews says that a Mohawk "Town or Castle" about "24 Miles from the ffort[sic] [Fort Hunter] called Eskahare [Schoharie]" has a population of "about 40".
Source: THE FAITHFUL MOHAWKS, BY JOHN WOLFE LYDEKKER. (PORT WASHINGTON, N.Y.: IRA J. FRIEDMAN, INC., 1968), (FIRST PUBLISHED IN 1938), P. 40.
Comment: Original manuscript is in Archives of the Society for the Propagation of the Gospel, 'A' MSS, Vol. 8, PP. 184f. Lydekker's book has excerpts of several of Andrews letters in Chapters 2 & 3. They contain some information about Mohawk culture.

Date: 1713,10,01
Description: Petition of Samuel Bayard about land granted to his father.
Source: N.Y.STATE ARCHIVES, ALBANY, N.Y.COL.MSS, INDORSED LAND PAPERS, 1643-1803, SERIES NO. A0272, DEPARTMENT OF STATE, APPLICATIONS FOR LAND GRANTS, VOL. 05, P. 181.
Comment: SEE 1695,09,28; 1695,12,12; 1698,05,31; 1698,10,19; 1699,05,19; 1709,05,27; 1710,07,24 (2); 1710,10,19; 1713,05,27; 1714,05,08; 1714,06,03; 1722,09,26.

Date: 1714,00,00°
Description: Tracing of survey by Thomas Machin, 1802, of the Old Schoharie Patent granted to Myndert Schuyler.
Source: SEE 1887,00,00-1888,00,00 (34).
Comment: Rufus Grider Collection. SEE 1710,10,19; 1714,11,03. For subsequent divisions of the land, see 1722,09,28; and a series of documents in 1736 and 1737 in Vol. 12 of N.Y.STATE ARCHIVES, ALBANY, N.Y.COL.MSS, INDORSED LAND PAPERS, 1643-1803, SERIES NO. A0272, DEPARTMENT OF STATE, APPLICATIONS FOR LAND GRANTS. (They are listed in this calendar.) See also, 1786,01,07; 1794,05,06; 1815,12,00.

Date: 1714,04,09
Description: Petition of Adam Vrooman (Vroman) for license to purchase 340 acres of land from Indians (at, or near, Onistagrawa), for a warrant to survey, and for a patent to 600 acres of land. Granted 9 Apr 1714.
Source: N.Y.STATE ARCHIVES, ALBANY, N.Y.COL.MSS, INDORSED LAND PAPERS, 1643-1803, SERIES NO. A0272, DEPARTMENT OF STATE, APPLICATIONS FOR LAND GRANTS, VOL. 06, P. 012.
Comment: A fairly detailed description of a tract of land reserved by Indians is included in this petition. SEE 1714,08,01.

Date: 1714,04,10
Description: Draft of Adam Vrooman's (Vroman's) license to purchase land bordered by Onitstagrawae (Onistagrawa) from the Indians.
Source: N.Y.STATE ARCHIVES, ALBANY, N.Y.COL.MSS, INDORSED LAND PAPERS, 1643-1803, SERIES NO. A0272, DEPARTMENT OF STATE, APPLICATIONS FOR LAND GRANTS, VOL. 06, P. 013.
Comment: This land was originally reserved by the Indians for themselves in grant of land from them to the Queen of England.

Date: 1714,04,10 (2)
Description: Warrant to Adam Vrooman (Vroman) to survey the land bordering Onitstagrawae (Onistagrawa).
Source: N.Y. STATE ARCHIVES, ALBANY, N.Y.COL.MSS, INDORSED LAND PAPERS, 1643-1803, SERIES NO. A0272, DEPARTMENT OF STATE, APPLICATIONS FOR LAND GRANTS, VOL. 06, P. 014.
Comment: Mentions land reserved by Indians. SEE 1714,04,09.

Date: 1714,04,10 (3)
Description: N.Y. Provincial Council Minutes. License to purchase Indian lands granted to Adam Vroman (Vrooman).
Source: N.Y.STATE ARCHIVES, ALBANY, N.Y.COUN.MIN., SERIES A1895, VOL. 11, P. 235.
Comment:

Date: 1714,04,13
Description: Indian deed for land in the Schoharie Valley to Adam Vrooman (Vroman) of Schenectady, 1714. Signed with totems.
Source: PIERPONT MORGAN LIBRARY, NEW YORK, NY, LITERARY AND HISTORICAL MANUSCRIPTS, OVERSIZE, ACCESSION # MA 948, ID 80124.
Comment: Original deed. In the Pierpont Morgan Library catalog, the date is listed as 13 Apr 1714. See 30 Apr 1714.

Date: 1714,04,30°
Description: Tracing of Indian deed for 340 acres in the Schoharie Valley to Adam Vrooman (Vroman) of Schenectady, 1714. Signed with totems.
Source: SEE 1887,00,00-1888,00,00 (38).
Comment: Rufus Grider Collection. SEE ALSO 1887,00,00-1888,00,00 (39); 1714,04,13.

Date: 1714,05,03
Description: Petition of Stevanus Groesbeck and John Dunbar, for license to purchase land one mile up the Schoharie Creek from the Mohaques (Mohawk) Castle, on the same side of the creek as the castle.
Source: N.Y.STATE ARCHIVES, ALBANY, N.Y.COL.MSS, INDORSED LAND PAPERS, 1643-1803, SERIES NO. A0272, DEPARTMENT OF STATE, APPLICATIONS FOR LAND GRANTS, VOL. 06, P. 023.
Comment:

Date: 1714,05,08
Description: Petition of Mynderdt (Myndert) Schuyler and others, for about 10,000 acres of land, formerly Nicholas Bayard's grant.
Source: N.Y.STATE ARCHIVES, ALBANY, N.Y.COL.MSS, INDORSED LAND PAPERS, 1643-1803, SERIES NO. A0272, DEPARTMENT OF STATE, APPLICATIONS FOR LAND GRANTS, VOL. 06, P. 024.
Comment: SEE 1710,10,19; 1714,11,03. For subsequent divisions of the land, see 1722,09,28; and a series of documents in 1736 and 1737 in Vol. 12 of N.Y.STATE ARCHIVES, ALBANY, N.Y.COL.MSS, INDORSED LAND PAPERS, 1643-1803, SERIES NO. A0272, DEPARTMENT OF STATE, APPLICATIONS FOR LAND GRANTS. (They are listed in this calendar.) See also, 1786,01,07; 1794,05,06; 1815,12,00.

Date: 1714,05,28
Description: Indian deed, dated 19 July 1710, to Evert Wendell, Harmanus Wendell, and Abraham Cuyler. Gift of land one mile along west side of Schoharie Creek, beginning at a stone called Keedsienoo, then to Netstograkaarawe Caghsoone creek and one mile from Schoharie creek to the woods. Deed was recorded 28 May 1714.
Source: ALBANY COUNTY CLERK'S OFFICE, ALBANY, N.Y., HALL OF RECORDS, DEEDS, BOOK 5, p. 227.
Comment:

Date: 1714,05,28 (2)
Description: Petition of Abraham Cuyler and others for confirmation of a gift of land on 19 July 1710 from native owners of Skohere (Schoharie). Indian deed included.
Source: N.Y.STATE ARCHIVES, ALBANY, N.Y.COL.MSS, INDORSED LAND PAPERS, 1643-1803, SERIES NO. A0272, DEPARTMENT OF STATE, APPLICATIONS FOR LAND GRANTS, VOL. 06, P. 26.
Comment: Land is about a mile in length on west side of Schoharie creek, running from a stone mountain called Onekeedsienos on the north up the creek to a run of water called Netstaghcokaarawe Caghsoone.

Date: 1714,06,03
Description: Warrant of survey of 10,000 acres of land of Mynderdt (Myndert) Schuyler and others; formerly Nicholas Bayard's grant.
Source: N.Y.STATE ARCHIVES, ALBANY, N.Y.COL.MSS, INDORSED LAND PAPERS, 1643-1803, SERIES NO. A0272, DEPARTMENT OF STATE, APPLICATIONS FOR LAND GRANTS, VOL. 06, P. 025.
Comment: For information on Bayard's grant, SEE 1695,09,28; 1695,12,12; 1698,05,31; 1698,10,19; 1699,05,19; 1709,05,27; 1710,07,24 (2); 1710,10,19; 1713,05,27; 1713,10,01; 1714,05,08; 1722,09,26.

Date: 1714,06,12
Description: N.Y. Provincial Council Minutes. Petition by Adam Vrooman (Vroman) about purchase of land to the west of Schoharie and north of Stony creek.
Source: N.Y.STATE ARCHIVES, ALBANY, N.Y.COUN.MIN., SERIES A1895, VOL. 11, P. 245 (D164/6).
Comment: SEE 1714,07,12; 1714,08,23; 1714,08,26.

Date: 1714,07,12
Description: Petition from Adam Vrooman (Vroman) for patent for land on Schoharie river near Onitstagrawae (Onistagrawa). Approved by Provincial Council of New York, 23 Aug 1714.
Source: N.Y. STATE ARCHIVES, ALBANY, N.Y.COL.MSS, INDORSED LAND PAPERS, 1643-1803, SERIES NO. A0272, DEPARTMENT OF STATE, APPLICATIONS FOR LAND GRANTS, VOL. 06, P. 034.
Comment: SEE 1714,08,26.

Date: 1714,08,01
Description: N.Y. Provincial Council Minutes. License to purchase Indian lands granted to Adam Vrooman (Vroman).
Source: N.Y.STATE ARCHIVES,ALBANY, N.Y.COUN.MIN., SERIES A1895, VOL. 11, P. 267.
Comment: SEE 1714,04,09.

Date: 1714,08,06°
Description: Date cited as being that of patent for Adam Vrooman (Vroman) for tract of land on Schoharie river.
Source: SEE 1726,10,21.
Comment: N.B. Discrepancy between this date and 26 Aug 1714 below.

Date: 1714,08,23°
Description: Petition of Adam Vrooman (Vroman) for patent for land on Schoharie river near Onitstagrawae (Onistagrawa) is approved.
Source: SEE 1714,06,12.
Comment: SEE ALSO 1714,07,12.

Date: 1714,08,26
Description: Warrant for patent for Adam Vrooman (Vroman) for land on Schoharie river near Onitstagrawae (Onistagrawa).
Source: N.Y. STATE ARCHIVES, ALBANY, N.Y.COL.MSS, INDORSED LAND PAPERS, 1643-1803, SERIES NO. A0272, DEPARTMENT OF STATE, APPLICATIONS FOR LAND GRANTS, VOL. 06, P. 036.
Comment: SEE 1714,07,12.

Date: 1714,08,26 (2)
Description: Grant of 600 acres of land on Schoharie river near Onitstagrawae (Onistagrawa) to Adam Vrooman (Vroman).
Source: N.Y. STATE ARCHIVES, ALBANY, N.Y.COL.MSS, INDORSED LAND PAPERS, 1643-1803, SERIES NO. A0272, DEPARTMENT OF STATE, APPLICATIONS FOR LAND GRANTS, VOL. 06, P. 064.
Comment: SEE 1714,07,12.

Date: 1714,08,26 (3)
Description: Patent of 600 acres of land to Adam Vrooman (Vroman).
Source: N.Y.STATE ARCHIVES, ALBANY, N.Y. LETTERS PATENT, 1664-1780, SERIES NO. 12590, BOOK 8, P. 092.
Comment:

Date: 1714,08,26 (4)
Description: N.Y. Provincial Council Minutes. Patent granted to Adam Vrooman (Vroman).
Source: N.Y.STATE ARCHIVES,ALBANY, N.Y.COUN.MIN., SERIES A1895, VOL. 11, P. 267.
Comment:

Date: 1714,08,26°
Description: Date of patent of Adam Vrooman (Vroman) for land on Schoharie river near Onitstagrawae (Onistagrawa).
Source: SEE 1726,10,17.
Comment:

Date: 1714,09,05
Description: Fees for patent of Adam Vrooman (Vroman) for land on Schoharie river near Onitstagrawae (Onistagrawa).
Source: N.Y. STATE ARCHIVES, ALBANY, N.Y.COL.MSS, INDORSED LAND PAPERS, 1643-1803, SERIES NO. A0272, DEPARTMENT OF STATE, APPLICATIONS FOR LAND GRANTS, VOL. 06, P. 037.
Comment: SEE 1714,07,12; 1714,08,26.

Date: 1714,11,03
Description: Petiton of Myndert Schuyler, Peter Van Brugh, Robert Livingston, Jr., John Schuyler, and Henry Wileman (Wildman), about patent for 10,000 acres at Schoharie pursuant to a warrant of a former petition.
Source: N.Y.STATE ARCHIVES, ALBANY, N.Y.COL.MSS, INDORSED LAND PAPERS, 1643-1803, SERIES NO. A0272, DEPARTMENT OF STATE, APPLICATIONS FOR LAND GRANTS,, VOL. 06, P. 078.
Comment: SEE 1714,05,08.

Date: 1714,11,03 (2)
Description: Warrant pertaining to 10,000 acres of land of Myndert Schuyler, Peter Van Brugh, Robert Livingston, Jr., John Schuyler, and Henry Wildman (Wileman).
Source: N.Y.STATE ARCHIVES, ALBANY, N.Y.COL.MSS, INDORSED LAND PAPERS, 1643-1803, SERIES NO. A0272, DEPARTMENT OF STATE, APPLICATIONS FOR LAND GRANTS, VOL. 06, P. 079.
Comment:

Date: 1714,11,03 (3)
Description: List of fees pertaining to 10,000 acres of land of Myndert Schuyer and others.
Source: N.Y.STATE ARCHIVES, ALBANY, N.Y.COL.MSS, INDORSED LAND PAPERS, 1643-1803, SERIES NO. A0272, DEPARTMENT OF STATE, APPLICATIONS FOR LAND GRANTS, VOL. 06, P. 80.
Comment:

Date: 1714,11,03 (4)
Description: Patent to Myndert Schuyler and others for 10,000 acres of land.
Source: N.Y.STATE ARCHIVES, ALBANY, N.Y. LETTERS PATENT, 1664-1780, SERIES NO. 12590, BOOK 8, P. 74.
Comment: See 1714,00,00; 1714,05,08. For subsequent divisions of the land, see 1722,09,28; and a series of documents in 1736 and 1737 in Vol. 12 of N.Y.STATE ARCHIVES, ALBANY, N.Y.COL.MSS, INDORSED LAND PAPERS, 1643-1803, SERIES NO. A0272, DEPARTMENT OF STATE, APPLICATIONS FOR LAND GRANTS. (They are listed in this calendar.) See also, 1786,01,07; 1794,05,06; 1815,12,00.

Date: 1714,11,03 (5)
Description: N.Y. Provincial Council Minutes. Mention is made of patent granted to Myndert Schuyler for land at Schoharie.
Source: N.Y.STATE ARCHIVES,ALBANY, N.Y.COUN.MIN., SERIES A1895, VOL. 11, P. 276 (D164/6).
Comment:

Date: 1714,11,11
Description: License to Samuel Staats and Rip Van Dam to purchase 2,000 acres of land at Foxes (Fox) Creek.
Source: N.Y.STATE ARCHIVES, ALBANY, N.Y.COL.MSS, INDORSED LAND PAPERS, 1643-1803, SERIES NO. A0272, DEPARTMENT OF STATE, APPLICATIONS FOR LAND GRANTS, VOL. 06, P. 096.
Comment:

Date: 1714,11,11 (2)
Description: Report of N.Y. Provincial Council, about license to Samuel Staats and Rip Van Dam to purchase 2,000 acres of land on Foxes (Fox) Creek.
Source: N.Y.STATE ARCHIVES, ALBANY, N.Y.COL.MSS, INDORSED LAND PAPERS, 1643-1803, SERIES NO. A0272, DEPARTMENT OF STATE, APPLICATIONS FOR LAND GRANTS, VOL. 06, P. 098.
Comment:

Date: 1715,02,25
Description: N.Y. Colonial Manuscripts. Affidavits from Lawrence Classen (Claus), Abraham Schuyler, and Grietje, wife of Adam Vrooman (Vroman), about the interference of John Visger (Weiser) with the Mohawk Indians.
Source: N.Y. STATE ARCHIVES, ALBANY, N.Y.COL.MSS., 1664-1776, VOL. 59, P. 172.
Comment:

Date: 1715,02,28
Description: N.Y. Provincial Council Minutes, report that complaints have been received from Albany about John Wizer (Weiser) and other Palatines settled at Schoharie as squatters.
Source: N.Y.STATE ARCHIVES,ALBANY, N.Y.COUN.MIN., SERIES A1895, VOL. 11, P. 288 (D164/6).
Comment: The document was very severely damaged by fire in 1911.

Date: 1715,06,09
Description: Memorial of Adam Vrooman (Vroman) to Robert Hunter, colonial governor of New York, complaining that John C. Weiser is causing problems for Vrooman at Schoharie. Vrooman suggests that Weiser and his son's influence among Indians may be troublesome to the colony's interests.
Source: N.Y. STATE ARCHIVES, ALBANY, N.Y.COL.MSS., 1664-1776, VOL. 60, P. 003a.
Comment: Weiser is a Palatine.

Date: 1715,07,09
Description: Letter from Adam Vrooman (Vroman) to N.Y. Provincial Governor Hunter, about threats from the Palatines. Vrooman says that John Conrad Weiser is the "Ring Leader". He reports that Weiser "has had his son some time to Live among the Indians and now he is turn'd their Interpreter so that this Wiser [sic] and his Son talk with the Indians very often and have made treates [sic] for them and have been busy to buy land at many places which is Contrary to your Excellencys Proclamation, and has made the Indians drunk to that degree to go and mark of [sic] Land with them. . ."
Source: THE DOCUMENTARY HISTORY OF THE STATE OF NEW YORK, ED. E.B. O'CALLAGHAN, (ALBANY; WEED, PARSONS, AND CO., CHARLES VAN BENTHUYSEN, 1849-1851), QUARTO ED., 3: 687-688.
Comment: N.B. This letter is followed in THE DOCUMENTARY HISTORY OF THE STATE OF NEW YORK by a warrant to arrest John Conrad Weiser.

Date: 1716,02,10
Description: Petiton of John Christian Garlach (Garlick) for license to purchase 150 acres on the east side of Skoheres (Schoharie) Creek.
Source: N.Y.STATE ARCHIVES, ALBANY, N.Y.COL.MSS, INDORSED LAND PAPERS, 1643-1803, SERIES NO. A0272, DEPARTMENT OF STATE, APPLICATIONS FOR LAND GRANTS, VOL. 06, 138.
Comment:

Date: 1716,02,14
Description: Patent to Johannes Harmense Fisher for land one mile from Fort Hunter.
Source: N.Y.STATE ARCHIVES, ALBANY, N.Y. LETTERS PATENT, 1664-1780, SERIES NO. 12590, BOOK 8, P. 144.
Comment:

Date: 1717,06,15
Description: Indian deed to Rip Van Damet [Van Dam], Peter Van Burgh, John Schuyler, Robert Livingston, George Clarke, Myndert Schuyler, and the heirs of Samuel Staats.
Source: ALBANY COUNTY CLERK'S OFFICE, ALBANY, N.Y., HALL OF RECORDS, DEEDS, BOOK 5, P. 370-371.
Comment:

Date: 1717,06,15°
Description: Two thousand acres of land at Schoharie adjoining that of Myndert Schuyler were purchased by Rip Van Dam and Phillip Schuyler from the Indians.
Source: SEE 1724,08,06.
Comment:

Date: 1718,07,07
Description: Letter from the N.Y. Provincial Governor Robert Hunter to the English Board of Trade. Hunter writes about the Palatines that about fifty families have moved against orders to Schoharie. Hunter considers them to be a very unsavory group. He writes, ". . .but one Wyser [Weiser] the constant ringleader of all mischief amongst them who is now gone for England, I know not for what purpose formed a party amongst them who would come to no terms. . ."
Source: DOCUMENTS RELATIVE TO THE COLONIAL HISTORY OF THE STATE OF NEW YORK, ED. BY E.B. O'CALLAGHAN AND BERTHOLD FERNOW, 15 VOL. (ALBANY, N.Y.: WEED, PARSONS, AND CO., 1856-87), 5: 507-511.
Comment: SEE 1720,08,02; 1720,09,06; 1720,11,01.

Date: 1720,00,00
Description: Document states the conditions, grievances, and oppressions of the Germans in the English Province of New York in America in 1720.
Source: THE DOCUMENTARY HISTORY OF THE STATE OF NEW YORK, ED. E.B. O'CALLAGHAN, (ALBANY; WEED, PARSONS, AND CO., CHARLES VAN BENTHUYSEN, 1849-1851), QUARTO ED., 3: 707-714.
Comment: N.B. Schoharie is written Schorie in this document.

Date: 1720,00,00-1792,00,00
Description: Manuscripts pertaining to highways in Schoharie, Saratoga, and other counties.
Source: ALBANY COUNTY CLERK'S OFFICE, HALL OF RECORDS, ALBANY, N.Y., REAL PROPERTY RECORDS, SCHOHARIE, SARATOGA AND OTHER COUNTIES (1720-1792), 1 VOLUME.
Comment: Contains nothing particular about Indians of Schoharie.

Date: 1720,06,03
Description: Draft of certificate for survey for John Peters Mebee (Maybe) of 608 acres on the west side of Schohare (Schoharie) Creek "called by the Indians Tiondorogue [Tienonderoge, Tienonderoga, Tionnonderoge]", purchased by him "of the Native Indian proprietors for a valuable Consideration in his Majestys [sic] Name".
Source: N.Y.STATE ARCHIVES, ALBANY, N.Y.COL.MSS, INDORSED LAND PAPERS, 1643-1803, SERIES NO. A0272, DEPARTMENT OF STATE, APPLICATIONS FOR LAND GRANTS, VOL. 09, P. 135.
Comment: SEE 1725,09,29; 1725,10,04; 1725,10,13; 1725,10,14. Is this for land in the Schoharie region? This document is filed in the N.Y. STATE ARCHIVES, ALBANY, N.Y.COL.MSS, INDORSED LAND PAPERS, 1643-1803, VOL. 9, P. 135, under the date 25 January 1725.

Date: 1720,07,26
Description: Letter from NY Provincial Governor Robert Hunter to William Popple, Secretary of the English Board of Trade, about Palatines.
Source: DOCUMENTS RELATIVE TO THE COLONIAL HISTORY OF THE STATE OF NEW YORK, ED. BY E.B. O'CALLAGHAN AND BERTHOLD FERNOW, 15 VOL. (ALBANY, N.Y.: WEED, PARSONS, AND CO., 1856-87), 5: 552-553.
Comment:

Date: 1720,08,02
Description: Petition of the New York Palatines to the English Board of Trade, stating, "That the Indians havg [sic] yielded to Her late Maty [sic]. . .a small Tract of Land called Schorie [Schoharie] for the use of the Palatines, they in fifteen days cleared a way of fifteen miles through the woods & settled fifty Families therein. . .in the following Spring the remainder. . .joined the said fifty families. . [at] . .Shorie [Schoharie] But that country being too small. . . they were constrained to purchase some Neighbouring Land of the Indians for which they were to giveThree hundd [sic] pieces of Eight."
Source: DOCUMENTS RELATIVE TO THE COLONIAL HISTORY OF THE STATE OF NEW YORK, ED. BY E.B. O'CALLAGHAN AND BERTHOLD FERNOW, 15 VOL. (ALBANY, N.Y.: WEED, PARSONS, AND CO., 1856-87), 5: 553-555.
Comment: The petition goes on to state that the Palatine settlement was contested by "some gentelmen[sic] of Albani [sic]" who declared that they themselves had purchased the land at Schoharie from the governor of New York. "The Indians were animated against the Palatines; but these found means to appease the Savages by giving them what they would of their own substance." SEE 1720,09,06.

Date: 1720,09,06
Description: Minutes of the English Board of Trade, about the Palatines.
Source: DOCUMENTS RELATIVE TO THE COLONIAL HISTORY OF THE STATE OF NEW YORK, ED. BY E.B. O'CALLAGHAN AND BERTHOLD FERNOW, 15 VOL. (ALBANY, N.Y.: WEED, PARSONS, AND CO., 1856-87), 5: 570.
Comment: SEE 1718,07,07; 1720,08,02; 1720,11,01.

Date: 1720,11,01
Description: Petition of Johannes Wilhelm Schefs, Agent for the Palatines, to the English Board of Trade. Mentions disagreement between Schefs and Weiser. Also gives information about population of Palatines in Schoharie River valley and Germans in the province of New York.
Source: DOCUMENTS RELATIVE TO THE COLONIAL HISTORY OF THE STATE OF NEW YORK, ED. BY E.B. O'CALLAGHAN AND BERTHOLD FERNOW, 15 VOL. (ALBANY, N.Y.: WEED, PARSONS, AND CO., 1856-87), 5: 574-576.
Comment: SEE 1718,07,07; 1720,08,02; 1720,09,06.

Date: 1721,08,29
Description: Statement of N.Y. Provincial Governor Robert Hunter. The report states, "In relation to the Palatines in the Province of New York, Brigadr Hunter acquainted their Lordships [the English Board of Trade and Plantations] that the greatest part of those who had settled at a place call'd Schorie [Schoharie], had agreed and submitted to his Proposals for the land they were upon, but durst no sign the agreement [sic] with the Proprietors, for fear of the Ring Leaders among themselves in the Disturbances about that Settlement."
Source: DOCUMENTS RELATIVE TO THE COLONIAL HISTORY OF THE STATE OF NEW YORK, ED. BY E.B. O'CALLAGHAN AND BERTHOLD FERNOW, 15 VOL. (ALBANY, N.Y.: WEED, PARSONS, AND CO., 1856-87), 5: 561.
Comment:

Date: 1721,09,02-09
Description: N.Y. Provincial Council Minutes, about Palatines at Schoharie.
Source: N.Y.STATE ARCHIVES,ALBANY, N.Y.COUN.MIN., SERIES A1895, VOL. 13, P. 143.
Comment:

Date: 1721,09,09
Description: N.Y. Provincial Council Minutes, about Palatines at Schoharie.
Source: N.Y.STATE ARCHIVES,ALBANY, N.Y.COUN.MIN., SERIES A1895, VOL. 13, P. 162.
Comment:

Date: 1721,10,16
Description: N.Y. Provincial Governor Burnet to English Board of Trade and Plantations. Proceedings in Albany, September 1721, are enclosed.
Source: PUBLIC RECORD OFFICE, KEW, ENGLAND, CO5/1053.
Comment: Reference made to land controversy of the Mohawks.

Date: 1721,10,16 (2)
Description: Letter from N.Y. Provincial Governor Burnet to the English Board of Trade, states that a license to purchase land from the Mohawks has been granted to Palatines "& those people seem very well pleased and satisfyed with what I have done and as proof of it all that did live in a lawless manner before on the Land at Schokery [Schoharie] which had been granted to other Proprietors have now actually taken leases from them and attorned [sic] Tenants to them."
Source: DOCUMENTS RELATIVE TO THE COLONIAL HISTORY OF THE STATE OF NEW YORK, ED. BY E.B. O'CALLAGHAN AND BERTHOLD FERNOW, 15 VOL. (ALBANY, N.Y.: WEED, PARSONS, AND CO., 1856-87), 5: 630-634.
Comment: Burnet writes, "I did intend to settle the Palatines as far as I could in the middle of our Indians, but finding the [sic] could not be brought to that I have granted their own request which was to have a license to purchase . . [land from the Mohawks] . ." The license came with the provision "that it be not nearer than a fall in the Mohocks River which is forty miles above Fort Hunter & four score from Albany by which the frontier will be so much extended . . ."

Date: 1722,03,09
Description: License to John Conrad Weiser, Jr., Peter Wagoner (Waggoner), and others to purchase land from the Indians land three miles from the Mohawk River and near the creek called Otqshage (Otsquage).
Source: N.Y.STATE ARCHIVES, ALBANY, N.Y.COL.MSS, INDORSED LAND PAPERS, 1643-1803, SERIES NO. A0272, DEPARTMENT OF STATE, APPLICATIONS FOR LAND GRANTS, VOL. 08, P. 138.
Comment:

Date: 1722,07,09
Description: Indian deed to John C. Weiser, Jr. and others for land on both sides of the Mohawk River.
Source: N.Y.STATE ARCHIVES, ALBANY, N.Y.COL.MSS, INDORSED LAND PAPERS, 1643-1803, SERIES NO. A0272, DEPARTMENT OF STATE, APPLICATIONS FOR LAND GRANTS, VOL. 08, P. 168.
Comment: Land is not in the Schoharie River Valley, but is land ceded to Palatines leaving Schoharie. Document contains Adam Vrooman's (Vroman's) signature, as well as marks (totems) of the Indians. N.B., signed by an Indian from each of the Five Nations. All but the Cayuga name are given, but the script makes it difficult to decipher some of the letters, particularly those of the Mohawk signers: _?__ry_?__(Mo), Kahyawgahrotun (Oa), Kaneigarah (Se), and Odaseatah (Oe). At least one, the Oneida, is a name on the Roll Call of Iroquois Chiefs (See THE ROLL CALL OF THE IROQUOIS CHIEFS by William N. Fenton, Smithsonian Miscellaneous Collections, Vol. 111, No. 15, Washington, D.C.)

Date: 1722,09,26
Description: Representation of the English Board of Trade to the King. Lists abuses through time of the power of New York provincial governors to dispose of land in the province. One listed is "To Nicholas Bayard, certain Tract of land called Skohaare beginning at the mouth of Skohaare River & runs to the head of said River, which by computation of those that have travelled those parts, is about forty miles in legth, the breadth is uncertain, being bounded by hills lying on the East & West Sides of the said River, which said tract of Land includes part of the Moquase or Mohacks land."
Source: DOCUMENTS RELATIVE TO THE COLONIAL HISTORY OF THE STATE OF NEW YORK, ED. BY E.B. O'CALLAGHAN AND BERTHOLD FERNOW, 15 VOL. (ALBANY, N.Y.: WEED, PARSONS, AND CO., 1856-87), 5: 650-654.
Comment: Discusses laws passed to prevent exorbitant land grants. "But we find . . . that several . . . formerly obtained without previous Survey are still remaining extended by great fraud & deceit . . ." SEE 1695,09,28; 1695,12,12; 1698,05,31; 1698,10,19; 1699,05,19; 1709,05,27; 1710,07,24 (2); 1710,10,19; 1713,05,27; 1713,10,01; 1714,05,08; 1714,06,03. The Six Nations are described as "being an honest warlike people beside that industrious planters."

Date: 1722,09,28
Description: N.Y. Colonial Manuscripts. Letter from Rip Van Dam, George Clarke and Philip Schuyler to Myndert Schuyler, Robert Livingston, Pieter Van Bergen, and John Schuyler about accounts and divisions of the Schoharie Patent.
Source: N.Y. STATE ARCHIVES, ALBANY, N.Y.COL.MSS., 1664-1776, VOL. 64, P. 137.
Comment: This document was destroyed by fire in 1911.

Date: 1723,02,06
Description: Deed, signed by Donachqua, Anharissa, DeGarydonde (Dagarytunteey), Danagerane, Dagnatagonghe (Dagnatagunoke), and Satergusqua to William York, Jacob Frederick Lawyer, and Nicholas York for land bordering that of Myndert Schuyler of the east side of the Schoharie and that of Adam Vrooman (Vroman) on the west side of the river.
Source: N.Y.STATE ARCHIVES, ALBANY, N.Y.COL.MSS, INDORSED LAND PAPERS, 1643-1803, SERIES NO. A0272, DEPARTMENT OF STATE, APPLICATIONS FOR LAND GRANTS, VOL. 09, P. 023.
Comment: SEE 1723,03,07; 1723,06,20; 1723,06,27. The Indian marks (totems) on the document show up clearly.

Date: 1723,02,06°
Description: Petition of William York, Jacob Federick Lawyer, and Nicholas York for a patent for land bordering that of Myndert Schuyler on the east side of the Schoharie and that of Adam Vrooman (Vroman) on the west side of the river. The land was purchased from the Indians, 6 February 1723.
Source: SEE 1723,03,07.
Comment:

Date: 1723,02,12
Description: Deed from Nascusaque (?sp), Johannes, Luykes (Lucas, Lucus), Jan, Cornelus (Cornelius), and Anthony "being empowered and authorized by the sachems of the Three Races [three clans] of ye Maquas [Mohawks]" to Christian Garlick (Garlach) and others for land upon Canada Creek.
Source: N.Y.STATE ARCHIVES, ALBANY,N.Y.COL.MSS, INDORSED LAND PAPERS, 1643-1803, SERIES NO. A0272, DEPARTMENT OF STATE, APPLICATIONS FOR LAND GRANTS, VOL. 09, P. 028.
Comment: Land is not in the Schoharie region, but Euroamericans involved are Schoharie Palatines. SEE 1723,08,00-09,00. Three clan marks can very clearly be seen on the document.

Date: 1723,03,04
Description: Petition of John Conrad Weiser, Jr., Peter Wagoner (Waggoner), and other Palatines for license to purchase from the Indians land three miles from the Mohawk River near Otqshage (Otsquage) Creek. Petition was approved by the N.Y. Provincial Council, 8 March 1723.
Source: N.Y.STATE ARCHIVES, ALBANY, N.Y.COL.MSS, INDORSED LAND PAPERS, 1643-1803, SERIES NO. A0272, DEPARTMENT OF STATE, APPLICATIONS FOR LAND GRANTS, VOL. 09, P. 037.
Comment: The land is not in the Schoharie region, but the Euroamericans involved are Schoharie Palatines. The land is nearer Canajoharie than Schoharie. SEE 1723,05,10; 1724,01,20.

Date: 1723,03,07
Description: Petition of William York, Jacob Federick Lawyer, and Nicholas York for a patent for land bordering that of Myndert Schuyler on the east side of the Schoharie and that of Adam Vrooman (Vroman) on the west side of the river. The land was purchased from the Indians, 6 February 1723.
Source: N.Y.STATE ARCHIVES, ALBANY, N.Y.COL.MSS, INDORSED LAND PAPERS, 1643-1803, SERIES NO. A0272, DEPARTMENT OF STATE, APPLICATIONS FOR LAND GRANTS, VOL. 08, P. 136.
Comment:

Date: 1723,03,09
Description: Warrant for survey of land on both sides of the Schoharie river purchased from the Indians by William York, Jacob Frederick Lawyer, and Nicholas York.
Source: N.Y.STATE ARCHIVES, ALBANY, N.Y.COL.MSS, INDORSED LAND PAPERS, 1643-1803, SERIES NO. A0272, DEPARTMENT OF STATE, APPLICATIONS FOR LAND GRANTS, VOL. 09, P. 093.
Comment:

Date: 1723,05,10
Description: Indian deed to J.C. Weisser (Weiser), Jr. for land at Otsquage (Otqshage).
Source: N.Y.STATE ARCHIVES, ALBANY, N.Y.COL.MSS, INDORSED LAND PAPERS, 1643-1803, SERIES NO. A0272, DEPARTMENT OF STATE, APPLICATIONS FOR LAND GRANTS, VOL. 09, P. 058.
Comment: The land is not in the Schoharie region, but Weiser is a Schoharie Palatine. SEE 1723,03,04; 1724,01,20. N.B., Indian marks (totems), and spelling of Indian names.

Date: 1723,06,00
Description: Draft of a patent to William York and others, for four tracts of land on Schoharie Creek.
Source: N.Y.STATE ARCHIVES, ALBANY, N.Y.COL.MSS, INDORSED LAND PAPERS, 1643-1803, SERIES NO. A0272, DEPARTMENT OF STATE, APPLICATIONS FOR LAND GRANTS, VOL. 09, P. 072.
Comment:

Date: 1723,06,20
Description: Description of a survey of land purchased by William York, Jacob Frederick Lawyer and Nicholas York along Schoharie Creek.
Source: N.Y.STATE ARCHIVES, ALBANY, N.Y.COL.MSS, INDORSED LAND PAPERS, 1643-1803, SERIES NO. A0272, DEPARTMENT OF STATE, APPLICATIONS FOR LAND GRANTS, VOL. 09, P. 071.
Comment: SEE 1723,03,07; 1723,06,27.

Date: 1723,06,20 (2)
Description: Warrant for a patent to William York, Jacob Frederick Lawyer, and Nicholas York for land at Schoharie. Also included is warrant to survey, dated 21 June 1723; and scrambled notes about insertion.
Source: N.Y.STATE ARCHIVES, ALBANY, N.Y.COL.MSS, INDORSED LAND PAPERS, 1643-1803, SERIES NO. A0272, DEPARTMENT OF STATE, APPLICATIONS FOR LAND GRANTS, VOL. 09, P. 073.
Comment: N.B., cryptic endorsement indicating that this, or related patent(s), should be dated 28 June 1723. SEE 1723,06,28.

Date: 1723,06,20 (3)
Description: Patent to Lewis Morris and others for 6,000 acres on the south side of the Mohawk River about thirteen miles above Fort Hunter.
Source: N.Y.STATE ARCHIVES, ALBANY, N.Y. LETTERS PATENT, 1664-1780, SERIES NO. 12590, Book 9, P. 44.

Date: 1723,06,21
Description: List of names to be inserted in patent for purchase of approximately 40,000 acres at Schoharie.
Source: N.Y.STATE ARCHIVES, ALBANY, N.Y.COL.MSS, INDORSED LAND PAPERS, 1643-1803, SERIES NO. A0272, DEPARTMENT OF STATE, APPLICATIONS FOR LAND GRANTS, VOL. 09: 072

Date: 1723,06,27
Description: Certificate of William York, Jacob Frederick Lawyer, and Nicholas York for land on both the east and west side of Schoharie river ("Skohare Kill") purchased from Donachqua and other Indians on 6 February 1723.
Source: N.Y.STATE ARCHIVES, ALBANY, N.Y.COL.MSS, INDORSED LAND PAPERS, 1643-1803, SERIES NO. A0272, DEPARTMENT OF STATE, APPLICATIONS FOR LAND GRANTS, VOL. 09, P. 079.
Comment: SEE 1723,02,06; 1723,06,20.

Date: 1723,06,28
Description: Patent to William York, Jacob Frederick Lawyer and Nicholas York for 600 acres of land south of Schoharie on the east side of Schoharie Kill. The acreage is divided into four tracts.
Source: N.Y.STATE ARCHIVES, ALBANY, N.Y. LETTERS PATENT, 1664-1780, SERIES NO. 12590, BOOK 09, P. 054.
Comment:

Date: 1723,08,00-09,00
Description: Description of Garlick (Garlach) land on Canada Creek.
Source: N.Y.STATE ARCHIVES, ALBANY, N.Y.COL.MSS, INDORSED LAND PAPERS, 1643-1803, SERIES NO. A0272, DEPARTMENT OF STATE, APPLICATIONS FOR LAND GRANTS, VOL. 09, P. 086, 087, 088.
Comment: Land is not in the Schoharie region, but the Euro-Americans involved are Schoharie Palatines. SEE 1723,02,12.

Date: 1723,11,13
Description: N.Y. Colonial Manuscripts. Letter from Isaac Bobin to George Clarke about a deed for Schoharie.
Source: N.Y. STATE ARCHIVES, ALBANY, N.Y.COL.MSS., 1664-1776, VOL. 66, P. 020.
Comment: The document was destroyed by fire, 1911.

Date: 1724,01,20
Description: Petition of J.C. Weisser (Weiser), Jr. concerning land at Otsquage (Otqshage).
Source: N.Y.STATE ARCHIVES, ALBANY, N.Y.COL.MSS, INDORSED LAND PAPERS, 1643-1803, SERIES NO. A0272, DEPARTMENT OF STATE, APPLICATIONS FOR LAND GRANTS, VOL. 09, P. 089.
Comment: The land is not in the Schoharie region, but Weiser is a Schoharie Palatine. SEE 1723,03,04; 1723,05,10.

Date: 1724,04,08
Description: Petition of Hartman Vindeker (Windecker) and other Schoharie Palatines for license to purchase land in Mohawk country.
Source: N.Y.STATE ARCHIVES, ALBANY, N.Y.COL.MSS, INDORSED LAND PAPERS, 1643-1803, SERIES NO. A0272, DEPARTMENT OF STATE, APPLICATIONS FOR LAND GRANTS, VOL. 09, P. 095,096.
Comment:

Date: 1724,08,06
Description: Petition of Lewis Morris, Jr., Andries Coeymans and others on behalf of the heirs of Samuel Staats for a warrant of survey of 2,000 acres of land at Schoharie, purchased from the Indians June 15, 1717 by Rip Van Dam and Phillip Schuyler. Also included is September 4, 1724 approval of the petition.
Source: N.Y.STATE ARCHIVES, ALBANY, N.Y.COL.MSS, INDORSED LAND PAPERS, 1643-1803, SERIES NO. A0272, DEPARTMENT OF STATE, APPLICATIONS FOR LAND GRANTS, VOL. 09, P. 119.
Comment: SEE 1717,06,15.

Date: 1724,09,04°
Description: Approval of petition of Lewis Morris, Jr. and Andries Coeymans on behalf of the heirs of Samuel Staats for a warrant of survey of 2,000 acres of land in Schoharie purchased from the Indians by Rip Van Dam and Phillip Schuyler.
Source: SEE 1724,08,06.
Comment:

Date: 1724,09,21
Description: Indian deed to John Peterse Mebee, for a tract of land on the west side of Tionondorogue creek.
Source: N.Y.STATE ARCHIVES, ALBANY, N.Y.COL.MSS, INDORSED LAND PAPERS, 1643-1803, SERIES NO. A0272, DEPARTMENT OF STATE, APPLICATIONS FOR LAND GRANTS, VOL. 9, P. 130.

Date: 1724,11,21
Description: Letter from N.Y. Provincial Governor Burnet to the English Board of Trade. Burnet reports that one of the regulations recently passed in the province was "An Act for laying out Public Highways at Schoharie in Albany county &c."
Source: DOCUMENTS RELATIVE TO THE COLONIAL HISTORY OF THE STATE OF NEW YORK, 15 VOL. (ALBANY, N.Y.: WEED, PARSONS, AND CO., 1856-87), 5: 734-740. THE REFERENCE TO SCHOHARIE IS ON p. 739.
Comment: A postmark to the letter is dated 28 Dec 1724. SEE 1720,00,00-1792,00,00.

Date: 1725,00,00°
Description: Description of a survey of 300 acres of land southward of Schoharie. Surveyed for William York and Lewis York by Phillip Verplank.
Source: SEE n.d.
Comment:

Date: 1725,01,00 [ ]
Description: Draft of a certificate to John Pieterse Mebee (Mebee; Maybe) for 680 acres of land at Tionondorogue on the west side of Schoharie Creek.
Source: N.Y.STATE ARCHIVES, ALBANY, N.Y.COL.MSS, INDORSED LAND PAPERS, 1643-1803, SERIES NO. A0272, DEPARTMENT OF STATE, APPLICATIONS FOR LAND GRANTS, VOL. 9, P. 135.
Comment: Date has been assigned on basis of placement of manuscript in Indorsed Land Papers, Vol. 9.

Date: 1725,01,25
Description: Warrant of survey of 600 acres of land on the west side of Tionondorogue Creek to John Peterse Mebee (Mebe; Maybe).
Source: N.Y.STATE ARCHIVES, ALBANY, N.Y.COL.MSS, INDORSED LAND PAPERS, 1643-1803, SERIES NO. A0272, DEPARTMENT OF STATE, APPLICATIONS FOR LAND GRANTS, VOL. 9, P. 134.
Comment:

Date: 1725,02,10
Description: Patent to Lewis York and William York for 300 acres of land south of Schoharie.
Source: N.Y.STATE ARCHIVES, ALBANY, N.Y. LETTERS PATENT, 1664-1780, SERIES NO. 12590, BOOK 09, P. 227.
Comment: The land is in Middleburgh. SEE 1725,10,28; 1725,11,02. Is the date 10 February 1725 correct, or should it be 10 February 1726? Check document carefully for date on it.

Date: 1725,04,03
Description: Warrant and certificate to J.C. Weiser, Jr., Johannis Lawyer, Jr. and Peter Wagoner (Waggoner) pertaining to land at Otsquage (Otqshage). A map is included.
Source: N.Y.STATE ARCHIVES, ALBANY, N.Y.COL.MSS, INDORSED LAND PAPERS, 1643-1803, SERIES NO. A0272, DEPARTMENT OF STATE, APPLICATIONS FOR LAND GRANTS, VOL. 09, P. 139, 140.
Comment: The land is not in the Schoharie region, but the Euro-Americans involved are Schoharie Palatines.

Date: 1725,09,29
Description: Petition of Peter Mabee (Maybe; Mebie) that the surveyor general be directed to make return of the warrant granted to his father before his death, for surveying a tract of land on Schoharie creek, in the petitioner's name so that he may obtain a patent for the land.
Source: N.Y.STATE ARCHIVES, ALBANY, N.Y.COL.MSS, INDORSED LAND PAPERS, 1643-1803, SERIES NO. A0272, DEPARTMENT OF STATE, APPLICATIONS FOR LAND GRANTS, VOL. 09, P. 148.
Comment: SEE 1720,06,03; 1725,10,04; 1725,10,13; 1725,10,14.

Date: 1725,10,04
Description: Description of a survey of 600 acres of land lying on the west side of Schoharie River, commonly called by the Indians Tiondorogue (Tienonderoge, Tienonderoga, Tionnonderoge), surveyed for Peter Mebee (Maybe; Mebie) by Cadwallader Colden, surveyor general.
Source: N.Y.STATE ARCHIVES, ALBANY, N.Y.COL.MSS, INDORSED LAND PAPERS, 1643-1803, SERIES NO. A0272, DEPARTMENT OF STATE, APPLICATIONS FOR LAND GRANTS, VOL. 09, P. 149.
Comment: SEE 1720,06,03; 1725, 09,29; 1725,10,13; 1725,10,14.

Date: 1725,10,13
Description: Warrant for a patent to Peter Mebee (Maybe, Mebie) for a tract of 600 acres of land on the Schoharie river, commonly called by the Indians Tiondorogue (Tienonderoge, Tienonderoga, Tionnonderoge).
Source: N.Y.STATE ARCHIVES, ALBANY, N.Y.COL.MSS, INDORSED LAND PAPERS, 1643-1803, SERIES NO. A0272, DEPARTMENT OF STATE, APPLICATIONS FOR LAND GRANTS, VOL. 09, P. 150.
Comment: SEE 1720,06,03; 1725,09,29; 1725,10,04; 1725,10,14. For a certificate accompanying the warrant, see 1725,10,14. The warrant includes an itemization of bills for obtaining the patent. A note added to the document says, "I Rec'd this wart [warrant] the 15. Apr. 1726. RCB." SEE n.d. for map that shows where Maybe's patent of 15 April 1726 is located.

Date: 1725,10,14
Description: Certificate to Peter Mebee (Maybe) for 600 acres of land on the Schoharie River, commonly called by the Indians Tiondorogue (Tienonderoge, Tienonderoga, Tionnonderoge). The certificate accompanies a warrant, dated 13 October 1725.
Source: N.Y.STATE ARCHIVES, ALBANY, N.Y.COL.MSS, INDORSED LAND PAPERS, 1643-1803, SERIES NO. A0272, DEPARTMENT OF STATE, APPLICATIONS FOR LAND GRANTS, VOL. 09, P. 150.
Comment: SEE 1720,06,03; 1725,09,29; 1725,10,04; 1725,10,13.

Date: 1725,10,28
Description: Petition of William York for Palatines and himself for land on the Mohawk River at Connajagara (Canajoharie)
Source: N.Y.STATE ARCHIVES, ALBANY, N.Y.COL.MSS, INDORSED LAND PAPERS, 1643-1803, SERIES NO. A0272, DEPARTMENT OF STATE, APPLICATIONS FOR LAND GRANTS, VOL. 09, P. 151.
Comment: The land is not in the Schoharie region. Palatines from Schoharie are involved, however.

Date: 1725,10,28 (2)
Description: Petition for a patent for 300 acres to William York and Lewis York for land on the south side of Schoharie adjoining that of Adam Vrooman (Vroman), purchased by them from the Indians, also warrants of survey.
Source: N.Y.STATE ARCHIVES, ALBANY, N.Y.COL.MSS, INDORSED LAND PAPERS, 1643-1803, SERIES NO. A0272, DEPARTMENT OF STATE, APPLICATIONS FOR LAND GRANTS, VOL. 09, P. 152, 153, 154.
Comment: SEE 1725,02,10.

Date: 1725,10,28 (3)
Description: Petition of Lewis Morris, Jr. and Andries Coeyman for license to purchase 1,500 acres of land on Jeux's creek adjacent to, and east of, Schoharie.
Source: N.Y.STATE ARCHIVES, ALBANY, N.Y.COL.MSS, INDORSED LAND PAPERS, 1643-1803, SERIES NO. A0272, DEPARTMENT OF STATE, APPLICATIONS FOR LAND GRANTS, VOL. 09, P. 155, 156.
Comment:

Date: 1725,11,00(?) [ ]
Description: Description of survey of 300 acres of land south of Schoharie, beginning at the southwest corner of Adam Vrooman's (Vroman's) land, on the north side of the Schoharie River, surveyed for William York and Lewis York, Palatines, by Phillip Verplank, deputy surveyor.
Source: N.Y.STATE ARCHIVES, ALBANY, N.Y.COL.MSS, INDORSED LAND PAPERS, 1643-1803, SERIES NO. A0272, DEPARTMENT OF STATE, APPLICATIONS FOR LAND GRANTS, VOL. 09, P. 154.
Comment:

Date: 1725,11,02
Description: Report of Lewis Morris, Jr. from the committee of the N.Y. Provincial Council to which the petition of William York and Lewis York for a patent for 300 acres of land lying on the south side of Schoharie adjoining that of Adam Vrooman (Vroman) was referred.
Source: N.Y.STATE ARCHIVES, ALBANY, N.Y.COL.MSS, INDORSED LAND PAPERS, 1643-1803, SERIES NO. A0272, DEPARTMENT OF STATE, APPLICATIONS FOR LAND GRANTS, VOL. 09, P. 152.
Comment:

Date: 1725,11,02 (2)
Description: Warrant of survey for 300 acres of land on the south side of Schoharie, adjoining land of Adam Vrooman (Vroman) for William York and Lewis York, Palatines.
Source: N.Y.STATE ARCHIVES, ALBANY, N.Y.COL.MSS, INDORSED LAND PAPERS, 1643-1803, SERIES NO. A0272, DEPARTMENT OF STATE, APPLICATIONS FOR LAND GRANTS, VOL. 09, P. 153.
Comment: SEE 1725,10,28 (2).

Date: 1725,11,02 (3)
Description: Report of Rip Van Dam, from the committee of the N.Y. Provincial Council concerning a petition of Lewis Morris, Jr. and Andries Coeyman for a license to purchase 1,500 acres of land adjacent to the bounds of Schoharie.
Source: N.Y.STATE ARCHIVES, ALBANY, N.Y.COL.MSS, INDORSED LAND PAPERS, 1643-1803, SERIES NO. A0272, DEPARTMENT OF STATE, APPLICATIONS FOR LAND GRANTS, VOL. 09, P. 155.
Comment:

Date: 1725,11,04
Description: Petition of Lewis Morris, Jr. and Andries Coeyman for a patent for 3,500 acres of land near a place called Schoharie.
Source: N.Y.STATE ARCHIVES, ALBANY, N.Y.COL.MSS, INDORSED LAND PAPERS, 1643-1803, SERIES NO. A0272, DEPARTMENT OF STATE, APPLICATIONS FOR LAND GRANTS, VOL. 09, P. 156.
Comment:

Date: 1725,11,04 (2)
Description: Report of F. Harrison, chairman of the committee of the N.Y. Provincial Council to which the petition of Lewis Morris, Jr. and Andries Coeyman for 3,500 acres of land near a place called Schoharie was referred.
Source: N.Y.STATE ARCHIVES, ALBANY, N.Y.COL.MSS, INDORSED LAND PAPERS, 1643-1803, SERIES NO. A0272, DEPARTMENT OF STATE, APPLICATIONS FOR LAND GRANTS, VOL. 09, P. 156.
Comment:

Date: 1726 (?) [ ]
Description: Cadwallader Colden's "Map of the Manorial Grants along the Hudson River".
Source: HENRY E. HUNTINGTON LIBRARY, SAN MARINO, CALIFORNIA, HUNTINGTON MISCELLANEOUS #15440.
Comment:

Date: 1726,02,03
Description: Certificate to William York and Lewis York for 300 acres of land south of Schoharie, beginning at the southwest corner of Adam Vrooman's (Vroman's) land on the north side of the Schoharie River.
Source: N.Y.STATE ARCHIVES, ALBANY, N.Y.COL.MSS, INDORSED LAND PAPERS, 1643-1803, SERIES NO. A0272, DEPARTMENT OF STATE, APPLICATIONS FOR LAND GRANTS, VOL. 09, P. 158.
Comment:

Date: 1726,02,04
Description: Warrant for patent to William York and Lewis York for a tract of 300 acres of land south of Schoharie, beginning at the southwest corner of Adam Vrooman's (Vroman's) land on the north side of the Schoharie River.
Source: N.Y.STATE ARCHIVES, ALBANY, N.Y.COL.MSS, INDORSED LAND PAPERS, 1643-1803, SERIES NO. A0272, DEPARTMENT OF STATE, APPLICATIONS FOR LAND GRANTS, VOL. 09, P. 157.
Comment: SEE 1725,10,28.

Date: 1726,02,04 (2)
Description: Certificate to William York and Lewis York, Palatines, for land to the southward of Schoharie, beginning at the southwest corner of Adam Vrooman's (Vroman's) land on the north side of the Schoharie River, containing 300 acres.
Source: N.Y.STATE ARCHIVES, ALBANY, N.Y.COL.MSS, INDORSED LAND PAPERS, 1643-1803, SERIES NO. A0272, DEPARTMENT OF STATE, APPLICATIONS FOR LAND GRANTS, VOL. 09, P. 158.
Comment:

Date: 1726,02,10°
Description: Patent to Lewis York and William York for 300 acres of land south of Schoharie.
Source: SEE 1725,02,10.
Comment: The land is in Middleburgh. SEE 1725,10,28; 1725,11,02. Is the date 10 February 1725 correct, or should it be 10 February 1726? Check document carefully for date on it.

Date: 1726,02,25°
Description: Warrant dated 25 February 1726 (should be 25 February 1727) for letters patent to a tract of land south of the Mohawk River for Robert Livingston, Jr. With the warrant, there is a return of survey, dated 24 November 1726, for William Burnet, Jr., Archibald Kennedy, Robert Livingston, Jr., and others for land of which Livingston's tract is a part.
Source: SEE 1727,02,25.
Comment:

Date: 1726,02,26
Description: Deed from Peter Vrooman (Vroman) to Adam Vrooman for twelve acres of land, as well as ten acres called "Brammatacha".
Source: ALBANY COUNTY CLERK'S OFFICE, ALBANY, N.Y., HALL OF RECORDS, DEEDS, BOOK 8, P. 369.
Comment:

Date: 1726,03,10
Description: Patent to Robert Livingston.
Source: N.Y.STATE ARCHIVES, ALBANY, N.Y. LETTERS PATENT, 1664-1780, SERIES NO. 12590, BOOK 9, P. 337.
Comment:

Date: 1726,03,30°
Description: Tracing of confirmation of purchases in 1711 and 1714 of land in the Schoharie Valley. Signed with totems, including that of Hendrick, 30 March 1726.
Source: SEE 1887,00,00-1888,00,00 (39).
Comment: Rufus Grider Collection. Traced by Grider from original in possession of A.G. Richmond.

Date: 1726,04,16
Description: Patent to Peter Mebee (Mebie; Maybe).
Source: N.Y.STATE ARCHIVES, ALBANY, N.Y. LETTERS PATENT, 1664-1780, SERIES NO. 12590, BOOK 9, P. 287.
Comment:

Date: 1726,04,17°
Description: Petition submitted by Adam Vrooman (Vroman) for resurvey of lands on Schoharie river near Onitstagrawae (Onistagrawa).
Source: SEE 1726,10,21.
Comment:

Date: 1726,04,30
Description: Survey description of two tracts of land on the west side of Schoharie Creek (Huntersfield). The second tract was laid out by Lewis Moore (Morris), Jr. and Coeymans.
Source: N.Y.STATE ARCHIVES, ALBANY, N.Y.COL.MSS, INDORSED LAND PAPERS, 1643-1803, SERIES NO. A0272, DEPARTMENT OF STATE, APPLICATIONS FOR LAND GRANTS, VOL. 10, P. 006.
Comment:

Date: 1726,04,30 (2)
Description: Certificate for two tracts of land for Lewis Morris, Jr. and Andries Coeyemans near Schoharie Creek "at a place called Huntersfield."
Source: N.Y.STATE ARCHIVES, ALBANY, N.Y.COL.MSS, INDORSED LAND PAPERS, 1643-1803, SERIES NO. A0272, DEPARTMENT OF STATE, APPLICATIONS FOR LAND GRANTS, VOL. 10, P. 007.
Comment:

Date: 1726,05,02
Description: Warrant of survey of two tracts of land on west side of Schoharie Creek.
Source: N.Y.STATE ARCHIVES, ALBANY, N.Y.COL.MSS, INDORSED LAND PAPERS, 1643-1803, SERIES NO. A0272, DEPARTMENT OF STATE, APPLICATIONS FOR LAND GRANTS, VOL. 10, P. 007.
Comment: SEE 1726,04,30.

Date: 1726,05,24
Description: Patent for two tracts of land containing 2,580 and 920 acres respectively to Lewis Morris, Jr. and Andries Coeymans.
Source: N.Y.STATE ARCHIVES, ALBANY, N.Y. LETTERS PATENT, 1664-1780, SERIES NO. 12590, BOOK 09, P. 296.
Comment: Known as the Morris and Coeymans Patent. The land is at Huntersfield. See 1725,10,28 (3); 1726,04,30; 1726,04,30 (2); 1726,05,02; n.d.; 1819,00,00. For subsequent divisions of the patent, see 1779,11,26; 1785,03,08; 1787,05,07; 1808,05,04; 1837,09,14.

Date: 1726,05,24°
Description: Statement of Peter Vroman (Vrooman) of Schoharie that he has secured commutation of quit rent and has settled with the State of New York for arrears due on 88 acres of land within the 3500 acre patent granted to Lewis Morris and others 24 May 1726.
Source: SEE 1787,05,07.
Comment:

Date: 1726,05,24°
Description: Map of patent granted in 1726 to Morris and Coeymans, resurveyed in November 1819 by Lawrence Vrooman and Tobias A. Stontenburgh. It shows old divided land laid out by Edward Collins in Knieskerns (Knisker, Kniskern, Knieskirk, Kneescarn, Knescarn, Kneiskerk) Dorp in 1729 and lots laid out by Isaac Vrooman in 1753. The map also shows the Schoharie Turnpike and Dorp Road.
Source: SEE 1819,00,00 [ ]; and 1720,00,00-1792,00,00.
Comment:

Date: 1726,07,20
Description: Deed to George Clarke for two tracts of land (one-seventh of the Morris Patent): one containing 2,580 acres and the other 920 acres.
Source: N.Y.STATE ARCHIVES, ALBANY, N.Y. DEEDS, SERIES NO. A 0453, BOOK 12, P. 189.
Comment:

Date: 1726,09,14
Description: Deed in Trust from three of the Five Nations to the King of England. Refers to the deed of 19 July 1701, whereby the Five Nations put their land under the protection of the King of England.
Source: DOCUMENTS RELATIVE TO THE COLONIAL HISTORY OF THE STATE OF NEW YORK, 15 VOL. (ALBANY, N.Y.: WEED, PARSONS, AND CO., 1856-87), 5: 800-801.
Comment:

Date: 1726,10,17
Description: Petition of Adam Vrooman (Vroman) for a resurvey of land on the Schoharie river near Onitstagrawae.
Source: N.Y.STATE ARCHIVES, ALBANY, N.Y.COL.MSS, INDORSED LAND PAPERS, 1643-1803, SERIES NO. A0272, DEPARTMENT OF STATE, APPLICATIONS FOR LAND GRANTS, VOL. 10, P. 015.
Comment:

Date: 1726,10,21
Description: Description of the survey of land of Adam Vrooman (Vroman) on the Schoharie river near Onitstagrawae. (Correction of original survey done after patent was granted in 1714.) Cites date of patent as being 6 Aug 1714.
Source: N.Y.STATE ARCHIVES, ALBANY, N.Y.COL.MSS, INDORSED LAND PAPERS, 1643-1803, SERIES NO. A0272, DEPARTMENT OF STATE, APPLICATIONS FOR LAND GRANTS, VOL. 10, P. 016.
Comment: N.B. Discrepancy between this date of patent and that of 26 Aug 1714. SEE 1714,08,26 (3).

Date: 1726,11,24°
Description: Warrant, dated 25 February 1726 (should be 25 February 1727) for letters patent to a tract of land south of the Mohawk River for Robert Livingston, Jr. With the warrant, there is a return of survey, dated 24 November 1726, for William Burnet, Jr., Archibald Kennedy, Robert Livingston, Jr., and others for land of which Livingston's tract is a part.
Source: SEE 1727,02,25; 1726,11,24.
Comment:

Date: 1726,12,20
Description: Letter from N.Y. Provincial Governor Burnet to the English Board of Trade. Burnet reports that a regulation that was recently passed in the province was an act ". . . for breaking up the Road in the winter time from Scohare to a place called the Verbergh."
Source: DOCUMENTS RELATIVE TO THE COLONIAL HISTORY OF THE STATE OF NEW YORK, 15 VOL. (ALBANY, N.Y.: WEED, PARSONS, AND CO., 1856-87), 5: 810-814. THE REFERENCE TO SCHOHARIE IS ON P. 813.
Comment: SEE 1720,00,00-1792,00,00.

Date: 1727,02,25; 1726,11,24
Description: Warrant, dated 25 February 1726 (should be 25 February 1727) for letters patent to a tract of land south of the Mohawk River for Robert Livingston, Jr. With the warrant, there is a return of survey, dated 24 November 1726, for William Burnet, Jr., Archibald Kennedy, Robert Livingston, Jr., and others for land of which Livingston's tract is a part.
Source: N.Y.STATE ARCHIVES, ALBANY, N.Y.COL.MSS, INDORSED LAND PAPERS, 1643-1803, SERIES NO. A0272, DEPARTMENT OF STATE, APPLICATIONS FOR LAND GRANTS, VOL. 10, P. 029.
Comment: Livingston's tract begins at the northwesternmost corner of the one designated for Archibald Kennedy. The land was purchased by Burnet, Kennedy, Livingston, David Provoost, Delia Provoost, Catherine Vanwy[ ]k, and Helena Santford (?) from "the Native Indians". The endorsement notes that Livingston's tract is 775 acres. Patent is in N.Y.STATE ARCHIVES, ALBANY, N.Y. LETTERS PATENT, 1664-1780, SERIES NO. 12590, BOOK 9, P. 315.

Date: 1727,05,06
Description: Petition to purchase Indian land on Cobellskill (Cobleskill) Creek between "Schohory [Schoharie] &"Canajoghory [Canajoharie], & about twelve Miles from a place called Antonios[?] Nose" for Robert Livingston, Jr., and Lancaster Syms, Jr.   N.Y.STATE ARCHIVES, ALBANY, N.Y.COL.MSS, INDORSED LAND PAPERS, 1643-1803, SERIES NO. A0272, DEPARTMENT OF STATE, APPLICATIONS FOR LAND GRANTS, VOL. 10, P. 030.   Petition was approved by N.Y. Provincial Council on 4 July 1727. See note on second page of document.
Source: N.Y.STATE ARCHIVES, ALBANY, N.Y.COL.MSS, INDORSED LAND PAPERS, 1643-1803, SERIES NO. A0272, DEPARTMENT OF STATE, APPLICATIONS FOR LAND GRANTS, VOL. 10, P. 029.
Comment: Livingston's tract begins at the northwesternmost corner of the one designated for Archibald Kennedy. The land was purchased by Burnet, Kennedy, Livingston, David Provoost, Delia Provoost, Catherine Vanwy[ ]k, and Helena Santford (?) from "the Native Indians". The endorsement notes that Livingston's tract is 775 acres.

Date: 1727,12,21
Description: Letter from N.Y. Provincial Governor Burnet to the English Board of Trade. Burnet reports that a recent regulation that was passed in the province was "An Act for reviving an Act entitled an Act for laying out and clearing the publick [sic] Highways in the Precinct at Schohere, in the County of Albany, and for exchanging some of the Commissioners."
Source: DOCUMENTS RELATIVE TO THE COLONIAL HISTORY OF THE STATE OF NEW YORK, 15 VOL. (ALBANY, N.Y.: WEED, PARSONS, AND CO., 1856-87), 5: 846-848. THE REFERENCE TO SCHOHARIE IS ON P. 847.
Comment: SEE 1720,00,00-1792,00,00.

Date: 1728,00,00 [ ]°
Description: Petition of Christian Castleman, William York, Jurian Pellenger (?sp), Phillip Crisler, Phillip Moor, Jacob Burst (Borst), John Lawyer, and Martin Burst (Borst) for land 18 miles above "Skohare"(Schoharie).
Source: SEE 1728,11,00(?) [ ].
Comment: The petition is undated, except for a date of 1728 in the margin apparently added by an archivist or researcher at the N.Y. State Archives. The date assigned to it here was chosen on the basis of its placement in Vol. 10 of the Land Papers. It is among documents dated November 1728.

Date: 1728,02,00
Description: Petition for patent for 1,000 acres of land between Cannajagara (Canajoharie) and Schoharie for William York, Phillip Moor, John Peter Zenger, Hans George Barneger, and Jacob Burst and others purchased from the Indian proprietors under a license from the N.Y. colonial governor.
Source: N.Y.STATE ARCHIVES, ALBANY, N.Y.COL.MSS, INDORSED LAND PAPERS, 1643-1803, SERIES NO. A0272, DEPARTMENT OF STATE, APPLICATIONS FOR LAND GRANTS, VOL. 10, P. 051.
Comment: See 1728,04,25; 1730,07,31.

Date: 1728,04,25
Description: Description of survey of land (about seven miles northwest of Huntersfield) for William York, Phillip Moore, John Peter Zenger, Hans Jury Barneger and Jacob Burst. The survey was done by Phillip Verplank.
Source: N.Y.STATE ARCHIVES, ALBANY, N.Y.COL.MSS, INDORSED LAND PAPERS, 1643-1803, SERIES NO. A0272, DEPARTMENT OF STATE, APPLICATIONS FOR LAND GRANTS, VOL. 10, P. 065.
Comment: SEE 1758,02; 1730,07,31. Mentions an Indian Path between Huntersfield and Canajoharie. One boundary of the land is the "brook by the Indians called Oscalleghe." The survey was done pursuant to a warrant dated 19 Dec 1727.

Date: 1728,07,13
Description: Petition of Philip Livingston, John Haskoll (Haskell[?]), and Isaac Bobin for land.
Source: N.Y.STATE ARCHIVES, ALBANY, N.Y.COL.MSS, INDORSED LAND PAPERS, 1643-1803, SERIES NO. A0272, DEPARTMENT OF STATE, APPLICATIONS FOR LAND GRANTS, VOL. 10, 069.
Comment: CALENDAR OF LAND PAPERS identifies this land as being in Albany County. It is unclear, however, whether or not it is in the Schoharie River Valley. N.B., Until 1795, Schoharie was in Albany County.

Date: 1728,08,28
Description: N.Y. Provincial Council Minutes. Petition of Johann Christian Garlach (Garlick), William and Nicholas York and Elias Garlach for license to purchase land at Skoharee (Schoharie) referred in Council.
Source: N.Y.STATE ARCHIVES,ALBANY, N.Y.COUN.MIN., VOL. 13, P. 345.
Comment:

Date: 1728,11,00(?) [ ]
Description: Petition of Christian Castleman, William York, Jurian Pellenger (?sp), Phillip[Crisler, Phillip Moor, Jacob Burst (Borst), John Lawyer, and Martin Burst (Borst) for land 18 miles above "Skohare" (Schoharie).
Source: N.Y.STATE ARCHIVES, ALBANY, N.Y.COL.MSS, INDORSED LAND PAPERS, 1643-1803, SERIES NO. A0272, DEPARTMENT OF STATE, APPLICATIONS FOR LAND GRANTS, VOL. 10, P. 079.
Comment: The petition is undated, except for a date of 1728 in the margin apparently added by an archivist or researcher at the N.Y. State Archives. The date assigned to it here comes from its placement in Vol. 10 of the Land Papers. It is among documents dated November 1728.

Date: 1728,11,07
Description: Petition of Andrew Nicholls, Evan Drummond, Edward Collins, John Wemp, and Cornelius Van Slyck to purchase Indian land.
Source: N.Y.STATE ARCHIVES, ALBANY, N.Y.COL.MSS, INDORSED LAND PAPERS, 1643-1803, SERIES NO. A0272, DEPARTMENT OF STATE, APPLICATIONS FOR LAND GRANTS, VOL. 10, P. 075.
Comment: CALENDAR OF LAND PAPERS identifies this land as being in Albany County. It is unclear, however, whether or not it is in the Schoharie River Valley. N.B., Until 1795 Schoharie was in Albany County.

Date: 1729,00,00°
Description: Map of patent granted in 1726 to Morris and Coeymans, resurveyed in November 1819 by Lawrence Vrooman (Vroman) and Tobias A. Stontenburgh. It shows old divided land laid out by Edward Collins in Knieskerns (Knisker, Kniskern, Knieskirk, Kneescarn, Kneiskerk, Knescarn) Dorp in 1729 and lots laid out by Isaac Vrooman in 1753. The map also shows the Schoharie Turnpike and Dorp Road.
Source: SEE 1819,00,00 [ ].
Comment: See also 1769,11,00.

Date: 1729,05,30
Description: Petition of Johan Peter Kniskern (Knisker, Knieskerk, Kneiskerk, Kneescarn, Knescarn), for a license to purchase 300 acres of land lying on Schoharie Creek.
Source: N.Y.STATE ARCHIVES, ALBANY, N.Y.COL.MSS, INDORSED LAND PAPERS, 1643-1803, SERIES NO. A0272, DEPARTMENT OF STATE, APPLICATIONS FOR LAND GRANTS, VOL. 10, P. 088.
Comment: SEE 1729,09,27; 1729,10,21.

Date: 1729,07,05°
Description: Petition of John Peter Kniskern (Knisker, Knieskerk, Kneescarn, Knescarn, Kneiskerk) for grant of land on both sides of Schoharie river.
Source: SEE 1730,09,29.
Comment:

Date: 1729,09,03
Description: Petition of Vincent Matthews, John Cornwell, Abraham Lodge, Samuel Heath, and others for a grant of 7,000 acres out of vacant lands in the province of New York.
Source: N.Y.STATE ARCHIVES, ALBANY, N.Y.COL.MSS, INDORSED LAND PAPERS, 1643-1803, SERIES NO. A0272, DEPARTMENT OF STATE, APPLICATIONS FOR LAND GRANTS, VOL. 10, P. 090-091.
Comment:

Date: 1729,09,27
Description: Indian deed to John Peter Knieskerk (Knisker, Kniskern, Kneescarn, Knescarn, Kneiskerk) for 300 acres of land on Schoharie Creek. Signed by Arrundias, Oquarady, and Sounistiowan.
Source: N.Y.STATE ARCHIVES, ALBANY, N.Y.COL.MSS, INDORSED LAND PAPERS, 1643-1803, SERIES NO. A0272, DEPARTMENT OF STATE, APPLICATIONS FOR LAND GRANTS, VOL. 10, P. 099.
Comment: SEE 1729,05,30; 1729,10,21; 1887,00,00-1888,00,00 (31). The marks of two of the Indian signers are on the document.

Date: 1729,10,21
Description: Petition of Johan Pieter Knieskerk (Knisker, Kniskern, Kneescarn, Knescarn, Kneiskerk) for a patent for 300 acres of land at Schoharie, beginning at the north bounds at a patent granted to Andries Coeymans and Lewis Morris, Jr., and running southerly on both sides of Schoharie creek.
Source: N.Y.STATE ARCHIVES, ALBANY, N.Y.COL.MSS, INDORSED LAND PAPERS, 1643-1803, SERIES NO. A0272, DEPARTMENT OF STATE, APPLICATIONS FOR LAND GRANTS, VOL. 10, P. 098.
Comment: SEE 1729,05,30; 1729,09,27. SEE 1726,06,24 for information on the patent of Coeymans and Morris.

Date: 1729,10,29°
Description: Description of survey of warrant for land to be granted to John Peter Kniskern (Knisker, Knieskirk, Kneescarn, Knescarn, Kneiskerk).
Source: SEE 1730,09,28.
Comment:

Date: 1729,11,00°
Description: Petition of Christian Castleman, J. Pellinger, Phillip Crisler, Phillip Moor, Jacob Burst, John Lawyer, and Martin Bourst for patent to 2,000 acres of land about 18 miles above Schoharie. Also with this document, although apparently unrelated to it, are a warrant and a certificate of Alexander Cosby dated 1 and 2 February 1730 for land on the east side of Schoharie River. The petition of Castleman and others is undated. It may have been written in November 1729.
Source: SEE 1730,02,01-02.
Comment:

Date: 1730,00,00-1752,03,19
Description: A list of names of persons received into the communion of the High Dutch Reformed Church from 1730 through 19 March 1752.
Source: N.Y.STATE LIBRARY, ALBANY, MANUSCRIPTS, 14192.
Comment:

Date: 1730,02,01-02
Description: Petition of Christian Castleman, J. Pellinger, Phillip Crisler, Phillip Moor, Jacob Burst, John Lawyer, and Martin Bourst for patent to 2,000 acres of land about 18 miles above Schoharie. Also with this document, although apparently unrelated to it, are a warrant and a certificate of Alexander Cosby dated 1 and 2 February 1730 for land on the east side of Schoharie River. The petition of Castleman and others is undated. It may have been written in November 1729.
Source: N.Y.STATE ARCHIVES, ALBANY, N.Y.COL.MSS, INDORSED LAND PAPERS, 1643-1803, SERIES NO. A0272, DEPARTMENT OF STATE, APPLICATIONS FOR LAND GRANTS, VOL. 10, P. 104.
Comment:

Date: 1730,02,10
Description: Patent to William York and Lewis York for 3,000 acres south of Schoharie.
Source: N.Y.STATE ARCHIVES, ALBANY, N.Y. LETTERS PATENT, 1664-1780, SERIES NO. 12590, BOOK 9, P. 227.
Comment:

Date: 1730,07,30
Description: Warrant for a patent for William York.
Source: N.Y.STATE ARCHIVES, ALBANY, N.Y.COL.MSS, INDORSED LAND PAPERS, 1643-1803, SERIES NO. A0272, DEPARTMENT OF STATE, APPLICATIONS FOR LAND GRANTS, VOL. 10, P. 125.
Comment:

Date: 1730,07,31
Description: Patent for a "tract of 1,000 acres of land northwest of Huntersfield on both sides of the Oscalleghe" to William York, Hans Jury Barneger, John Peter Zenger, and others.
Source: N.Y.STATE ARCHIVES, ALBANY, N.Y. LETTERS PATENT, 1664-1780, SERIES NO. 12590, BOOK 10, P. 123.
Comment: See 1728,02,00; 1728,04,25.

Date: 1730,09,28
Description: Description of survey of 300 acres of land on both sides of Schoharie river to be granted to John Peter Kniskern (Knisker, Knieskirk, Kneescarn, Knescarn, Kneiskerk).
Source: N.Y.STATE ARCHIVES, ALBANY, N.Y.COL.MSS, INDORSED LAND PAPERS, 1643-1803, SERIES NO. A0272, DEPARTMENT OF STATE, APPLICATIONS FOR LAND GRANTS, VOL. 10, P. 139.
Comment:

Date: 1730,09,29
Description: Warrant for patent for John Peter Kniskern (Knisker, Knieskirk, Kneescarn, Knescarn, Kneiskerk) for 300 acres of land on both sides of Schoharie river.
Source: N.Y.STATE ARCHIVES, ALBANY, N.Y.COL.MSS, INDORSED LAND PAPERS, 1643-1803, SERIES NO. A0272, DEPARTMENT OF STATE, APPLICATIONS FOR LAND GRANTS, VOL. 10, P. 143.
Comment: SEE 1730,10,29; 1720,07,05.

Date: 1730,09,29 (2)
Description: Deed to John Peter Kniskorn by John Montgomerie and others, for 300 acres of land near Schoharie.
Source: N.Y.STATE LIBRARY, ALBANY, MANUSCRIPTS, 7977.
Comment:

Date: 1730,10,29
Description: Description of Kniskern (Knisker, Knieskirk, Kneescarn, Knescarn, Kneiskerk) survey.
Source: N.Y.STATE ARCHIVES, ALBANY, N.Y.COL.MSS, INDORSED LAND PAPERS, 1643-1803, SERIES NO. A0272, DEPARTMENT OF STATE, APPLICATIONS FOR LAND GRANTS, VOL. 10, P. 139.
Comment: SEE 1730,09,29; 1729,07,05.

Date: 1731,00,00°
Description: Tracing of a map of a grant of land in 1711 from the Indians to Adam Vrooman (Vroman) and Martinus Van Slyck.
Source: SEE 1887,00,00-1888,00,00 (41).
Comment: Rufus Grider Collection.

Date: 1731,02,12°
Description: Tracing of a map by William Cockburn "of the lands mentioned in the different releases". Latest date on map is 12 February 1731, but the map itself is undated. Shows Vrooman (Vroman) lands.
Source: SEE 1887,00,00-1888,00,00 (42).
Comment: Rufus Grider Collection. Traced by Grider, 1887-1888, from original in possession of A.G. Richmond. SEE 1731,07,12; 1770,11,15; n.d.; 1770,00,00. Referred to as the "Old Bowry" map.

Date: 1731,05,20
Description: Articles of agreement between Phillip Livingston and David Schuyler for the purchase of Mohawk land.
Source: N.Y.STATE ARCHIVES, ALBANY, N.Y.COL.MSS, INDORSED LAND PAPERS, 1643-1803, SERIES NO. A0272, DEPARTMENT OF STATE, APPLICATIONS FOR LAND GRANTS, VOL. 10, P. 153.
Comment:

Date: 1731,06,03
Description: Petition of John Lindsay, Walter Butler, William Dick, James Stephenson, Joseph Warrel, Charles Home, James Henderson, George Ingoldsby, Archibald Kennedy, Jr., Edward Collins, Thomas Butler, John Avery, and Ballard Beckford to purchase land in Mohawk country from the "Native Indians".
Source: N.Y.STATE ARCHIVES, ALBANY, N.Y.COL.MSS, INDORSED LAND PAPERS, 1643-1803, SERIES NO. A0272, DEPARTMENT OF STATE, APPLICATIONS FOR LAND GRANTS, VOL. 10, P. 155.
Comment:

Date: 1731,06,24
Description: Petition of Petrus Van Driessen for land.
Source: N.Y.STATE ARCHIVES, ALBANY, N.Y.COL.MSS, INDORSED LAND PAPERS, 1643-1803, SERIES NO. A0272, DEPARTMENT OF STATE, APPLICATIONS FOR LAND GRANTS, VOL. 10, P. 162.
Comment: SEE 1731,09,25; 1732,05,09; 1732,09,15. Land is not in the Schoharie River Valley. However, Van Driessen and Ehle (with whom he sought land) were missionaries among the Mohawks. Ehle ministered at Schoharie at one point.

Date: 1731,07,12
Description: Map done by William Cockburn of the lands mentioned in different releases. Referred to as The Old Bowry Map.
Source: SCHOHARIE COUNTY HISTORICAL REVIEW, "VROOMAN'S LAND", MAY 1950, P. 23.
Comment: Conveyed by Wouter Vroman (Vrooman). SEE 1770,11,15 for other information about Cockburn. SEE ALSO 1887,00,00-1888,00,00 (42); n.d.; 1770,00,00. N.B., date on the map. Grider cites the date as being 12 February 1731.

Date: 1731,07,13
Description: Petition of Jennike Cregier to purchase 2,000 acres on the southeast side of Schoharie River above Kadasede, beginning at said river at a place called Yagoughsitawawanie running upstream to a place called Chenochquatha and then into the woods on both sides.
Source: N.Y.STATE ARCHIVES, ALBANY, N.Y.COL.MSS, INDORSED LAND PAPERS, 1643-1803, SERIES NO. A0272, DEPARTMENT OF STATE, APPLICATIONS FOR LAND GRANTS, VOL. 10, P. 168.
Comment: Petition granted 7 September 1731 (see endorsement),

Date: 1731,09,25
Description: Petition of Petrus Van Driessen and Ehl/Ehle for 2,000 acres of land south of the Mohawk.
Source: N.Y.STATE ARCHIVES, ALBANY, N.Y.COL.MSS, INDORSED LAND PAPERS, 1643-1803, SERIES NO. A0272, DEPARTMENT OF STATE, APPLICATIONS FOR LAND GRANTS, VOL. 11, P. 6.
Comment: SEE 1731,06,24; 1732,05,09; 1732,09,15. Land is not in the Schoharie River Valley. However, Van Driessen and Ehle were missionaries among the Indians. Ehle ministered at Schoharie at one point.

Date: 1732,05,09
Description: Deed to ministers of the gospel Petrus Van Driessen and Johannes Ehl (Ehle) for land. Signed by Lourence (Lawrence), Symon, Moses, Anthony, Eliza, _an, Gideon, Johannes, Adam, Willem, Nicholaes (Nicholas), A__iadikha, Abraham, Onichanorum, Targioris, Annanias, Seth, and Hendrick.The names are listed in three columns. At the head of each is a sketch of an animal. Each of the Indians also used their own marks (not animal totems, or clan designations, but rather single stroke marks, often the first letter of their name) on the document.
Source: N.Y.STATE ARCHIVES, ALBANY, N.Y.COL.MSS, INDORSED LAND PAPERS, 1643-1803, SERIES NO. A0272, DEPARTMENT OF STATE, APPLICATIONS FOR LAND GRANTS, VOL. 11, P. 038.
Comment: SEE 1731,06,24; 1732,09,25; 1732,09,15. Land is not in the Schoharie River Valley. However, Van Driessen and Ehle were missionaries among the Mohawks; and Ehle ministered at Schoharie at one point.

Date: 1732,09,15
Description: Petition of Petrus Van Driesson and Johannes Ehl/Ehle. Plus warrant.
Source: N.Y.STATE ARCHIVES, ALBANY, N.Y.COL.MSS, INDORSED LAND PAPERS, 1643-1803, SERIES NO. A0272, DEPARTMENT OF STATE, APPLICATIONS FOR LAND GRANTS, VOL. 11, PP. 45, 49.
Comment: SEE 1731,06,24; 1731,09,25; 1732,05,09. Not Schoharie land; but Van Driessen and Ehle were missionaries among the Mohawks. Ehle ministered at Schoharie at one point.

Date: 1732,09,25
Description: Petition from Peter Van Brugh and others of Huntersfield for 400 acres of land on the west side of Schoharie.
Source: N.Y.STATE ARCHIVES, ALBANY, N.Y.COL.MSS, INDORSED LAND PAPERS, 1643-1803, SERIES NO. A0272, DEPARTMENT OF STATE, APPLICATIONS FOR LAND GRANTS, VOL. 11, P. 043.
Comment:

Date: 1733,03,26
Description: Release of Bardrom Eutus by Hendrick Hauck (Houck) and wife Anna Vroneger of several parcels of land in that part of Schoharie called Knickskerksdorf (Kniskerdorp; Knisker Dorp; Knieskirk Dorp; Kniskern Dorp, Kneisker Dorp, Kneescarn Dorp, Knescarn Dorp), being one-half of lot 3 of Knickersksdorf, except 3 morgens reserved by Hauck; and annual quitrent of 2 s, 8d is also reserved. The parties are yeomen of Schoharie.
Source: N.Y.STATE LIBRARY, ALBANY, MANUSCRIPTS, SCHOHARIE COUNTY, PATENTEES, LAND RECORDS, DW10738.
Comment:

Date: 1733,09,18
Description: Deed from Johannes de Wilt, Thomas, Hendrick, Sett (Seth), Aurey (Arey), Assarus (Asarus), Gideon, Brant, Jaromme (Yacomine[?]), Rebecca, and "the rest whose Hands are hereunto Subscribed of the Several Tribes [Clans or Lineages] of the Turtle, Bear, and Wolf Mohocks [Mohawks]" to Walter Butler and others for 86,000 acres of land south of the Mohawk, to Schoharie and to Schenectady.
Source: N.Y.STATE ARCHIVES, ALBANY, N.Y.COL.MSS, INDORSED LAND PAPERS, 1643-1803, SERIES NO. A0272, DEPARTMENT OF STATE, APPLICATIONS FOR LAND GRANTS, VOL. 11, P. 066.
Comment: Indian marks are clear on the deed; and seals are present. Note, women signers. In addition to the Indians listed above, the following also signed, Mitchell Manture, Maria, Wistray, Johannes, Thouwistaras, Petrus, Konyiwanoe, Hannah, Mary, Mosses (Moses), Nel[or t]tia, Yacomine, Cartrine, Sarrah, Wary, Margarte, Handedick, Alida, Mary, Catarinet, Wary, __?__. SEE 1733,10,16; 1737,07,26; 1737,11,12; 1738,07,00 [ ]; 1738,10,28; 1753,02,05; 1887,00,00-1888,00,00 (25).

Date: 1733,09,18°
Description: Rufus Grider tracing of deed from Mohawks Indians to Walter Butler for land south of the Mohawk, 18 September 1733.
Source: SEE 1887,00,00-1888,00,00 (25).
Comment: Traced from original in N.Y.STATE LAND PAPERS, VOL. 11, P. 065. Compare Grider's tracing with the original (1733,09,18)..

Date: 1733,10,16
Description: Petition of Walter Butler and others for a patent for 86,000 acres of land south of the Mohawk River. The tract runs from the "flatts or lowland of Tienonderoga", beginning "at the Land in possession of David Carvik", alongTienonderoga Creek (Schoharie River) to Schoharie, then along the bounds of Schoharie as they run "Southerly and easterly" to the bounds of Schenectady, then round the "bounds of other patented lands to the place where it first began".
Source: N.Y.STATE ARCHIVES, ALBANY, N.Y.COL.MSS, INDORSED LAND PAPERS, 1643-1803, SERIES NO. A0272, DEPARTMENT OF STATE, APPLICATIONS FOR LAND GRANTS, VOL. 11, P. 065.
Comment: Patent granted. (See note with endorsement.) For deed, SEE 1733,09,18.

Date: 1733,10,16°
Description: Rufus Grider tracing of deed from Mohawks Indians to Walter Butler for land south of the Mohawk, 1733.
Source: SEE 1887,00,00-1888,00,00 (25).
Comment: Traced from original in N.Y.STATE LAND PAPERS, VOL. 11, P. 065. Compare Grider's tracing with the original (1733,09,18).

Date: 1733,11,03
Description: Petition to purchase 15,000 acres on Schoharie Creek from the "Native Indians".
Source: N.Y.STATE ARCHIVES, ALBANY, N.Y.COL.MSS, INDORSED LAND PAPERS, 1643-1803, SERIES NO. A0272, DEPARTMENT OF STATE, APPLICATIONS FOR LAND GRANTS, VOL. 11, P. 075.
Comment: N.B. Two copies of the petition are contained in this document. In one, the names of the petitioners are written: "Abraham Glen, Abraham Truax(?), and Phillip Schuyler in behalf of themselves and five other persons". In the other, they are written: "Jacob Glen, John Schuyler, and Arent Bratt in behalf of themselves and five other persons".

Date: 1733,11,14
Description: Petition of George Clarke for 900 acres at Schoharie.
Source: N.Y.STATE ARCHIVES, ALBANY, N.Y.COL.MSS, INDORSED LAND PAPERS, 1643-1803, SERIES NO. A0272, DEPARTMENT OF STATE, APPLICATIONS FOR LAND GRANTS, VOL. 11, 084.
Comment:

Date: 1734,00,00 [ ]
Description: Petition of sachems of Schoharie Mohawk Indians, on behalf of themselves and their castles, about 6,000 acres of land which has been stolen from them by the River Indians (Mahicans) and sold to Vincent Matthews, Michael Dunning, and Daniel Denton; with map showing Schoharie "wigwams". The Indians signing the petition are Agarhetonthea, Chan_anguina, and Seth. Their marks are on the document.
Source: N.Y.STATE ARCHIVES, ALBANY, N.Y.COL.MSS, INDORSED LAND PAPERS, 1643-1803, SERIES NO. A0272, DEPARTMENT OF STATE, APPLICATIONS FOR LAND GRANTS, VOL. 11, P. 106.
Comment: The land is on west side of Hudson River and Blew Hills of Kattskill (Katskill) along each side of Chawtickagnack creek to the Schoharies Creek to the nearer falls to Schoharie, containing about 6,000 acres. The land is on the east side of the Schoharie. The petition is presented by the "Sachems or Chiefs of the Schoharie Mohawk Indians in behalf of them and their castles." N.B., Use of the plural: "castles". Also note that the directions [(N,S, E, & W] given on the mark are correct. When the map is viewed with north at the top, the illustrations are upside down, however.) SEE 1734,08,07; 1734,10,03; 1734,10,05; 1734,10,12; 1887,00,00-1888,00,00 (40).

Date: 1734,00,00°
Description: William Johnson to John Bradstreet, about Hardenburgh Patent dispute. Johnson writes that in 1734, Indians of Schoharie met with Esopus or Delawares and told them not to attempt to sell land westward of Catskill Hills.
Source: SEE 1769,05,17.
Comment:

Date: 1734,04,18
Description: Deed from Arondiack, Thom., and Hendrick of Canajoharie to Mr. Cosby for land on south side of the Mohawk River. The land borders tracts of land owned by Colden, Alexander, Bleeker, and others. The marks of the three Indians ceding the land are clearly visible. (In Dutch or German.)
Source: N.Y.STATE ARCHIVES, ALBANY, N.Y.COL.MSS, INDORSED LAND PAPERS, 1643-1803, SERIES NO. A0272, DEPARTMENT OF STATE, APPLICATIONS FOR LAND GRANTS, VOL. 11, P. 087.
Comment: A note, in English, at the end of the document lists patents that border the tract ceded. The script is unclear at the end of the name Arondiack. Another letter appears to be at the end of the name. The compiler of this calendar is uncertain about the location of this land.

Date: 1734,05,30
Description: Description of survey of George Clark's patent west of Schoharie River.
Source: N.Y.STATE ARCHIVES, ALBANY, N.Y.COL.MSS, INDORSED LAND PAPERS, 1643-1803, SERIES NO. A0272, DEPARTMENT OF STATE, APPLICATIONS FOR LAND GRANTS, VOL. 11, P. 096.
Comment: SEE 1773,11,14.

Date: 1734,05,30 (2)
Description: Warrant of Anne Willmot for patent for land near Fort Hunter between Schoharie and the Mohawk River.
Source: N.Y.STATE ARCHIVES, ALBANY, N.Y.COL.MSS, INDORSED LAND PAPERS, 1643-1803, SERIES NO. A0272, DEPARTMENT OF STATE, APPLICATIONS FOR LAND GRANTS, VOL. 11, P. 097.
Comment:

Date: 1734,07,09
Description: Indian deed to David Schuyler for all that tract of land on the south side of the "Mohocks" (Mohawk) River, beginning a little above a place called Onawedake.
Source: N.Y.STATE ARCHIVES, ALBANY, N.Y.COL.MSS, INDORSED LAND PAPERS, 1643-1803, SERIES NO. A0272, DEPARTMENT OF STATE, APPLICATIONS FOR LAND GRANTS, VOL. 11, P. 127.
Comment: It is unclear to the compiler of this calendar whether or not this land is in the Schoharie River Valley.

Date: 1734,07,15
Description: Certificate to George Clark for patent for land near Schoharie.
Source: N.Y.STATE ARCHIVES, ALBANY, N.Y.COL.MSS, INDORSED LAND PAPERS, 1643-1803, SERIES NO. A0272, DEPARTMENT OF STATE, APPLICATIONS FOR LAND GRANTS, VOL. 11, P. 142.
Comment:

Date: 1734,08,07
Description: Indian deed to Daniel Denton for tract of land on west side of Hudson River on west side of the Blew Hills of Cattskill (Katskill), bounded on each side of Chawtickignank Creek to the Schowherre (Schoharie) Creek.
Source: N.Y.STATE ARCHIVES, ALBANY, N.Y.COL.MSS, INDORSED LAND PAPERS, 1643-1803, SERIES NO. A0272, DEPARTMENT OF STATE, APPLICATIONS FOR LAND GRANTS, VOL. 11, P. 104.
Comment: SEE 1734,00,00 [ ]; 1734,10,03.

Date: 1734,08,07 (2)
Description: Indian deed to Michael Dunning for tract of land on the west side of Hudson River on the west side of the Blew Hills of Cattskill (Katskill), bounded on each side of Chawtickignank Creek to Schowherres (Schoharie) Creek.
Source: N.Y.STATE ARCHIVES, ALBANY, N.Y.COL.MSS, INDORSED LAND PAPERS, 1643-1803, SERIES NO. A0272, DEPARTMENT OF STATE, APPLICATIONS FOR LAND GRANTS, VOL. 11, P. 105.
Comment: SEE 1734,00,00 [ ]; 1734,10,03.

Date: 1734,10,03
Description: Petition of Vincent Matthews, Michael Dunning and Daniel Denton for patent for 6,000 acres of land on the west side of Hudson River.
Source: N.Y.STATE ARCHIVES, ALBANY, N.Y.COL.MSS, INDORSED LAND PAPERS, 1643-1803, SERIES NO. A0272, DEPARTMENT OF STATE, APPLICATIONS FOR LAND GRANTS, VOL. 11, P. 114.
Comment: Schoharie Mohawks contested sale of land by River Indians (Mahicans) to Matthews, Dunning, and Denton. SEE 1734,00,00 [ ]; 1734,08,07; 1734,10,05; 1734,10,12.

Date: 1734,10,03 (2)
Description: Petition of Thomas Williams and Edward Collins for 8,000 acres of land on the west side of Hudson River.
Source: N.Y.STATE ARCHIVES, ALBANY, N.Y.COL.MSS, INDORSED LAND PAPERS, 1643-1803, SERIES NO. A0272, DEPARTMENT OF STATE, APPLICATIONS FOR LAND GRANTS, VOL. 11, P. 115.
Comment:

Date: 1734,10,03 (3)
Description: Petition of Johannes Lansingh (Lansing) and company for a patent for 6,000 acres of land west of Hudson River and west of Katts Kill (Catskill).
Source: N.Y.STATE ARCHIVES, ALBANY, N.Y.COL.MSS, INDORSED LAND PAPERS, 1643-1803, SERIES NO. A0272, DEPARTMENT OF STATE, APPLICATIONS FOR LAND GRANTS, VOL. 11, P. 116.
Comment:

Date: 1734,10,05
Description: Description of survey for Matthews, Dunning, and Denton for 6,000 acres of land, consisting of several tracts, on the west side of Catskill Mountians on a creek called Chawtiekignack and Schoharie Kill.
Source: N.Y.STATE ARCHIVES, ALBANY, N.Y.COL.MSS, INDORSED LAND PAPERS, 1643-1803, SERIES NO. A0272, DEPARTMENT OF STATE, APPLICATIONS FOR LAND GRANTS, VOL. 11, P. 120.
Comment: SEE 1734,00,00 [ ]; 1734,08,07; 1734,10,03; 1734,10,12.

Date: 1734,10,12
Description: Warrant for patent for several tracts of land, consisting of 6,000 acres on the west side of Catskill Mountains on a creek called Chawtiekignack and east side of Schoharie Kill, for Matthews, Dunning, and Denton.
Source: N.Y.STATE ARCHIVES, ALBANY, N.Y.COL.MSS, INDORSED LAND PAPERS, 1643-1803, SERIES NO. A0272, DEPARTMENT OF STATE, APPLICATIONS FOR LAND GRANTS, VOL. 11, P. 123.
Comment: SEE 1734,00,00 [ ]; 1734, 08,07; 1734, 10,03; 1734,10,05.

Date: 1734,10,26
Description: Description of survey of land for William Cosby, Jr. and others near Fort Hunter between the Schoharie and Mohawk rivers.
Source: N.Y.STATE ARCHIVES, ALBANY, N.Y.COL.MSS, INDORSED LAND PAPERS, 1643-1803, SERIES NO. A0272, DEPARTMENT OF STATE, APPLICATIONS FOR LAND GRANTS, VOL. 11, P. 133.
Comment: Also named with William Cosby, Jr. are Henry Cosby, Phillis Hanson, Edward Hanson, Elizabeth Guerin, Menard Guerin, Charles Williams, John White, Thomas Cooper, Thomas Corksill (?sp.), Anne Wilmott, Peter Bard, Capt. William Cosby, and Bernice Bard. N.B. Indian place names for a river and a brook.

Date: 1734,11,05
Description: Petition of William Corry for 100,000 acres of land near Aries Creek, Tienonderoga, and Schoharie creek.
Source: N.Y.STATE ARCHIVES, ALBANY, N.Y.COL.MSS, INDORSED LAND PAPERS, 1643-1803, SERIES NO. A0272, DEPARTMENT OF STATE, APPLICATIONS FOR LAND GRANTS, VOL. 11, P. 140.
Comment: 1737,08,02.

Date: 1734,11,11
Description: Warrant for a patent to George Clark for land near Schoharie.
Source: N.Y.STATE ARCHIVES, ALBANY, N.Y.COL.MSS, INDORSED LAND PAPERS, 1643-1803, SERIES NO. A0272, DEPARTMENT OF STATE, APPLICATIONS FOR LAND GRANTS, VOL. 11, P. 143.
Comment:

Date: 1734,11,12
Description: Petition of William Cosby, Henry Cosby and John Holton to purchase land in Mohawk country from Schoharie Mohawks.
Source: N.Y.STATE ARCHIVES, ALBANY, N.Y.COL.MSS, INDORSED LAND PAPERS, 1643-1803, SERIES NO. A0272, DEPARTMENT OF STATE, APPLICATIONS FOR LAND GRANTS, VOL. 11, P 144, 145.
Comment:

Date: 1734,11,21
Description: Patent for a tract of 900 acres of land adjoining Huntersfield to George Clarke.
Source: N.Y.STATE ARCHIVES, ALBANY, N.Y. LETTERS PATENT, 1664-1780, SERIES NO. 12590, BOOK 11, P. 154.
Comment: The land is in Middleburgh and Schoharie.

Date: 1734,12,00 [ ]
Description: Division of six tracts of 28,000 acres between the Mohawk and Schoharie rivers. The boundaries of each tract are stated.
Source: N.Y.STATE ARCHIVES, ALBANY, N.Y.COL.MSS, INDORSED LAND PAPERS, 1643-1803, SERIES NO. A0272, DEPARTMENT OF STATE, APPLICATIONS FOR LAND GRANTS, VOL. 11, P. 157.
Comment: Date assigned on basis of the specific placement of the manuscript in the Indorsed Land Papers, vol. 11.

Date: 1734,12,11
Description: Deed to William Cosby, Jr. and others for a tract of land west of Hudson River between Cattskill (Catskill) Creek and the hills lying on the west side of the Schoharie River, the former called Kahosetthare River and the latter Gataraga Hill. Signed by George, Mary, Seth, Joseph, and Lawrence, all of whom put their mark on the document.
Source: N.Y.STATE ARCHIVES, ALBANY, N.Y.COL.MSS, INDORSED LAND PAPERS, 1643-1803, SERIES NO. A0272, DEPARTMENT OF STATE, APPLICATIONS FOR LAND GRANTS, VOL. 11, P. 153.
Comment: Mines, minerals, and ore, and "all other the Hereditaments and Appurtenances to the said tract or parcel of land" are included in the cession. SEE 1887,00,00-1888,00,00 (32). N.B., A woman, Mary, signed the deed.

Date: 1734,12,11 (2)
Description: Indian deed from "the Native Indians and sole and absolute proprietors of Schohary [Schoharie]", Mary, Seth, Joseph, and Lawrence, to William Cosby, Jr. Henry Cosby, John Felton, and others. The tract of land ceded is west of Hudson River between the Katts Kill (Catskill) Creek and the Schoharie River and between the Schoharie River and two hills on the west side of that river, one called by the Indians Kahosetthare and the other Gataraga Hill.
Source: N.Y.STATE ARCHIVES, ALBANY, SERIES #450, DOS PATENT BOOK 11, PP. 185-186 (D244/4).
Comment: "Mines Minerals or Ore of any Kind soever . . . and all other Hereditaments and Appurtenances to the said Tract or parcell of Land" are specifically included in this deed. Note, the Indians signed with their marks. This is a contemporary copy of the original deed.

Date: 1735,02,15
Description: Warrant and certificate for a patent for Anne Willmott for 2,000 acres of land near Fort Hunter between Schoharie and the Mohawk River. With this is a copy of the patent of land issued to Walter Butler, John Lyndesay, James Stephenson, Joseph Warrell, Charles Home, James Henderson, John Avery, and Ballard Beckford on behalf of themselves and 35 others. The patent contains the issuance of land named in the warrant to Anne Willmott.
Source: N.Y.STATE ARCHIVES, ALBANY, N.Y.COL.MSS, INDORSED LAND PAPERS, 1643-1803, SERIES NO. A0272, DEPARTMENT OF STATE, APPLICATIONS FOR LAND GRANTS, VOL. 11, P. 161.
Comment: SEE 1735,06,10 (2).

Date: 1735,02,15 (2)
Description: Warrant for a patent for Charles Williams and others for 14,000 acres of land near Fort Hunter between the Schoharie and Mohawk rivers. With this is a copy of the patent of land issued to Walter Butler, John Lyndesay, James Stephenson, Joseph Warrell, Charles Home, James Henderson, John Avery, and Ballard Beckford on behalf of themselves and 35 others. The patent contains the issuance of land named in the warrant to Charles Williams and others.
Source: N.Y.STATE ARCHIVES, ALBANY, N.Y.COL.MSS, INDORSED LAND PAPERS, 1643-1803, SERIES NO. A0272, DEPARTMENT OF STATE, APPLICATIONS FOR LAND GRANTS, VOL. 11, p. 162.
Comment: Note endorsement at end of the document for the date. SEE 1735,06,10 (4).

Date: 1735,02,15 (3)
Description: Warrant for Maynard and Elizabeth Guerin for land near Fort Hunter between the Schoharie and Mohawk rivers. With this is a copy of the patent of land issued to Walter Butler, John Lyndesay, James Stephenson, Joseph Warrell, Charles Home, James Henderson, John Avery, and Ballard Beckford on behalf of themselves and 35 others. The patent contains the issuance of land named in the warrant to M. and E. Guerin.
Source: N.Y.STATE ARCHIVES, ALBANY, N.Y.COL.MSS, INDORSED LAND PAPERS, 1643-1803, SERIES NO. A0272, DEPARTMENT OF STATE, APPLICATIONS FOR LAND GRANTS, VOL. 11, P. 163.
Comment: SEE 1735,06,10.

Date: 1735,02,15 (4)
Description: Warrant to Edward and P. Harrison for land near Fort Hunter between the Schoharie and Mohawk rivers.
Source: N.Y.STATE ARCHIVES, ALBANY, N.Y.COL.MSS, INDORSED LAND PAPERS, 1643-1803, SERIES NO. A0272, DEPARTMENT OF STATE, APPLICATIONS FOR LAND GRANTS, VOL. 11, p. 164.
Comment:

Date: 1735,04,03
Description: Petition of William Cosby, Jr., Henry Cosby, and John Holton on behalf of themselves and four others for a 14,000 acre tract of land between Schoharie River and Katts Kill (Catskill) Creek.
Source: N.Y.STATE ARCHIVES, ALBANY, N.Y.COL.MSS, INDORSED LAND PAPERS, 1643-1803, SERIES NO. A0272, DEPARTMENT OF STATE, APPLICATIONS FOR LAND GRANTS, VOL. 11, P. 165.
Comment:

Date: 1735,06,10
Description: Warrant and certificate for a patent for Maynard and Elizabeth Guerin for 4,000 acres of land on the Schoharie river. The Guerins's warrant is for a small portion of land issued in a patent to Walter Butler, John Lyndesay, James Stephenson, Joseph Warrell, Charles Home, James Henderson, John Avery, and Ballard Beckford on behalf of themselves and 35 others. A copy of the patent is attached to the warrant.
Source: N.Y.STATE ARCHIVES, ALBANY, N.Y.COL.MSS, INDORSED LAND PAPERS, 1643-1803, SERIES NO. A0272, DEPARTMENT OF STATE, APPLICATIONS FOR LAND GRANTS, VOL. 11, P. 170.
Comment: SEE 1735,02,15.

Date: 1735,06,10 (2)
Description: Warrant and certificate for patent for Anne Wilmot for 2,000 acres of land. Wilmot's warrant is for a small portion of land issued in a patent to Walter Butler, John Lyndesay, James Stephenson, Joseph Warrell, Charles Home, James Henderson, John Avery, and Ballard Beckford on behalf of themselves and 35 others. A copy of the patent is attached to the warrant.
Source: N.Y.STATE ARCHIVES, ALBANY, N.Y.COL.MSS, INDORSED LAND PAPERS, 1643-1803, SERIES NO. A0272, DEPARTMENT OF STATE, APPLICATIONS FOR LAND GRANTS, VOL. 11, P. 171.
Comment: SEE 1735,02,15.

Date: 1735,06,10 (3)
Description: Warrant for patent for Edward and Phillis Harrison for 4,000 acres of land on Schoharie River on the south corner of the Williams tract. The Harrisons's warrant is for a small portion of land issued in a patent to Walter Butler, John Lyndesay, James Stephenson, Joseph Warrell, Charles Home, James Henderson, John Avery, and Ballard Beckford on behalf of themselves and 35 others. A copy of the patent is attached to the warrant.
Source: N.Y.STATE ARCHIVES, ALBANY, N.Y.COL.MSS, INDORSED LAND PAPERS, 1643-1803, SERIES NO. A0272, DEPARTMENT OF STATE, APPLICATIONS FOR LAND GRANTS, VOL. 11, P. 172.
Comment: SEE 1735,02,15.

Date: 1735,06,10 (4)
Description: Warrant and certificate for a patent for Charles Williams and others for 14,000 acres on Schoharie River. Williams's warrant is for a small portion of land issued in a patent to Walter Butler, John Lyndesay, James Stephenson, Joseph Warrell, Charles Home, James Henderson, John Avery, and Ballard Beckford on behalf of themselves and 35 others. A copy of the patent is attached to the warrant.
Source: N.Y.STATE ARCHIVES, ALBANY, N.Y.COL.MSS, INDORSED LAND PAPERS, 1643-1803, SERIES NO. A0272, DEPARTMENT OF STATE, APPLICATIONS FOR LAND GRANTS, VOL. 11, P. 174.
Comment:

Date: 1735,06,10 (5)
Description: Warrant for Henry Cosby for 2,000 acres of land. Cosby's warrant is for a small portion of land issued in a patent to Walter Butler, John Lyndesay, James Stephenson, Joseph Warrell, Charles Home, James Henderson, John Avery, and Ballard Beckford on behalf of themselves and 35 others. A copy of the patent is attached to the warrant.
Source: N.Y.STATE ARCHIVES, ALBANY, N.Y.COL.MSS, INDORSED LAND PAPERS, 1643-1803, SERIES NO. A0272, DEPARTMENT OF STATE, APPLICATIONS FOR LAND GRANTS, VOL. 11, P. 175.
Comment:

Date: 1735,06,27 [ ]
Description: Division of four lots (4,000 acres) granted to Capt. Butler and company. Lot No. 1 is designated for Mr. Miln or Mr. Wiliams; Lot No. 2, for Marianne Scott; Lot No. 3 for Capt. Butler; and Lot No. 4 for Mr. Miln or Mr. Williams. The first three border in part on land formerly granted to Edward Collins. The fourth begins at the northwest corner of land granted to Hendrick and Hans Hansen.
Source: N.Y.STATE ARCHIVES, ALBANY, N.Y.COL.MSS, INDORSED LAND PAPERS, 1643-1803, SERIES NO. A0272, DEPARTMENT OF STATE, APPLICATIONS FOR LAND GRANTS, VOL. 11, P. 178.
Comment: Land is identified in the CALENDAR OF LAND PAPERS as being in the Schoharie region.

Date: 1735,07,04
Description: Petition of Lieut. Walter Butler and Grietje Vrouman (Vrooman), widow, for license to purchase 600 acres in Schoharie.
Source: N.Y.STATE ARCHIVES, ALBANY, N.Y.COL.MSS, INDORSED LAND PAPERS, 1643-1803, SERIES NO. A0272, DEPARTMENT OF STATE, APPLICATIONS FOR LAND GRANTS, VOL. 11, P. 182.
Comment: SEE 1735,07,05.

Date: 1735,07,05
Description: License to Lieut. Walter Butler and Grietje Vrouman (Vrooman), widow, to purchase 600 acres at Schoharie.
Source: N.Y.STATE ARCHIVES, ALBANY, N.Y.COL.MSS, INDORSED LAND PAPERS, 1643-1803, SERIES NO. A0272, DEPARTMENT OF STATE, APPLICATIONS FOR LAND GRANTS, VOL. 11, p. 183.
Comment: SEE 1735,07,04.

Date: 1735,08,29
Description: Patent to William Cosby, Jr.
Source: N.Y.STATE ARCHIVES, ALBANY, N.Y. LETTERS PATENT, 1664-1780, SERIES NO. 12590, BOOK 11, P. 201.
Comment: SEE 1735,04,30.

Date: 1735,08,29 (2)
Description: Patent to Maynard Guerin and Elizabeth Guerin for 4,000 acres of Walter Butler's 86,000 acre grant.
Source: N.Y.STATE ARCHIVES, ALBANY, N.Y. LETTERS PATENT, 1664-1780, SERIES NO. 12590, BOOK 11, P. 210.
Comment: SEE 1733,09,18; 1733,10,16; 1735,06,10; 1735,02,15 (3).

Date: 1735,08,29 (3)
Description: Patent to Anne Willmot.
Source: N.Y.STATE ARCHIVES, ALBANY, N.Y. LETTERS PATENT, 1664-1780, SERIES NO. 12590, BOOK 11, P. 218.
Comment: SEE 1735,06,10 (2); 1735,02,10.

Date: 1735,09,10°
Description: Certificate for a patent to Thomas Freeman and others for 5,000 acres of land on the south side of the Mohawk River.
Source: SEE 1735,10,07.
Comment:

Date: 1735,10,07
Description: Warrant for patent for Thomas Freeman and others for 5,000 acres of land on the south side of the Mohawk River to the flats or lowlands of Tienonderoga, round these flats to Tienonderoga (Schoharie) Creek to Schoharie, then along the bounds of Schoharie as they run southward and eastward to the bounds of Schenectady, then round the bounds of other patented lands there to where this tract first began. Also included is a certificate, dated 10 Sept 1735.
Source: N.Y.STATE ARCHIVES, ALBANY, N.Y.COL.MSS, INDORSED LAND PAPERS, 1643-1803, SERIES NO. A0272, DEPARTMENT OF STATE, APPLICATIONS FOR LAND GRANTS, VOL. 11, p. 189.
Comment: For identification of Tienonderoga Creek as the Schoharie River, SEE 1737,10,12; 1754,10,25.

Date: 1735,10,11
Description: Patent to Edward Harrison and Phillas Harrison for 4,000 acres out of Walter Butler's 86,000 acre grant.
Source: N.Y.STATE ARCHIVES, ALBANY, N.Y. LETTERS PATENT, 1664-1780, SERIES NO. 12590, BOOK 11, P. 187.
Comment: SEE 1735,02,15 (4); 1735,06,10 (3).

Date: 1735,12,24
Description: Deed from Johannes, Gideon, Asarias (Asaras), Sett (Seth), Joseph, and Thomas to Walter Butler for land near Aries Creek, Fort Hunter, Tiononderoga (Lower Mohawk Village), and Schoharie Creek.
Source: N.Y.STATE ARCHIVES, ALBANY, N.Y.COL.MSS, INDORSED LAND PAPERS, 1643-1803, SERIES NO. A0272, DEPARTMENT OF STATE, APPLICATIONS FOR LAND GRANTS, VOL. 12, P. 086.
Comment: Contains marks of Indian signers.

Date: 1735,12,24 (2)
Description: Deed from Johannes, Gideon, Asaras, Seth, Joseph, and Thomas "Native Indians and Sole and absolute proprietors of the Mohawk Country" to the King of England, conveyed thereupon to James DeLancey, Jacob Glen, John Lyndsay, and Pashal Nelson. The land conveyed is south of the Mohawk River, beginning at a place called by the Indians Aries Creek along the edge of the flats at Fort Hunter, then following other creeks named in the deed to Schoharie.
Source: N.Y.STATE ARCHIVES, ALBANY, SERIES #453, DOS DEED BOOK 13, PP. 118-122.
Comment: Mines, minerals, ores, etc. also ceded. Note, Indians signed with their marks.

Date: 1736,04,14
Description: Description of survey for John DePeyster and Johannes Lawyer of 1,500 acres of land at Schoharie.
Source: N.Y.STATE ARCHIVES, ALBANY, N.Y.COL.MSS, INDORSED LAND PAPERS, 1643-1803, SERIES NO. A0272, DEPARTMENT OF STATE, APPLICATIONS FOR LAND GRANTS, VOL. 12, P. 072.
Comment: SEE 1736,05,13; 1737,05,04; 1737,10,15.

Date: 1736,05,13
Description: Petition of John DePeyster and Johannes Lawyer for patent for 1,500 acres at Schoharie, part of land purchased by Myndert Schuyler, Peter Van Brugh and Robert Livingston in 1714. Patent was granted 15 October 1737.
Source: N.Y.STATE ARCHIVES, ALBANY, N.Y.COL.MSS, INDORSED LAND PAPERS, 1643-1803, SERIES NO. A0272, DEPARTMENT OF STATE, APPLICATIONS FOR LAND GRANTS, VOL. 12, P. 011.
Comment: SEE 1736,04,14; 1737,05,04; 1737,10,15; 1714,05,08; 1714,11,03.

Date: 1736,06,10
Description: Petition of Walter Butler to purchase 2,000 acres of land at Schoharie.
Source: N.Y.STATE ARCHIVES, ALBANY, N.Y.COL.MSS, INDORSED LAND PAPERS, 1643-1803, SERIES NO. A0272, DEPARTMENT OF STATE, APPLICATIONS FOR LAND GRANTS, VOL. 12, P. 016.
Comment: SEE 1736,06,12; 1736,06,26; 1738,03,31; 1738,04,21; 1751,09,17.

Date: 1736,06,12
Description: License of Walter Butler to purchase 2,000 acres at Schoharie.
Source: N.Y.STATE ARCHIVES, ALBANY, N.Y.COL.MSS, INDORSED LAND PAPERS, 1643-1803, SERIES NO. A0272, DEPARTMENT OF STATE, APPLICATIONS FOR LAND GRANTS, VOL. 12, P. 015.
Comment: SEE 1736,06,10; 1736,06,26; 1738,03,31; 1738,04,21; 1751,09,17.

Date: 1736,06,17
Description: Map of 4,000 acres of Timothy Bagley's land and 2,000 acres of William Crosby's land.
Source: MIX'S CATALOG OF MAPS AND SURVEYS IN OFFFICES OF THE SECRETARY OF STATE, STATE ENGINEER AND SURVEYOR AND COMPTROLLER AND N.Y. STATE LIBRARY, 1859, REFERENCES THIS MAP, LISTING IT AS BEING IN THE OFFICES OF THE N.Y. STATE DEPARTMENT OF TAXATION & FINANCE, MAP #152.
Comment:

Date: 1736,06,25°
Description: Map of 4,000 acres of Timothy Bagley's land and 2,000 acres of William Crosby's land.
Source: SEE 1736,06,17.
Comment:

Date: 1736,06,25 (2)
Description: Patent to Timothy Bagley for 6,000 acres on both sides of the Mohawk River.
Source: N.Y.STATE ARCHIVES, ALBANY, N.Y. LETTERS PATENT, 1664-1780, SERIES NO. 12590, BOOK 11, P. 260.
Comment: SEE 1736,06,17; 1736,06,25; 1738,10,28.

Date: 1736,06,26
Description: Petition of Walter Butler for patent for 2,000 acres within Indian purchase at Schoharie, south of the Lawyer and York patent.
Source: N.Y.STATE ARCHIVES, ALBANY, N.Y.COL.MSS, INDORSED LAND PAPERS, 1643-1803, SERIES NO. A0272, DEPARTMENT OF STATE, APPLICATIONS FOR LAND GRANTS, VOL. 12, P. 031.
Comment: SEE 1736,06,10; 1736,06,12; 1736,06,26; 1738,03,31; 1738,04,21; 1751,09,17.

Date: 1736,08,13
Description: Deed from Sett (Seth), Asurus (Asarus, Asarius, Asaras), Cornelus (Cornelius), Thomas, Abraham, Lourence (Lawrence), and Aria to John Wemp for land south of the Mohawk River, by a rock called by the Mohawks Estaghrogon, plus three small islands in the Mohawk River, opposite land held by Wouter Swart.
Source: N.Y.STATE ARCHIVES, ALBANY, N.Y.COL.MSS, INDORSED LAND PAPERS, 1643-1803, SERIES NO. A0272, DEPARTMENT OF STATE, APPLICATIONS FOR LAND GRANTS, VOL. 12, P. 038.
Comment: Note, marks of the Indians on the deed. SEE 1737,11,12 (2).

Date: 1736,09,23
Description: Petition of Wooter Vrooman (Vroman) for a license to purchese 2,000 acres of a tract of land between the Manor of Renslaerwick and the township of Schenectady.
Source: N.Y.STATE ARCHIVES, ALBANY, N.Y.COL.MSS, INDORSED LAND PAPERS, 1643-1803, SERIES NO. A0272, DEPARTMENT OF STATE, APPLICATIONS FOR LAND GRANTS, VOL. 12, P. 043.
Comment:

Date: 1736,12,02°
Description: On 2 December 1736 the Committee of the N.Y. Provincial Council passed a regulation requiring "an actual survey in the presence of the Indians."
Source: SEE 1785,09,20
Comment:

Date: 1737,05,04
Description: A warrant for a patent to John DePeyster and Johannes Lawyer for 1,500 acres of land at Schoharie, being part of the land purchased in the year 1714 from "the Native Indian proprietors" by Myndert Schuyler, Peter Van Brugh, and others. A copy of a certificate, dated 19 April 1737, describing the bounds of the land is attached.
Source: N.Y.STATE ARCHIVES, ALBANY, N.Y.COL.MSS, INDORSED LAND PAPERS, 1643-1803, SERIES NO. A0272, DEPARTMENT OF STATE, APPLICATIONS FOR LAND GRANTS, VOL. 12, P. 077.
Comment: A detailed description of the land is given in the certificate. Some of the reference points mentioned are Fauxes (Fox) Creek, and land formerly granted to Lewis Morris, Jr. and Andries Coeman (Coeyman, Coeymans). The endorsement on this document notes that the patent is dated 16 June 1737 (cf. 1737,10,15). SEE 1714,05,08; 1714,11,03; 1736,04,14; 1736,05,13.

Date: 1737,06,16°
Description: A patent is granted to John DePeyster and Johannes Lawyer for 1,500 acres of land at Schoharie, being part of the land purchased in the year 1714 from "the Native Indian proprietors" by Myndert Schuyler, Peter Van Brugh, and others.
Source: SEE 1737,05,04.
Comment: SEE ALSO 1737,10,15.

Date: 1737,07,26
Description: Warrant for letters patent to be issued to George Ingoldsby, Frederick Morris, Timothy Bagly (Bagley), Daniel Bagly (Bagley), and Richard Nicolls for a tract of 10,000 acres of land, being part of a 86,000 tract of land purchased on 16 October 1733 from the Indians by Walter Butler, John Lyndesay, James Stevenson, Joseph Warrel, Charles Home, James Henderson, John Avory (Avery) and Ballard Beckford. A copy of a certificate, dated 25 July 1737, describing the bounds of the land is attached.
Source: N.Y.STATE ARCHIVES, ALBANY, N.Y.COL.MSS, INDORSED LAND PAPERS, 1643-1803, SERIES NO. A0272, DEPARTMENT OF STATE, APPLICATIONS FOR LAND GRANTS, VOL. 12, P. 090.
Comment: SEE 1733,09,18; 1733,10,16; 1737,07,26; 1737,11,12; 1738,10,28.

Date: 1737,07,28
Description: Patent to George Ingoldsby and four others to land from Walter Butler's 86,000 acre grant.
Source: N.Y.STATE ARCHIVES, ALBANY, N.Y. LETTERS PATENT, 1664-1780, SERIES NO. 12590, BOOK 11, P. 381.
Comment: SEE 1737,07,28.

Date: 1737,08,02
Description: N.Y. Provincial Council Minutes, about a patent granted to William Corry for land at or near Aries creek, Tienonderoga (Schoharie) Creek, and Schoharie Creek.
Source: N.Y.STATE ARCHIVES,ALBANY, N.Y.COUN.MIN., VOL. 17, P. 173.
Comment: SEE 1734,11,05.

Date: 1737,09,26
Description: Petition of __?__ Corry for land south of the Mohawk.
Source: N.Y.STATE ARCHIVES, ALBANY, N.Y.COL.MSS, INDORSED LAND PAPERS, 1643-1803, SERIES NO. A0272, DEPARTMENT OF STATE, APPLICATIONS FOR LAND GRANTS, VOL. 12, P. 094.
Comment:

Date: 1737,10,12
Description: Description of a survey for Samuel Heath, William English, John Dyer, Francis Silvestor (Sylvestor), Catharine Corry, William Cosby, Elizabeth Mills, William Corry, Catharine Huit, Timothy Bagly (Bagley), Charles Oneil (O'Neil), Sarah Huit, and Daniel Bagly (Bagley) of 24,000 acres for Samuel Heath, south of the Mohawk River, west of Schoharie River, also "called Tienonderoga (Tienonderoge, Tionnderoga, Tionnonderoge) Kill or Creek Beginning at a certain large tree formerly marked & painted by the Indians standing near the fort path from Fort Hunter to Scohary [Schoharie]".
Source: N.Y.STATE ARCHIVES, ALBANY, N.Y.COL.MSS, INDORSED LAND PAPERS, 1643-1803, SERIES NO. A0272, DEPARTMENT OF STATE, APPLICATIONS FOR LAND GRANTS, VOL. 12, P. 045.
Comment: N.B. Apparently, Schoharie creek was also called Tienonderoga creek. SEE 1737,10,25; 1754,10,25.

Date: 1737,10,15
Description: Patent for three tracts of land together containing 1,500 acres to Johannes Lawyer and John DePeyster, part of land purchased by Myndert Schuyler, Peter Van Brugh and Robert Livingston in 1714.
Source: N.Y.STATE ARCHIVES, ALBANY, N.Y. LETTERS PATENT, 1664-1780, SERIES NO. 12590, BOOK 11, P. 388.
Comment: SEE 1736,04,14; 1736,05,13; 1737,05,04; 1714,05,08; 1714,11,03. The land is in Schoharie. N.B., Date of patent is cited as 16 June 1737 in endorsement of document dated 4 May 1737.

Date: 1737,10,25
Description: Warrant to Samuel Heath, William English, John Dyer, Francis Silvester (Sylvester), Catharine Corry, William Cosby, Elizabeth Mills, William Corry, Catharine Huit, Timothy Bagley (Bagley), Charles ONeil (Oneil, O'Neil), Sara Huit, and Daniel Bagly (Bagley) for a patent for 25,400 acres of land south of the Mohawk River, west of the Schoharie River. A copy of a certificate, dated 24 October 1737, describing the bounds of the land is attached.
Source: N.Y.STATE ARCHIVES, ALBANY, N.Y.COL.MSS, INDORSED LAND PAPERS, 1643-1803, SERIES NO. A0272, DEPARTMENT OF STATE, APPLICATIONS FOR LAND GRANTS, VOL. 12, P. 102.
Comment: SEE 1737,10,12.

Date: 1737,11,12
Description: Warrant for letters patent to be issued to Aron Bradt (Bratt) and John Wemp for land "beginning at the Southwest Corner of the Township of Schenectady" and encompassing a tract of 500 acres of land formerly granted to Arent Van Patten (Patton) and John Dellemont. The land being patented is part of a 86,000 tract purchased on 16 October 1733 from the Indians by Walter Butler, and others. A copy of a certificate, dated 11 November 1737, describing the bounds of the land is attached.
Source: N.Y.STATE ARCHIVES, ALBANY, N.Y.COL.MSS, INDORSED LAND PAPERS, 1643-1803, SERIES NO. A0272, DEPARTMENT OF STATE, APPLICATIONS FOR LAND GRANTS, VOL. 12, P. 109.
Comment: SEE 1733,09,18; 1733,10,16; 1737,07,26.

Date: 1737,11,12 (2)
Description: Warrant for letters patent to be issued to John Wemp for land south of the Mohawk River near the lowlands or flats at Fort Hunter. A copy of a certificate, dated 11 November 1737, describing the bounds of the land is attached.
Source: N.Y.STATE ARCHIVES, ALBANY, N.Y.COL.MSS, INDORSED LAND PAPERS, 1643-1803, SERIES NO. A0272, DEPARTMENT OF STATE, APPLICATIONS FOR LAND GRANTS, VOL. 12, P. 110.
Comment: One point of references used in the description in the certificate is "a Rock on the Bank of Said River Called by the Indians Estagrogan". Three small islands "in the Said Mohawks River Lying opposite to the Land Belonging to Wouter Swart where he now Dwells" are also included in the tract. The endorsement on this document notes that the patent is dated 17 November 1737. SEE 1736,08,13.

Date: 1737,11,19
Description: Patent to William Correy.
Source: N.Y.STATE ARCHIVES, ALBANY, N.Y. LETTERS PATENT, 1664-1780, SERIES NO. 12590, BOOK 11, P. 433.
Comment: SEE 1737,08,02; 1737,09,26.

Date: 1737,12,06
Description: Petition of Timothy Green and Martin Van Bergen for a license to purchase land near Kattskill (Catskill) Hills.
Source: N.Y.STATE ARCHIVES, ALBANY, N.Y.COL.MSS, INDORSED LAND PAPERS, 1643-1803, SERIES NO. A0272, DEPARTMENT OF STATE, APPLICATIONS FOR LAND GRANTS, VOL. 12, P. 119.
Comment: East of the mouth of Schoharie river.

Date: 1737,12,16
Description: Patent to Aaron Bradt and John Wemp.
Source: N.Y.STATE ARCHIVES, ALBANY, N.Y. LETTERS PATENT, 1664-1780, SERIES NO. 12590, BOOK 11, P. 404.
Comment: SEE 1737,11,12.

Date: 1738,02,09
Description: Patent to Alexander, Philip, and William Cosby.
Source: N.Y.STATE ARCHIVES, ALBANY, N.Y. LETTERS PATENT, 1664-1780, SERIES NO. 12590, BOOK 11, P. 514.
Comment:

Date: 1738,03,16
Description: Petition of Henry Van Renselaer (Rensselaer), Jr., Hendrick Wemp, Abraham Truax, and Arent Stevens to purchase 8,000 acres of land south of the Mohawk "as yet unpurchased of the Native Indian proprietors".
Source: N.Y.STATE ARCHIVES, ALBANY, N.Y.COL.MSS, INDORSED LAND PAPERS, 1643-1803, SERIES NO. A0272, DEPARTMENT OF STATE, APPLICATIONS FOR LAND GRANTS, VOL. 12, P. 127.
Comment: This land may not be in the Schoharie River Valley.

Date: 1738,03,16 (2)
Description: Petition of Arent Bradt (Bratt) and Hendrick Vroman (Vrooman) to purchase 20,000 acres on the south side of the Mohawk River.
Source: N.Y.STATE ARCHIVES, ALBANY, N.Y.COL.MSS, INDORSED LAND PAPERS, 1643-1803, SERIES NO. A0272, DEPARTMENT OF STATE, APPLICATIONS FOR LAND GRANTS, VOL. 12, P. 129.
Comment: This land may not be in the Schoharie River Valley.

Date: 1738,03,31
Description: Return of survey of 2,000 acres of land on both sides of Schoharie river for Walter Butler.
Source: N.Y.STATE ARCHIVES, ALBANY, N.Y.COL.MSS, INDORSED LAND PAPERS, 1643-1803, SERIES NO. A0272, DEPARTMENT OF STATE, APPLICATIONS FOR LAND GRANTS, VOL. 12, P. 130.
Comment: See 1736,06,10; 1736,06,12; 1736,06,26; 1738,03,31; 1738,04,21; 1751,09,17.

Date: 1738,03,31 (2)
Description: Warrant and certificate for survey of 2,000 acres of land of Walter Butler on both sides of the Schoharie river.
Source: N.Y.STATE ARCHIVES, ALBANY, N.Y.COL.MSS, INDORSED LAND PAPERS, 1643-1803, SERIES NO. A0272, DEPARTMENT OF STATE, APPLICATIONS FOR LAND GRANTS, VOL. 12, P. 131.
Comment: SEE 1736,06,10; 1736,06,12; 1736,06,26; 1738,04,21; 1751,09,17.

Date: 1738,04,10
Description: Deed, signed by Johannis (Johannes), Seth (Sett) and Hans (Hance) Jury (Ury), to A. Bratt (Bradt) and others for land west of Huntersfield.
Source: N.Y.STATE ARCHIVES, ALBANY, N.Y.COL.MSS, INDORSED LAND PAPERS, 1643-1803, SERIES NO. A0272, DEPARTMENT OF STATE, APPLICATIONS FOR LAND GRANTS, VOL. 13, P. 030.
Comment: This document is dated 10 Apr 1749 in the CALENDAR OF N.Y. COLONIAL MANUSCRIPTS INDORSED LAND PAPERS IN THE OFFICE OF THE SECRETARY OF STATE 1643-1803, (Albany: Weed, Parsons and Company, 1864) (Hereinafter referred to as the CALENDAR OF LAND PAPERS). The date written on the document looks more like 10 Apr 1738, however. N.B. Indian marks on the deed. The mark next to the name Seth is not that of a Turtle.) This document has the same page number as the petition of A. Bratt (Bradt) and Volkert Van Veghton for two tracts of land west of Huntersfield, dated 1739,05,17 [ ].

Date: 1738,04,21
Description: Patent to Walter Butler containing 2,000 acres of land.
Source: N.Y.STATE ARCHIVES, ALBANY, N.Y. LETTERS PATENT, 1664-1780, SERIES NO. 12590, BOOK 11, P. 429.
Comment: Known as Butler's Purchase. The land is in Fulton/Blenheim. SEE 1736,06,10; 1736,06,12; 1736,06,26; 1738,03,31; 1751,09,17.

Date: 1738,05,05°
Description: Petiton of A. Bratt and Volkert Van Veghton "on behalf of themselves and Company" for a patent for two tracts of land west of Huntersfield. The petition itself is not dated, except for a 5 May 1738 date in the margin apparently added by an archivist or researcher at the N.Y. State Archives. The endorsement, however, has the date 17 May 1739 with the note: "was referred & reported by Mr. Horsmanden in fav[o]r of the pet[itio]n".
Source: SEE 1739,05,17 (3).
Comment:

Date: 1738,06,22
Description: Return of Survey of tract of 6,000 acres of land on east side o the Schoharie River for Alexander, William and Phillip Cosby.
Source: N.Y.STATE ARCHIVES, ALBANY, N.Y.COL.MSS, INDORSED LAND PAPERS, 1643-1803, SERIES NO. A0272, DEPARTMENT OF STATE, APPLICATIONS FOR LAND GRANTS, VOL. 12, P. 140.
Comment:

Date: 1738,07,00 [ ]
Description: Draft of certificate to Alexander Cosby and others for 6,000 acres on the east side of Schoharie creek, part of a 86,000 acre tract purchased by Walter Butler, John Lindesay and company in 1733.
Source: N.Y.STATE ARCHIVES, ALBANY, N.Y.COL.MSS, INDORSED LAND PAPERS, 1643-1803, SERIES NO. A0272, DEPARTMENT OF STATE, APPLICATIONS FOR LAND GRANTS, VOL. 12, P. 146.
Comment: SEE 1733,09,18; 1733,10,16.

Date: 1738,08,30
Description: Letter from the New York Commissioners of Indian Affairs to Lieutenant-Governor Clarke, about French "encroachments".
Source: DOCUMENTS RELATIVE TO THE COLONIAL HISTORY OF THE STATE OF NEW YORK, ED. BY E.B. O'CALLAGHAN AND BERTHOLD FERNOW, 15 VOL. (ALBANY, N.Y.: WEED, PARSONS, AND CO., 1856-87), 6: 131-132.
Comment: Editor's footnote indicates that one of the commissioners, John DePeyster, was a patentee of lands in Schoharie. The document itself does not refer to Schoharie.

Date: 1738,09,06
Description: Deed to Edward Clarke for a tract of 2,000 acres.
Source: N.Y.STATE ARCHIVES, ALBANY, N.Y. DEEDS, SERIES NO. A0453, BOOK 15, P. 180.
Comment: Recorded by the N.Y. Provincial Secretary August 15, 1752.

Date: 1738,09,25
Description: Petition of Edward Clarke to purchase 1,200 acres of land at Schoharie from "the Native Indian Proprietors".
Source: N.Y.STATE ARCHIVES, ALBANY, N.Y.COL.MSS, INDORSED LAND PAPERS, 1643-1803, SERIES NO. A0272, DEPARTMENT OF STATE, APPLICATIONS FOR LAND GRANTS, VOL. 12, P. 163.
Comment: SEE 1739,07,07; 1739,08,25.

Date: 1738,10,05
Description: Certificate to Cadwallader Colden for land south of the Mohawk River near Canajoharie; plus instructions to Richard Bradley, dated 24 October 1738, to prepare a draft of letters patent for Cadwallader Colden and Conradt Rightmyer for the land.
Source: N.Y.STATE ARCHIVES, ALBANY, N.Y.COL.MSS, INDORSED LAND PAPERS, 1643-1803, SERIES NO. A0272, DEPARTMENT OF STATE, APPLICATIONS FOR LAND GRANTS, VOL. 13, P. 003.
Comment: Land borders patent of Jacob Lansing and others, patent of Abraham Van Horne and others, and a brook called by the Indians Otsquaghe (Otqshage, Otsquage).

Date: 1738,10,20
Description: Deed, signed by Mary, Joseph, Lowrence (Lawrence), Sett (Seth), Johan Jurie (Hans, Hance Ury, Jury, Yurry, Yury, Ury), and Jacob "Native Indians of Schohare [Schoharie]", to Edward Clark for land on both sides of Schoharie Creek, beginning at a tract recently granted to Walter Butler. Attached is also a receipt to Capt. E. Clarke for payment for this land: seven miles long and one mile wide on both sides of Schoharie Creek, and another tract along Stone Creek.
Source: N.Y.STATE ARCHIVES, ALBANY, N.Y.COL.MSS, INDORSED LAND PAPERS, 1643-1803, SERIES NO. A0272, DEPARTMENT OF STATE, APPLICATIONS FOR LAND GRANTS, VOL. 13, P. 002.
Comment: N.B. Indian marks on receipt. Also, a woman, Mary, is among the signers of the deed. All of the Indians are identified as being of Schoharie. "Woods, Underwoods, Trees, Mines, Minerals, Quarries", etc. are all included in the deed.

Date: 1738,10,24°
Description: Certificate to Cadwallader Colden for land south of the Mohawk River near Canajoharie; plus instructions to Richard Bradley, dated 24 October 1738, to prepare a draft of letters patent for Cadwallader Colden and Conradt Rightmyer for the land.
Source: SEE 1738,10,05.
Comment: Land borders patent of Jacob Lansing and others, patent of Abraham Van Horne and others, and a brook called by the Indians Otsquaghe.

Date: 1738,10,28
Description: Petition of Timothy Bagley and others, for a patent for 6,000 acres of land in the county of Albany, being part of a large tract purchased by Lieut. Walter Butler from the native Indians, in the year 1733.
Source: N.Y.STATE ARCHIVES, ALBANY, N.Y.COL.MSS, INDORSED LAND PAPERS, 1643-1803, SERIES NO. A0272, DEPARTMENT OF STATE, APPLICATIONS FOR LAND GRANTS, VOL. 13, P. 006.
Comment: SEE 1733,09,18; 1733,10,16; 1736,06,25 (2); 1737,07,26. A patent for 6,000 acres of land was granted on June 25, 1736. Are these parcels of land related to one another; or is this 6,000 another parcel, perhaps part of one referred to in the petition of July 26, 1737?

Date: 1739,01,04
Description: Description of tracts granted to Henry and William Cosby, plus abstract of land titles. One of the tracts runs south of the Mohawk along Tienonderoga (Tienonderoge, Tionnonderoge, Tiononderoga, Tiondorogue) Creek to Schoharie then "along the bounds of Schoharie as they run southerly and Easterly thence to the bounds of Schenectady . . ."
Source: N.Y.STATE ARCHIVES, ALBANY, N.Y.COL.MSS, INDORSED LAND PAPERS, 1643-1803, SERIES NO. A0272, DEPARTMENT OF STATE, APPLICATIONS FOR LAND GRANTS, VOL. 13, PP. 13, 15.
Comment: SEE 1739,04,02. For identification of Tienonderoga Creek as the Schoharie river, SEE 1737,10,12; 1754,10,25.

Date: 1739,02,09
Description: Petition of George Ingoldsby, Timothy Bagley, Richard Nicholls, Frederick Morris, Richard Shuckburgh, and others to purchase land on one side of the Mohawk River from the Indians.
Source: N.Y.STATE ARCHIVES, ALBANY, N.Y.COL.MSS, INDORSED LAND PAPERS, 1643-1803, SERIES NO. A0272, DEPARTMENT OF STATE, APPLICATIONS FOR LAND GRANTS, VOL. 13, P. 18.
Comment: SEE 1739,08,01. Others named in the petition are: Alexander Colhoun (Calhoun), Charles O'Neill, James Lyne, Arent Stephens, Leendert (?) Lansing, John Baptist Van Eps, Jr., Dow Fonda, Abraham Truaz (Truax), Robert Todd, William English, and Alexander Malcom. This land may be near the junction of the Mohawk and Schoharie Rivers. However, its location is unclear to the compiler of this calendar.

Date: 1739,04,10°
Description: Indian deed to Arent (Bradt) and others for land ceded in West Huntersfield.
Source: SEE 1738,04,10.
Comment: This document is dated 10 Apr 1739 in CALENDAR OF LAND PAPERS. The date on the document looks more like 10 Apr 1738, however. Therefore, it has been so dated in this calendar.

Date: 1739,04,12
Description: Instructions to Richard Bradley to prepare a draft of letters patent for Walter Butler, John Miln, and Thomas Scurlock to land south of the Mohawk River.
Source: N.Y.STATE ARCHIVES, ALBANY, N.Y.COL.MSS, INDORSED LAND PAPERS, 1643-1803, SERIES NO. A0272, DEPARTMENT OF STATE, APPLICATIONS FOR LAND GRANTS, VOL. 13, P. 023.
Comment: SEE 1739,01,04. A warrant is attached. It describes the land as being south of the Mohawk along Tienonderoga (Tienonderoge, Tiononderoga, Tionnonderoga, Tiondorogue, Tiononderoga) Creek to Schoharie then "along the bounds of Schoharie as they run southerly and Easterly thence to the bounds of Schenectady . . ." Tienonderoga Creek is the Schoharie River (SEE 1737,10,12; 1754,10,25).

Date: 1739,05,17 (3)
Description: Petiton of A. Bratt (Bradt) and Volkert Van Veghton "on behalf of themselves and Company" for a patent for two tracts of land west of Huntersfield.
Source: N.Y.STATE ARCHIVES, ALBANY, N.Y.COL.MSS, INDORSED LAND PAPERS, 1643-1803, SERIES NO. A0272, DEPARTMENT OF STATE, APPLICATIONS FOR LAND GRANTS, VOL. 13, P. 030.
Comment: N.B. This document has the same page number as the Indian deed to Bratt and others, dated 1730,04,10. SEE also 1739,05,17 [ ]. The petition itself is not dated, except for a 5 May 1738 date in the margin apparently added by an archivist or researcher at the N.Y. State Archives. The endorsement, however, has the date 17 May 1739 with the note: "was referred & reported by Mr. Horsmanden in fav[o]r of the pet[itio]n".

Date: 1739,05,17 (4)
Description: Minutes of New York Provincial Council with petitions from Edward Clarke, James Henderson and Phillip Livingston, and A. Bratt and Company for land.
Source: N.Y.STATE ARCHIVES, ALBANY, N.Y.COL.MSS, INDORSED LAND PAPERS, 1643-1803, SERIES NO. A0272, DEPARTMENT OF STATE, APPLICATIONS FOR LAND GRANTS, VOL. 13, P. 032.
Comment:

Date: 1739,05,17 (5)
Description: Petition of Jeremiah Dunbar for 6,000 acres of land south of the Mohawk purchased by him from Walter Butler, John Miln and Thomas Scurlock. Answer of Cadwallader Colden to the petition is with this document and is dated May 21. Also included is an affidavit to Jeremiah Dunbar.
Source: N.Y.STATE ARCHIVES, ALBANY, N.Y.COL.MSS, INDORSED LAND PAPERS, 1643-1803, SERIES NO. A0272, DEPARTMENT OF STATE, APPLICATIONS FOR LAND GRANTS, VOL. 13, PP. 034, 035, 036.
Comment: These manuscripts present an interesting discussion of procedures of marking land, and establishing proof thereof.

Date: 1739,05,17 [ ]
Description: Petition of Edward Clarke for a patent for 600 acres of land on both sides of Schoharie Creek.
Source: N.Y.STATE ARCHIVES, ALBANY, N.Y.COL.MSS, INDORSED LAND PAPERS, 1643-1803, SERIES NO. A0272, DEPARTMENT OF STATE, APPLICATIONS FOR LAND GRANTS, VOL. 13, P. 028.
Comment: The petition itself is undated. The endorsement, however, has the date 17 May 1739 with the note: "was referred & reported by Mr. Horsmanden in favor of the pet[itio]n".

Date: 1739,05,17 [ ] (2)
Description: Petition of James Henderson and Phillip Livingston for 2,000 acres of land south of the Mohawk.
Source: N.Y.STATE ARCHIVES, ALBANY, N.Y.COL.MSS, INDORSED LAND PAPERS, 1643-1803, SERIES NO. A0272, DEPARTMENT OF STATE, APPLICATIONS FOR LAND GRANTS, VOL. 13, P. 029.
Comment:

Date: 1739,05,21°
Description: Petition of Jeremiah Dunbar for 6,000 acres of land south of the Mohawk purchased by him from Walter Butler, John Miln and Thomas Scurlock. Answer of Cadwallader Colden to the petition is with this document and is dated May 21. Also included is an affidavit to Jeremiah Dunbar.
Source: SEE 1739,05,17 (5).
Comment: These manuscripts present an interesting discussion of procedures of marking land, and establishing proof thereof.

Date: 1739,06,15
Description: Warrant for patent for land of Edward Collins.
Source: N.Y.STATE ARCHIVES, ALBANY, N.Y.COL.MSS, INDORSED LAND PAPERS, 1643-1803, SERIES NO. A0272, DEPARTMENT OF STATE, APPLICATIONS FOR LAND GRANTS, VOL. 13, P. 40.
Comment: CALENDAR OF LAND PAPERS identifies this land as being in Albany County. It is uncertain, however, whether or not it is in the Schoharie River Valley. N.B., Until 1795 Schoharie was in Albany County.

Date: 1739,06,28 [ ]
Description: Petition of Edward Clarke for 400 more acres of land, making the total of of his land 1,000 acres.
Source: N.Y.STATE ARCHIVES, ALBANY, N.Y.COL.MSS, INDORSED LAND PAPERS, 1643-1803, SERIES NO. A0272, DEPARTMENT OF STATE, APPLICATIONS FOR LAND GRANTS, VOL. 13, P. 042.
Comment: N.B. The petition itself is not dated. The date, 28 June 1739, shows up on the endorsement with the note: "read & referred & reported by Mr. Horsmanden in fav[o]r of the pet[itio]n".

Date: 1739,07,07
Description: Return of survey of Edward Clarke's land.
Source: N.Y.STATE ARCHIVES, ALBANY, N.Y.COL.MSS, INDORSED LAND PAPERS, 1643-1803, SERIES NO. A0272, DEPARTMENT OF STATE, APPLICATIONS FOR LAND GRANTS, VOL. 13, 046.
Comment: SEE 1738,09,25; 1738,10,20; 1739,05,17 [ ]; 1739,06,28.

Date: 1739,08,01
Description: Patent of George Ingoldesby for 32,000 acres of land on the Mohawk.
Source: N.Y.STATE ARCHIVES, ALBANY, N.Y.COL.MSS, INDORSED LAND PAPERS, 1643-1803, SERIES NO. A0272, DEPARTMENT OF STATE, APPLICATIONS FOR LAND GRANTS, VOL. 13, P. 047.
Comment: SEE 1739,02,09. The location of this land is uncertain to the compiler of this calendar. It is possible that it is near the conjunction of the Mohawk and Schoharie Rivers.

Date: 1739,08,08
Description: Petition of J. Gillam, pertaining to land south of the Mohawk.
Source: N.Y.STATE ARCHIVES, ALBANY, N.Y.COL.MSS, INDORSED LAND PAPERS, 1643-1803, SERIES NO. A0272, DEPARTMENT OF STATE, APPLICATIONS FOR LAND GRANTS, VOL. 13, P. 048.
Comment: This land may be near the conjunction of the Mohawk and Schoharie Rivers. However, the compiler of this calendar is uncertain of its location.

Date: 1739,08,08 (2)
Description: Warrant for patent of J. Henderson for four tracts of land.
Source: N.Y.STATE ARCHIVES, ALBANY, N.Y.COL.MSS, INDORSED LAND PAPERS, 1643-1803, SERIES NO. A0272, DEPARTMENT OF STATE, APPLICATIONS FOR LAND GRANTS, VOL. 13, P. 049.
Comment:

Date: 1739,08,25
Description: Warrant for patent to Edward Clarke, and certificate.
Source: N.Y.STATE ARCHIVES, ALBANY, N.Y.COL.MSS, INDORSED LAND PAPERS, 1643-1803, SERIES NO. A0272, DEPARTMENT OF STATE, APPLICATIONS FOR LAND GRANTS, VOL. 13, 052.
Comment: SEE 1738,09,25; 1738,10,20; 1739,05,17 [ ]; 1739,06,28; 1739,07,07.

Date: 1739,08,29
Description: Patent to Edward Clarke for two tracts of land totalling 2,000 acres bordering the Schoharie River.
Source: N.Y.STATE ARCHIVES, ALBANY, N.Y. LETTERS PATENT, 1664-1780, SERIES NO. 12590, BOOK 12, P. 68.
Comment: This land is in the towns of Blenheim and Fulton(?).

Date: 1740,04,03
Description: Petition of the Rev. H. Barclay for license to purchase a tract of land south of the Mohawk.
Source: N.Y.STATE ARCHIVES, ALBANY, N.Y.COL.MSS, INDORSED LAND PAPERS, 1643-1803, SERIES NO. A0272, DEPARTMENT OF STATE, APPLICATIONS FOR LAND GRANTS, VOL. 13, P. 63.
Comment:

Date: 1740,07,26
Description: Petition of Volkert Oothout and others for patent for land south of the Mohawk bordering J. Lindesay's land.
Source: N.Y.STATE ARCHIVES, ALBANY, N.Y.COL.MSS, INDORSED LAND PAPERS, 1643-1803, SERIES NO. A0272, DEPARTMENT OF STATE, APPLICATIONS FOR LAND GRANTS, VOL. 13, P. 068.
Comment: SEE 1741,08,01; 1741,08,17.

Date: 1740,11,24
Description: Indian deed to the Rev. Henry Barclay for land south of the Mohawk. Signed by John Sejehowane, Gidion Dewighnidoge, and Esras Tikjerere/Tekjerere.
Source: N.Y.STATE ARCHIVES, ALBANY, N.Y.COL.MSS, INDORSED LAND PAPERS, 1643-1803, SERIES NO. A0272, DEPARTMENT OF STATE, APPLICATIONS FOR LAND GRANTS, VOL. 13, P. 069.
Comment: Contains marks of Indian signers.

Date: 1741,10,10
Description: Return of survey for Rev. Barclay of land south of the Mohawk River near Fort Hunter, near Wemp's land.
Source: N.Y.STATE ARCHIVES, ALBANY, N.Y.COL.MSS, INDORSED LAND PAPERS, 1643-1803, SERIES NO. A0272, DEPARTMENT OF STATE, APPLICATIONS FOR LAND GRANTS, VOL. 13, P. 098.
Comment: SEE 1741,10,19.

Date: 1741,10,19
Description: Warrant and certificate to Rev. Barclay for land.
Source: N.Y.STATE ARCHIVES, ALBANY, N.Y.COL.MSS, INDORSED LAND PAPERS, 1643-1803, SERIES NO. A0272, DEPARTMENT OF STATE, APPLICATIONS FOR LAND GRANTS, VOL. 13, P. 103.
Comment: SEE 1741,10,10.

Date: 1742,00,00-1748,00,00 [ ] °
Description: Transcription of an extract from a manuscript book of notes taken down by Christopher Pyrlaus between the Years 1742 and 1748 while in the country of the Five Nations. The extract was apparently copied by John Heckewelder. It appears to be in his handwriting (SEE 1820,03,04). Pyrlaus explains that the names of the founders of the League of the Iroquois have been passed down to their successors. He received his information from an Indian named Sganarady.
Source: SEE 1820,00,00 [ ].
Comment: Transcription was probably done ca. 1820.

Date: 1742,07,14
Description: Petition of Jeronimus Greslaer (Crissler, Greslar, Kreisler), in behalf of himself and others, for a license to purchase a tract of land, lying near a hill called by the Indians Onentadego, and to another hill called Janaentadego.
Source: N.Y.STATE ARCHIVES, ALBANY, N.Y.COL.MSS, INDORSED LAND PAPERS, 1643-1803, SERIES NO. A0272, DEPARTMENT OF STATE, APPLICATIONS FOR LAND GRANTS, VOL. 13, P. 124.
Comment:

Date: 1742,08,30
Description: Deed from Indians of Schoharie to Bartholomew Vroman (Vrooman) and others including Josaias Swart. A creek called Jutrachcogte (Iutrachcogte[?]) by the Indians and a hill called Janoentago (Ianoentago[?]) are used as points of reference in the deed.
Source: N.Y.STATE ARCHIVES, ALBANY, N.Y.COL.MSS, INDORSED LAND PAPERS, 1643-1803, SERIES NO. A0272, DEPARTMENT OF STATE, APPLICATIONS FOR LAND GRANTS, VOL. 13, P. 126.
Comment: N.B. Three Indians (Schanewisse, Jttegarehontie[Ittegarehontie(?)], Cinsjacqua[?sp.]) signed the deed, using their marks to do so. SEE 1742,10,13.

Date: 1742,10,02
Description: Petition of William Bauch and Jacob Frederick Lawyer for license to purchase 4,000 acres of land at Schoharie.
Source: N.Y.STATE ARCHIVES, ALBANY, N.Y.COL.MSS, INDORSED LAND PAPERS, 1643-1803, SERIES NO. A0272, DEPARTMENT OF STATE, APPLICATIONS FOR LAND GRANTS, VOL. 13, P. 129.
Comment: SEE 1744,04,14; 1744,04,17; 1752,10,04; 1752,10,05; 1752,09,18; 1753,04,10; 1753,05,06; 1754,09,30. SEE ALSO 1743,11,02.

Date: 1742,10,02 (2)
Description: Petition of Johannes Lawyer, Jr., Nicholas York, John Eckerson, Peter Sillye, and Jeronimus Gresler (Greslaer, Kreisler, Crissler) for license to purchase 9,000 acres southwest of Schoharie.
Source: N.Y.STATE ARCHIVES, ALBANY, N.Y.COL.MSS, INDORSED LAND PAPERS, 1643-1803, SERIES NO. A0272, DEPARTMENT OF STATE, APPLICATIONS FOR LAND GRANTS, VOL. 13, P. 130.
Comment:

Date: 1742,10,13
Description: Petition of Bartholomew Vrooman (Vroman), Martinus Vroman, Barent Vroman, Josaias Swart, and Jeronimas Greslaer (Kreisler, Greslar, Crissler) for a patent of 800 acres of land near the creek called by the Indians Jutrachcogte (Iutrachcogte[?]).
Source: N.Y.STATE ARCHIVES, ALBANY, N.Y.COL.MSS, INDORSED LAND PAPERS, 1643-1803, SERIES NO. A0272, DEPARTMENT OF STATE, APPLICATIONS FOR LAND GRANTS, VOL. 13, P. 131.
Comment: SEE 1742,08,30.

Date: 1743,00,00°
Description: Rufus Grider Collection. Watercolor drawing of the First Lutheran Church, Schoharie Village, 1743.
Source: SEE 1887,00,00-1888,00,00.
Comment:

Date: 1743,06,21
Description: Return of survey for Bartholomew Vrooman (Vroman), Martinus Vrooman, Barent Vrooman, Josaias Swart, and Heronimus (Jeronimus) Greslar (Greslaer, Kreisler, Crissler) of land twenty-four miles west of Schoharie on a brook called by the Indians Tagquatainigo.
Source: N.Y.STATE ARCHIVES, ALBANY, N.Y.COL.MSS, INDORSED LAND PAPERS, 1643-1803, SERIES NO. A0272, DEPARTMENT OF STATE, APPLICATIONS FOR LAND GRANTS, VOL. 13, P. 151.
Comment: SEE 1743,07,12.

Date: 1743,07,12
Description: Warrant and certificate to Bartholomew Vrooman (Vroman) for land twenty-miles west of Schoharie.
Source: N.Y.STATE ARCHIVES, ALBANY, N.Y.COL.MSS, INDORSED LAND PAPERS, 1643-1803, SERIES NO. A0272, DEPARTMENT OF STATE, APPLICATIONS FOR LAND GRANTS, VOL. 13, P. 155.
Comment: SEE 1743,06,21.

Date: 1743,07,14
Description: Patent to Barent Vrooman, Bartholomew Vrooman, Martinus Vroman, and others for a tract of 800 acres of land west of Schoharie. Known as the Mine Patent.
Source: N.Y.STATE ARCHIVES, ALBANY, N.Y. LETTERS PATENT, 1664-1780, SERIES NO. 12590, BOOK 12, P. 182.
Comment: This land may be further west than the Schoharie River Valley.

Date: 1743,11,02
Description: License to William Bauch and J.F. Lawyer to purchase 4,000 acres of land at Schoharie contiguous to land possessed by Bauch and Sawyer (Lawyer[?]).
Source: N.Y.STATE ARCHIVES, ALBANY, N.Y.COL.MSS, INDORSED LAND PAPERS, 1643-1803, SERIES NO. A0272, DEPARTMENT OF STATE, APPLICATIONS FOR LAND GRANTS, VOL. 13.
Comment: SEE 1742,10,02.

Date: 1744,04,14
Description: Cession of land south and southwest of Schoharie by Seth, Hans Ury, and others to Jacob Frederick Lawyer, William Bauch, and others; with statement attached, dated 4 Oct 1752, about legitimacy of deed.
Source: N.Y. STATE ARCHIVES, ALBANY, INDIAN TREATIES & DEEDS, SERIES #448.
Comment: Compare the marks at end of deed with the names at the beginning, among which are those of Indian women. N.B. Hints of link between kinship and land holding can be found in statement at the end of the document. Also, date of deed, 14 Apr 1744, does not match 16 Apr 1744 date in the statement at the end of the document. SEE 1742,10,02.

Date: 1744,04,16°
Description: Account of money paid the Indians for land round and between the patent of Nicholas York, Jacob Frederick Lawyer and others.
Source: SEE 1752,09,18.
Comment: SEE ALSO: 1744,04,17; 1752,10,04; 1752,10,05; 1753,04,10; 1753,05,06.

Date: 1744,04,17
Description: Indian deed to Jacob Frederick Lawyer, William Bauch and Heronimus Kreisler (Greslar, Greslaer, Crissler) for land south and southwest of Schoharie. Points of reference in the deed are the foot of a hill called Furberg (where the tract begins), the patent granted to Edward Clarke, the Schoharie creek, another creek called Oneyagine by the Indians and Stone creek by the Euroamericans, and "the great patent of Schoharie, granted to Myndert Schuyler, Peter Vonbrugh and others".
Source: N.Y.STATE ARCHIVES, ALBANY, N.Y.COL.MSS, INDORSED LAND PAPERS, 1643-1803, SERIES NO. A0272, DEPARTMENT OF STATE, APPLICATIONS FOR LAND GRANTS, VOL. 15, P. 015.
Comment: Also included is a certificate of Johannes Lawyer of the same date attesting that the Indians received full payment for the land. Land was in dispute in later years: SEE 1742,10,02; 1752,09,18; 1752,10,04; 1752,10,05; 1744,04,16; 1753,04,10; 1753,05,06; 1754,09,30.

Date: 1744,05,11
Description: Petition of John Baptist Van Rensselaer and others for license to purchase 16,000 acres of vacant land in the county of Albany.
Source: N.Y.STATE ARCHIVES, ALBANY, N.Y.COL.MSS, INDORSED LAND PAPERS, 1643-1803, SERIES NO. A0272, DEPARTMENT OF STATE, APPLICATIONS FOR LAND GRANTS, VOL. 13, P. 162.
Comment:

Date: 1744,05,18
Description: Petition of Stephen Bayard and others for a license to purchase 28,000 acres of land on the south side of the Mohawk River.
Source: N.Y.STATE ARCHIVES, ALBANY, N.Y.COL.MSS, INDORSED LAND PAPERS, 1643-1803, SERIES NO. A0272, DEPARTMENT OF STATE, APPLICATIONS FOR LAND GRANTS, VOL. 13, P. 164.
Comment:

Date: 1744,09,02
Description: Deed to Jacob Frederick Lawyer, William Bauch, Nicholas York, and Heronimus Kreisler (Greslar, Greslaer, Crissler) for land in the southwest part of Schoharie. Signed by Seth, Lawrence, Ana, Magritta, Maria, Cathrina, John, and Andone.
Source: N.Y.STATE ARCHIVES, ALBANY, N.Y.COL.MSS, INDORSED LAND PAPERS, 1643-1803, SERIES NO. A0272, DEPARTMENT OF STATE, APPLICATIONS FOR LAND GRANTS, VOL. 13, P. 166.
Comment: N.B. Indian marks on the document. Four women are among the signers. N.B. Cathrina is identified as Seth's wife.

Date: 1744,10,15
Description: Petition of John Becker and Johannes Eckerson for license to purchase from "the Native Indians" 4,000 acres on the Schoharie river, southeast of Schoharie.
Source: N.Y.STATE ARCHIVES, ALBANY, N.Y.COL.MSS, INDORSED LAND PAPERS, 1643-1803, SERIES NO. A0272, DEPARTMENT OF STATE, APPLICATIONS FOR LAND GRANTS, VOL. 13, P. 167.
Comment: SEE 1753,04,10.

Date: 1746,07,07
Description: Richard Shuckburgh to William Johnson. "John a Schory [Schoharie] Indian has kill'd & scalp'd a Cagnawaga [Caughnawaga] Indian near Still Water."
Source: THE PAPERS OF SIR WILLIAM JOHNSON. ED. BY JAMES SULLIVAN, ET AL. ALBANY: STATE UNIVERSITY OF NEW YORK, 14 VOLS., 1921-1965, 01: 0053-0054
Comment:

Date: 1746,07,28
Description: Richard Shuckburgh to William Johnson, informing him that an officer and 25 men from Schoharie are being sent to protect William Johnson and adjacent settlement in face of rumor of attack.
Source: THE PAPERS OF SIR WILLIAM JOHNSON. ED. BY JAMES SULLIVAN, ET AL. ALBANY: STATE UNIVERSITY OF NEW YORK, 14 VOLS., 1921-1965, 01: 0055.
Comment:

Date: 1746,12,13-1747,11,07
Description: An account of expenses, with receipt, enclosed in a letter from George Clinton to William Johnson, dated 28 July 1748. It reports that supplies were given on 29 April 1747 to Indians of Schoharie who were going out fighting.
Source: THE PAPERS OF SIR WILLIAM JOHNSON. ED. BY JAMES SULLIVAN, ET AL. ALBANY: STATE UNIVERSITY OF NEW YORK, 14 VOLS., 1921-1965, 09: 0015-0031.
Comment:

Date: 1747,04,29°
Description: An account of expenses from 13 Dec 1746-7 Nov 1747 enclosed in letter from George Clinton to William Johnson, dated 28 July 1748. Supplies are given to Indians of Schoharie who are going out fighting.
Source: SEE 1748,07,28.
Comment:

Date: 1747,06,16
Description: John H Lydius to William Johnson. Mentions "the Schoharie Partie John, the Rever [River] Indian" is on scout [around Crown Point?]
Source: THE PAPERS OF SIR WILLIAM JOHNSON. ED. BY JAMES SULLIVAN, ET AL. ALBANY: STATE UNIVERSITY OF NEW YORK, 14 VOLS., 1921-1965, 01: 0100
Comment:

Date: 1748,02,04
Description: Albert Van Slyck to William Johnson. The minister, the Reverend Mr. Schuyler of Schoharie, is to begin coming to the Indians "two 3 or 4 Time In one Year."
Source: THE PAPERS OF SIR WILLIAM JOHNSON. ED. BY JAMES SULLIVAN, ET AL. ALBANY: STATE UNIVERSITY OF NEW YORK, 14 VOLS., 1921-1965, 01: 0130.
Comment: It is not clear whether the Indians mentioned are Indians of Schoharie, or Mohawks near Johnson.

Date: 1748,07,28
Description: An account of expenses from 13 Dec 1746-7 Nov 1747, with receipt. Enclosed in letter from George Clinton to William Johnson. Supplies were given on 29 April 1747 to Indians of Schoharie who were going out fighting.
Source: THE PAPERS OF SIR WILLIAM JOHNSON. ED. BY JAMES SULLIVAN, ET AL. ALBANY: STATE UNIVERSITY OF NEW YORK, 14 VOLS., 1921-1965, 09: 0015-0031.
Comment: Original is in William L. Clements Library, Ann Arbor, Michigan.

Date: 1750,02,04
Description: Petition of Benjamin Nicoll and Co., for a license to purchase 12,000 acres of land, lying to the southeast of Schoharie on both side of Foxes (Fox) creek.
Source: N.Y.STATE ARCHIVES, ALBANY, N.Y.COL.MSS, INDORSED LAND PAPERS, 1643-1803, SERIES NO. A0272, DEPARTMENT OF STATE, APPLICATIONS FOR LAND GRANTS, VOL. 14, P. 104.
Comment:

Date: 1750,05,16°
Description: Tracing of a map showing lots and locations along the Schoharie River. A note on the map states, "This Division was made, 16 May Anno 1750".
Source: SEE 1887,00,00-1888,00,00 (46).
Comment: This is a tracing by Rufus Grider Rufus Grider done in 1887 from the original which was in the possession of Henry Cady of Schoharie at the time.

Date: 1750,05,22
Description: George Clinton to William Johnson, telling him to assure the Five Nations that they will be assisted if attacked by any enemy; and that they may consult with officers of the militia on the Mohawk River and Schoharie.
Source: THE PAPERS OF SIR WILLIAM JOHNSON. ED. BY JAMES SULLIVAN, ET AL. ALBANY: STATE UNIVERSITY OF NEW YORK, 14 VOLS., 1921-1965, 01: 0280-0281.
Comment: Contains no specific information about Indians of Schoharie.

Date: 1750,08,25-10,13
Description: A journal of the proceedings of Conrad Weiser in his journey to Onondaga. On 29 August, Weiser reported that he took a "Ride to a small Indian Mohocks (Mohawks) Town. . .as I had lived from the Year 1714, 'till the Year 1729, within Two Miles of their Town." Talked with Indians there.
Source: HISTORICAL SOCIETY OF PENNSYLVANIA, PHILADELPHIA, PENN MSS, INDIAN AFFAIRS I, 1687-1753, VOL. 1, 66 [24 pages].
Comment: The town that Weiser visited is Schoharie. It is said to be about 36 miles from Albany. SEE 1753,09,02.

Date: 1750,09,11
Description: Petition of John Becker and Johannis (Johannes) Eckerson for a license to purchase 4,000 acres on a branch of Schoharie Creek, southeast of Schoharie.
Source: N.Y.STATE ARCHIVES, ALBANY, N.Y.COL.MSS, INDORSED LAND PAPERS, 1643-1803, SERIES NO. A0272, DEPARTMENT OF STATE, APPLICATIONS FOR LAND GRANTS, VOL. 14, P. 080.
Comment: In the document, it is said that it is a "dangerous time to make survey on account of the war. . ."

Date: 1750,11,29
Description: Petition of Johannis (Johannes) Becker and Johannis (Johannes) Eckerson that 4,000 acres purchased by them on the east side of Schoharie creek, a little above Schoharie, be excluded from any license granted to Hieronimus Crissler (Kriesler, Greslar, Greslaer) and others to purchase on the east side of the creek.
Source: N.Y.STATE ARCHIVES, ALBANY, N.Y.COL.MSS, INDORSED LAND PAPERS, 1643-1803, SERIES NO. A0272, DEPARTMENT OF STATE, APPLICATIONS FOR LAND GRANTS, VOL. 14, P. 097.
Comment:

Date: 1750,12,14
Description: Petition of William Bauch and Frederick Lawyer for a license to purchase, with Nicholas York, and Jeronimus Greslaer (Kreisler, Greslar, Crissler), 5,000 acres of land on both sides of Schoharie Creek, back of lands on the west side of the creek granted to Johannis (Johannes) Lawyer and John DePeyster, back to land on the east side of the creek to Adam Vroman's (Vrooman's) land and northeast to lands granted to Walter Butler, now owned by E. Clarke.
Source: N.Y.STATE ARCHIVES, ALBANY, N.Y.COL.MSS, INDORSED LAND PAPERS, 1643-1803, SERIES NO. A0272, DEPARTMENT OF STATE, APPLICATIONS FOR LAND GRANTS, VOL. 14, P. 093.
Comment: SEE 1752,10,04; 1752,10,05; 1752,09,18; 1753,04,10; 1753,05,06. For information on the Lawyer and DePeyster grant, SEE 1737,10,15.

Date: 1751,00,00 [ ]
Description: Letter from William Johnson to G. Banyar to make out a petition for a license to purchase a tract of land southwest of Schoharie where two Indian paths meet. One path goes to Skenewaseys (Sonowesie's[?]) house, the other to Onaoghduagey and the area of Charolotte Creek where "Germans made canoes".
Source: N.Y.STATE ARCHIVES, ALBANY, N.Y.COL.MSS, INDORSED LAND PAPERS, 1643-1803, SERIES NO. A0272, DEPARTMENT OF STATE, APPLICATIONS FOR LAND GRANTS, VOL. 14, P. 113.
Comment: SEE 1751,05,06; 1770,03,00; 1770,04,12.

Date: 1751,00,00°
Description: Indian deed to William Johnson for land south and southwest of Schoharie. Included with certificate dated March 1770 stating that Peter Schuyler and Robert Adams were present when Canajoharie Indians agreed to sell above land on branch of river Adagegtinge.
Source: SEE 1770,03,00.
Comment:

Date: 1751,00,00°
Description: Letter from William Johnson to G. Banyar to make out a petition for a license to purchase a tract of land southwest of Schoharie where two Indian paths meet. One path goes to Skenewaseys (Sonowesie's[?]) house, the other to Onaoghduagey and the area of Charolotte Creek where "Germans made canoes".
Source: SEE 1751,00,00 [ ].
Comment: SEE 1751,05,06; 1770,03,00; 1770,04,12.

Date: 1751,01,31
Description: Petition of Jacob Borst (Burst) and others for a license to purchase a 20,000 acre tract of woodland six miles west of Schoharie between the mountains of Schoharie and the hills called Onuntadass (Onuntadasha, Onuntadashe, Onuntadagka) by the Indians.
Source: N.Y.STATE ARCHIVES, ALBANY, N.Y.COL.MSS, INDORSED LAND PAPERS, 1643-1803, SERIES NO. A0272, DEPARTMENT OF STATE, APPLICATIONS FOR LAND GRANTS, VOL. 14, P. 102.
Comment:

Date: 1751,02,04
Description: Petition of Benjamin Nicoll and company for a license to purchase 12,000 acres of land southeast of Schoharie on both sides of Foxes (Fox) Creek.
Source: N.Y.STATE ARCHIVES, ALBANY, N.Y.COL.MSS, INDORSED LAND PAPERS, 1643-1803, SERIES NO. A0272, DEPARTMENT OF STATE, APPLICATIONS FOR LAND GRANTS, VOL. 14, 104.
Comment:

Date: 1751,03,22
Description: Petition of William Bauch and Jacob Frederick Lawyer to purchase land from the Indians.
Source: N.Y.STATE ARCHIVES, ALBANY, N.Y.COL.MSS, INDORSED LAND PAPERS, 1643-1803, SERIES NO. A0272, DEPARTMENT OF STATE, APPLICATIONS FOR LAND GRANTS, VOL. 14, P. 107.
Comment:

Date: 1751,04,03
Description: Petition of Luykas Johannis (Johannes) Wyngaard, John Garret Roseboom, Jacob Merkell, and Nicholas Jacobus Lydius for a license to purchase 10,000 acres of vacant land between the patent of Schoharie and the patent of John Lindesay "in his Majesty's Name" from "the Native Indian Proprietors".
Source: N.Y.STATE ARCHIVES, ALBANY, N.Y.COL.MSS, INDORSED LAND PAPERS, 1643-1803, SERIES NO. A0272, DEPARTMENT OF STATE, APPLICATIONS FOR LAND GRANTS, VOL. 14, P. 109.
Comment:

Date: 1751,05,06
Description: Description of a 130,000 acre tract of land south and southwest of Schoharie beginning where two roads or Indian paths meet, one leading from "Scoharee (Schoharie) to the House of Skenewaseys (Sonowesie[?]) an Indian", and the other to Ona'Ogh'da'gey (Onondaga[?]). William Johnson and company request 100,000 acres of this.
Source: N.Y.STATE ARCHIVES, ALBANY, N.Y.COL.MSS, INDORSED LAND PAPERS, 1643-1803, SERIES NO. A0272, DEPARTMENT OF STATE, APPLICATIONS FOR LAND GRANTS, VOL. 14, P. 113.
Comment: A detailed description of the location of the tract is given, including Indian names for landmarks. N.B., reference to a "place where the Germans formerly made Canoes to go to Conas'to'gey [Conastoga]". SEE 1751,00,00 [ ]; 1770,03,00; 1770,04,12.

Date: 1751,05,06 (2)
Description: William Johnson to Goldsbrow Banyar, about a deed of land to the south and southwest of Schoharie.
Source: THE PAPERS OF SIR WILLIAM JOHNSON. ED. BY JAMES SULLIVAN, ET AL. ALBANY: STATE UNIVERSITY OF NEW YORK, 14 VOLS., 1921-1965,: 01: 0921-0922.
Comment: Original document is in N.Y.STATE ARCHIVES, ALBANY, N.Y.COL.MSS, INDORSED LAND PAPERS, 1643-1803, SERIES NO. A0272, DEPARTMENT OF STATE, APPLICATIONS FOR LAND GRANTS, VOL. 14, P. 113.

Date: 1751,05,08
Description: Arent Stevens to William Johnson. Stevens writes that he has questioned Hendrick (of Canajoharie) about who owns land that Johnson wants to buy. Hendrick said that the land is not owned by Oneidas, but by Indians of Canajoharie; "and there cannot be any dispute about it, he [Hendrick] says he wishes to have the Bargain made as soon as possible, I told Hendrick to send to Scoharee [Schoharie] for Seth [Sett], and likewise for Sonewesie [Skenewaseys(?)] that we may meet at your house as soon as possible: that they may make an end of the Affair . . ."
Source: THE PAPERS OF SIR WILLIAM JOHNSON. ED. BY JAMES SULLIVAN, ET AL. ALBANY: STATE UNIVERSITY OF NEW YORK, 14 VOLS., 1921-1965, 01: 0330-0331.
Comment:

Date: 1751,05,18
Description: Letter from Goldsbrow Banyar to William Johnson. Outlines the procedure for obtaining a patent.
Source: THE PAPERS OF SIR WILLIAM JOHNSON. ED. BY JAMES SULLIVAN, ET AL. ALBANY: STATE UNIVERSITY OF NEW YORK, 14 VOLS., 1921-1965, 01: 0334-0335.
Comment:

Date: 1751,05,23
Description: Cession by Seth, John, Lawrence and others to Jacob Borst (Burst), Jeronimus (Heronimus) Gresler (Greslar, Greslaer, Crissler, Kreisler), and others of land six miles west of Schoharie between mountains of Schoharie and hill called Onuntadasha (Onuntadass, Onuntadashe, Onuntadagka) on the west side of a creek called Oscalleghe (Otsgarage, Aschalege, Oscallaghe, Oschaleghe, Otsgarrege, Cobleskill).
Source: N.Y. STATE ARCHIVES, ALBANY, INDIAN TREATIES & DEEDS, SERIES #448, (1748-1810).
Comment: Compare names at beginning of document with those signed at end. N.B., Survey was done in the presence of the Indians.

Date: 1751,05,23 (2)
Description: Deed signed by Seth, John, Lawrence, Joseph and others to Jacob Borst (Burst) et al. Deed is to 25,000 acres of land six miles west of Schoharie between the mountains of Schoharie and the hill called by the Indians Onuntadashe (Onuntadass, Onuntadasha, Onuntadagka) and the brook called Oscallaghe (Oscalleghe, Oschaleghe, Otsgarege, Otsgarrege, Otsgarage, Aschalege, Cobleskill).
Source: N.Y.STATE ARCHIVES, ALBANY, N.Y.COL.MSS, INDORSED LAND PAPERS, 1643-1803, SERIES NO. A0272, DEPARTMENT OF STATE, APPLICATIONS FOR LAND GRANTS, VOL. 14, P. 116.
Comment: N.B. List of Indians at beginning of the document does not correspond exactly to that of Indians who signed, using their marks.

Date: 1751,06,10
Description: Petition of Jacob Borst, Jeronimus Greslaer (Kreisler, Gresler, Greslar, Crissler), Mathias Bowman, Barent Keiser, Hendrick Hens, Adam Zehe, Robert Stuert (Stewart), Barent Ten Eyck, and Jacob C. Ten Eyck for letters patent for land about six miles west of Schoharie between the mountains of Schoharie and the hill called by the Indians Onuntadasha(Onuntadashe, Onuntadass, Onuntadagka).
Source: N.Y.STATE ARCHIVES, ALBANY, N.Y.COL.MSS, INDORSED LAND PAPERS, 1643-1803, SERIES NO. A0272, DEPARTMENT OF STATE, APPLICATIONS FOR LAND GRANTS, VOL. 14, P. 122.
Comment: SEE 1751,09,18; 1751,10,05.

Date: 1751,06,12
Description: Petition of Mathew Ferrall for license to purchase 130,000 acres of land southwest of Schoharie. Also included is license for the purchase.
Source: N.Y.STATE ARCHIVES, ALBANY, N.Y.COL.MSS, INDORSED LAND PAPERS, 1643-1803, SERIES NO. A0272, DEPARTMENT OF STATE, APPLICATIONS FOR LAND GRANTS, VOL. 14, P. 124, 125.
Comment: SEE 1785,09,20. On 21 November 1752, Ferrall and his associates applied for a subsequent license to purchase the land because the one issued on 12 June 1751 had expired. SEE ALSO 1752,11,21; 1754,03,01; 1754,03,05.

Date: 1751,08,24
Description: Deed of land south and southwest of Schoharie from Indians of Schoharie and others.
Source: THE PAPERS OF SIR WILLIAM JOHNSON. ED. BY JAMES SULLIVAN, ET AL. ALBANY: STATE UNIVERSITY OF NEW YORK, 14 VOLS., 1921-1965, 13: 0015-0019.
Comment: Clan totems are used for some of the Indian marks at the end of the document. Original is in N.Y.STATE ARCHIVES, ALBANY, N.Y.COL.MSS, INDORSED LAND PAPERS, 1643-1803, SERIES NO. A0272, DEPARTMENT OF STATE, APPLICATIONS FOR LAND GRANTS, Vol. 26, P. 127. SEE 1770,03,00. Footnote in THE PAPERS OF SIR WILLIAM JOHNSON. ED. BY JAMES SULLIVAN, ET AL. ALBANY: STATE UNIVERSITY OF NEW YORK, 14 VOLS., 1921-1965, gives brief history of the deed.

Date: 1751,08,24°
Description: Indian deed to William Johnson for a tract of land on the south and southwest side of Schoharie.
Source: SEE 1770,03,00.
Comment:

Date: 1751,09,17
Description: Return of survey of Thomas Braine for 2,000 acres of land near Schoharie purchased from the Indians by Walter Butler and others.
Source: N.Y.STATE ARCHIVES, ALBANY, N.Y.COL.MSS, INDORSED LAND PAPERS, 1643-1803, SERIES NO. A0272, DEPARTMENT OF STATE, APPLICATIONS FOR LAND GRANTS, VOL. 14, P. 130.
Comment: 1736,06,10; 1736,06,12; 1736,06,26; 1738,03,31; 1738,04,21.

Date: 1751,09,18
Description: Return of survey for Jacob Borst (Burst), Jeronimus (Heronimus) Greslar (Greslaer, Kreisler, Gresler, Crissler), Mathias Bowman, Barent Keiser, Hendrick Hens, Adam Zehe, Robert Stuert (Stewart), Barent Ten Eyck, and Jacob C. Ten Eyck for two tracts of 18,000 acres of land between the mountains of Schoharie and the hill called Onuntadagka (Onuntadass, Onuntadasha, Ountadashe) on a creek called Oschaleghe (Oscalleghe, Oscallaghe, Otsgarrege, Otsgarege, Otsgarage, Aschalege, Cobleskill).
Source: N.Y.STATE ARCHIVES, ALBANY, N.Y.COL.MSS, INDORSED LAND PAPERS, 1643-1803, SERIES NO. A0272, DEPARTMENT OF STATE, APPLICATIONS FOR LAND GRANTS, VOL. 14, P. 132.
Comment: SEE 1751,10,05; 1751,06,10.

Date: 1751,10,00
Description: Petition of Stephen Bayard and others to purchase 28,000 acres of land on the south side of the Mohawk River.
Source: N.Y.STATE ARCHIVES, ALBANY, N.Y.COL.MSS, INDORSED LAND PAPERS, 1643-1803, SERIES NO. A0272, DEPARTMENT OF STATE, APPLICATIONS FOR LAND GRANTS, VOL. 14, P. 137.
Comment:

Date: 1751,10,05
Description: Petition of Jacob (Burst) and others for patent for 18,000 acres of land westward of Schoharie.
Source: N.Y.STATE ARCHIVES, ALBANY, N.Y.COL.MSS, INDORSED LAND PAPERS, 1643-1803, SERIES NO. A0272, DEPARTMENT OF STATE, APPLICATIONS FOR LAND GRANTS, VOL. 14, P. 134.
Comment: Borst's associates are: Mathias Bowman, Barent Keiser, Hendrick Hens, Adam Zehe, Robert Stuert (Stewart), Barent Ten Eyck, and Jacob C. Ten Eyck. Jeronimus (Heronimus) Greslaer (Kreisler, Gresler, Greslar, Crissler), one of the associates among those who acquired the land, is deceased. The petitioners request that the name of his widow Maria Margrieta Greslaer be inserted in the letters patent. SEE 1769,09,18; 1751,06,10.

Date: 1751,10,07
Description: Petition of John Frederick Bauch, Christian Zehe, Johannis Zehe, Michael Wanner, and Johannes Knisker (Kniskern, Knieskirk, Kniskern, Kneiskerk, Kneescarns, Kniskorn, Knescarn) to purchase from the Indians 12,000 acres of land twelve miles west of Schoharie on a creek called Otsgarege (Oscalleghe, Oscallaghe, Oschaleghe, Otsgarrege, Otsgarage, Ascallege, Cobleskill).
Source: N.Y.STATE ARCHIVES, ALBANY, N.Y.COL.MSS, INDORSED LAND PAPERS, 1643-1803, SERIES NO. A0272, DEPARTMENT OF STATE, APPLICATIONS FOR LAND GRANTS, VOL. 14, P. 135.
Comment: SEE 1753,07,16; 1752,11,09; 1753,11,30.

Date: 1751,10,08
Description: Petition of John Lawyer and Phillip Berg (Bergh) to purchase 4,000 acres of land from the Indians. One tract is north of Schoharie Patent on the west side of M. Coeymans patent. The second is at or near the Myndert Schuyler Patent. The third tract is between the first two tracts and Renselaerswyck. Also included is a short description of the lands in a script different from that used in the petition.
Source: N.Y.STATE ARCHIVES, ALBANY, N.Y.COL.MSS, INDORSED LAND PAPERS, 1643-1803, SERIES NO. A0272, DEPARTMENT OF STATE, APPLICATIONS FOR LAND GRANTS, VOL. 14, P. 136.
Comment: Lists surrounding patents in description of tracts.

Date: 1751,11,07
Description: Petition of John Beeker (Becker) and Johannes Eckerson to purchase 4,000 acres of land southeast of Schoharie on a branch of Schoharie Creek.
Source: N.Y.STATE ARCHIVES, ALBANY, N.Y.COL.MSS, INDORSED LAND PAPERS, 1643-1803, SERIES NO. A0272, DEPARTMENT OF STATE, APPLICATIONS FOR LAND GRANTS, VOL. 14, P. 139.
Comment:

Date: 1752,00,00 [ ]
Description: Petition of Johannes Lawyer, Jr., Nicholas York, John Ackerson, and Peter Uscily for a patent for 6,000 acres of land, purchased from the Indians, lying south and southwest from Schoharie, beginning at a place on the Schoharie creek called Jothahoike by the Indians.
Source: N.Y.STATE ARCHIVES, ALBANY, N.Y.COL.MSS, INDORSED LAND PAPERS, 1643-1803, SERIES NO. A0272, DEPARTMENT OF STATE, APPLICATIONS FOR LAND GRANTS, VOL. 15, P. 012.
Comment:

Date: 1752,00,00 [ ] (2)
Description: Petition of Jacob Frederick Lawyer and Hieronimus Kreisler (Greslar, Crissler) for a patent for 4,000 acres of land purchased from the Indians, lying south and southwest of Schoharie.
Source: N.Y.STATE ARCHIVES, ALBANY, N.Y.COL.MSS, INDORSED LAND PAPERS, 1643-1803, SERIES NO. A0272, DEPARTMENT OF STATE, APPLICATIONS FOR LAND GRANTS, VOL. 15, P. 013.
Comment: The document provides a fairly detailed description of land boundaries. The tract begins at the foot of a "Hill called Der furbery" then proceeds to the northeast corner of a patent "lately granted to Captain Edward Clarke". It comes at some point to Stone Creek which is said to be called Oneye(or c)ajine by the Indians and then proceeds easterly to the southwest corner of "the great patent of Schoharie granted to Collo. Myndert Schuyler, Peter Van Brugh and others".

Date: 1752,01,08
Description: Petition of Goldsbrow Banyar and others for patent for 6,000 acres of land west of Schoharie between two tracts laid out for Jacob Borst (Burst) and others.
Source: N.Y.STATE ARCHIVES, ALBANY, N.Y.COL.MSS, INDORSED LAND PAPERS, 1643-1803, SERIES NO. A0272, DEPARTMENT OF STATE, APPLICATIONS FOR LAND GRANTS, VOL. 14, P. 141.
Comment:

Date: 1752,02,21
Description: Patent to Jacob Borst (Burst), Mathias Bown, Adam Zehe, and others for two tracts of land west of Schoharie.
Source: N.Y.STATE ARCHIVES, ALBANY, N.Y. LETTERS PATENT, 1664-1780, SERIES NO. 12590, BOOK 12, P. 400.
Comment:

Date: 1752,05,01
Description: Deed to Johannes Lawyer and Phillip Bergh (Berg) for tracts near Schoharie. One tract is 2,800 acres, four miles east of Schoharie, beginning at land granted to Lewis Moriss (Morris) and Andries Coeiman (Coeyman, Coeman, Coeymans). The other is 200 acres, one mile west of Schoharie. The marks of Seth, Hans Ury (Yury, Yurry, Jury, Jurie), John, Anthony, and Joseph are on the deed.
Source: N.Y.STATE ARCHIVES, ALBANY, N.Y.COL.MSS, INDORSED LAND PAPERS, 1643-1803, SERIES NO. A0272, DEPARTMENT OF STATE, APPLICATIONS FOR LAND GRANTS, V0L. 14, P. 146.
Comment: Cadwallader Colden, Jr. certifies that the land was surveyed and boundaries marked in the presence of Seth, John, and Anthony; that the purchase money was paid to them and the other Indian grantees; and that the deed was sealed and delivered in Colden's presence. Peter Vroman (Vrooman) attests that the boundaries were inserted in the deed, the money paid, and the deed sealed and delivered in his presence. Maria Right[m]yer was interpreter. Boundaries are clearly described in the deed.

Date: 1752,05,01 (2)
Description: Deed from Seth, Hans, John, Anthony, and Joseph "Native Indians of the Province of New York & sole and absolute Proprietors" conveying two tracts of land to Johannes Lawyer and Phillip Bergh (Berg). One tract of 2,800 acres is four miles east from Schoharie, and the other of 200 acres is one mile west from Schoharie.
Source: N.Y.STATE ARCHIVES, ALBANY, INDIAN TREATIES & DEEDS, SERIES #448, VOL. 1, PP. 011-013. (D246/4).
Comment: Note, the marks of the Indians. This document is a contemporary copy of the original deed. Therefore, it is not sealed, but is marked LS in places where seals are located in the original deed.

Date: 1752,05,07
Description: Petition of Jacob Starnbergh (Starnberg) to purchase 500 acres of land at Schoharie between two patents of (Knisker, Kniskern, Kniskorn, Knieskerk, Knieskerk, Knieskirk, Knescarn, Kneescarn) Town.
Source: N.Y.STATE ARCHIVES, ALBANY, N.Y.COL.MSS, INDORSED LAND PAPERS, 1643-1803, SERIES NO. A0272, DEPARTMENT OF STATE, APPLICATIONS FOR LAND GRANTS, VOL. 14, P. 148.
Comment:

Date: 1752,05,25
Description: Petition of Augustus Van Cortlandt for patent to tract of 887 acres of land at Schoharie between the patents of Myndert Schuyler and others, and Lewis Morris (Moriss) and others.
Source: N.Y.STATE ARCHIVES, ALBANY, N.Y.COL.MSS, INDORSED LAND PAPERS, 1643-1803, SERIES NO. A0272, DEPARTMENT OF STATE, APPLICATIONS FOR LAND GRANTS, VOL. 14, P. 154.
Comment:

Date: 1752,06,24
Description: Petition of Johannes Lawyer and Phillip Bergh (Berg) for two tracts of land (3,000 acres) near Schoharie.
Source: N.Y.STATE ARCHIVES, ALBANY, N.Y.COL.MSS, INDORSED LAND PAPERS, 1643-1803, SERIES NO. A0272, DEPARTMENT OF STATE, APPLICATIONS FOR LAND GRANTS, VOL. 14, P. 159.
Comment:

Date: 1752,06,24 (2)
Description: Petition of A. Van Cortlandt for patent for 2,000 acres of Schoharie land.
Source: N.Y.STATE ARCHIVES, ALBANY, N.Y.COL.MSS, INDORSED LAND PAPERS, 1643-1803, SERIES NO. A0272, DEPARTMENT OF STATE, APPLICATIONS FOR LAND GRANTS, VOL. 14, P. 160.
Comment:

Date: 1752,08,01
Description: Return of survey for Johannes Lawyer and Phillip Berg (Bergh) of two tracts of land at Schoharie: one, four miles east of Schoharie on the road to Albany; the other, one mile west of Schoharie. Two thousand six hundred forty acres acres total..
Source: N.Y.STATE ARCHIVES, ALBANY, N.Y.COL.MSS, INDORSED LAND PAPERS, 1643-1803, SERIES NO. A0272, DEPARTMENT OF STATE, APPLICATIONS FOR LAND GRANTS, VOL. 14, P. 175.
Comment: SEE 1753,02,06.

Date: 1752,08,14
Description: Petition of Samuel Auchmuty and eight others for a patent for 18,000 acres of land being part of two tracts: one purchased in 1733 from the Indians by Walter Butler, and the other purchased in 1734 from the Indians by Jacob Glen and others.
Source: N.Y.STATE ARCHIVES, ALBANY, N.Y.COL.MSS, INDORSED LAND PAPERS, 1643-1803, SERIES NO. A0272, DEPARTMENT OF STATE, APPLICATIONS FOR LAND GRANTS, VOL. 15, P. 006.
Comment:

Date: 1752,09,18
Description: Certificate of Direck (Dirck) Hagadorn and Lodowig Reikert, that they were sent by Nicholas York, William Bauch and Jacob Frederick Lawyer to Johannes Becker requesting that he go along with them to New York to appear before the governor and council, and bring with him all his writings concerning the land in dispute between him and York, Bauch, and Lawyer. Included is a list of expenses incurred 16 Apr 1744.
Source: N.Y.STATE ARCHIVES, ALBANY, N.Y.COL.MSS, INDORSED LAND PAPERS, 1643-1803, SERIES NO. A0272, DEPARTMENT OF STATE, APPLICATIONS FOR LAND GRANTS, VOL. 15, P. 016.
Comment: SEE 1752,10,04; 1752,10,05; 1753,04,10; 1753,05,06; 1744,04,17; 1742,10,02.

Date: 1752,09,22
Description: Return of survey for Augustus Van Cortlandt, of a tract of land containing 1,270 acres at Schoharie, between a tract of land granted to Myndert Schuyler et al. and another to Lewis Morris, Jr.
Source: N.Y.STATE ARCHIVES, ALBANY, LAND PAPERS, VOL. 15, P. 009.
Comment: SEE 1753,02,19.

Date: 1752,10,04
Description: Acknowledgement of Edward Holland that the Indian deed to Jacob Frederick Lawyer, William Bauch, and Heronimus Kreisler (Greslar, Greslaer, Crissler) for land south and southwest of Schoharie (17 April 1744) was duly executed by the Indians.
Source: N.Y.STATE ARCHIVES, ALBANY, N.Y.COL.MSS, INDORSED LAND PAPERS, 1643-1803, SERIES NO. A0272, DEPARTMENT OF STATE, APPLICATIONS FOR LAND GRANTS, VOL. 15, P. 015.
Comment: SEE 1744,04,14; 1744,04,17; 1752,10,05; 1752, 09,18; 1753,04,10; 1753,05,06.

Date: 1752,10,04°
Description: Date of statement about legitimacy of cession of land by Indians to J.F. Lawyer, William Bauch, and others.
Source: SEE 1744,04,14; 1744,04,17; 1752,10,05; 1752,09,18; 1753,04,10; 1753,05,06; 1742,10,02.
Comment:

Date: 1752,10,05
Description: Petition of William Bauch, Jacob Frederick Lawyer, Nicholas York, and Thomas Eckerson for patent for about 6,000 acres of land on both sides of Schoharie creek, and contiguous to several small tracts of land granted to William York and others, and also for three small islands in the creek containing together about twelve acres.
Source: N.Y.STATE ARCHIVES, ALBANY, N.Y.COL.MSS, INDORSED LAND PAPERS, 1643-1803, SERIES NO. A0272, DEPARTMENT OF STATE, APPLICATIONS FOR LAND GRANTS, VOL. 15, P. 014.
Comment: SEE 1752,09,18; 1752,10,04; 1744,04,16; 1744,04,17; 1753,04,10; 1753,05,06; 1742,10,02. Note, Bauch, York, and Eckerson sign the petition with their marks.

Date: 1752,11,09
Description: Deed from Lawrence, Seth (Sett), Hans (Hance) Yurry (Yury, Jury, Jurie, Ury), Joseph, John, Anthony, Margeret (Margaret), Maria, and Cathrina (Catherine[?]) "sole & absolute proprietors" to John Frederick Bauch, Christian Zehe, Johannes Zehe, Michael Wanner & Johannis Knisker (Kniskern) of about 4,000 acres of land west of Schoharie and south of creek called Otsgarege (Oscalleghe, Cobleskill). Also included is a certificate of Cadwallader Colden attesting that the bounds described in the deed are correct, that the purchase money has been paid, and that the deed is legally executed.
Source: N.Y. STATE ARCHIVES, ALBANY, INDIAN TREATIES & DEEDS, SERIES #448, VOL. 1, PP. 019-021. (D246/4).
Comment: N.B, Marks of Indians at end of deed. Compare names of signers with those listed at beginning of document, among which are names of Indian women. Women listed at beginning of deed did not sign the deed. Survey was done in presence of the Indians. Seth is identified as "the Chief Indian or Sachem of the Schoharie Castle". Anna Maria Rightmeir (Rightmeyer, Rightmyer) is interpreter. This is not the original deed. It is a contemporary copy. SEE 1751,10,07; 1753,07,16; 1752,11,30; 1887,00,00-1888,00,00 (30).

Date: 1752,11,09 (2)
Description: Indian deed to John Frederick Bauch, Christian Zehe, Johannes Zehe, Michael Wanner & Johannis Knisker (Kniskern, Knieskirk, Kniskorn, Kneescarns, Kneiskerk, Knieskerk, Knescarn) for a tract of about 4,000 acres of land to the westward of Schoharie and on the south side of a creek called Otsgarege (Oscalleghe, Oscallaghe, Oschaleghe, Ascschalege) by the Indians and Cobus Kill (Cobleskill) by the Euroamericans. Also included is a certificate of Cadwallader Colden attesting that the bounds described in the deed are correct, the purchase money has been paid, and the deed is legally executed.
Source: N.Y.STATE ARCHIVES, ALBANY, N.Y.COL.MSS, INDORSED LAND PAPERS, 1643-1803, SERIES NO. A0272, DEPARTMENT OF STATE, APPLICATIONS FOR LAND GRANTS, VOL. 15, P. 019.
Comment: SEE 1751,10,07; 1753,07,16; 1752,11,30; 1887,00,00-1888,00,00 (30).

Date: 1752,11,13
Description: Petition of Lambertus Starnbergh (Starnberg) for a license to purchase 2,000 acres of vacant lands on the east of the large Schoharie patent, and on the north and south of Fox's kill, and also a small piece lying on Cobus kill (Cobleskill), near Hendrick Stubragh's land.
Source: N.Y.STATE ARCHIVES, ALBANY, N.Y.COL.MSS, INDORSED LAND PAPERS, 1643-1803, SERIES NO. A0272, DEPARTMENT OF STATE, APPLICATIONS FOR LAND GRANTS, VOL. 15, P. 020.
Comment:

Date: 1752,11,13 (2)
Description: Petition of Lawrence Lawyer for a license to purchase 2,000 acres of vacant land between Schoharie and Cobus kill (Cobleskill).
Source: N.Y.STATE ARCHIVES, ALBANY, N.Y.COL.MSS, INDORSED LAND PAPERS, 1643-1803, SERIES NO. A0272, DEPARTMENT OF STATE, APPLICATIONS FOR LAND GRANTS, VOL. 15, P. 021.
Comment:

Date: 1752,11,13 (3)
Description: Petition of Johannes Becker, Jr., Johannes Schafer, Jr., Hendrick Schafer, Jr., and Jacob Schafer for a license to purchase 6,000 acres of vacant land on the north side of Cobus kill (Cobleskill) and on the east of the patent near Schoharie granted to Jacob Borst (Burst), Jacob C. Ten Eyke and others.
Source: N.Y.STATE ARCHIVES, ALBANY, N.Y.COL.MSS, INDORSED LAND PAPERS, 1643-1803, SERIES NO. A0272, DEPARTMENT OF STATE, APPLICATIONS FOR LAND GRANTS, VOL. 15, P. 023.
Comment: SEE 1753,07,18; 1753,05,19; 1753,09,10.

Date: 1752,11,16
Description: N.Y. Provincial Council Minutes. Licenses to purchase Indian lands are granted: south of the Mohawk river and west of Schoharie to John Christopher Hardwick (Hartwick) and others; on Otsego lake and Adaquicktinge creek to Frederick Miller, and others; between Schoharie and Cobus Kill (Cobleskill) to Lawrence Lawyer, to Johannis Becker, Jr., J. Shafer, Jr., H. Shafter, Jr., and J. Shafer, to L. Starnberg (Starnberg), to J. Miller. Patent granted to Arent Stevens, B. Vrooman (Vroman), M. Ferral (Ferrall), R. Adams, C. Colden, Jr., J. Young, J. Sewell, E. Arnold, D. Fonda and J. Fonda.
Source: N.Y.STATE ARCHIVES,ALBANY, N.Y.COUN.MIN., VOL. 23, P. 045.
Comment:

Date: 1752,11,21
Description: Petition of Mathew Ferrall (Ferral) and associates to purchase 130,000 acres of land southwest of Schoharie. A license of 12 June 1751 to purchase the same tract of land had expired because "all of the six Nations of Indians are the Proprietors of the said Tract of Land, with whom your Petitioner must be obliged to Agree severally. which he has not as yet been able to do". The endorsement on the document notes that the license was granted.
Source: N.Y.STATE ARCHIVES, ALBANY, N.Y.COL.MSS, INDORSED LAND PAPERS, 1643-1803, SERIES NO. A0272, DEPARTMENT OF STATE, APPLICATIONS FOR LAND GRANTS, VOL. 15, P. 028.
Comment: This license granted 21 November 1752 also expired because the survey could not be done on time. SEE 1751,06,12; 1785,09,20.

Date: 1752,11,30
Description: Petition of John Frederick Bauch, Christian Zehe, Johannes Zehe, Michael Wanner, and Johannis Knisker (Kniskern, Knieskirk, Kneescarns, Kniskorn, Knieskerk, Kneiskerk, Knescarn) for a patent for about 4,800 acres of land to the westward of Schoharie, on the south side of a creek called Otsgarage (Oscalleghe, Oscallaghe, Oschaleghe, Otsgarrege, Otsgarege, Aschalege) by the Indians and Cobus kill (Cobleskill) by the Euroamericans.
Source: N.Y.STATE ARCHIVES, ALBANY, N.Y.COL.MSS, INDORSED LAND PAPERS, 1643-1803, SERIES NO. A0272, DEPARTMENT OF STATE, APPLICATIONS FOR LAND GRANTS, VOL. 15, P. 030.
Comment: SEE 1751,10,07; 1752,11,09; 1753,07,16.

Date: 1752,11,30 (2)
Description: Return of survey for Goldsbrow Banyar, John Benson and Joseph Webb, Jr. of a tract of about 4,000 acres of land eight miles west from Schoharie.
Source: N.Y.STATE ARCHIVES, ALBANY, N.Y.COL.MSS, INDORSED LAND PAPERS, 1643-1803, SERIES NO. A0272, DEPARTMENT OF STATE, APPLICATIONS FOR LAND GRANTS, VOL. 15, P. 031.
Comment: Bordered in part by two different tracts of land granted to Jacob Borst (Burst) and others. SEE 1753,04,14.

Date: 1752,12,01
Description: N.Y. Provincial Council Minutes. Patent granted to John Frederick Bauch, Christian Zehe, Johannes Zehe, Michael Wanner (Warner[?]), and Johannis Knisker (Kniskern, Knieskirk, Kniskorn, Kneiskerk, Knieskerk, Kneescarns).
Source: N.Y.STATE ARCHIVES,ALBANY, N.Y.COUN.MIN., VOL. 23, P. 051.
Comment:

Date: 1752,12,06
Description: Letter from Cadwallader Colden to Goldsbrow Banyar, secretary of the province, directing him to change the course of a certain patent.
Source: N.Y.STATE ARCHIVES, ALBANY, N.Y.COL.MSS, INDORSED LAND PAPERS, 1643-1803, SERIES NO. A0272, DEPARTMENT OF STATE, APPLICATIONS FOR LAND GRANTS, VOL. 15, P. 033.
Comment: SEE 1752,11,30.

Date: 1753,00,00°
Description: Map of patent granted in 1726 to Morris and Coeymans, resurveyed in November 1819 by Lawrence Vrooman [Vroman] and Tobias A. Stontenburgh. It shows old divided land laid out by Edward Collins in Knieskerns (Knisker, Kniskern, Knieskirk) Dorp in 1729 and lots laid out by Isaac Vrooman in 1753. The map also shows the Schoharie Turnpike and Dorp Road.
Source: SEE 1819,00,00 [ ].
Comment: See also 1769,11,00.

Date: 1753,00,00°
Description: A letter from Gideon Hawley, missionary. Hawley visited Schoharie in 1753, and writes about his visit in detail.
Source: SEE 1794,07,31.
Comment:

Date: 1753,02,05
Description: Return of survey for Samuel Auchmuty, John Burges, William Ogilvie, Anne Avery, Morley Harrison, Josiah Crane, William Mitchel, Hendrick Cropsy (? sp.), and John Bickerton of tracts of land containing 18,000 acres. The tracts are taken from two larger parcels of land, both purchased from the "Native Indians", the first in 1733 by Walter Butler and others, and the second in 1734 by John Glen and others. A map of each of these is included.
Source: N.Y.STATE ARCHIVES, ALBANY, N.Y.COL.MSS, INDORSED LAND PAPERS, 1643-1803, SERIES NO. A0272, DEPARTMENT OF STATE, APPLICATIONS FOR LAND GRANTS, VOL. 15, P. 035.
Comment: Pertains to Walter Butler's tract at Duanesburgh, Schoharie County and Jacob Glen's purchase at Fairfield, Herkimer County. Contains maps of the tracts of land. SEE 1733,09,18.

Date: 1753,02,06
Description: Patent for two tracts of land together containing 2,640 acres of land to Philip Bergh (Berg) and Johannes Lawyer.
Source: N.Y.STATE ARCHIVES, ALBANY, N.Y. LETTERS PATENT, 1664-1780, SERIES NO. 12590, BOOK 12, P. 469.
Comment: Known as Lawyer's Patent. The land is in Schoharie. SEE 1752,08,01.

Date: 1753,02,19
Description: Patent for a tract of 1,270 acres of land to Augustus Van Cortlandt.
Source: N.Y.STATE ARCHIVES, ALBANY, N.Y. LETTERS PATENT, 1664-1780, SERIES NO. 12590, BOOK 12, P. 463.
Comment: SEE 1752,09,22. The land is in Schoharie.

Date: 1753,03,11
Description: Peppercorn lease for one year to Edward Holland by Augustus Van Cortlandt for a parcel of land in Schoharie containing 1,270 acres of land with the usual allowance for highways. The parties to the agreement are gentlemen of New York City.
Source: N.Y.STATE LIBRARY, ALBANY, MANUSCRIPTS, SCHOHARIE COUNTY, PATENTEES, LAND RECORDS, DW10738.
Comment:

Date: 1753,04,00
Description: A map of a tract of land about ten miles west of Schoharie on a place called New Durlach.
Source: N.Y.STATE LIBRARY, ALBANY, MANUSCRIPTS, JOHANNES LAWYER AND OTHERS, MAPS AND DEEDS OF SCHOHARIE VALLEY, ACC. NO. 16469, MAP #2.
Comment:

Date: 1753,04,10
Description: Answer and petition of John Becker and Johannes Eckerson, showing why the petition of William Bauch and others ought not to be granted, and requesting a patent for 3,000 acres of a tract of land purchased by them from the Indians.
Source: N.Y.STATE ARCHIVES, ALBANY, N.Y.COL.MSS, INDORSED LAND PAPERS, 1643-1803, SERIES NO. A0272, DEPARTMENT OF STATE, APPLICATIONS FOR LAND GRANTS, VOL. 15, P. 043.
Comment: SEE 1752,09,18; 1752, 10,04; 1752,10,15; 1744,04,16; 1744, 04,17; 1753,05,06; 1742,10,02. Pertains to land at Middleburgh.

Date: 1753,04,14
Description: Map of 40,000 acres for Banyar, Benson, and Webb.
Source: MIX'S CATALOG OF MAPS AND SURVEYS IN OFFFICES OF THE SECRETARY OF STATE, STATE ENGINEER AND SURVEYOR AND COMPTROLLER AND N.Y. STATE LIBRARY, 1859, REFERENCES THIS MAP, LISTING IT AS BEING IN THE OFFICES OF THE N.Y. STATE DEPARTMENT OF TAXATION & FINANCE, MAP # 7.
Comment: SEE 1752,11,30.

Date: 1753,04,14 (2)
Description: Map of part of a tract of land situate in the county of Schoharie, granted on April 14, 1753 to Goldsbrow Banyar and others.
Source: N.Y.STATE LIBRARY, ALBANY, MANUSCRIPTS, JOHANNES LAWYER AND OTHERS, MAPS AND DEEDS OF SCHOHARIE VALLEY, ACC. NO. 16469, MAP #3.
Comment: See 1752,11,30 (2).

Date: 1753,04,14 (3)
Description: Patent to Goldsbrow Banyar, John Benson, and others for tract of 4,000 acres of land west of Schoharie.
Source: N.Y.STATE ARCHIVES, ALBANY, N.Y. LETTERS PATENT, 1664-1780, SERIES NO. 12590, BOOK 12, P. 484.
Comment:

Date: 1753,05,00°
Description: Tracing of a map showing the division of Fountain's Town or Brunnen Dorf, now Schoharie Village, copied from a map made in May 1753 by John Rutse Bleeker, Surveyor. There is a water color inset of the Lutheran parsonage.
Source: SEE 1887,00,00-1888,00,00 (45).
Comment:

Date: 1753,05,06
Description: Draft of the land patented to William Bauch and others, and of the lands adjacent thereto, claimed by Johannes Becker and Teunis Eckerson, as having been conveyed and confirmed to them by purchase, and a deed of gift from the Indians. Map included.
Source: N.Y.STATE ARCHIVES, ALBANY, N.Y.COL.MSS, INDORSED LAND PAPERS, 1643-1803, SERIES NO. A0272, DEPARTMENT OF STATE, APPLICATIONS FOR LAND GRANTS, VOL. 15, P. 050.
Comment: SEE 1753,04,10; 1752,09,18; 1752,10,04; 1752,10,05; 1744,04,16; 1744,04,17; 1742,10,02. Pertains to land at Middleburgh.

Date: 1753,05,10
Description: Message from Schoharie Indians.
Source: CLEMENTS LIBRARY, ANN ARBOR, MICHIGAN, GEORGE CLINTON PAPERS.
Comment:

Date: 1753,05,19
Description: Deed from Lowrence (Lawrence), Seth (Sett), Hans (Hance) Yurry (Yury, Jury, Jurie, Ury), Seth the Younger, and Jacob to Lambartus Starnbergh (Starnberg) for two tracts of land lying at Schoharie; and certificate of Cadwallader Colden, Jr. that the bounds described therein are correct.
Source: N.Y.STATE ARCHIVES, ALBANY, N.Y.COL.MSS, INDORSED LAND PAPERS, 1643-1803, SERIES NO. A0272, DEPARTMENT OF STATE, APPLICATIONS FOR LAND GRANTS, VOL. 15, P. 051.
Comment: N.B. Indian marks. Hans has written his own name on the document. SEE 1753,07,18; 1753,09,10.

Date: 1753,05,19 (2)
Description: Indian deed to Johannes Becker and others, for a 6,000 acre tract of land about six miles west of Schoharie on the northeast side of the creek called Aschalege (Oscalleghe, Oscallaghe, Oschaleghe, Otsgarrege, Otsgarege, Otsgarage) by the Indians and Cobus kill (Cobleskill) by the Euroamericans. Also included is a certificate of Cadwallader Colden, Jr., attesting that the purchase money was paid to the Indians in his presence.
Source: N.Y.STATE ARCHIVES, ALBANY, N.Y.COL.MSS, INDORSED LAND PAPERS, 1643-1803, SERIES NO. A0272, DEPARTMENT OF STATE, APPLICATIONS FOR LAND GRANTS, VOL. 15, P. 052.
Comment: SEE 1753,07,18. Pertains to land in Carlisle and Cobleskill. N.B. Marks of the Indians on the deed.

Date: 1753,05,19 (3)
Description: Deed from Lawrence, Seth (Sett), Hans(Hance) Yurry (Yury, Jury, Jurie, Ury), Seth the Younger, and Jacob to Lambartus Starnbergh (Starnberg) of two tracts of land lying at Schoharie; and certificate of Cadwallader Colden, Jr. that the bounds described therein are correct.
Source: N.Y.STATE ARCHIVES, ALBANY, INDIAN TREATIES & DEEDS, SERIES #448, VOL. 1, PP. 022-023.(D246/4).
Comment: N.B. Indian marks. SEE 1753,07,18; 1753,09,10. This is not the original deed. This is a contemporary copy.

Date: 1753,05,29
Description: Petition of Annatie U. Ziellie, David Becker, Abraham Becker, Johannes Becker, Jr., John Van Dyck, and Peter U. Ziellie, freeholders and inhabitants upon the low lands at Schoharie, for a grant of 1,000 acres of woodland adjoining their land at Schoharie. The land has been petitioned for by Thomas Eckerson and others, but, if granted to them, "would prove ruinous to Your Petitioners."
Source: N.Y.STATE ARCHIVES, ALBANY, N.Y.COL.MSS, INDORSED LAND PAPERS, 1643-1803, SERIES NO. A0272, DEPARTMENT OF STATE, APPLICATIONS FOR LAND GRANTS, VOL. 15, P. 053.
Comment: Pertains to land at Middleburgh.

Date: 1753,05,29 (2)
Description: Caveat entered on behalf of Annatie V. Ziellie, widow, David Becker and others, against Thomas Eckerson and others obtaining a grant of the unpatented lands adjoining their land at Schoharie, until their petition for the same be heard.
Source: N.Y.STATE ARCHIVES, ALBANY, N.Y.COL.MSS, INDORSED LAND PAPERS, 1643-1803, SERIES NO. A0272, DEPARTMENT OF STATE, APPLICATIONS FOR LAND GRANTS, VOL. 15, P. 054.
Comment: Pertains to land in Middleburgh.

Date: 1753,06,06
Description: Petition of Jacob Starnberger (Starnberg, Starnbergh), George Zimmer, Hendrick Weaver, and Jacob Zimmer for a license to purchase from the Indians 8,000 acres of land at Schoharie between the large patent of Schoharie and the patent of Renselaerwyck, on both sides of Foxes' (Fox) creek.
Source: N.Y.STATE ARCHIVES, ALBANY, N.Y.COL.MSS, INDORSED LAND PAPERS, 1643-1803, SERIES NO. A0272, DEPARTMENT OF STATE, APPLICATIONS FOR LAND GRANTS, VOL. 15, P. 055.
Comment: SEE 1754,06,06; 1761,10,02; 1765,09,17, 1766,07,07; 1769,09,20; 1769,09,30.

Date: 1753,07,16
Description: Return of survey for John Frederick Bauch, Christian Zehe, Johannes Zehe, Michal (Michael) Warner (Wanner), and Johannes Knisker (Kniskern, Knieskirk Knieskerk, Kneiskerk, Kniskorn, Kneescarns) of a tract of land containing 36,000 acres to the westward of Schoharie on the south side of a creek called Otsgarage (Oscalleghe, Oscallaghe, Oschaleghe, Otsgarrege, Otsgarege, Aschalege) by the Indians and Cobus kill (Cobleskill) by the Euroamericans.
Source: N.Y.STATE ARCHIVES, ALBANY, N.Y.COL.MSS, INDORSED LAND PAPERS, 1643-1803, SERIES NO. A0272, DEPARTMENT OF STATE, APPLICATIONS FOR LAND GRANTS, VOL. 15, P. 058.
Comment: SEE 1751,10,07; 1752,11,09; 1752,11,30. Patents bordering the tract of land are listed.

Date: 1753,07,18
Description: Petition of Johannes Becker, Jr., Johannes Schafer, Jr., Hendrick Schafer, Jr., and Jacob Schafer for a patent for a 6,000 acre tract of land about six miles west of Schoharie on the north side of a creek called Aschalege (Oscalleghe, Oscallaghe, Oschaleghe, Otsgarrege, Otsgarege, Otsgarage) by the Indians and Cobus kill (Cobleskill) by the Euroamericans.
Source: N.Y.STATE ARCHIVES, ALBANY, N.Y.COL.MSS, INDORSED LAND PAPERS, 1643-1803, SERIES NO. A0272, DEPARTMENT OF STATE, APPLICATIONS FOR LAND GRANTS, VOL. 15, P. 059.
Comment: SEE 1753,05,19; 1753,09,10; 1752,11,13.

Date: 1753,07,18 (2)
Description: Petition of Lambertus Starnbergh and Adam Starnbergh (Starnberg) for a patent for tracts of land at Schoharie containing about 3,100 acres.
Source: N.Y.STATE ARCHIVES, ALBANY, N.Y.COL.MSS, INDORSED LAND PAPERS, 1643-1803, SERIES NO. A0272, DEPARTMENT OF STATE, APPLICATIONS FOR LAND GRANTS, VOL. 15, P. 060.
Comment: SEE 1753,09,10; 1754,03,19.

Date: 1753,07,20
Description: Petition of Johannes Lawyer, Jr., Jacob Borst (Burst), Jr., George Forster, and Reinhart Heints (Hiets) for license to purchase from the Indians 8,000 acres of land about twelve miles west of Schoharie on the west and north side of the patent granted to Jacob Borst, Mathew Bowman and others.
Source: N.Y.STATE ARCHIVES, ALBANY, N.Y.COL.MSS, INDORSED LAND PAPERS, 1643-1803, SERIES NO. A0272, DEPARTMENT OF STATE, APPLICATIONS FOR LAND GRANTS, VOL. 15, P. 062.
Comment: CALENDAR OF LAND PAPERS notes that the land is in Sharon, Schoharie County. SEE 1753,07,28; 1764,06,06; 177[ ],05,23.

Date: 1753,07,28
Description: License to Johannes Lawyer, Jr., Jacob Borst (Burst), Jr., George Forster, and Reinhart Heints (Hiets) to purchase 8,000 acres of land from the Indians, the land being about twelve miles west of Schoharie on the west and north side of a patent granted to Jacob Borst, Mathew Bowman and others.
Source: N.Y.STATE ARCHIVES, ALBANY, N.Y.COL.MSS, INDORSED LAND PAPERS, 1643-1803, SERIES NO. A0272, DEPARTMENT OF STATE, APPLICATIONS FOR LAND GRANTS, VOL. 15, P. 063.
Comment: CALENDAR OF LAND PAPERS notes that the land is in Sharon, Schoharie County. SEE 1753,07,20; 1764,06,06; 177[ ],05,23.

Date: 1753,08,27
Description: Petition of Ury Rightmeyer (Rightmyer, Rightmeir) and Hendrick Weaver on behalf of themselves and others for a license to purchase from "the native Indian Proprietors" 32,000 acres of land to the southward of Schoharie beginning at the southernmost bounds of a patent called Breakabine (Breakabeen) and running from thence up along both sides of Schoharie creek to the patent of the Vanbergens, running ten miles into the woods on each side of said creek.
Source: N.Y.STATE ARCHIVES, ALBANY, N.Y.COL.MSS, INDORSED LAND PAPERS, 1643-1803, SERIES NO. A0272, DEPARTMENT OF STATE, APPLICATIONS FOR LAND GRANTS, VOL. 15, P. 066.
Comment: SEE 1753,09,01; 1753,10,26; 1754,05,01. CALENDAR OF LAND PAPERS notes that the land is in Blenheim and Broome, Schoharie County.

Date: 1753,08,31
Description: Petition of Augustine Moore and John Meyer for a patent for 4,000 acres of land on the south side of the Mohawk river about twelve miles from that river, to the west of a tract granted to Peter Wagener, David Schuyler and others, and to the southeast of a tract granted to James Henderson and others.
Source: N.Y.STATE ARCHIVES, ALBANY, N.Y.COL.MSS, INDORSED LAND PAPERS, 1643-1803, SERIES NO. A0272, DEPARTMENT OF STATE, APPLICATIONS FOR LAND GRANTS, VOL. 15, P. 067.
Comment: CALENDAR OF LAND PAPERS identifies the land in this document as being in Blenheim and Broome, Schoharie County. Are these not further than twelve miles from the Mohawk river, however?

Date: 1753,09,01
Description: License to Ury Righmeyer (Rightmyer, Rightmeir) and Hendrick Weaver on behalf of themselves and their associates to purchase from the Indians 32,000 acres of land southward of Schoharie beginning at the southernmost bounds of a patent called Breakabine (Breakabeen) granted to Edward Clarke and others and running from thence up along both sides of Schoharie creek to the patent of the Vanbergens, running ten miles into the woods on each side of the creek. Also included is a document, dated 7 September, from Cadwallader Colden and Alexander Colden appointing John Dies as deputy surveyor to survey the land.
Source: N.Y.STATE ARCHIVES, ALBANY, N.Y.COL.MSS, INDORSED LAND PAPERS, 1643-1803, SERIES NO. A0272, DEPARTMENT OF STATE, APPLICATIONS FOR LAND GRANTS, VOL. 15, P. 069.
Comment: SEE 1753,08,27; 1753,10,26; 1754, 05,01.

Date: 1753,09,02
Description: Journal of Conrad Weiser's visit to the Mohawks, 24 July-30 August 1753. On August 7, Weiser wrote, "... the Woman [an Indian woman meeting with New York Commissioners of Indian Affairs in Albany about prisoners from Canada] asked me where I lived, because I could talk their Language so well, she wondered that I was never heard of. I told her I lived at Shohary [Schoharie] and travelled up and down among the Indians, and so forth." Contains much information about Weiser's conversations with Mohawks, summarizing their positions and concerns as reported by Weiser.
Source: DOCUMENTS RELATIVE TO THE COLONIAL HISTORY OF THE STATE OF NEW YORK, ED. BY E.B. O'CALLAGHAN AND BERTHOLD FERNOW, 15 VOL. (ALBANY, N.Y.: WEED, PARSONS, AND CO., 1856-87), 6: 795-799.
Comment: N.B. Weiser did not live at the time at Schoharie, although he did live there from 1714 until 1729, according to his journal of 1750 (SEE 1750,08,25-10,13).

Date: 1753,09,07°
Description: Date of appointment of John Dies by Cadwallader and Alexander Colden to serve as deputy surveyor to survey 32,000 acres of land to be purchased from the Indians by Ury Rightmeyer (Rightmyer, Rightmeir) and Hendrick Weaver.
Source: SEE 1753,09,01.
Comment:

Date: 1753,09,10
Description: Return of survey for Lambertus Starnbergh (Starnberg) and Adam Starnbergh of two tracts of land containing together 3,000 acres of land at Schoharie.
Source: N.Y.STATE ARCHIVES, ALBANY, N.Y.COL.MSS, INDORSED LAND PAPERS, 1643-1803, SERIES NO. A0272, DEPARTMENT OF STATE, APPLICATIONS FOR LAND GRANTS, VOL. 15, P. 072.
Comment: SEE 1753,07,18; 1754,03,19. Patents bordering the tracts are listed in the survey.

Date: 1753,09,10 (2)
Description: Return of survey for Johannes Becker, Jr., Johannes Schafer, Jr., Hendrick Schafer, Jr., and Jacob Schafer of a 6,000 acre tract of land about six miles west of Schoharie on the north side of a creek called Aschalege (Oscalleghe, Oscallaghe, Oschaleghe, Otsgarrege, Otsgarege, Otsgarage) by the Indians and Cobus kill (Cobleskill) by the Euroamericans.
Source: N.Y.STATE ARCHIVES, ALBANY, N.Y.COL.MSS, INDORSED LAND PAPERS, 1643-1803, SERIES NO. A0272, DEPARTMENT OF STATE, APPLICATIONS FOR LAND GRANTS, VOL. 15, P. 073.
Comment: SEE 1753,07,18; 1753,05,19; 1752,11,13.

Date: 1753,09,13
Description: Bond from John Van Dyck and Jacob Van Dyck attesting that John Van Dyck will pay Thomas Eckerson, Nicholas York, Jacob Frederick Lawyer, and William Bauch the costs and charges that may be awarded to Eckerson and the others by reason of a caveat entered by John Van Dyck on behalf of himself and others against granting a patent for a certain tract of land lying on both sides of Schoharie creek to Thomas Eckerson and others.
Source: N.Y.STATE ARCHIVES, ALBANY, N.Y.COL.MSS, INDORSED LAND PAPERS, 1643-1803, SERIES NO. A0272, DEPARTMENT OF STATE, APPLICATIONS FOR LAND GRANTS, VOL. 15, P. 075.
Comment:

Date: 1753,10,18°
Description: Indian deed to Ury Rightmeyer (Rightmyer, Rightmeir), Hendrick Weaver, and others to land south of Schoharie.
Source: SEE 1753,10,26.
Comment:

Date: 1753,10,26
Description: Petition of Ury Rightmeyer (Rightmeir, Rightmyer), Hendrick Weaver, John Lansing, Abraham Lott, Jr., Isaac Goelet, and Edward Taylor for a patent for 8,000 acres of land about eight miles southward of Schoharie between the lands patented to Edward Clarke and to Garet Van Bergen, Francis Salsbury, and others. This land was purchased by the petitioners from "the native Indian Proprietors". Document refers to Indian deed of "the eighteenth day of October last".
Source: N.Y.STATE ARCHIVES, ALBANY, N.Y.COL.MSS, INDORSED LAND PAPERS, 1643-1803, SERIES NO. A0272, DEPARTMENT OF STATE, APPLICATIONS FOR LAND GRANTS, VOL. 15, P. 076.
Comment: Some of the tract is in Blenheim, Schoharie County. SEE 1754,01,11; 1754,03,01; 1754,05,01; 1753,09,01; 1753,08,27.

Date: 1754,00,00
Description: Indian council held near site at Mill lane and Route 30, north of Middleburgh.
Source: HISTORICAL MARKER AT MILL LANE & ROUTE 30, NORTH OF MIDDLEBURGH, NEW YORK. ERECTED BY THE N.Y. STATE DEPARTMENT OF EDUCATION, 1932.
Comment: Documentary evidence is not cited on the marker.

Date: 1754,00,00-1755,00,00°
Description: Rufus Grider Collection. Map of the Schoharie River Valley showing "Plan of the Indian Castel[sic]" at Vrooman's (Vroman's) land about 1754-1755, and plan and elevation of the "New Fort" never erected. From original in the British Museum, London. Pen and ink tracing for which Grider paid $27.
Source: SEE 1887,00,00-1888,00,00 (10).
Comment: SEE ALSO 1758,00,00 [ ].

Date: 1754,01,11
Description: N.Y. Provincial Council Minutes. Petition of Ury Rightmeyer (Rightmyer, Rightmeir), Hendrick Weaver, John Lansing, Abraham Lott, Jr., Isaac Goelet and Edward Taylor for land south the of Schoharie referred by the N.Y. Provincial Council.
Source: N.Y.STATE ARCHIVES,ALBANY, N.Y.COUN.MIN., VOL. 23, P. 134.
Comment: SEE 1754,03,01.

Date: 1754,03,01
Description: Petition of Mathew Ferrall (Ferral) on behalf of himself and company for a license to purchase of the Six Nations Indians 130,000 acres of a tract of land south and southwest of Schoharie.
Source: N.Y.STATE ARCHIVES, ALBANY, N.Y.COL.MSS, INDORSED LAND PAPERS, 1643-1803, SERIES NO. A0272, DEPARTMENT OF STATE, APPLICATIONS FOR LAND GRANTS, VOL. 15, P. 092.
Comment: CALENDAR OF LAND PAPERS notes that this document pertains to land in Ephrata, Fulton County. SEE 1751,06,12; 1752,11,21; 1754,03,05; 1785,09,20.

Date: 1754,03,01 (2)
Description: Report of the committee to whom was referred the petition of Mathew Ferrall (Ferral) and others for a license to purchase 130,000 acres of land from the Indians.
Source: N.Y.STATE ARCHIVES, ALBANY, N.Y.COL.MSS, INDORSED LAND PAPERS, 1643-1803, SERIES NO. A0272, DEPARTMENT OF STATE, APPLICATIONS FOR LAND GRANTS, VOL. 15, P. 094.
Comment: CALENDAR OF LAND PAPERS notes that this document pertains to land in Ephrata, Fulton County. SEE 1751,06,12; 1752,11,21; 1754,03,05; 1785,09,20.

Date: 1754,03,01 (3)
Description: N.Y. Provincial Council Minutes. Mention is made that patent was granted to Ury Rightmeyer (Rightmyer, Rightmeir) and associates for 8,000 acres of land.
Source: N.Y.STATE ARCHIVES,ALBANY, N.Y.COUN.MIN., VOL. 23, P. 142.
Comment: SEE 1753,10,26; 1754,01,11; 1754,05,01.

Date: 1754,03,05
Description: Affidavit of William Johnson to prove the purchase by Mathew Ferrall (Ferral) of 130,000 acres of land south and southwest of Schoharie from the Six Nations Indians.
Source: N.Y.STATE ARCHIVES, ALBANY, N.Y.COL.MSS, INDORSED LAND PAPERS, 1643-1803, SERIES NO. A0272, DEPARTMENT OF STATE, APPLICATIONS FOR LAND GRANTS, VOL. 15, P. 093.
Comment: CALENDAR OF LAND PAPERS notes that this document pertains to land in Ephrata, Fulton County. SEE 1751,06,12; 1752,11,21; 1754, 03,01; 1785,09,20.

Date: 1754,03,13°
Description: Copy of a report of N. Y. Provincial Council Meeting, attended by the Lieutenant Governor of New York, James DeLancey and Council members, about a petition of Mathew Ferrall (Ferral) in behalf of himself and others for a license to purchase 130,000 acres of "a large tract of vacant land lying . . . south and southwest of Schohary (Schoharie)". The date of the Council Meeting is 13 March 1754. The document states that the Council advised that the license be granted. The copy is certified as being true on 19 and 20 September 1985.
Source: SEE 1785,09,20.
Comment:

Date: 1754,03,19
Description: Patent to John F. Bauch, Christian Zehe, Johannes Zehe, and others for 3,600 acres of land.
Source: N.Y.STATE ARCHIVES, ALBANY, N.Y. LETTERS PATENT, 1664-1780, SERIES NO. 12590, BOOK 13, P. 023.
Comment: The land is in Cobleskill.

Date: 1754,03,19 (2)
Description: Patent for two tracts of land containing 3,000 acres to Lambertus Starnbergh and Adam Starnbergh (Starnberg).
Source: N.Y.STATE ARCHIVES, ALBANY, N.Y. LETTERS PATENT, 1664-1780, SERIES NO. 12590, BOOK 13, P. 30.
Comment: SEE 1753,07,18; 1753,09,10. The land is in Schoharie.

Date: 1754,03,19 (3)
Description: Patent to Johannes Becker, Jr. and others for a tract of 6,000 acres of land.
Source: N.Y.STATE ARCHIVES, ALBANY, N.Y. LETTERS PATENT, 1664-1780, SERIES NO. 12590, BOOK 13, P. 037.
Comment:

Date: 1754,04,27
Description: Deed from Lowrance (Lawrence), Seth, Joseph, Johannes Canajosery, Joseph, Jr., Seth, Jr., Jacob, Lowrence (Lawrence), Jr. to Johannes S. Pruyn and Dirck B. Van Sconover, for three tracts of land to the west of Schoharie.
Source: N.Y.STATE ARCHIVES, ALBANY, N.Y.COL.MSS, INDORSED LAND PAPERS, 1643-1803, SERIES NO. A0272, DEPARTMENT OF STATE, APPLICATIONS FOR LAND GRANTS, VOL. 15, P. 100.
Comment: Indian marks were used in signing the deed. SEE 1755,02,05.

Date: 1754,05,01
Description: Return of survey for Ury Rightmeyer (Rightmyer, Rightmeir), Hendrick Weaver, John Lansingh, Abraham Lott, Jr., Isaac Goelett, and Edward Taylor of three tracts of land containing together 8,000 acres, about eight miles southward of Schoharie between the lands granted to Edward Clarke and to Garret Vanbergen, Francis Salisbury and others.
Source: N.Y.STATE ARCHIVES, ALBANY, N.Y.COL.MSS, INDORSED LAND PAPERS, 1643-1803, SERIES NO. A0272, DEPARTMENT OF STATE, APPLICATIONS FOR LAND GRANTS, VOL. 15, P. 101.
Comment: SEE 1753,10,26; 1753,09,01; 1753, 08,27; 1754,01,11; 1754,03,01; 1754,05,01.

Date: 1754,05,06
Description: Patent to Ury Rightmeyer and others for three tracts of land, 8,000 acres total. Known as Righmeyer's Patent.
Source: N.Y.STATE ARCHIVES, ALBANY, N.Y. LETTERS PATENT, 1664-1780, SERIES NO. 12590, BOOK 13, P. 50.
Comment:

Date: 1754,06,06
Description: Indian deed to Johannes Lawyer, Jr., and others for land west of Schoharie, beginning on the east side of a creek called Otsgarrege (Oscalleghe, Oscallaghe, Oschaleghe, Otsgarege, Otsgarage, Aschalege) and containing 13,000 acres.
Source: N.Y.STATE ARCHIVES, ALBANY, N.Y.COL.MSS, INDORSED LAND PAPERS, 1643-1803, SERIES NO. A0272, DEPARTMENT OF STATE, APPLICATIONS FOR LAND GRANTS, VOL. 15, P. 108.
Comment: Indians signed the deed with their marks. N.B. A woman, Catherine, was among the signers.

Date: 1754,06,06 (2)
Description: Certificate of Cadwallader Colden, Jr. that a tract of land westward of Schoharie, beginning on the east side of a creek called Otsgarrege (Oscallghe, Oscallaghe, Oschaleghe, Otsgarage, Aschalege, Cobleskill), and containing 13,000 acres, deeded by the Indians to Johannes Lawyer, Jr., Jacob Borst (Burst), and Reinhart H[ein([?)]ts, was surveyed and the purchase money mentioned in the deed paid to the Indians Seth, Joseph, Anthony, and Lowrance [Lawrence] in Colden's presence.
Source: N.Y.STATE ARCHIVES, ALBANY, N.Y.COL.MSS, INDORSED LAND PAPERS, 1643-1803, SERIES NO. A0272, DEPARTMENT OF STATE, APPLICATIONS FOR LAND GRANTS, VOL. 15, P. 108.
Comment: N.B. Indian marks.

Date: 1754,06,06 (3)
Description: Certificate of John Baptist Van Eps, justice of the peace, that an Indian deed of land to Johannes Lawyer, Jr. and others was duly executed in his presence.
Source: N.Y.STATE ARCHIVES, ALBANY, N.Y.COL.MSS, INDORSED LAND PAPERS, 1643-1803, SERIES NO. A0272, DEPARTMENT OF STATE, APPLICATIONS FOR LAND GRANTS, VOL. 15, P. 108.
Comment:

Date: 1754,06,06 (4)
Description: Deed to George Zemer (Zimmer), Jacob Sternberger (Starnberg, Starnbergh[?]), Hendrick Wever (Weaver), and Jacob Zemer (Zimmer) for a tract of land lying on the east side of Schoharie creek. The marks of Seth, Joseph, Anthony, Lowrance (Lawrence), and Catherine are on the deed.
Source: N.Y.STATE ARCHIVES, ALBANY, N.Y.COL.MSS, INDORSED LAND PAPERS, 1643-1803, SERIES NO. A0272, DEPARTMENT OF STATE, APPLICATIONS FOR LAND GRANTS, VOL. 15, P. 109.
Comment: N.B. Indian marks on the deed. Attached to the deed is certification by Cadwallader Colden, Jr. that the land was surveyed in the presence of "Seth and two young Indians". Also included is certification by J.B.V. Eps that the bounds of the land mentioned in the deed were inserted in his presence before execution of the deed and the "Consideration Money" paid to the Indians. Anna Maria Rightmeir (Rightmeyer, Rightmyer) was interpreter.

Date: 1754,06,06 (5)
Description: Certificate of Cadwallader Colden, Jr. that land on the east side of Schoharie creek, ceded by the Indians to George Zemer (Zimmer) and others, was surveyed and the purchase money mentioned in the deed was paid in his presence.
Source: N.Y.STATE ARCHIVES, ALBANY, N.Y.COL.MSS, INDORSED LAND PAPERS, 1643-1803, SERIES NO. A0272, DEPARTMENT OF STATE, APPLICATIONS FOR LAND GRANTS, VOL. 15, P. 109.
Comment:

Date: 1754,06,06 (6)
Description: Certificate of John Baptist Van Eps, justice of the peace, that deed for land on the east side of Schoharie creek, ceded by the Indians to George Zemer (Zimmer) and others, was duly executed.
Source: N.Y.STATE ARCHIVES, ALBANY, N.Y.COL.MSS, INDORSED LAND PAPERS, 1643-1803, SERIES NO. A0272, DEPARTMENT OF STATE, APPLICATIONS FOR LAND GRANTS, VOL. 15, P. 109.
Comment:

Date: 1754,06,06 (7)
Description: Copy of and Indian deed to Jacob Zimmer (Zemer) and Jacob Starnberger (Starnberg, Starnbergh[?]), conveying land on the east side of Schoharie.
Source: N.Y.STATE ARCHIVES, ALBANY, N.Y.COL.MSS, INDORSED LAND PAPERS, 1643-1803, SERIES NO. A0272, DEPARTMENT OF STATE, APPLICATIONS FOR LAND GRANTS, VOL. 19, P. 158.
Comment: SEE 1753,06,06; 1761,10,02; 1765,09,17; 1766,07,07; 1769,09,20; 1769,09,30.

Date: 1754,07,27
Description: N.Y. Provincial Council Minutes. Order on application made by Hendrick, Paulus, and Nickus from Canajoharie that a patent for 1,000 acres be granted to Coenradt Mattys (Matice, Mattice).
Source: N.Y.STATE ARCHIVES,ALBANY, N.Y.COUN.MIN., VOL. 23, P. 210.
Comment:

Date: 1754,08,04
Description: N.Y. Colonial Manuscripts. Letter from William Johnson to Governor Hardy about Pottman and Elwood's account for building Mohawk fort.
Source: N.Y. STATE ARCHIVES, ALBANY, N.Y.COL.MSS., 1664-1776, VOL. 83, P. 040.
Comment: This document was destroyed by fire in 1911.

Date: 1754,08,06
Description: Pennsylvania Provincial Council Minutes, including proceedings of a treaty at Albany.
Source: PENNSYLVANIA HISTORICAL & MUSEUM COMMISSION, HARRISBURG, PA., PENNSYLVANIA PROVINCIAL RECORDS, VOL. M, PP. 339-388.
Comment: Printed in PENNSYLVANIA ARCHIVES, Series 1, 02: 166-167. Indians of Schoharie were present at the Albany conference.

Date: 1754,09,30
Description: Petition of William Bauch and Jacob Frederick Lawyer for a patent for three tracts of land on both sides of Schoharie creek, except for a part lying to the northeast and southeast of little Schoharie or Mill creek, and controverted by Johannes Becker and Johannes Eckerson, and the petitioner on behalf of Thomas Eckerson; and also for three small islands in the Schoharie river, containing altogether 4,000 acres.
Source: N.Y.STATE ARCHIVES, ALBANY, N.Y.COL.MSS, INDORSED LAND PAPERS, 1643-1803, SERIES NO. A0272, DEPARTMENT OF STATE, APPLICATIONS FOR LAND GRANTS, VOL. 15, P. 121.
Comment: Land involved in this grant is in Middleburgh. License to purchase land was granted 2 November 1743, purchase from Indians dated 16 April 1744. SEE 1743,11,02; 1744,04,16; 1744,04,17.

Date: 1754,10,25
Description: Indian deed to Richard Shuckburgh, for a certain tract of land, lying in the Mohawk's country, about four miles above the Mohawk castle (Lower Mohawk Village), on the west side of Tienonderoge (Tienonderoga, Tionnonderoge, Tiondorogue, Tiononderoga), alias Schohoree (Schoharie) creek, being bounded on the north by the patents of John P. Maybe and Jacob Glen and company, southwesterly by the patent of William Corry, and easterly by the Tienonderoge or Schoharee (Schoharie) creek.
Source: N.Y.STATE ARCHIVES, ALBANY, N.Y.COL.MSS, INDORSED LAND PAPERS, 1643-1803, SERIES NO. A0272, DEPARTMENT OF STATE, APPLICATIONS FOR LAND GRANTS, VOL. 15, P. 123.
Comment: N.B. Data that this document presents about the name Schoharie. Schoharie creek is identified as an alias for Tienonderoge creek. Schoharie may have been term used for broad region along Schoharie creek from confluence of Mohawk and Schoharie rivers (village of Tienonderoge/Lower Mohawk Village/Fort Hunter) to the mouth of the river, south of present day Schoharie. Contains marks of Indian signers: Candagaia alias Hance (Hans) the Wilt (Wild), Cornelius, and Cajiguate.

Date: 1754,10,25 (2)
Description: Indian deed to Richard Shuckburgh, for a certain tract of land, lying in the Mohawk's country, about four miles above the Mohawk castle (Lower Mohawk Village), on the west side of Tienonderoge, alias Schohoree (Schoharie) creek, being bounded on the north by the patents of John P. Maybe and Jacob Glen and company, southwesterly by the patent of William Corry, and easterly by the Tienonderoge (Tienonderoga, Tionnonderoge, Tiondorogue, Tiononderoga) or Schoharee (Schoharie) creek.
Source: N.Y. STATE ARCHIVES, ALBANY, INDIAN TREATIES & DEEDS, SERIES #448.
Comment:

Date: 1754,11,01
Description: Petition of Richard Shuckburgh and Jacobus Van Dyck for a patent for 1,166 acres of land about four miles above the Mohawk Castle (Lower Mohawk Village) on the west side of Tienonderoga (Tienonderoge, Tionnonderoge, Tiondorogue, Tiononderoga) or Schohary (Schoharie) creek, bounded northward by lands granted to James De Lancey and others, southerly by lands granted to William Correy and others, and eastwardly by the Schoharie creek, and also for a small tract on the south side of the Mohawk river on both sides of a creek called Aries creek.
Source: N.Y.STATE ARCHIVES, ALBANY, N.Y.COL.MSS, INDORSED LAND PAPERS, 1643-1803, SERIES NO. A0272, DEPARTMENT OF STATE, APPLICATIONS FOR LAND GRANTS, VOL. 15, P. 124.
Comment: CALENDAR OF LAND PAPERS notes that this document pertains to land in Glen, Montgomery County. Note, identification of Schoharie creek with Tienonderoge.

Date: 1754,11,06
Description: Covenant of William Bauch and Nicholas York on behalf of themselves and Jacob Frederick Lawyer to convey to Johan Joost Mattys and Johan Nicholas Mattys (Matice, Mattice), fifty acres out of the far eastern end and one hundred acres out of the far western end of three tracts of land lying on both sides of Schoharie creek upon their obtaining a patent for this land.
Source: N.Y.STATE ARCHIVES, ALBANY, N.Y.COL.MSS, INDORSED LAND PAPERS, 1643-1803, SERIES NO. A0272, DEPARTMENT OF STATE, APPLICATIONS FOR LAND GRANTS, VOL. 15, P. 125.
Comment: SEE 1755,09,00.

Date: 1754,12,05
Description: Release and quitclaim to Johannes Marckell (Merckell, Mirakle) by Lambert Starenbergh (Starnberg, Starnbergh) and others of several woodland and lowland lots at the lower end of Schoharie along the Schoharie and adjoining Marckell's property, being Lot 12, containing 20 acres and Lots 13 and 14, containing nearly 60 acres, together with Lot 18 at the lower end of Cniskernsdorp (Kniskernsdorp; Knisker Dorp; Knieskirk Dorp; Knickskerksdorf), containing about 20 acres.
Source: N.Y.STATE LIBRARY, ALBANY, MANUSCRIPTS, SCHOHARIE COUNTY, PATENTEES, LAND RECORDS, DW10738.
Comment:

Date: 1755,02,05
Description: Petition of Johannes Samuel Pruyn and Dirck Bratt (Bradt) Van Schoonhoven (Sconover) for a patent for three tracts of land on the west side of Schoharie, containing together about 3,600 acres.
Source: N.Y.STATE ARCHIVES, ALBANY, N.Y.COL.MSS, INDORSED LAND PAPERS, 1643-1803, SERIES NO. A0272, DEPARTMENT OF STATE, APPLICATIONS FOR LAND GRANTS, VOL. 15, P. 134.
Comment: SEE 1754,04,27.

Date: 1755,02,28
Description: Petition of Johannes Becker, Johannes Eckerson and Thomas Eckerson for a patent for three tracts of land at Schoharie. The first begins at the southwest corner of the Myndert Schuyler's patent of Schoharie. It is on the north side of a brook called the Mill creek or little Schoharie. The second begins at the same place and runs south thirty-eight degrees. The third is a small tract known by the name of Hunters land (Huntersfield[?]), lying on both sides of Mill creek. The total amount of land involved is 2,330 acres.
Source: N.Y.STATE ARCHIVES, ALBANY, N.Y.COL.MSS, INDORSED LAND PAPERS, 1643-1803, SERIES NO. A0272, DEPARTMENT OF STATE, APPLICATIONS FOR LAND GRANTS, VOL. 15, P. 136.
Comment: CALENDAR OF LAND PAPERS notes that this document pertains to land in Middleburgh.

Date: 1755,03,00-1756,10,00
Description: William Johnson's Account of Indian Expenses, including several references to Schoharie.
Source: THE PAPERS OF SIR WILLIAM JOHNSON. ED. BY JAMES SULLIVAN, ET AL. ALBANY: STATE UNIVERSITY OF NEW YORK, 14 VOLS., 1921-1965, 02: 0566-0646.
Comment: References to Schoharie: 24 May, 1 June, 2, 19, 20, 27 July, 7 Aug (2 references), 3 Sept, 8 Oct, 20 Dec 1755, 24 Apr, 14 May, 30 July, 6 Aug, 10, 14 (2 references), 26 Sept, and 3 October 1756.

Date: 1755,05,02
Description: Patent to Johannes Becker and others for a tract of 485 acres of land.
Source: N.Y. STATE ARCHIVES, ALBANY, N.Y. LETTERS PATENT, 1664-1780, SERIES NO. 12590, BOOK 13, P. 134.
Comment:

Date: 1755,05,24°
Description: William Johnson's Account of Indian Expenses. Money is given to Schoharie John, an Indian, to purchase provisions.
Source: SEE 1755,03,00-1756,10,00.
Comment:

Date: 1755,05,31
Description: Patent for three tracts of land on both sides of the Schoharie River to William Bauch, J.F. Lawyer, and Nicholas York.
Source: N.Y. STATE ARCHIVES, ALBANY, N.Y. LETTERS PATENT, 1664-1780, SERIES NO. 12590, BOOK 13, P. 124.
Comment:

Date: 1755,06,01°
Description: William Johnson's Account of Indian Expenses. Seth, the Schoharie sachem, and his family are given unspecified goods by William Johnson.
Source: SEE 1755,03,00-1756,10,00.
Comment:

Date: 1755,06,02
Description: William Johnson to James DeLancey, about complaints of Indian leaders including Seth "the head Sachem" of Indians living near Schoharie, concerning the sale of rum to the Indians.
Source: THE PAPERS OF SIR WILLIAM JOHNSON. ED. BY JAMES SULLIVAN, ET AL. ALBANY: STATE UNIVERSITY OF NEW YORK, 14 VOLS., 1921-1965, 01: 0560-0561.
Comment: Also printed in THE DOCUMENTARY HISTORY OF THE STATE OF NEW YORK, ED. E.B. O'CALLAGHAN, (ALBANY; WEED, PARSONS, AND CO., CHARLES VAN BENTHUYSEN, 1849-1851), QUARTO ED., 02: 656-657.

Date: 1755,06,02 (2)
Description: Patent to Johannes Becker and Johannes Eckerson for 485 acres of land.
Source: N.Y. STATE ARCHIVES, ALBANY, N.Y. LETTERS PATENT, 1664-1780, SERIES NO. 12590, BOOK 13, P. 134.
Comment: The land is in Middleburgh.

Date: 1755,06,02 (3)
Description: William Johnson to James DeLancey, about complaints of Indian leaders including Seth "the head Sachem" of Indians living near Schoharie, concerning the sale of rum to the Indians.
Source: THE DOCUMENTARY HISTORY OF THE STATE OF NEW YORK, ED. E.B. O'CALLAGHAN, (ALBANY; WEED, PARSONS, AND CO., CHARLES VAN BENTHUYSEN, 1849-1851), QUARTO ED., 02: 656-657.
Comment:

Date: 1755,09,00
Description: Petition of Mohawk Indians living in Schoharie to Charles Hardy, colonial governor of New York, complaining that Johannes Lawyer is using land that is not his. The land was reserved by the Indians for use by Nicholas Matice (Mattys, Mattice).
Source: N.Y. STATE ARCHIVES, ALBANY, COLONIAL MANUSCRIPTS, VOL. 81, P. 135.
Comment: SEE 1754,11,06.

Date: 1755,09,24
Description: Goldsbrow Banyar to William Johnson. Mentions that messengers are sent to Indian villages, including Schoharie and Oquaga (Onoquaga), to condole the dead and urge Indians to join English against French.
Source: THE PAPERS OF SIR WILLIAM JOHNSON. ED. BY JAMES SULLIVAN, ET AL. ALBANY: STATE UNIVERSITY OF NEW YORK, 14 VOLS., 1921-1965, 02: 0085-0088.
Comment:

Date: 1755,09,24 (2)
Description: Message to Indians of several villages, including Schoharie.
Source: THE PAPERS OF SIR WILLIAM JOHNSON. ED. BY JAMES SULLIVAN, ET AL. ALBANY: STATE UNIVERSITY OF NEW YORK, 14 VOLS., 1921-1965, 02: 0092-0094.
Comment: Original document is in N.Y.STATE ARCHIVES, ALBANY, COUN.MIN., VOL. 25, PP. 083-084.

Date: 1756,00,00°
Description: A colored map of the Schoharie river, "drawn on a scale of two miles to an inch, with a plan and elevation of the new fort to 35 feet to the inch". Provides also a sketch of the plan of the "Indian Castel [sic]" and shows its location on the map.
Source: SEE 1758,00,00 [ ]
Comment: Notes in the Crown Collection of photographs give the date of the map as being ca. 1758. It may be 1756 instead, however. SEE 1756,05,28. Size 11 in. x 10 in. The Indian "castle" is shown on the west side of the river. (N.B. A copy of this map is in the Rufus Grider Collection. The New York State Library list of items in the Grider Collection gives ca. 1754-1755 as the date of the map and states that Grider paid $27 for the pen and ink drawing. It is noted that the original is in the British Museum. SEE 1887,00,00-1788,00,00 (10) for reference to Grider drawing. SEE 1758,00,00 (2) [ ] for reference to the Crown Collection photograph.

Date: 1756,02,27
Description: Report of a conference at which Adam, the speaker from Onoquoaga (Oquaga) asks that a trading house be built at Onoquaga and provided with a "constant supply of goods." He says that it would "increase our numbers, as it would draw Indians from all parts within 100 miles of us, to settle among us."
Source: THE PAPERS OF SIR WILLIAM JOHNSON. ED. BY JAMES SULLIVAN, ET AL. ALBANY: STATE UNIVERSITY OF NEW YORK, 14 VOLS., 1921-1965, 09: 0387-0392.
Comment:

Date: 1756,03,05-05,26
Description: Journal of Sir William Johnson's Indian Transactions. On 5 May and on 21 May, Indians of Schoharie are listed as being present On 21 May, a former split at Schoharie is mentioned "into two parties at the head of which were Seth and David two of their cheif [sic] men". David gives a speech on the evening of the 21st. He states, ". . . all former misunderstandings are now removed and an entire end put to every kind of quarrel amongst us." He requests that a "Fort [be] built for us" and asks that Johnson "supply the wants of those the River Indians who have lately come to settle amongst us. . ."
Source: DOCUMENTS RELATIVE TO THE COLONIAL HISTORY OF THE STATE OF NEW YORK, ED. BY E.B. O'CALLAGHAN AND BERTHOLD FERNOW, 15 VOL. (ALBANY, N.Y.: WEED, PARSONS, AND CO., 1856-87), 7: 091-116.
Comment: David states in his speech, "We are besides in hopes that when we have a Fort it will be the means of drawing many Indians who now live dispersed on the Delaware & Susquehana [sic] Rivers to come and live amongst us which will add to our strength and consequence." Was the split at Schoharie perhaps engendered by the arrival of the River Indians? N.B., David says, ". . . we had a general Meeting of all Women & children belonging to our settlement together with the River Indians who were lately come to live amongst us and all former misunderstandings are now removed,. . ."

Date: 1756,04,03
Description: William Johnson to William Shirley, reporting that "[T]he Indians of Scohare [Schoharie] (altho but few) have begged to have a place of Safety, which I promised them, and this Day they asked for Men to Garrison it."
Source: THE PAPERS OF SIR WILLIAM JOHNSON. ED. BY JAMES SULLIVAN, ET AL. ALBANY: STATE UNIVERSITY OF NEW YORK, 14 VOLS., 1921-1965, 09: 0414-0417.
Comment: Original is in the HENRY E. HUNTINGTON LIBRARY, SAN MARINO, CALIFORNIA.

Date: 1756,04,22
Description: William Johnson to William Shirley, saying that he is in the process of arranging for a person to build a fort for the Indians of Schoharie (as well as one for the Oneidas, Onondagas, Senecas, and Indians of Oquaga (Onoquaga) who have requested such.
Source: THE PAPERS OF SIR WILLIAM JOHNSON. ED. BY JAMES SULLIVAN, ET AL. ALBANY: STATE UNIVERSITY OF NEW YORK, 14 VOLS., 1921-1965, 09: 0437-0441.
Comment: Original is in HENRY E. HUNTINGTON LIBRARY, SAN MARINO, CA. BARY, SAN MARINO, CALIFORNIA.

Date: 1756,05,21°
Description: Document mentions splits ("factions") among Indians at Schoharie.
Source: SEE 1756,03,05-05,26.
Comment:

Date: 1756,05,28
Description: Letter from William Johnson to the English Board of Trade. A note at the end of the letter states, "Forts are now building in the Seneca's Country, at Onondaga, Oneida & Schohere [Schoharie]". A memorandum on the back of the letter gives dimensions of the forts.
Source: THE DOCUMENTARY HISTORY OF THE STATE OF NEW YORK, ED. E.B. O'CALLAGHAN, (ALBANY; WEED, PARSONS, AND CO., CHARLES VAN BENTHUYSEN, 1849-1851), 2: 418-423.
Comment:

Date: 1756,05,28 (2)
Description: Letter from William Johnson to the English Board of Trade. A note at the end of the letter states, "Forts are now building in the Seneca's Country, at Onondaga, Oneida & Schohere [Schoharie]".
Source: DOCUMENTS RELATIVE TO THE COLONIAL HISTORY OF THE STATE OF NEW YORK, ED. BY E.B. O'CALLAGHAN AND BERTHOLD FERNOW, 15 VOL. (ALBANY, N.Y.: WEED, PARSONS, AND CO., 1856-87), 7: 086-091.
Comment:

Date: 1756,05,28 (3)
Description: Letter from William Johnson to the English Board of Trade. A note at the end of the letter states, "Forts are now building in the Seneca's Country, at Onondaga, Oneida & Schohere [Schoharie]". A memorandum on the back of the letter gives dimensions of the forts.
Source: THE DOCUMENTARY HISTORY OF THE STATE OF NEW YORK, ED. E.B. O'CALLAGHAN, (ALBANY; WEED, PARSONS, AND CO., CHARLES VAN BENTHUYSEN, 1849-1851), QUARTO ED., 2: 717-726.
Comment:

Date: 1756,07,00
Description: Notice to inhabitants of "Scohare" (Schoharie) announcing the construction of a new road from German Flats to Oswego. All who want to work on it should come to Fort Johnson.
Source: THE PAPERS OF SIR WILLIAM JOHNSON. ED. BY JAMES SULLIVAN, ET AL. ALBANY: STATE UNIVERSITY OF NEW YORK, 14 VOLS., 1921-1965, 02: 0533.
Comment:

Date: 1756,11,00
Description: Warrant of survey of Lewis Morris (Moriss), Jr. and Coeymans (Coeman, Coeyman) for 1,500 acres of land.
Source: N.Y.STATE ARCHIVES, ALBANY, N.Y.COL.MSS, INDORSED LAND PAPERS, 1643-1803, SERIES NO. A0272, DEPARTMENT OF STATE, APPLICATIONS FOR LAND GRANTS, VOL. 10, P. 005.
Comment:

Date: 1756,11,00-1757,03,00
Description: Account of Indian expenses, including some references to Schoharie.
Source: THE PAPERS OF SIR WILLIAM JOHNSON. ED. BY JAMES SULLIVAN, ET AL. ALBANY: STATE UNIVERSITY OF NEW YORK, 14 VOLS., 1921-1965, 09: 0646-0658.
Comment: Original is in HENRY E. HUNTINGTON LIBRARY, SAN MARINO, CALIFORNIA. References to Schoharie: 13, 23 Jan 1757; 10, 28 Feb 1757.

Date: 1757,01,15-25
Description: Journal of Indian Proceedings. David, a Schoharie chief, reports at Fort Johnson on 21 January that since last summer "we lost Seth our Chief Sachem and now are in darkness." William Johnson offers condolence. He wipes tears from eyes, clear throats, gives clothing.
Source: THE PAPERS OF SIR WILLIAM JOHNSON. ED. BY JAMES SULLIVAN, ET AL. ALBANY: STATE UNIVERSITY OF NEW YORK, 14 VOLS., 1921-1965, 09: 0585-0593.
Comment: Original is in PUBLIC ARCHIVES OF CANADA, OTTAWA, INDIAN RECORDS, VOL. 04. Johnson advocates unanimity during these proceedings. He announces that he will appoint another in Seth's place at next general meeting of all the nations.

Date: 1757,02,20-04,01
Description: Journal of Indian Proceedings, Fort Johnson. Indians of Schoharie speak on 28 February about replacing Seth, a chief sachem who has died.
Source: THE PAPERS OF SIR WILLIAM JOHNSON. ED. BY JAMES SULLIVAN, ET AL. ALBANY: STATE UNIVERSITY OF NEW YORK, 14 VOLS., 1921-1965, 09: 0616-0624.
Comment: Original copy is in PUBLIC ARCHIVES OF CANADA, OTTAWA, INDIAN RECORDS, VOL. 04. N.B. Information on condolence/choosing new chief, on "Our Young Men," and on relations between Schoharie and the Six Nations. "Our Young Men are not so well pleased as they ought to be, they think the Six Nations have been taken more notice of than they, altho not so deserving, which makes them discontented." (Compare last with reference to Oquaga (Onoquaga), THE PAPERS OF SIR WILLIAM JOHNSON. ED. BY JAMES SULLIVAN, ET AL. ALBANY: STATE UNIVERSITY OF NEW YORK, 14 VOLS., 1921-1965,, dated 2 May 1757).

Date: 1757,05,01
Description: Indian Proceedings. Adam of Onoquaga (Oquaga) requests twelve hoes and twelve hatchets for River Indians (Mahicans, Mahickanders) at Onoquaga who are too poor to buy what they need to cultivate "the Land they had newly come on." Provisions are ordered at Schoharie.
Source: THE PAPERS OF SIR WILLIAM JOHNSON. ED. BY JAMES SULLIVAN, ET AL. ALBANY: STATE UNIVERSITY OF NEW YORK, 14 VOLS., 1921-1965, 09: 0707-0713.
Comment:

Date: 1757,05,02
Description: Indian proceedings of a meeting of deputies of Onoquagas (Oquagas) and others at Fort Johnson. Speaker says that Parson Schuyler of Schoharie demanded land for ministering to Indians of Onoquaga. Land was given, but now Schuyler is no longer a minister to them. They are taking the land back.
Source: THE PAPERS OF SIR WILLIAM JOHNSON. ED. BY JAMES SULLIVAN, ET AL. ALBANY: STATE UNIVERSITY OF NEW YORK, 14 VOLS., 1921-1965, 09: 0714-0716.
Comment: Original proceedings are in PUBLIC ARCHIVES OF CANADA, OTTAWA, INDIAN RECORDS, VOL. 5. Schuyler was a Presbyterian minister at Schoharie. SEE 1775,02,10-16. N.B., Interesting comment: Adam, the speaker, states at one point, "You desired we should go up to Onondaga to the Council to be held there. You told us we were wise Men & might do good as much depends on the result of that Meeting. Brother the People who are to compose that Council think themselves too wise to be directed by us..."

Date: 1757,05,04-12
Description: Journal of Indian Affairs. On 9 May, two River Indians (Mahicans) from Schoharie let William Johnson "know by several Strings of Wampum their Poverty & at the same time their readiness to join our Arms..." Johnson gave them provisions and "recommended Industry & Planting Corn to them..."
Source: THE PAPERS OF SIR WILLIAM JOHNSON. ED. BY JAMES SULLIVAN, ET AL. ALBANY: STATE UNIVERSITY OF NEW YORK, 14 VOLS., 1921-1965, 09: 0720-0721.
Comment: Original is in PUBLIC ARCHIVES OF CANADA, OTTAWA, INDIAN RECORDS, VOL. 5. N.B. Johnson recommends that River Indians plant corn. Were they not doing so?

Date: 1757,05,24
Description: Extract from Journal for Indian Affairs, Fort Johnson. David of Schoharie and nine others arrive at Fort Johnson on way to secure prisoners or scalps, one to be given in place of deceased chief sachem, Seth. William Johnson gives 2,000 black wampum to be given with prisoner or scalp.
Source: THE PAPERS OF SIR WILLIAM JOHNSON. ED. BY JAMES SULLIVAN, ET AL. ALBANY: STATE UNIVERSITY OF NEW YORK, 14 VOLS., 1921-1965, 09: 0770.
Comment: Original copy is in PUBLIC ARCHIVES OF CANADA, OTTAWA, INDIAN RECORDS, VOL. 05. N.B. Information about warfare (size of war party, motivation) and condolence.

Date: 1757,05,27-06,07
Description: Journal of Indian Affairs. From 31 May through 7 June, a number of Indians, some of whom are from Schoharie, are at Fort Johnson in war parties.
Source: THE PAPERS OF SIR WILLIAM JOHNSON. ED. BY JAMES SULLIVAN, ET AL. ALBANY: STATE UNIVERSITY OF NEW YORK, 14 VOLS., 1921-1965, 09: 0779-0782.
Comment: Original copy is in PUBLIC ARCHIVES OF CANADA, OTTAWA, INDIAN RECORDS, VOL. 5. N.B. information about size and composition of war parties; mention of feasting and war dance. Seth's Hans (Hance) of Schoharie is identified as being of Turtle Clan.

Date: 1757,06,26-30
Description: Journal of Indian Affairs. On 27 June, an Indian of Schoharie who had been scouting at Crown Point arrived at Fort Johnson announcing that his party had captured a Frenchman and would be arriving at Fort Johnson shortly.
Source: THE PAPERS OF SIR WILLIAM JOHNSON. ED. BY JAMES SULLIVAN, ET AL. ALBANY: STATE UNIVERSITY OF NEW YORK, 14 VOLS., 1921-1965, 09: 0788-0792.
Comment: Original is in PUBLIC ARCHIVES OF CANADA, OTTAWA, INDIAN RECORDS, VOL. 5.

Date: 1757,07,18-31
Description: Journal of Indian Affairs. Indians of Onoquaga (Oquaga) and others request that "somebody might be appointed at Schohere (Schoharie) to assist them with Provisions, when they came backwards & forwards to & from Fort Johnson."
Source: THE PAPERS OF SIR WILLIAM JOHNSON. ED. BY JAMES SULLIVAN, ET AL. ALBANY: STATE UNIVERSITY OF NEW YORK, 14 VOLS., 1921-1965, 09: 0802-0808.
Comment: Original copy is in PUBLIC ARCHIVES OF CANADA, OTTAWA, INDIAN RECORDS, VOL. 5. There is no direct evidence in this particular document that Indians of Schoharie were present at the meeting with William Johnson at Fort Johnson. SEE 1757,08,23-29, for answer to request.

Date: 1757,08,01-21
Description: Journal of Indian Affairs. On 1 August, William Johnson sent a black belt to the Indians of Schoharie and others "inviting them to come and join him."
Source: THE PAPERS OF SIR WILLIAM JOHNSON. ED. BY JAMES SULLIVAN, ET AL. ALBANY: STATE UNIVERSITY OF NEW YORK, 14 VOLS., 1921-1965, 09: 0809-0811.
Comment: Original is in PUBLIC ARCHIVES OF CANADA, OTTAWA, INDIAN RECORDS, VOL. 5.

Date: 1757,08,23-29
Description: Proceedings of an Indian council at Fort Johnson. In answer to a previous request from Indians that provisions be made available, William Johnson noted on 24 August that he has employed two men of Schoharie to supply those Indians who come to him on public business.
Source: THE PAPERS OF SIR WILLIAM JOHNSON. ED. BY JAMES SULLIVAN, ET AL. ALBANY: STATE UNIVERSITY OF NEW YORK, 14 VOLS., 1921-1965, 09: 0811-0822.
Comment: Original copy is in PUBLIC ARCHIVES OF CANADA, OTTAWA, INDIAN RECORDS, VOL. 5. SEE 1757,07,18-31, for request.

Date: 1757,09,15-20
Description: Indian Proceedings at Fort Johnson between Oneidas, Senecas, Cayugas, Cherokees, River Indians (Mahicans, Mahickanders) and William Johnson about French advances on German Flats and Five Nations country.
Source: THE PAPERS OF SIR WILLIAM JOHNSON. ED. BY JAMES SULLIVAN, ET AL. ALBANY: STATE UNIVERSITY OF NEW YORK, 14 VOLS., 1921-1965, 09: 0831-0853.
Comment: A number of River Indians are said to reside "about Scohere [Schoharie] and Kats Kiln [Catskill]."

Date: 1757,09,16
Description: William Johnson to James Abercromby. "About Schohere [Schoharie] & Kats Kiln [Catskill] live a number of Mohikander & River Indians (Mahicans)."
Source: THE PAPERS OF SIR WILLIAM JOHNSON. ED. BY JAMES SULLIVAN, ET AL. ALBANY: STATE UNIVERSITY OF NEW YORK, 14 VOLS., 1921-1965, 02: 0739-0741.
Comment:

Date: 1757,09,28
Description: William Johnson to the English Board of Trade, states, "A number of the six nations who are settled at Aughquaga (Oquaga) on the Susquehanna River, also a small body settled at Schoherie. . . have always, and during this War constantly, shewn themselves firmly attached to our Interest, & no Indians have been more ready on every summons to come and join His Majesty's Arms. They are a flourishing & encreasing [sic] people for many of our friend Indians amongst the Six nations, who are disgusted with the ruling Politics of their people, leave their castles & go and settle at Aughquaga."
Source: DOCUMENTS RELATIVE TO THE COLONIAL HISTORY OF THE STATE OF NEW YORK, ED. BY E.B. O'CALLAGHAN AND BERTHOLD FERNOW, 15 VOL. (ALBANY, N.Y.: WEED, PARSONS, AND CO., 1856-87), 7: 276-279.
Comment: Johnson writes, ". . .if measures were fallen upon to satisfy the Indians with regard to their lands, and remove the prevailing Jealousy they have of our views of settling their hunting grounds we might not only releive [sic] our frontiers from calamaties. . . but be able to draw off many Indians from the French Influence. . ."

Date: 1757,10,19
Description: Order from William Johnson to Captains Starmbergh (Sternberger) and Swart at Schoharie to search for, and arrest, if found, two Frenchmen who escaped from Albany.
Source: THE PAPERS OF SIR WILLIAM JOHNSON. ED. BY JAMES SULLIVAN, ET AL. ALBANY: STATE UNIVERSITY OF NEW YORK, 14 VOLS., 1921-1965, 02: 0748. Noted, but not printed, in THE PAPERS OF SIR WILLIAM JOHNSON. ED. BY JAMES SULLIVAN, ET AL. ALBANY: STATE UNIVERSITY OF NEW YORK, 14 VOLS., 1921-1965,.
Comment: No information about Indians of Schoharie. Manuscript destroyed by fire.

Date: 1757,10,21
Description: William Johnson to James Abercromby, informing him that Johnson has sent Capt. Thomas Butler to Schoharie with a message to Officers of the Militia to search for two Frenchmen, DeQuayne and La Force.
Source: THE PAPERS OF SIR WILLIAM JOHNSON. ED. BY JAMES SULLIVAN, ET AL. ALBANY: STATE UNIVERSITY OF NEW YORK, 14 VOLS., 1921-1965, 02: 0748-0749.
Comment: Manuscript is in HISTORICAL SOCIETY OF PENNSYLVANIA, PHILADELPHIA, AUTOGRAPH COLLECTION. No information about Indians of Schoharie.

Date: 1757,12,27
Description: James Abercromby to William Johnson, about affairs at Schoharie. Mentions subject of control of fortifications at the Schoharie (Schohang) Indian settlement. ". . .they seem to imagine that their Indians would not consent, to their taking possession of the Castle because it was built for the Indians, it makes it necessary that that matter should be explained, that the inhabitants may at all times have free acsess [sic] to this Fort. . ."
Source: THE PAPERS OF SIR WILLIAM JOHNSON. ED. BY JAMES SULLIVAN, ET AL. ALBANY: STATE UNIVERSITY OF NEW YORK, 14 VOLS., 1921-1965, 02: 0768-0769.
Comment: Original is at NEWBERRY LIBRARY, CHICAGO, IL.

Date: 1757,12,27 (2)
Description: James Abercromby to William Johnson, about alarm at Skoery (Schoharie). Abercromby thinks the alarm will prove groundless, but "in Order to make people easy," he is sending a Command there "to assist and direct" the people of Schoharie "in throwing up some breastwork for their defense."
Source: THE PAPERS OF SIR WILLIAM JOHNSON. ED. BY JAMES SULLIVAN, ET AL. ALBANY: STATE UNIVERSITY OF NEW YORK, 14 VOLS., 1921-1965, 13: 0101-0102.
Comment: Manuscript in N.Y. STATE LIBRAY, ALBANY, TAYLOR-COOPER COLLECTION.

Date: 1757,12,28
Description: William Johnson to James Abercromby, informing Abercromby that Johnson finds the report of an alarm at Schoharie to be surprising. Johnson has gotten no hint of it from Indians of Schoharie or Onoquaga (Oquaga) who are trusted friends. Moreover, George Croghan just returned from bringing clothing to Indians of Schoharie and was at Lawyer's house. He was not informed of any alarm. Johnson will send Croghan and two Indian officers to Schoharie to discover the truth.
Source: THE PAPERS OF SIR WILLIAM JOHNSON. ED. BY JAMES SULLIVAN, ET AL. ALBANY: STATE UNIVERSITY OF NEW YORK, 14 VOLS., 1921-1965, 13: 0103.
Comment: Manuscript in NEW JERSEY HISTORICAL SOCIETY, NEWARK, N.J..

Date: 1758,00,00 [ ]
Description: A colored map of the Schoharie river, "drawn on a scale of two miles to an inch, with a plan and elevation of the new fort to 35 feet to the inch". Provides also a sketch of the plan of the "Indian Castel [sic]" and shows its location on the map.
Source: BRITISH MUSEUM, LONDON, ENGLAND, MANUSCRIPTS. A photograph of the original was published in THE CROWN COLLECTION OF PHOTOGRAPHS OF AMERICAN MAPS, SELECTED AND EDITED BY ARCHER BUTLER HULBERT. CLEVELAND, OHIO: THE ARTHUR CLARK COMPANY, 1907, SERIES 1, VOL. 2, #42 (RIVER SCHOHARIE, CROWN cxxi, 33).
Comment: Notes in the Crown Collection of photographs give the date of the map as being ca. 1758. It may be 1756 instead, however. SEE 1756,05,28. Size 11 in. x 10 in. The Indian "castle" is shown on the west side of the river. (N.B. A copy of this map is in the Rufus Grider Collection. The New York State Library list of items in the Grider Collection gives ca. 1754-1755 as the date of the map and states that Grider paid $27 for the pen and ink drawing. It is noted that the original is in the British Museum. SEE 1887,00,00-1788,00,00 (10) for reference to Grider drawing. SEE 1758,00,00 (2) [ ] for reference to Crown Collection photograph.

Date: 1758,00,00 [ ] (2)
Description: A colored map of the Schoharie river, "drawn on a scale of two miles to an inch, with a plan and elevation of the new fort to 35 feet to the inch". Provides also a sketch of the plan of the "Indian Castel [sic]" and shows its location on the map.
Source: Photograph of original, published in THE CROWN COLLECTION OF PHOTOGRAPHS OF AMERICAN MAPS, SELECTED AND EDITED BY ARCHER BUTLER HULBERT. CLEVELAND, OHIO: THE ARTHUR CLARK COMPANY, 1907, SERIES 1, VOL. 2, #42 (RIVER SCHOHARIE, CROWN cxxi, 33). Original map is in the manuscripts collection of the BRITISH MUSEUM, LONDON, ENGLAND.
Comment: Notes in the Crown Collection publication of photographs give the date of the map as being ca. 1758. Size 11 in. x 10 in. It may be 1756 instead, however. SEE 1756,05,28. The Indian "castle" is shown on the west side of the river. (N.B. A copy of this map is in the Rufus Grider Collection. The New York State Library list of items in the Grider Collection gives ca. 1754-1755 as the date of the map and states that Grider paid $27 for the pen and ink drawing. It is noted that the original is in the British Museum. SEE 1887,00,00-1788,00,00 (10) for reference to Grider drawing.)

Date: 1758,00,00°
Description: Rufus Grider Collection. Map of the Schoharie River Valley showing "Plan of the Indian Castel[sic]" at Vrooman's (Vroman's) land about 1754-1755, and plan and elevation of the "New Fort" never erected. From original in the British Museum, London. Pen and ink tracing for which Grider paid $27.
Source: SEE 1887,00,00-1888,00,00 (10).
Comment: Notes in the Crown Collection publication of photographs of original maps in the British Museum give the date of the map as being ca. 1758. Size 11 in. x 10 in. SEE 1758,00,00 [ ]. The date of the map may be 1756 instead, however. SEE 1756,05,28.

Date: 1758,03,11-14
Description: Report of an Indian conference. On 14 March, Johnson warns Schoharie and "Mohickon" (Mahican, Mahickander) Indians of possibility of attack by the enemy. He admonishes them ". . . to Collect your Scattered people together. . ." ". . .then your tribes will become once More a respectable body . . ."
Source: THE PAPERS OF SIR WILLIAM JOHNSON. ED. BY JAMES SULLIVAN, ET AL. ALBANY: STATE UNIVERSITY OF NEW YORK, 14 VOLS., 1921-1965, 09: 0879-0886.
Comment: Original is in PUBLIC RECORD OFFICE, KEW, ENGLAND, W.O. 34, VOL. 39.

Date: 1758,05,17
Description: William Johnson to James Abercromby. Identifies Schoharie as a settlement of primarily Mohawk Indians about 40 miles from Albany. Discusses disposition of Indians of Oquaga (Onoquaga) [and Schoharie(?)] vis-a-vis the Six Nations proper.
Source: THE PAPERS OF SIR WILLIAM JOHNSON. ED. BY JAMES SULLIVAN, ET AL. ALBANY: STATE UNIVERSITY OF NEW YORK, 14 VOLS., 1921-1965, 09: 0901-0906.
Comment: Original is in HENRY E. HUNTINGTON LIBRARY, SAN MARINO, CALIFORNIA. Copy in PUBLIC RECORD OFFICE, KEW, ENGLAND, WO34, VOL. 39 is dated 17 Mar 1758.

Date: 1758,05,30
Description: Extract from Journal of Indian Affairs. Contains information about the number of individuals in, and composition of, a war party comprised of several Indians of Schoharie.
Source: THE PAPERS OF SIR WILLIAM JOHNSON. ED. BY JAMES SULLIVAN, ET AL. ALBANY: STATE UNIVERSITY OF NEW YORK, 14 VOLS., 1921-1965, 09: 0914.
Comment: Original copy is in PUBLIC ARCHIVES OF CANADA, OTTAWA, INDIAN RECORDS, VOL. 5.

Date: 1758,06,21-07,01
Description: Indian Proceedings at Fort Johnson. Indians are coming to Fort Johnson to consider joining English in warfare against the French. A party of 23 Indians from the Lower Mohawk Village and from Schohary (Schoharie) is mentioned on 24 June. They have been scouting around Ticonderoga/Crown Point. On 29 June, Indians of Schoharie arrive to meet with Johnson.
Source: THE PAPERS OF SIR WILLIAM JOHNSON. ED. BY JAMES SULLIVAN, ET AL. ALBANY: STATE UNIVERSITY OF NEW YORK, 14 VOLS., 1921-1965, 09: 0934-0940.
Comment: Manuscript is in PULBIC ARCHIVES OF CANADA, OTTAWA, INDIAN RECORDS, VOL. 5. Contains information about William Johnson as a military man and Indians as warriors.

Date: 1758,07,02-11
Description: Journal of Indian Affairs. On 3 July, it is noted that a report has been received from Mr. Vrooman (Vroman) of Schoharie "that a party of Tuscarores [Tuscaroras] from Aughquaga [Onoquaga, Oquaga], some Nanticokes and several Mahickanders (Mahicans, Mohicans) from Otsiningto were expected there every hour." A message was sent to Vrooman "to send the Men forward by way of Albany to Lake George & give the Women Provisions to carry them home."
Source: THE PAPERS OF SIR WILLIAM JOHNSON. ED. BY JAMES SULLIVAN, ET AL. ALBANY: STATE UNIVERSITY OF NEW YORK, 14 VOLS., 1921-1965, 09: 0942-0944.
Comment: Manuscript is in PUBLIC ARCHIVES OF CANADA, OTTAWA, INDIAN RECORDS, VOL. 5.

Date: 1758,07,16
Description: A list of the number of Indians who joined William Johnson and the British Army under General Abercromby, 8 July, at the Saw Mills near Ticonderoga/Crown Point. The number of Schoharie Indians was said to be 18. An additional note says that the day after action was taken, 25 Mohawks and Schoharie Indians joined the Advance Guard.
Source: THE PAPERS OF SIR WILLIAM JOHNSON. ED. BY JAMES SULLIVAN, ET AL. ALBANY: STATE UNIVERSITY OF NEW YORK, 14 VOLS., 1921-1965, 09: 0944-0945.
Comment: Original copy is in PUBLIC ARCHIVES OF CANADA, OTTAWA, INDIAN RECORDS VOL. 5, P. 263.

Date: 1758,11,00-1759,12,00
Description: William Johnson's account of Indian expenses, including several references to Schoharie. One pertains to money given to David of Schoharie to bring more Indians to a settlement that he is starting at Avigo on the Susquehanna River.
Source: THE PAPERS OF SIR WILLIAM JOHNSON. ED. BY JAMES SULLIVAN, ET AL. ALBANY: STATE UNIVERSITY OF NEW YORK, 14 VOLS., 1921-1965, 03: 0149-0182.
Comment: Manuscript is in PUBLIC RECORD OFFICE, KEW, ENGLAND, CO 5/57. ENCLOSED IN LETTER FROM JEFFREY AMHERST TO WILLIAM PITT, DATED 9 JANUARY 1760. References to Schoharie: 20 Nov (2 references), 25 Nov, 13, 26 Dec 1758, 23, 25 Jan, 7 Feb, 1, 27 April, 1, 2, 13 May, 10 Nov 1759.

Date: 1758,11,18-12,04
Description: Journal of Indian Affairs. On 19 November, Seth, a chief of Schoharie, came to Fort Johnson to complain that Germans are settled on lands belonging to the Indians. He explained that the Germans claim they were settled there by the Patroon of Albany, Stephen Van Rensselaer, 2nd, but that Hans (Hance) Lawyer of Schoharie showed the Indians a map of Schoharie that indicated that the Patroon "had no right or Title to said Lands." Indians of Schoharie also ask for clothing for their women and children.
Source: THE PAPERS OF SIR WILLIAM JOHNSON. ED. BY JAMES SULLIVAN, ET AL. ALBANY: STATE UNIVERSITY OF NEW YORK, 14 VOLS., 1921-1965, 10: 0057-0060.
Comment: "[T]wo Horse Loads of Goods" were sent by William Johnson "to cloath [clothe] the Women & Children of that Settlement, being in number 18 Women & 33 Children" on 21 November.

Date: 1758,12,05-09
Description: Journal of Indian Affairs. Report by Oneida hunting near Schoharie that settlers are ill-tempered because of some pigs killed lately by some Indians and will not provide any food to the Indians who are starving because of the scarcity of game.
Source: THE PAPERS OF SIR WILLIAM JOHNSON. ED. BY JAMES SULLIVAN, ET AL. ALBANY: STATE UNIVERSITY OF NEW YORK, 14 VOLS., 1921-1965, 10: 0063-0064.
Comment: Original is in PUBLIC ARCHIVES OF CANADA, OTTAWA, INDIAN RECORDS, VOL. 5, ENCLOSED IN JOHNSON TO MCAULAY, 5 DEC 1758. It is not clear if rthe Oneidas are from Schoharie or if they are just hunting there.

Date: 1758,12,09
Description: Instructions from William Johnson to Jelles Fonda, who is going to Schoharie. Johnson instructs Fonda to urge non-Indian inhabitants of Schoharie to maintain good relations with all Indians who reside at, or pass through, Schoharie.
Source: THE PAPERS OF SIR WILLIAM JOHNSON. ED. BY JAMES SULLIVAN, ET AL. ALBANY: STATE UNIVERSITY OF NEW YORK, 14 VOLS., 1921-1965, 10: 0064-0065.
Comment: Original copy in PUBLIC ARCHIVES OF CANADA, OTTAWA, INDIAN RECORDS, VOL. 5. SEE 1758,12,16-18.

Date: 1758,12,16-18
Description: Journal of Indian Affairs. Jelles Fonda reports to William Johnson about meeting at Schoharie at which he gave instructions from Johnson dated 9 Dec 1758. Indians and Euro-Americans were both present at the meeting at Schoharie.
Source: THE PAPERS OF SIR WILLIAM JOHNSON. ED. BY JAMES SULLIVAN, ET AL. ALBANY: STATE UNIVERSITY OF NEW YORK, 14 VOLS., 1921-1965, 10: 0079-0080.
Comment: SEE 1758,12,09.

Date: 1759,02,03-10
Description: Journal of Indian Affairs. On 10 February, it is reported at Fort Johnson that Capt. Butler is being sent to Schoharie in order to recruit warriors.
Source: THE PAPERS OF SIR WILLIAM JOHNSON. ED. BY JAMES SULLIVAN, ET AL. ALBANY: STATE UNIVERSITY OF NEW YORK, 14 VOLS., 1921-1965, 10: 0097-0099.
Comment: Original is in PUBLIC ARCHIVES OF CANADA, OTTAWA, INDIAN RECORDS, VOL. 5.

Date: 1759,02,10
Description: Instructions for John Butler, about recruiting Indians of Schoharie. They should "take their Snow Shoes." Also, mentions complaints by Indians against "one Becker [Nicholas(?)] a German keeping & planting some of their Land."
Source: THE PAPERS OF SIR WILLIAM JOHNSON. ED. BY JAMES SULLIVAN, ET AL. ALBANY: STATE UNIVERSITY OF NEW YORK, 14 VOLS., 1921-1965, 10: 0100.
Comment: Original is in PUBLIC ARCHIVES OF CANADA, OTTAWA, INDIAN RECORDS, VOL. 5.

Date: 1759,02,11-23
Description: Journal of Indian Affairs. William Johnson wants to recruit warriors from Schoharie, 12 February. Fourteen warriors from Schoharie arrive with several of their women and children at Fort Johnson on 17 February. Warriors will scout at Ticonderoga.
Source: THE PAPERS OF SIR WILLIAM JOHNSON. ED. BY JAMES SULLIVAN, ET AL. ALBANY: STATE UNIVERSITY OF NEW YORK, 14 VOLS., 1921-1965, 10: 0105-0107.
Comment: Original in PUBLIC ARCHIVES OF CANADA, OTTAWA, INDIAN RECORDS, VOL. 5.

Date: 1760,04,05
Description: Petition of William Winne, John Winne and thirty-eight others for a license to purchase from the Indians a tract of unpatented lands lying between the western bounds of the manor of Renslaerwyck and the tract commonly called the Schoharie Patent (of Myndert Schuyler), and then running along the western boundary of the manor Renslaerwyck to the southwest corner of the manor and along the south line thereof to the tract commonly called Coyerman's (Coeyman, Coeman) patent, and enclosed by lines parallel to the southwest boundary of the manor of Renslaerwick, at a distance of four miles from that boundary.
Source: N.Y.STATE ARCHIVES, ALBANY, N.Y.COL.MSS, INDORSED LAND PAPERS, 1643-1803, SERIES NO. A0272, DEPARTMENT OF STATE, APPLICATIONS FOR LAND GRANTS, VOL. 15, P. 172.
Comment:

Date: 1760,06,29-1761,07,03
Description: Journal of Warren Johnson, brother of Sir William Johnson. Contains several observations of and comments about Indian dress, customs, etc. Examples: "An Indian Letter or Message is A String of Wampum;" "the Indians goe in Mourning for their Relations, the white people condole with them by clearing their throats to make them Speak, they wipe away the Tears from their Eyes, & the Blood of the Deceased from their Bed. & out of their Sight, that their Hearts may be chearful: this is done by giving them Strings of Wampum, & black Strouds, & . . ."
Source: THE PAPERS OF SIR WILLIAM JOHNSON. ED. BY JAMES SULLIVAN, ET AL. ALBANY: STATE UNIVERSITY OF NEW YORK, 14 VOLS., 1921-1965, 13: 0180-0214.
Comment:

Date: 1760,08,05
Description: Census of Indians, dated at Oswego, 5 August 1760. Indians of Schoharie are said to number 22.
Source: THE PAPERS OF SIR WILLIAM JOHNSON. ED. BY JAMES SULLIVAN, ET AL. ALBANY: STATE UNIVERSITY OF NEW YORK, 14 VOLS., 1921-1965, 10: 0175.
Comment: Original is in PUBLIC RECORD OFFICE, KEW, ENGLAND, WO34, VOL. 39. The figure given in this document seems very low for a total population count. What is the context? It is most likely fighting men and their families.

Date: 1760,09,09
Description: Petition of Ten Eyck and others to purchase 5,000 acres north of Huntersfield or Schoharie on both sides of Schoharie river adjoining tract of Myndert Schuyler and Peter Van Burgh.
Source: N.Y.STATE ARCHIVES, ALBANY, N.Y.COL.MSS, INDORSED LAND PAPERS, 1643-1803, SERIES NO. A0272, DEPARTMENT OF STATE, APPLICATIONS FOR LAND GRANTS, VOL. 16, P. 004.
Comment: CALENDAR OF LAND PAPERS identifies the land as being in the town of Esperance, Schoharie County. SEE 1760,12,31; 1761,04,16.

Date: 1760,09,13
Description: A list of Indians who proceeded with the British Army under General Amherst from Fort William Augustus to Montreal.
Source: THE PAPERS OF SIR WILLIAM JOHNSON. ED. BY JAMES SULLIVAN, ET AL. ALBANY: STATE UNIVERSITY OF NEW YORK, 14 VOLS., 1921-1965, 10: 0180-0185.
Comment: SEE 1760,10,00. "Mohickans"(Mahicans, Mahickanders) are designated as "River Indians" on the October 1760 list. The last nine names under "Mohawks" on the 13 September 1760 list appear as "Indians of Schoharie" on the October 1760 list.

Date: 1760,10,00
Description: List of Indians who joined William Johnson for march to Montreal. Includes personal names (both Indian and Christian) of nine Indians of Schoharie and sixteen River Indians (Mahicans).
Source: THE PAPERS OF SIR WILLIAM JOHNSON. ED. BY JAMES SULLIVAN, ET AL. ALBANY: STATE UNIVERSITY OF NEW YORK, 14 VOLS., 1921-1965, 13: 0173-0178.
Comment: Manuscript in N.Y. HISTORICAL SOCIETY, NEW YORK, N.Y. Bound with Jelles Fonda Journal dated 29 June-23 October 1760, but in the handwriting of Daniel Claus. For another list of the same Indians, SEE 1760,09,13. In that list, Indian names only are given. River Indians appear under the heading "Mohickans"; those designated as Indians of Schoharie on the October 1760 list, appear as the last nine names under "Mohawks" on the 13 September 1760 list.

Date: 1760,12,31
Description: License to Jacob Ten Eyck and others to purchase land.
Source: N.Y.STATE ARCHIVES, ALBANY, N.Y.COL.MSS, INDORSED LAND PAPERS, 1643-1803, SERIES NO. A0272, DEPARTMENT OF STATE, APPLICATIONS FOR LAND GRANTS, VOL. 16, P. 025.
Comment: SEE 1760,09,09; 1761,04,16. CALENDAR OF LAND PAPERS notes that the land involved in this document is in Esperance, Schoharie County.

Date: 1761,01,28
Description: William Johnson to Alexander Colden, requesting detailed survey of land on both sides of the Mohawk River, Schoharie, Stonaraby, and Cherry Valley with the patentees names, the quantity and year patented, and what belongs to the Indians. Johnson says he wants to satisfy Indians as to the land they have left and prevent them from being imposed upon.
Source: THE PAPERS OF SIR WILLIAM JOHNSON. ED. BY JAMES SULLIVAN, ET AL. ALBANY: STATE UNIVERSITY OF NEW YORK, 14 VOLS., 1921-1965, 03: 0311-0314.
Comment: Manuscript destroyed by fire.

Date: 1761,01,28 (2)
Description: Godsbrow Banyar to William Johnson. Mentions two petitions for 25,000 acres of land westward of Schoharie that have been granted. It is Banyar's opinion that the petitioners will "hardly find so much land."
Source: THE PAPERS OF SIR WILLIAM JOHNSON. ED. BY JAMES SULLIVAN, ET AL. ALBANY: STATE UNIVERSITY OF NEW YORK, 14 VOLS., 1921-1965, 03: 0396-0398.
Comment: Manuscript destroyed by fire.

Date: 1761,04,07°
Description: Confirmation of sale to John Markell (Merckell; Marckell; Mirakle), yeoman, by his late father, Lambert Sternberger (Starnberg), April 7, 1761, of Lot 17 in Kniskerns (Kneescarns, Kniskorn, Knieskerk, Knieskerk, Knieskirk) Town (Knisker Dorp), on the east side of Schoharie Creek, containing about 20 acres.
Source: SEE 1768,06,21.
Comment:

Date: 1761,04,16
Description: Appointment of John R. Bleeker to survey tracts of land for Jacob Ten Eyck and others.
Source: N.Y.STATE ARCHIVES, ALBANY, N.Y.COL.MSS, INDORSED LAND PAPERS, 1643-1803, SERIES NO. A0272, DEPARTMENT OF STATE, APPLICATIONS FOR LAND GRANTS, VOL. 16, P. 025.
Comment: SEE 1760,09,09; 1760,12,31. CALENDAR OF LAND PAPERS notes that this document pertains to land in Esperance, Schoharie County.

Date: 1761,06,00 [ ]°
Description: Caveat on behalf of the City of Albany against granting 500 acres of land at Schaahtecoghe (Scaticoke) and 1,000 acres at Tionnondorage.
Source: SEE n.d.
Comment: This manuscript is found in Vol. 16 of the Indorsed Land Papers at the N.Y. State Archives in Albany, NY, between documents dated June 15, 1761 and June 17, 1761.

Date: 1761,06,15
Description: Petition of Johannes Lawyer for patent of 11,000 acres west of Schoharie Creek, formerly land of J. Borst and B. Huser(?sp.).
Source: N.Y.STATE ARCHIVES, ALBANY, N.Y.COL.MSS, INDORSED LAND PAPERS, 1643-1803, SERIES NO. A0272, DEPARTMENT OF STATE, APPLICATIONS FOR LAND GRANTS, VOL. 16, 058.
Comment: CALENDAR OF LAND PAPERS notes that this document pertains to land in Sharon. SEE 1761,06.27.

Date: 1761,06,27
Description: Return of survey of a 7,000 acre tract of land for Johannes Lawyer, Jr., and six others. The land is to the westward of Schoharie, on the north and west sides of a tract of 15,000 acres, formerly granted to Jacob Borst (Burst) and others.
Source: N.Y.STATE ARCHIVES, ALBANY, N.Y.COL.MSS, INDORSED LAND PAPERS, 1643-1803, SERIES NO. A0272, DEPARTMENT OF STATE, APPLICATIONS FOR LAND GRANTS, VOL. 16, P. 066.
Comment: CALENDAR OF LAND PAPERS notes that this document pertains to land in Sharon. SEE 1761, 06,15.

Date: 1761,06,29
Description: Petition of William Van Bergen, Martin Garetse Van Bergen and James Umphry, Jr. for a license to purchase 3,000 acres of land on the west side of Hudson's River, between Cattskill (Catskill) Creek and Schoharie near Batavia.
Source: N.Y.STATE ARCHIVES, ALBANY, N.Y.COL.MSS, INDORSED LAND PAPERS, 1643-1803, SERIES NO. A0272, DEPARTMENT OF STATE, APPLICATIONS FOR LAND GRANTS, VOL. 16, P. 067.
Comment: SEE 1761,12,23.

Date: 1761,07,08
Description: Petition of J. Ten Eyck and others for land west of Schoharie.
Source: N.Y.STATE ARCHIVES, ALBANY, N.Y.COL.MSS, INDORSED LAND PAPERS, 1643-1803, SERIES NO. A0272, DEPARTMENT OF STATE, APPLICATIONS FOR LAND GRANTS, VOL. 16, P. 071.
Comment: CALENDAR OF LAND PAPERS identifies land as being in Esperance and Duanesburgh. SEE 1761,08,24.

Date: 1761,08,14
Description: Patent to Jacob Borst, William Bornheyer, and others for 7,000 acres of land.
Source: N.Y.STATE ARCHIVES, ALBANY, N.Y. LETTERS PATENT, 1664-1780, SERIES NO. 12590, BOOK 13, P. 406.
Comment: CALENDAR OF LAND PAPERS identifies land as being in Sharon, Schoharie County.

Date: 1761,08,14°
Description: Map of a patent granted August 14, 1761 to Johannes Lawyer, Jr. and others. Map made October 6, 1763; made over again November 11, 1786 by Johannes Lawyer, Jr. for his own use.
Source: SEE 1786,11,11.
Comment:

Date: 1761,08,24
Description: Return of survey for J. Ten Eyck and others of land west of Schoharie.
Source: N.Y.STATE ARCHIVES, ALBANY, N.Y.COL.MSS, INDORSED LAND PAPERS, 1643-1803, SERIES NO. A0272, DEPARTMENT OF STATE, APPLICATIONS FOR LAND GRANTS, VOL. 16, P. 082.
Comment: SEE 1761,07,08.

Date: 1761,09,00
Description: Return of survey of land for F. Young and others.
Source: N.Y.STATE ARCHIVES, ALBANY, N.Y.COL.MSS, INDORSED LAND PAPERS, 1643-1803, SERIES NO. A0272, DEPARTMENT OF STATE, APPLICATIONS FOR LAND GRANTS, VOL. 16, P. 092.
Comment: CALENDAR OF LAND PAPERS identifies the land as being in Cherry Valley, Sharon, Otsego, and Schoharie.

Date: 1761,09,01
Description: Petition of Henry Van Driesen and others for land.
Source: N.Y.STATE ARCHIVES, ALBANY, N.Y.COL.MSS, INDORSED LAND PAPERS, 1643-1803, SERIES NO. A0272, DEPARTMENT OF STATE, APPLICATIONS FOR LAND GRANTS, VOL. 16, P. 083.
Comment: CALENDAR OF LAND PAPERS identifies the land as being in the towns of Carlisle in Schoharie County and Charlestown in Montgomery County.

Date: 1761,09,12
Description: Petition of Josiah Swart and others for 8,000 acres west of Schoharie and Breakaben (Breakabeen).
Source: N.Y.STATE ARCHIVES, ALBANY, N.Y.COL.MSS, INDORSED LAND PAPERS, 1643-1803, SERIES NO. A0272, DEPARTMENT OF STATE, APPLICATIONS FOR LAND GRANTS, VOL. 16, P. 092.
Comment:

Date: 1761,09,17
Description: Patent to Jacob Hendrick Ten Eyck and others land. Known as the Ten Eyck Patent.
Source: N.Y.STATE ARCHIVES, ALBANY, N.Y. LETTERS PATENT, 1664-1780, SERIES NO. 12590, BOOK 13, P. 434
Comment:

Date: 1761,09,25-1771,10,13
Description: Extracts from the Account Book of John Butler. On 30 April 1766, Butler notes disbursement of funds for "sundrys" going to Schoharie. On [2 December] 1766, he paid money for an express sent to Schoharie to John Lawyer. On 28 September 1766, he paid cash to Hendrick Wemple for "going Express to Schohary [Schoharie]". On 24 April 1767, he disbursed funds for "Sundry Expenses agoing to Schohary with Capt Fry & yeats [Yates]" and for "sundrys" coming from Schoharie.
Source: THE PAPERS OF SIR WILLIAM JOHNSON. ED. BY JAMES SULLIVAN, ET AL. ALBANY: STATE UNIVERSITY OF NEW YORK, 14 VOLS., 1921-1965, 13: 0506-0521.
Comment: Manuscript in N.Y. STATE LIBRARY, ALBANY, MANUSCRIPTS.

Date: 1761,10,02
Description: Document about land east of Schoharie involving Jacob Starnberger and others.
Source: N.Y.STATE ARCHIVES, ALBANY, N.Y.COL.MSS, INDORSED LAND PAPERS, 1643-1803, SERIES NO. A0272, DEPARTMENT OF STATE, APPLICATIONS FOR LAND GRANTS, VOL. 16, P. 098.
Comment: SEE 1753,06,06; 1754,06,06; 1765,09,17; 1766,07,07; 1769,09,20; 1769,09,30.

Date: 1761,12,01
Description: Caveat of Richard Morris against purchase of land.
Source: N.Y.STATE ARCHIVES, ALBANY, N.Y.COL.MSS, INDORSED LAND PAPERS, 1643-1803, SERIES NO. A0272, DEPARTMENT OF STATE, APPLICATIONS FOR LAND GRANTS, VOL. 16, P. 105.
Comment: CALENDAR OF LAND PAPERS notes that this document pertains to land in Broome, Schoharie County.

Date: 1761,12,23
Description: Deed from the "Katskill [Catskill] Indians" to William Van Bergen, Martin G. Van Bergen, James _?_mphrey (Umphrey, Humphrey), Jr.and others. Schoharie Creek is listed as a boundary point several times in the deed. The marks of Tamphampamet, Panenamet, Nishogkampewine, Cankeskoha, and Shepokass are on the deed.
Source: N.Y.STATE ARCHIVES, ALBANY, N.Y.COL.MSS, INDORSED LAND PAPERS, 1643-1803, SERIES NO. A0272, DEPARTMENT OF STATE, APPLICATIONS FOR LAND GRANTS, VOL. 16, P. 106.
Comment: The land was surveyed, and boundaries marked, in the presence of the Indians. SEE 1761,06,29.

Date: 1762,01,16
Description: Documents pertaining to F. Sauldsberry and M. Van Bergen land.
Source: N.Y.STATE ARCHIVES, ALBANY, N.Y.COL.MSS, INDORSED LAND PAPERS, 1643-1803, SERIES NO. A0272, DEPARTMENT OF STATE, APPLICATIONS FOR LAND GRANTS, VOL. 16, P. 107,108.
Comment: CALENDAR OF LAND PAPERS notes that the land is north of Windham (Batavia).

Date: 1762,03,10
Description: __?__ Ackeson resists license to Adam Zielle for a tract of land at Schoharie.
Source: N.Y.STATE ARCHIVES, ALBANY, N.Y.COL.MSS, INDORSED LAND PAPERS, 1643-1803, SERIES NO. A0272, DEPARTMENT OF STATE, APPLICATIONS FOR LAND GRANTS, VOL. 16, P. 111.
Comment:

Date: 1762,03,20
Description: Release to Jacob Enders by Hendrick Hauck (Houck) and others of a lot in Kniskern's town (Kniskernsdorp; Kniskern Dorp; Knisker Dorp; Knickskerksdorf), on and along the east side of the Schoharie River between Lots 18 and 19, containing 120 acres. The parties to the agreement are yeoman of Schoharie.
Source: N.Y.STATE LIBRARY, ALBANY, MANUSCRIPTS, SCHOHARIE COUNTY, PATENTEES, LAND RECORDS, DW10738.
Comment:

Date:	1762,07,16
Description:	Petition of Spornheyer and Heints for a patent of land near Schoharie.
Source:	N.Y.STATE ARCHIVES, ALBANY, N.Y.COL.MSS, INDORSED LAND PAPERS, 1643-1803, SERIES NO. A0272, DEPARTMENT OF STATE, APPLICATIONS FOR LAND GRANTS, VOL. 16, P. 117.
Comment:	SEE 1762,09,25.

Date:	1762,09,20
Description:	Petition of Starnberger (Starnberg, Starnbergh[?]) and others for patent to land east of Schoharie Creek.
Source:	N.Y.STATE ARCHIVES, ALBANY, N.Y.COL.MSS, INDORSED LAND PAPERS, 1643-1803, SERIES NO. A0272, DEPARTMENT OF STATE, APPLICATIONS FOR LAND GRANTS, VOL. 16, P. 121.
Comment:	N.B. Land is EAST of Schoharie Creek. SEE 1769,09,30; 1753,06,06; 1754,06,06; 1761,10,02; 1765,09,17; 1766,07,07.

Date:	1762,09,25
Description:	Return of survey of land for Spornheyer. A map is included.
Source:	N.Y.STATE ARCHIVES, ALBANY, N.Y.COL.MSS, INDORSED LAND PAPERS, 1643-1803, SERIES NO. A0272, DEPARTMENT OF STATE, APPLICATIONS FOR LAND GRANTS, VOL. 16, P. 123.
Comment:	SEE 1762,07,16. CALENDAR OF LAND PAPERS notes that land is in Sharon, Schoharie County.

Date:	1763,00,00
Description:	A deed that mentions the Dove-Gatt. This deed is for a tract of land on the west side of the Schoharie River. One of the landmarks mentioned in it is the Dove-Gatt. Another is a house occupied by To-gri-hed-en-tis. The deed is dated 1763.
Source:	OLD STONE CHURCH AND FORTRESS, SCHOHARIE, N.Y., CATALOGUE AND HISTORICAL NOTES, 1933, DEED # 323.
Comment:	This reference states, "When the early Dutch settlers came to the Schoharie Valley, most of them about the year 1720, they found two of these Dove-Gatts in the valley, one in Vrooman's land (Fulton) and the other a short distance down the valley north of (the Stone Fort) building. Dove-Gatt is the Dutch name for a slender bay of water extending out from the main stream and having the form of the letter L..."

Date:	1763,05,19
Description:	Patent to William Ernst Sporhnheyer and William Heints for two tracts of land, 2,000 acres total.
Source:	N.Y.STATE ARCHIVES, ALBANY, N.Y. LETTERS PATENT, 1664-1780, SERIES NO. 12590, BOOK 13, P. 511.
Comment:	

Date:	1763,10,04-17
Description:	Journal of Indian Affairs. On 17 October, a number of chiefs of Canajoharie, Lower Mohawk Village, Schoharie, Oquaga (Onoquaga, Aughquago, Aquago, Onoquoaga), and Chugnut assembled at Johnson Hall for meeting about Delaware and Shawnee hostilities.
Source:	THE PAPERS OF SIR WILLIAM JOHNSON. ED. BY JAMES SULLIVAN, ET AL. ALBANY: STATE UNIVERSITY OF NEW YORK, 14 VOLS., 1921-1965, 10: 0891-0900.
Comment:	

Date:	1763,10,06
Description:	Transfer of lots within Lawyer's Patent from Johannes Lawyer and others to Jacob Borst, Jr. and to William Bornheyer.
Source:	N.Y.STATE ARCHIVES, ALBANY, N.Y. DEEDS, SERIES NO. A0453, BOOK 17, P. 150.
Comment:	Recorded by the N.Y. Provincial Secretary October 28, 1765.

Date: 1763,10,06°
Description: Map of a patent granted August 14, 1761 to Johannes Lawyer, Jr. and others. Map made October 6, 1763; made over again November 11, 1786 by Johannes Lawyer, Jr. for his own use.
Source: SEE 1786,11,11.
Comment:

Date: 1763,10,07°
Description: Proclamation of King of England about acquisition of land from Indians in the English colonies in North America.
Source: SEE 1766,10,03; 1768,04,29.
Comment:

Date: 1763,11,05
Description: Deed granting a lot in the Hardenbergh Patent to David Brown and others.
Source: N.Y. STATE ARCHIVES, ALBANY, N.Y. DEEDS, SERIES NO. A0453, BOOK 16, P 304.
Comment: Recorded by the N.Y. Provincial Secretary November 16, 1763.

Date: 1763,11,07-24
Description: Report of an Indian conference at which Indians of Onoquaga were present. They were thanked on 15 November by William Johnson for their vigilance in preventing attacks by Indian hostiles upon the villages of Cherry Valley, Schoharie, etc.
Source: THE PAPERS OF SIR WILLIAM JOHNSON. ED. BY JAMES SULLIVAN, ET AL. ALBANY: STATE UNIVERSITY OF NEW YORK, 14 VOLS., 1921-1965, 10: 0930-0935.
Comment: Manuscripts of this report are in PUBLIC ARCHIVES OF CANADA, OTTAWA, INDIAN RECORDS, VOL. 7 AND VOL. 9.

Date: 1763,11,18
Description: Enumeration of Indians within the English Northern Department of Indian Affairs. Lists Mohawks as comprising 160 men, being in "Two villages on the Mohawk River, with a few Emigrants at Scohare about 16. miles from Fort Hunter."
Source: DOCUMENTS RELATIVE TO THE COLONIAL HISTORY OF THE STATE OF NEW YORK, 15 VOL. (ALBANY, N.Y.: WEED, PARSONS, AND CO., 1856-87), 7: 582-584.
Comment: Population.

Date: 1763,11,18 [ ]
Description: Draft of a memorandum on the Six Nations and other confederates. It lists the Mohawks as consisting of "Two Villages on the Mohock [Mohawk] River & a few Emigrants at Scohare [Schoharie] 16 m. distant". The total Mohawk population is given as 160.
Source: THE PAPERS OF SIR WILLIAM JOHNSON. ED. BY JAMES SULLIVAN, ET AL. ALBANY: STATE UNIVERSITY OF NEW YORK, 14 VOLS., 1921-1965, 04: 0240-0246.
Comment:

Date: 1763,12,05-22
Description: Journal of Indian conference at Johnson Hall. On 7 December, David of Schoharie arrives with five others. They discuss possiblility of moving from Schoharie should fear of attack from hostile Indians necessitate it. Barent Vrooman (Vroman) is eager to buy their land. On 14 December, a message comes from Euroamerican settlers at Schoharie that Delawares have been in the settlement, have behaved badly, and made threats upon leaving. William Johnson told Indians then at Johnson Hall that no destruction of Schoharie or any other settlement would be tolerated.
Source: THE PAPERS OF SIR WILLIAM JOHNSON. ED. BY JAMES SULLIVAN, ET AL. ALBANY: STATE UNIVERSITY OF NEW YORK, 14 VOLS., 1921-1965, 10: 0957-0972.
Comment: Original copy is in PUBLIC ARCHIVES OF CANADA, OTTAWA, INDIAN RECORDS, VOL. 7.

Date: 1763,12,07
Description: Letter from Lieutenant Governor Cadwallader Colden to William Johnson, sending blank warrants and commissions for officers to command two companies for the defense of Schoharie and Cherry Valley.
Source: THE PAPERS OF SIR WILLIAM JOHNSON. ED. BY JAMES SULLIVAN, ET AL. ALBANY: STATE UNIVERSITY OF NEW YORK, 14 VOLS., 1921-1965, 04: 0263. REFERENCE ONLY. MANUSCRIPT WAS DESTROYED BY FIRE IN 1911.
Comment:

Date: 1763,12,08
Description: Letter from Captain John Duncan at Corrysbush to William Johnson. Mentions road to Schoharie.
Source: THE PAPERS OF SIR WILLIAM JOHNSON. ED. BY JAMES SULLIVAN, ET AL. ALBANY: STATE UNIVERSITY OF NEW YORK, 14 VOLS., 1921-1965, 04: 0266-0267. REFERENCE ONLY. MANUSCRIPT WAS DESTROYED BY FIRE IN 1911.
Comment:

Date: 1763,12,19
Description: Letter from Cadwallader Colden to William Johnson.
Source: THE PAPERS OF SIR WILLIAM JOHNSON. ED. BY JAMES SULLIVAN, ET AL. ALBANY: STATE UNIVERSITY OF NEW YORK, 14 VOLS., 1921-1965, 02: 0956-0957.
Comment:

Date: 1763,12,23
Description: Letter from William Johnson to Major General Gage, among other things characterizing the Assembly's measures for the defense of Schoharie and Cherry Valley.
Source: THE PAPERS OF SIR WILLIAM JOHNSON. ED. BY JAMES SULLIVAN, ET AL. ALBANY: STATE UNIVERSITY OF NEW YORK, 14 VOLS., 1921-1965, 04: 0272--0273. REFERENCE ONLY. MANUSCRIPT WAS DESTROYED BY FIRE IN 1911.
Comment:

Date: 1763,12,25
Description: Samuel Dunlop of Cherry Valley to William Johnson, informing him that the people of Cherry Valley feel deserted. They fear that they will be attacked "and Schoharry's [Schoharie's] being warned off we take to be a bad Omen of our approaching Ruin."
Source: THE PAPERS OF SIR WILLIAM JOHNSON. ED. BY JAMES SULLIVAN, ET AL. ALBANY: STATE UNIVERSITY OF NEW YORK, 14 VOLS., 1921-1965, 10: 0986-0988.
Comment: Manuscript destroyed by fire. Printed in DIARY OF THE SIEGE OF DETROIT, ED. HOUGH, PP. 218-220.

Date: 1764,01,02-31
Description: Journal of Indian Affairs at Johnson Hall. On 29 January, seven Indians of Schoharie meet with William Johnson about land. They have appointed Joseph alias Attrewaghti, a young man, to be their headman. Johnson gives them ammunition, paint, liquor; and orders clothing for women and children.
Source: THE PAPERS OF SIR WILLIAM JOHNSON. ED. BY JAMES SULLIVAN, ET AL. ALBANY: STATE UNIVERSITY OF NEW YORK, 14 VOLS., 1921-1965, 11: 0024-0035.
Comment: Original copy is in PUBLIC ARCHIVES OF CANADA, OTTAWA, INDIAN RECORDS, VOL. 7.

Date: 1764,01,15
Description: Letter from Robert McKean to William Johnson "to say that he has completed his company and to ask that he may be quartered at Schoharey [Schoharie] and the lieutenant governor informed that the company is ready".
Source: THE PAPERS OF SIR WILLIAM JOHNSON. ED. BY JAMES SULLIVAN, ET AL. ALBANY: STATE UNIVERSITY OF NEW YORK, 14 VOLS., 1921-1965, 04: 0297. REFERENCE ONLY. MANUSCRIPT DESTROYED BY FIRE IN 1911.
Comment:

Date: 1764,01,20
Description: Letter from William Johnson to David Vander Heyden. Johnson is sending Captain John Hansen and Company to march to Schoharie "for the protection of that settlement".
Source: THE PAPERS OF SIR WILLIAM JOHNSON. ED. BY JAMES SULLIVAN, ET AL. ALBANY: STATE UNIVERSITY OF NEW YORK, 14 VOLS., 1921-1965, 04: 0301.
Comment:

Date: 1764,01,27
Description: Letter from William Johnson to Cadwallader Colden. Johnson sends the muster rolls of two companies sent to Schoharie and Cherry Valley to protect settlements.
Source: THE PAPERS OF SIR WILLIAM JOHNSON. ED. BY JAMES SULLIVAN, ET AL. ALBANY: STATE UNIVERSITY OF NEW YORK, 14 VOLS., 1921-1965, 04: 0305-0307.
Comment:

Date: 1764,02,01
Description: John R. Hansen to William Johnson, about mustering of militia at Schoharie. Hansen writes, "there's no Possibility of getting any Snow Shoes, at this Place, if they shou'd be wanted."
Source: THE PAPERS OF SIR WILLIAM JOHNSON. ED. BY JAMES SULLIVAN, ET AL. ALBANY: STATE UNIVERSITY OF NEW YORK, 14 VOLS., 1921-1965, 11: 0035.
Comment: Printed in DIARY OF THE SEIGE OF DETROIT, ED. HOUGH. The original was destroyed in the N.Y. State Library fire in 1911.

Date: 1764,02,01-04
Description: Report of an Indian Conference at which eighty-four Indians of Onoquaga (Oquaga, Onoquoaga, Aquago, Aughquago) and their chiefs are present. Adam, the speaker, petitions to have a fort built at Onoquaga for the protection of the Indians there, and requests that some men from Schoharie and Cherry Valley be posted there "to cover our old People, and Children whilst our Young Men are against our Enemies." Adam points out that Onoquaga serves as a barrier should the Enemy (Delawares, Senecas, Mingoes from Kanisteo) try to approach Schoharie, Cherry Valley, or the Mohawk River Valley.
Source: THE PAPERS OF SIR WILLIAM JOHNSON. ED. BY JAMES SULLIVAN, ET AL. ALBANY: STATE UNIVERSITY OF NEW YORK, 14 VOLS., 1921-1965, 11: 0037-0041.
Comment:

Date: 1764,02,21
Description: Henry Montour, William Hare, John Johnston to William Johnson, advising him to be on guard at every part of the Mohawk River Valley, the Schoharie River Valley, Stone Arabia, and Cherry Valley.
Source: THE PAPERS OF SIR WILLIAM JOHNSON. ED. BY JAMES SULLIVAN, ET AL. ALBANY: STATE UNIVERSITY OF NEW YORK, 14 VOLS., 1921-1965, 11: 0074-0076.
Comment: Manuscript destroyed by fire. Printed in DIARY OF THE SIEGE OF DETROIT, ED. HOUGH, PP. 247-249. Montour, Hare, and Johnston are leading a contingent against Delawares/Senecas/Mingoes of the village of Kanisteo.

Date: 1764,02,27 [ ]
Description: Letter from David Van Der Heyden to William Johnson, February 27, [1764], correcting an error in a previous account and sending a new account involving the Indians of Schoharie.
Source: THE PAPERS OF SIR WILLIAM JOHNSON. ED. BY JAMES SULLIVAN, ET AL. ALBANY: STATE UNIVERSITY OF NEW YORK, 14 VOLS., 1921-1965, 04: 0342. REFERENCE ONLY. MANUSCRIPT WAS DESTROYED BY FIRE IN 1911.
Comment:

Date: 1764,02,28
Description: Henry Montour, William Hare, John Johnston to William Johnson, informing him about part of the success of their expedition against Kanisteo. They are sending prisoners to William Johnson. They note that if they had failed, some parts of the Mohawk and Schoharie River Valleys and Cherry Valley would have suffered.
Source: THE PAPERS OF SIR WILLIAM JOHNSON. ED. BY JAMES SULLIVAN, ET AL. ALBANY: STATE UNIVERSITY OF NEW YORK, 14 VOLS., 1921-1965, 11: 0086.
Comment:

Date: 1764,03,05-23
Description: Journal of Indian Affairs at Johnson Hall. On 17 March, William Johnson clothes and arms twelve Mohickanders (Mahicans, Mahickanders) of Schoharie and Catskill for war. They are to join the Oneidas.
Source: THE PAPERS OF SIR WILLIAM JOHNSON. ED. BY JAMES SULLIVAN, ET AL. ALBANY: STATE UNIVERSITY OF NEW YORK, 14 VOLS., 1921-1965, 11: 0105-0115.
Comment: Original copy is in PUBLIC ARCHIVES OF CANADA, OTTAWA, INDIAN RECORDS, VOL. 7.

Date: 1764,03,10
Description: Letter from Thomas Ackeson of Schoharie to William Johnson "about men who joined Captain Honsan's [Hansen's(?)] company; Indians of Schohary [Schoharie] who will go to war, and supplies for Indians who are on the war path".
Source: THE PAPERS OF SIR WILLIAM JOHNSON. ED. BY JAMES SULLIVAN, ET AL. ALBANY: STATE UNIVERSITY OF NEW YORK, 14 VOLS., 1921-1965, 04: 0363. REFERENCE ONLY. MANUSCRIPT DESTROYED BY FIRE IN 1911.
Comment:

Date: 1764,03,12
Description: Letter from Joseyas (Josias) Swart of Schoharie to William Johnson, "writing in favor of two Indians sent as prisoners to Johnson by Captain Hanson [Hansen]".
Source: THE PAPERS OF SIR WILLIAM JOHNSON. ED. BY JAMES SULLIVAN, ET AL. ALBANY: STATE UNIVERSITY OF NEW YORK, 14 VOLS., 1921-1965, 04: 0363-0364. REFERENCE ONLY. MANUSCRIPT WAS DESTROYED BY FIRE IN 1911.
Comment:

Date: 1764,04,22
Description: Letter from Cadwallader Colden to William Johnson. Mentions act providing one captain, two lieutenants, and 47 privates from Albany, Cherry Valley and Schoharie (from May 1 - August 1) for scouting frontiers.
Source: THE PAPERS OF SIR WILLIAM JOHNSON. ED. BY JAMES SULLIVAN, ET AL. ALBANY: STATE UNIVERSITY OF NEW YORK, 14 VOLS., 1921-1965, 04: 0400-0401.
Comment:

Date: 1764,04,24-05,11 [ ]
Description: Contemporary copy of Journal of Indian Affairs. Chiefs from Oghquago (Oquaga) and Schohare (Schoharie) meet with William Johnson at Johnson Hall on April 27th.
Source: THE PAPERS OF SIR WILLIAM JOHNSON. ED. BY JAMES SULLIVAN, ET AL. ALBANY: STATE UNIVERSITY OF NEW YORK, 14 VOLS., 1921-1965, 11: 0180-0189.
Comment: Original is in the PUBLIC ARCHIVES OF CANADA, OTTOWA, INDIAN RECORDS, VOL. 7.

Date: 1764,06,06
Description: Indian deed, dated 6 June 1764, conveying land west of Schoharie on the northwest side of the Borst-Keyser Tract, and on the east side of Cobleskill (Ostgarrege, Oscalleghe, Oscallaghe, Oschaleghe, Otsgarege, Otsgarage, Aschalege).
Source: N.Y. STATE ARCHIVES, ALBANY, INDIAN TREATIES & DEEDS, SERIES #448.
Comment:

Date: 1764,06,06°
Description: Extract of Indian deed, dated 6 June 1764, to Lawyer, Borst (Burst), Foster, and Hiets (Heints), conveying land west of Schoharie. Extract was made 23 May 177[ ].
Source: SEE 177[ ],05,23
Comment: SEE 1764,06,06 for reference to the complete deed. SEE ALSO 1753,07,20; 1753,07,28.

Date: 1764,07,00
Description: Numbers of Indians at conference at Niagara. Fourteen Indians of Schoharie are reported to be present.
Source: THE PAPERS OF SIR WILLIAM JOHNSON. ED. BY JAMES SULLIVAN, ET AL. ALBANY: STATE UNIVERSITY OF NEW YORK, 14 VOLS., 1921-1965, 11: 0276.
Comment: Printed in "JOURNALS OF CAPT. JOHN MONTRESSOR," in N.Y. HISTORICAL SOCIETY COLLECTIONS,1881, P. 275.

Date: 1765,02,27
Description: New York Council Minutes. Patents granted to Jacob Starnberger, George Zimmer, Hendrick Weaver, Jacob Zimmer, John Joost Becker, William Zimmer, John Schever, and Petrus Zimmer for land adjoining Schoharie patent.
Source: N.Y.STATE ARCHIVES, ALBANY, N.Y.COUNCIL MINUTES, VOL. 29, P. 064.
Comment:

Date: 1765,09,17
Description: Return of survey of Jacob Starnberger, George Zimmer, and others of 8,000 acres of land on the east side of Schoharie granted to them by "the Native Indian Proprietors" 6 June 1754. Map is included.
Source: N.Y.STATE ARCHIVES, ALBANY, N.Y.COL.MSS, INDORSED LAND PAPERS, 1643-1803, SERIES NO. A0272, DEPARTMENT OF STATE, APPLICATIONS FOR LAND GRANTS, VOL. 19, P. 153.
Comment: SEE 1753,06,06; 1754,06,06; 1761,10,02; 1766,07,07; 1769,09,20; 1769,09,30. N.B. Although, the document is dated 17 Sept 1766, the endorsement gives the date as 17 Sept 1765. It is found in the N.Y.STATE ARCHIVES, ALBANY, N.Y.COL.MSS, INDORSED LAND PAPERS, 1643-1803, SERIES NO. A0272, DEPARTMENT OF STATE, APPLICATIONS FOR LAND GRANTS, in chronological order under 17 Sept 1765.

Date: 1765,09,22
Description: Draft of a letter from the land office to the surveyor general about the laying out of lands. The claim of Robert Lettice Hooper and associates, under an Indian deed to Sir William Johnson is rejected, and their claim for 2,000 acres of land, under the military right of John Morris is granted.
Source: N.Y.STATE ARCHIVES, ALBANY, N.Y.COL.MSS, INDORSED LAND PAPERS, 1643-1803, SERIES NO. A0272, DEPARTMENT OF STATE, APPLICATIONS FOR LAND GRANTS, VOL. 39, P. 093.
Comment: N.B. Reference to military right (bounty lands).

Date: 1765,09,30
Description: Letter from John Duncan to William Johnson "about a certificate of land near Schohary [Schoharie], sold by the Indians", etc.
Source: THE PAPERS OF SIR WILLIAM JOHNSON. ED. BY JAMES SULLIVAN, ET AL. ALBANY: STATE UNIVERSITY OF NEW YORK, 14 VOLS., 1921-1965, 04: 0851. REFERENCE ONLY. DOCUMENT WAS DESTROYED BY FIRE IN 1911.
Comment:

Date: 1765,10,11
Description: Patent for 20,00 acres of land, some of which is in the Schoharie River Valley. Known as Young's Patent.
Source: N.Y.STATE ARCHIVES, ALBANY, N.Y. LETTERS PATENT, 1664-1780, SERIES NO. 12590, BOOK 14, P. 120.
Comment:

Date: 1766,00,00 [ ]
Description: Caveats by J. Duane about land.
Source: N.Y.STATE ARCHIVES, ALBANY, N.Y.COL.MSS, INDORSED LAND PAPERS, 1643-1803, SERIES NO. A0272, DEPARTMENT OF STATE, APPLICATIONS FOR LAND GRANTS, VOL. 21, P. 095.
Comment: SEE 1766,05,17. CALENDAR OF LAND PAPERS notes that the land is in Duanesburgh.

Date: 1766,04,30 [ ]°
Description: Account of the disbursement of funds for "sundrys" pertaining to Schoharie, in Extracts from the Account Book of John Butler.
Source: SEE 1761,09,21-1771,10,13.
Comment: There are no details illuminating what the "sundrys" were, or what they were for.

Date: 1766,05,17
Description: Petition of James Duane and others to purchase land north of Schoharie from the Indians.
Source: N.Y.STATE ARCHIVES, ALBANY, N.Y.COL.MSS, INDORSED LAND PAPERS, 1643-1803, SERIES NO. A0272, DEPARTMENT OF STATE, APPLICATIONS FOR LAND GRANTS, VOL. 20, P. 169, 170.
Comment: CALENDAR OF LAND PAPERS notes that the land is in Duanesburgh.

Date: 1766,05,19
Description: Indian Proceedings at Johnson Hall. It is reported that on 19 September, eighty Oneidas arrived at Johnson Hall. After waiting fourteen days for N.Y. Governor Henry Moore's arrival, they ceded land near Oriskany. "The Mohawks and Conjohares [Canajoharies] did at the same time dispose of sundry tracts to Scohare [Schoharie] People, and others."
Source: THE PAPERS OF SIR WILLIAM JOHNSON. ED. BY JAMES SULLIVAN, ET AL. ALBANY: STATE UNIVERSITY OF NEW YORK, 14 VOLS., 1921-1965, 12: 0183-0185.
Comment: Manuscript is in PUBLIC ARCHIVES OF CANADA, OTTAWA, INDIAN RECORDS, VOL. 7.

Date: 1766,05,24-27
Description: Indian Proceedings at Johnson Hall. William Johnson is given a mine as a gift from "Old Laurence, chief of Schohare[sic] aged 78 Years." Laurence (Lawrence) is accompanied by his "Wife, and Nephew named Nicolas (Nicholas) son of Catherine chief Woman of Schohare."
Source: THE PAPERS OF SIR WILLIAM JOHNSON. ED. BY JAMES SULLIVAN, ET AL. ALBANY: STATE UNIVERSITY OF NEW YORK, 14 VOLS., 1921-1965, 12: 0094-0097.
Comment: Original copy is in PUBLIC ARCHIVES OF CANADA, OTTAWA, INDIAN RECORDS, VOL. 7. N.B. Possible matrilineal link, i.e., Laurence, a chief of Schoharie, comes with his nephew who is son of Catherine a chief woman of Schoharie. It is likely that Catherine is Laurence's sister.

Date: 1766,06,14
Description: Letter from Johannes Lawyer and Jacob Zimmer to William Johnson, about a petition for land in Schoharie.
Source: SIR WILLIAM JOHNSON. ED. BY JAMES SULLIVAN, ET AL. ALBANY: STATE UNIVERSITY OF NEW YORK, 14 VOLS., 1921-1965, 05: 0265-0266.
Comment: SEE 1766,10,03 (5); 1768,08,02; 1768,12,01.

Date: 1766,07,02°
Description: Petition of Josiah Banks for land adjacent to Schoharie.
Source: SEE 1766,08,20.
Comment:

Date: 1766,07,07
Description: Report about interference with a tract held by Starnberger and others.
Source: N.Y.STATE ARCHIVES, ALBANY, N.Y.COL.MSS, INDORSED LAND PAPERS, 1643-1803, SERIES NO. A0272, DEPARTMENT OF STATE, APPLICATIONS FOR LAND GRANTS, VOL. 20, P. 176.
Comment: SEE 1753,06,06; 1754,06,06; 1765,09,17; 1766,07,07; 1769,09,20; 1769,09,30.

Date: 1766,08,13-30
Description: Report of an Indian Congress. On 30 August, it is reported that [Johannes] Lawyer arrives at the conference with three others from "Scohare [Schoharie] to purchase about 3 M Acres of Woodland there from the Mohawks, but could not agree about the Price, and departed." The Indians expected that the purchasers would pay them more than Lawyer and his associates apparently were prepared to do.
Source: THE PAPERS OF SIR WILLIAM JOHNSON. ED. BY JAMES SULLIVAN, ET AL. ALBANY: STATE UNIVERSITY OF NEW YORK, 14 VOLS., 1921-1965, 12: 0167-0170.
Comment: Manuscript is in PUBLIC ARCHIVES OF CANADA, OTTAWA, INDIAN RECORDS, VOL. 7.

Date: 1766,08,20
Description: Petition of Josiah Banks for land adjacent to Schoharie.
Source: N.Y.STATE ARCHIVES, ALBANY, N.Y.COL.MSS, INDORSED LAND PAPERS, 1643-1803, SERIES NO. A0272, DEPARTMENT OF STATE, APPLICATIONS FOR LAND GRANTS, VOL. 21, P. 125.
Comment:

Date: 1766,08,25
Description: Caveat of J. Duane about land.
Source: N.Y.STATE ARCHIVES, ALBANY, N.Y.COL.MSS, INDORSED LAND PAPERS, 1643-1803, SERIES NO. A0272, DEPARTMENT OF STATE, APPLICATIONS FOR LAND GRANTS, VOL. 22, P. 015.
Comment: SEE 1766,05,17. CALENDAR OF LAND PAPERS notes that the land is in Duanesburgh.

Date: 1766,09,05-19 [ ]
Description: Contemporary copy of Indian Proceedings at Johnson Hall. Iroquois of the Lower Mohawk Village and of Canajoharie "dispose of sundry tracts to Schohare [Schoharie] people".
Source: THE PAPERS OF SIR WILLIAM JOHNSON. ED. BY JAMES SULLIVAN, ET AL. ALBANY: STATE UNIVERSITY OF NEW YORK, 14 VOLS., 1921-1965, 12: 0183-0185.
Comment: Original is in PUBLIC ARCHIVES OF CANADA, OTTAWA, INDIAN RECORDS, VOL. 7.

Date: 1766,09,22
Description: William Johnson to Goldsbrow Banyar. Johnson comments on Indian cession of land at Schoharie.
Source: THE PAPERS OF SIR WILLIAM JOHNSON. ED. BY JAMES SULLIVAN, ET AL. ALBANY: STATE UNIVERSITY OF NEW YORK, 14 VOLS., 1921-1965, 12: 0191-0192.
Comment: Original is in N.Y. HISTORICAL SOCIETY, NEW YORK, N.Y., BANYAR PAPERS.

Date: 1766,09,26
Description: Quitclaim deed to Hendrick Kniskern (Knisker; Knieskirk, Kniskorn, Knieskerk, Kneiskerk, Kneescarns) by Jost Kniskern of Lots 2, 4, 7, 8 and 10 at Kniskerns dorp in Schoharry (Schoharie), all on or near Schoharie Creek or Kill, containing respectively 8 3/4 acres, 10 acres, 8 acres, 9 acres, and one-half acre, more or less. The parties to the agreement are yeomen of Schoharie.
Source: N.Y.STATE LIBRARY, ALBANY, MANUSCRIPTS, SCHOHARIE COUNTY, PATENTEES, LAND RECORDS, DW10738.
Comment:

Date: 1766,09,28 [ ]°
Description: Account of the cash paid to Hendrick Wemple for "going Express to Schohary [Schoharie]", in Extracts from the Account Book of John Butler.
Source: SEE 1761,09,21-1771,10,13.
Comment: The document does not disclose the reason for Wemple's trip to Schoharie.

Date: 1766,10,03
Description: Indian deed for 10,000 acres of land from Breakabeen Creek to Stony Creek at Schoharie to be granted to Michael Byrne, France Rupert, Lucas Vedder, and associates.
Source: N.Y. STATE ARCHIVES, ALBANY, INDIAN TREATIES & DEEDS, SERIES #448, VOL. 1. (D246/4).
Comment:

Date: 1766,10,03 (2)
Description: Indian deed for 10,000 acres of land from Breakabeen Creek to Stony Creek at Schoharie to be granted to Michael Byrne, France (Francis) Rupert, Lucas Vedder, and associates.
Source: N.Y.STATE ARCHIVES, ALBANY, N.Y.COL.MSS, INDORSED LAND PAPERS, 1643-1803, SERIES NO. A0272, DEPARTMENT OF STATE, APPLICATIONS FOR LAND GRANTS, VOL. 21, P. 163.
Comment: SEE 1766,10,18; 1767,12,14.

Date: 1766,10,03 (3)
Description: Indian deed to Nicholas Matthias (Matice, Mattice) and Lawrence Lawyer for Schoharie land. The marks of three men of the Mohawk Castle: Aughnoura alias Daniel, "chief of the Turtle Tribe", Tiyorhasara alias Abraham, "chief of the Wolf Tribe", and Canadagaia alias Hans, "chief of the Bear Tribe" are on the deed.
Source: N.Y.STATE ARCHIVES, ALBANY, N.Y.COL.MSS, INDORSED LAND PAPERS, 1643-1803, SERIES NO. A0272, DEPARTMENT OF STATE, APPLICATIONS FOR LAND GRANTS, VOL. 21, P. 164.
Comment: N.B. Receipt to Indians for money/goods paid for the land; clan designations of Indian signers; signature of one of the Indians, Daniel. SEE 1766,10,18; 1767,04,04; 1768,00,00; 1768,08,13; 1768,08,23.

Date:	1766,10,03 (4)
Description:	Indian deed to Prym (Pruyn[?]) for Schoharie land.
Source:	N.Y.STATE ARCHIVES, ALBANY, N.Y.COL.MSS, INDORSED LAND PAPERS, 1643-1803, SERIES NO. A0272, DEPARTMENT OF STATE, APPLICATIONS FOR LAND GRANTS, VOL. 21, P. 165.
Comment:	N.B. Receipt from Indians for money/goods paid for the land. SEE 1785,10,01.

Date:	1766,10,03 (5)
Description:	Indian deed to Johannes Lawyer, Jacob Zimmer, Moses Abbit, Jacob Enter, and others for two tracts of land containing 24,000 acres. The first is north[?] of Schoharie Creek. The second is west of a tract granted to George Clark and others.
Source:	N.Y.STATE ARCHIVES, ALBANY, N.Y.COL.MSS, INDORSED LAND PAPERS, 1643-1803, SERIES NO. A0272, DEPARTMENT OF STATE, APPLICATIONS FOR LAND GRANTS, VOL. 21, P. 166.
Comment:	Signed by three Indians: Daniel, chief of the new Turtle Tribe, Abraham, chief of the new Wolf Tribe, and Hans Chriss(?), chief of the new Bear Tribe. Their marks are on the document. See 1768,08,02; 1785,00,00-1791,00,00; 1794,05,05.

Date:	1766,10,03 (6)
Description:	Indian deed to H. Heegar (Heeger, Heger) and others for land south of the York patent.
Source:	N.Y.STATE ARCHIVES, ALBANY, N.Y.COL.MSS, INDORSED LAND PAPERS, 1643-1803, SERIES NO. A0272, DEPARTMENT OF STATE, APPLICATIONS FOR LAND GRANTS, VOL. 21, P. 167.
Comment:	N.B. Receipt for Indians for money/goods paid for the land. SEE 1768,12,01; 1766, 10,18.

Date:	1766,10,03 (7)
Description:	Indian deed to land at the mouth of Salm Creek (?), running up Schoharie Creek.
Source:	N.Y. STATE ARCHIVES, ALBANY, INDIAN TREATIES & DEEDS, SERIES #448.
Comment:	

Date:	1766,10,03 (8)
Description:	Indian deed to land at Schoharie Creek beginning at the western corner of the York Patent, and running south to the west corner of the Bouck Patent and east across the mountain called Ogshontau(?).
Source:	N.Y. STATE ARCHIVES, ALBANY, INDIAN TREATIES & DEEDS, SERIES #448.
Comment:	

Date:	1766,10,03 (9)
Description:	Indian deed to land on the north side of Schoharie Creek which empties into the large Schoharie Creek (?) near Schoharie.
Source:	N.Y. STATE ARCHIVES, ALBANY, INDIAN TREATIES & DEEDS, SERIES #448.
Comment:	

Date:	1766,10,03°
Description:	Date of purchase from Indians by J.N. Matthias (Matice, Mattice) and others of tract of land on the Schoharie river.
Source:	SEE 1768,06,06.
Comment:	

Date:	1766,10,18
Description:	Petition of Vaughn for land south of the Mohawk River.
Source:	N.Y.STATE ARCHIVES, ALBANY, N.Y.COL.MSS, INDORSED LAND PAPERS, 1643-1803, SERIES NO. A0272, DEPARTMENT OF STATE, APPLICATIONS FOR LAND GRANTS, VOL. 22, P. 010.
Comment:	

Date: **1766,10,18 (2)**
Description: Petition of Byrne, Heeger (Heger, Heegar) and others for land.
Source: N.Y.STATE ARCHIVES, ALBANY, N.Y.COL.MSS, INDORSED LAND PAPERS, 1643-1803, SERIES NO. A0272, DEPARTMENT OF STATE, APPLICATIONS FOR LAND GRANTS, VOL. 12, P. 011, 012.
Comment: SEE 1766,10,03; 1768,12,01.

Date: **1766,10,18 (3)**
Description: Petition of Prim (Pruyn) for land.
Source: N.Y.STATE ARCHIVES, ALBANY, N.Y.COL.MSS, INDORSED LAND PAPERS, 1643-1803, SERIES NO. A0272, DEPARTMENT OF STATE, APPLICATIONS FOR LAND GRANTS, VOL. 22, P. 013.
Comment:

Date: **1766,10,18 (4)**
Description: Petition of Bayard for land.
Source: N.Y.STATE ARCHIVES, ALBANY, N.Y.COL.MSS, INDORSED LAND PAPERS, 1643-1803, SERIES NO. A0272, DEPARTMENT OF STATE, APPLICATIONS FOR LAND GRANTS, VOL. 12, P. 014.
Comment:

Date: **1766,10,18 (5)**
Description: Petition of Johannes Lawyer for land.
Source: N.Y.STATE ARCHIVES, ALBANY, N.Y.COL.MSS, INDORSED LAND PAPERS, 1643-1803, SERIES NO. A0272, DEPARTMENT OF STATE, APPLICATIONS FOR LAND GRANTS, VOL. 22, P. 015.
Comment: SEE 1766,10,03.

Date: **1766,10,18 (6)**
Description: Petition of Matthis (Matice, Mattice) and Lawyer for land.
Source: N.Y.STATE ARCHIVES, ALBANY, N.Y.COL.MSS, INDORSED LAND PAPERS, 1643-1803, SERIES NO. A0272, DEPARTMENT OF STATE, APPLICATIONS FOR LAND GRANTS, VOL. 22, P. 017.
Comment: SEE 1766,10,03; 1767,04,04; 1768,00,00; 1768,08,13; 1768,08,23.

Date: **1766,11,03°**
Description: Date of warrant from N.Y. Provincial Council to Surveyor General by which a parcel of land purchased from Indians at Schoharie was surveyed into two tracts, the first for J.N. Mathias (Matice, Mattice) et al. and the other for L. Lawyer.
Source: SEE 1768,06,06.
Comment:

Date: **1766,11,20**
Description: Return of survey for Brewer. Map included.
Source: N.Y.STATE ARCHIVES, ALBANY, N.Y.COL.MSS, INDORSED LAND PAPERS, 1643-1803, SERIES NO. A0272, DEPARTMENT OF STATE, APPLICATIONS FOR LAND GRANTS, VOL. 22, P. 066.
Comment: CALENDAR OF LAND PAPERS notes that land is in Duanesburgh.

Date: **1766,11,20 (2)**
Description: Return of survey of land for Butler.
Source: N.Y.STATE ARCHIVES, ALBANY, N.Y.COL.MSS, INDORSED LAND PAPERS, 1643-1803, SERIES NO. A0272, DEPARTMENT OF STATE, APPLICATIONS FOR LAND GRANTS, VOL. 22, P. 067.
Comment: CALENDAR OF LAND PAPERS notes that the land is in Duanesburgh.

Date: 1766,12,02 [ ]°
Description: Account of the cost of an express to John Lawyer at Schoharie, in Extracts from the Account Book of John Butler.
Source: SEE 1761,09,21-1771,10,13.
Comment: No note is made in the document about the subject of the express.

Date: 1766,12,27 [ ]
Description: Letter from Peter Vergerau to William Johnson, about land in area near "BreakaBeen [Breakabeen], Schohare [Schoharie], or Cobustkill [Cobleskill]", to be acquired from the Indians.
Source: THE PAPERS OF SIR WILLIAM JOHNSON. ED. BY JAMES SULLIVAN, ET AL. ALBANY: STATE UNIVERSITY OF NEW YORK, 14 VOLS., 1921-1965, 05: 0456-0457.
Comment:

Date: 1766,12,27°
Description: Letter from Peter Vergerau to William Johnson, about land in area near "BreakaBeen [Breakabeen], Schohare [Schoharie], or Cobustkill [Cobleskill]", to be acquired from the Indians.
Source: SEE 1766,12,27.
Comment:

Date: 1767,00,00
Description: Petition of Vergereau for land east and west of Schoharie River.
Source: N.Y.STATE ARCHIVES, ALBANY, N.Y.COL.MSS, INDORSED LAND PAPERS, 1643-1803, SERIES NO. A0272, DEPARTMENT OF STATE, APPLICATIONS FOR LAND GRANTS, VOL. 24, P. 057.
Comment:

Date: 1767,00,00 (2)
Description: Map of three tracts of land.
Source: N.Y.STATE ARCHIVES, ALBANY, N.Y.COL.MSS, INDORSED LAND PAPERS, 1643-1803, SERIES NO. A0272, DEPARTMENT OF STATE, APPLICATIONS FOR LAND GRANTS, VOL. 63, P. 157.
Comment: According to CALENDAR OF LAND PAPERS the land is in present day Conesville, Schoharie County.

Date: 1767,02,02
Description: Petition of David Smith for land.
Source: N.Y.STATE ARCHIVES, ALBANY, N.Y.COL.MSS, INDORSED LAND PAPERS, 1643-1803, SERIES NO. A0272, DEPARTMENT OF STATE, APPLICATIONS FOR LAND GRANTS, VOL. 23, P. 004.
Comment: CALENDAR OF LAND PAPERS notes that land is in town of Sharon.

Date: 1767,03,29
Description: Letter from Sir William Johnson about mistake by Bayard in making purchase of land from Indians.
Source: N.Y.STATE ARCHIVES, ALBANY, N.Y.COL.MSS, INDORSED LAND PAPERS, 1643-1803, SERIES NO. A0272, DEPARTMENT OF STATE, APPLICATIONS FOR LAND GRANTS, VOL. 23, P. 088.
Comment:

Date: 1767,04,04°
Description: Explanation of lands on Schoharie river laid out for J. Nicholas Mathias (Matice, Mattice) and Lawrence Lawyer.
Source: SEE 1768,00,00.
Comment: SEE 1766,10,03; 1766,10,18; 1767,04,04; 1768,08,13; 1768,08,23.

Date: 1767,04,08
Description: William Johnson to Goldbrow Banyar, about division of a tract of land purchased by Johannes Lawyer and others in October 1766. Johnson writes that the Indians are determined to see that the land is divided according to the terms of their cession. They "will not dispose of a foot more of land as they Say, to any Man."
Source: THE PAPERS OF SIR WILLIAM JOHNSON. ED. BY JAMES SULLIVAN, ET AL. ALBANY: STATE UNIVERSITY OF NEW YORK, 14 VOLS., 1921-1965, 12: 0297-0298.
Comment: Manuscript is in N.Y. HISTORICAL SOCIETY, NEW YORK, N.Y. BANYAR PAPERS.

Date: 1767,04,09
Description: Speech of the Mohawk and Schoharie Indians, about land sold by them last fall to Hannis Lawyer and his associates. They hear that Lawyer and his associates are to have only half of it, and do not understand why this is so.
Source: THE DOCUMENTARY HISTORY OF THE STATE OF NEW YORK, ED. E.B. O'CALLAGHAN, (ALBANY; WEED, PARSONS, AND CO., CHARLES VAN BENTHUYSEN, 1849-1851), QUARTO ED., 3: 847-848.
Comment:

Date: 1767,04,24 [ ]°
Description: Account of the disbursement of funds for "sundrys agoing to Schohary with Capt Fry & yeats [Yates]" and for "Sundrys aComing [sic] from Schohary [Schoharie]", in Extracts from the Account Book of John Butler.
Source: SEE 1761,09,21-1771,10,13.
Comment: There are no details illuminating what the "sundrys" were, or what they were for.

Date: 1767,04,27
Description: William Johnson to Goldsbrow Banyar, about the patent of Johannes Lawyer and others.
Source: THE PAPERS OF SIR WILLIAM JOHNSON. ED. BY JAMES SULLIVAN, ET AL. ALBANY: STATE UNIVERSITY OF NEW YORK, 14 VOLS., 1921-1965, 12: 0301-0302.
Comment: Original is in N.Y. HISTORICAL SOCIETY, NEW YORK, N.Y., BANYAR PAPERS. SEE 1768,11,13; 1768,11,24; 1769,01,05; 1769,01,29; 1769,02,10; 1774,03,24.

Date: 1767,05,11
Description: Letter from Thomas Gage to William Johnson about a land dispute between James Duane and the people of Schoharie.
Source: THE PAPERS OF SIR WILLIAM JOHNSON. ED. BY JAMES SULLIVAN, ET AL. ALBANY: STATE UNIVERSITY OF NEW YORK, 14 VOLS., 1921-1965, 05: 547.
Comment:

Date: 1767,06,00
Description: Survey map of the land of Livingston, Debo_?_s, and Young on Cobleskill Creek.
Source: MIX'S CATALOG OF MAPS AND SURVEYS IN OFFFICES OF THE SECRETARY OF STATE, STATE ENGINEER AND SURVEYOR AND COMPTROLLER AND N.Y. STATE LIBRARY, 1859, REFERENCES THIS MAP, LISTING IT AS BEING IN THE OFFICES OF GENERAL SERVICES, NEW YORK STATE, MAP #100.
Comment: SEE n.d.

Date: 1767,07,06
Description: Petition of Volkert Douw and others for land south of the Mohawk river.
Source: N.Y.STATE ARCHIVES, ALBANY, N.Y.COL.MSS, INDORSED LAND PAPERS, 1643-1803, SERIES NO. A0272, DEPARTMENT OF STATE, APPLICATIONS FOR LAND GRANTS, VOL. 23, P. 162.
Comment:

Date: 1767,07,28
Description: William Johnson to Goldsbrow Banyar, asking Banyar to let him know about a patent for the "Tract of Byrn's at Schohare [sic]."
Source: THE PAPERS OF SIR WILLIAM JOHNSON. ED. BY JAMES SULLIVAN, ET AL. ALBANY: STATE UNIVERSITY OF NEW YORK, 14 VOLS., 1921-1965, 12: 0343-0344
Comment: Original is in N.Y. HISTORICAL SOCIETY, NEW YORK, N.Y., BANYAR PAPERS.

Date: 1767,08,29
Description: Return of survey of land on the west side of Schoharie for Pruym (Pruyn). Map included.
Source: N.Y.STATE ARCHIVES, ALBANY, N.Y.COL.MSS, INDORSED LAND PAPERS, 1643-1803, SERIES NO. A0272, DEPARTMENT OF STATE, APPLICATIONS FOR LAND GRANTS, VOL. 24, P. 020.
Comment: 1766,10,03; 1766,10,18; 1785,10,01.

Date: 1767,12,14
Description: Return of survey for Byrne and others of land at Breakabeen and Stoney (Stony) Creek.
Source: N.Y.STATE ARCHIVES, ALBANY, N.Y.COL.MSS, INDORSED LAND PAPERS, 1643-1803, SERIES NO. A0272, DEPARTMENT OF STATE, APPLICATIONS FOR LAND GRANTS, VOL. 24, P. 048.
Comment: SEE 1766,10,03.

Date: 1768,00,00
Description: Map and explanation of the lands laid out for Nicholas Mathias (Matice, Mattice) and Lawrence Lawyer on Schoharie river to the south of the land called Huntersfield formerly granted to Myndert Schuyler, Peter Van Brugh, and others, 4 Apr 1767. Attested to, by John Glen, 23 Aug 1768.
Source: N.Y.STATE ARCHIVES, ALBANY, N.Y.COL.MSS, INDORSED LAND PAPERS, 1643-1803, SERIES NO. A0272, DEPARTMENT OF STATE, APPLICATIONS FOR LAND GRANTS, VOL. 24, P. 133.
Comment: Map shows land on east side of the Schoharie reserved to Indians. SEE 1766,10,03; 1766,10,18; 1767,04,04; 1768,08,13; 1768,08,23.

Date: 1768,00,00 [ ]
Description: Map of the Byrne Patent.
Source: MIX'S CATALOG OF MAPS AND SURVEYS IN OFFFICES OF THE SECRETARY OF STATE, STATE ENGINEER AND SURVEYOR AND COMPTROLLER AND N.Y. STATE LIBRARY, 1859, REFERENCES THIS MAP, LISTING IT AS BEING IN THE OFFICES OF THE N.Y. STATE DEPARTMENT OF TAXATION & FINANCE, MAP #261.
Comment: SEE 1768,03,25.

Date: 1768,01,09
Description: Sir Henry Moore to William Johnson, about proposed reorganization of militia, the proposed partition of a tract of land north of the Hudson, and proceedings concerning the Schoharie tract.
Source: THE PAPERS OF SIR WILLIAM JOHNSON. ED. BY JAMES SULLIVAN, ET AL. ALBANY: STATE UNIVERSITY OF NEW YORK, 14 VOLS., 1921-1965, 06: 0075. Noted only; document is not printed in THE PAPERS OF SIR WILLIAM JOHNSON. ED. BY JAMES SULLIVAN, ET AL. ALBANY: STATE UNIVERSITY OF NEW YORK, 14 VOLS., 1921-1965,. It was destroyed by fire.
Comment:

Date: 1768,01,21
Description: List of the associates of Byrn (Byrne) on patent for land at Schoharie.
Source: N.Y.STATE ARCHIVES, ALBANY, N.Y.COL.MSS, INDORSED LAND PAPERS, 1643-1803, SERIES NO. A0272, DEPARTMENT OF STATE, APPLICATIONS FOR LAND GRANTS, VOL. 24, P. 069.
Comment:

Date: 1768,01,22
Description: William Johnson to Sir Henry Moore, about "the Scohare [Schohari] tracts and Mr. Ranslaer's [Rensselaer's] caveat, the Michl Byrne tract at Scohare," among other things.
Source: THE PAPERS OF SIR WILLIAM JOHNSON. ED. BY JAMES SULLIVAN, ET AL. ALBANY: STATE UNIVERSITY OF NEW YORK, 14 VOLS., 1921-1965, 06: 0083. Noted only; document is not printed in THE PAPERS OF SIR WILLIAM JOHNSON. ED. BY JAMES SULLIVAN, ET AL. ALBANY: STATE UNIVERSITY OF NEW YORK, 14 VOLS., 1921-1965,. It was destroyed by fire.
Comment:

Date: 1768,02,18
Description: William Johnson to Henry Moore. Refers to Lawyer tract in Schoharie County, New York.
Source: THE PAPERS OF SIR WILLIAM JOHNSON. ED. BY JAMES SULLIVAN, ET AL. ALBANY: STATE UNIVERSITY OF NEW YORK, 14 VOLS., 1921-1965, 06: 0116-0117.
Comment: SEE 1768,11,13; 1768,11,24; 1769,01,05; 1769,01,29; 1769,02,10; 1774,03,24.

Date: 1768,03,02
Description: Petition of Scott and others for 1,000 acres between Schoharie Kill and Kattskill (Catskill) Mountain.
Source: N.Y.STATE ARCHIVES, ALBANY, N.Y.COL.MSS, INDORSED LAND PAPERS, 1643-1803, SERIES NO. A0272, DEPARTMENT OF STATE, APPLICATIONS FOR LAND GRANTS, VOL. 24, P. 086.
Comment: SEE 1768,03,02; 1769,06,29; 1770,01,02; 1771,05,03; 1806,00,00; n.d.

Date: 1768,03,25
Description: Patent to Michael Byrne, France Rupert, Lucas Vedder, Moses Ibbit, Ed Roach, John Michum, John Brackan, Gilbert Tice, Andrew Hanlon, Achilles Preston, Joseph Irwin, Jonathan Runnion, William Philips, Benjamin Phillips, John Frazer, William Frazer, William McIntire, and Daniel Campbell for 18,000 acres of land.
Source: N.Y.STATE ARCHIVES, ALBANY, N.Y. LETTERS PATENT, 1664-1780, SERIES NO. 12590, BOOK 14, P. 259.
Comment: Known as the Byrne Patent or Stony Hill Tract. The land is in mainly in Fulton, Schoharie County. SEE 1768,00,00 [ ].

Date: 1768,03,25 (2)
Description: Fulton Patent Survey done for Michael Byrne, Francis Ruport (Rupert), and Lucas Veder.
Source: MIX'S CATALOG OF MAPS AND SURVEYS IN OFFFICES OF THE SECRETARY OF STATE, STATE ENGINEER AND SURVEYOR AND COMPTROLLER AND N.Y. STATE LIBRARY, 1859, REFERENCES THIS MAP, LISTING IT AS BEING IN THE OFFICE OF THE N.Y. SECRETARY OF STATE, FIELDBOOK # 21, SUBDIVISION D, P. 329.
Comment:

Date: 1768,04,17
Description: Petition of T. Eckerson and others for a patent to land in Schoharie.
Source: N.Y.STATE ARCHIVES, ALBANY, N.Y.COL.MSS, INDORSED LAND PAPERS, 1643-1803, SERIES NO. A0272, DEPARTMENT OF STATE, APPLICATIONS FOR LAND GRANTS, VOL. 24, P. 111, 112.
Comment: SEE 1768,07,16; 1768,08,11; 1770,03,00.

Date: 1768,04,29
Description: Petition of William Smith, late Drummer in the third Battalion of the King of England's Sixtieth Regiment of Foot, for land east of Schoharie river. Refers to Proclamation of 7 Oct 1763.
Source: N.Y.STATE ARCHIVES, ALBANY, N.Y.COL.MSS, INDORSED LAND PAPERS, 1643-1803, SERIES NO. A0272, DEPARTMENT OF STATE, APPLICATIONS FOR LAND GRANTS, VOL. 24, P. 120.
Comment: SEE 1768,11,08. Bounty land.

Date: 1768,06,06
Description: Petition of Johan Nicholas Matthias (Matice, Mattice), Johan Nicholas Matthias, Jr., and Volkert P. Douw for a grant of 1,457 acres of land at the Schoharie river. Boundaries are described. Granted 21 Nov 1768.
Source: N.Y.STATE ARCHIVES, ALBANY, N.Y.COL.MSS, INDORSED LAND PAPERS, 1643-1803, SERIES NO. A0272, DEPARTMENT OF STATE, APPLICATIONS FOR LAND GRANTS, VOL. 24, P. 132.
Comment:

Date: 1768,06,08-28
Description: Report of an Indian Congress. On 10 June, it was noted that "Sale was made of one thousand Acres at Schohare, to Vroman (Vrooman), in the presence of his Excellency [Sir Henry Moore]" (THE PAPERS OF SIR WILLIAM JOHNSON. ED. BY JAMES SULLIVAN, ET AL. ALBANY: STATE UNIVERSITY OF NEW YORK, 14 VOLS., 1921-1965, 12: 0538).
Source: THE PAPERS OF SIR WILLIAM JOHNSON. ED. BY JAMES SULLIVAN, ET AL. ALBANY: STATE UNIVERSITY OF NEW YORK, 14 VOLS., 1921-1965, 12: 0529-0543.
Comment: Manuscript is in PUBLIC ARCHIVES OF CANADA, OTTAWA, INDIAN RECORDS, VOL. 8.

Date: 1768,06,10
Description: Deed from Abraham alias Teahansera (Tiyahasara, Tiyahassary, Tyrohannea[?], Tiyorhasara), Hans (Hance) alias Canadajaya (Canadagaia, Candagaie, Kanchdegawa), and Hendrick alias Tiendaghe (Tiendega, Tiendaga, Teyendacha) to Adam Vrooman (Vroman) and others for 1,000 acres of land on the west side of Schoharie river, on the north side of Stony (Stoney) creek, adjacent to land purchased by Thomas Eakeson (Eckerson).
Source: N.Y.STATE ARCHIVES, ALBANY, N.Y.COL.MSS, INDORSED LAND PAPERS, 1643-1803, SERIES NO. A0272, DEPARTMENT OF STATE, APPLICATIONS FOR LAND GRANTS, VOL. 24, P. 135.
Comment: Deed is signed and sealed. N.B. Indian marks. SEE 1769,04,17; 1770,03,19.

Date: 1768,06,10 (2)
Description: Indian deed to land on the west side of Schoharie Creek and the north side of Stoney (Stony) Creek.
Source: N.Y. STATE ARCHIVES, ALBANY, INDIAN TREATIES & DEEDS, SERIES #448.
Comment: SEE 1769,04,17.

Date: 1768,06,11
Description: Deed to John Rightmyer (Rightmeyer, Rightmeir). The marks of three Indians of the Mohawk Castle, Abraham alias Tiyahasara (Teahansera, Tyrohannea[?], Tiyorhasara, Tiyahassary), Hans (Hance) alias Canadagaia (Canadajaya, Candagaie, Kanachdegawa), and Hendick alias Tiendega (Tiendaga, Tiendaghe, Teyendacha), are on the deed.
Source: N.Y.STATE ARCHIVES, ALBANY, N.Y.COL.MSS, INDORSED LAND PAPERS, 1643-1803, SERIES NO. A0272, DEPARTMENT OF STATE, APPLICATIONS FOR LAND GRANTS, VOL. 24, P. 134.
Comment: N.B. The signature of Abraham alias Tiyahasara. He writes it in Mohawk, using different orthography from that used by the scribe of the deed.

Date: 1768,06,14°
Description: Deed, signed by Abraham alias Tiyahassary (Tiyahasara, Tyrohannea[?], Tiyorhasara, Teahansera), Hendrick alias Tiendaga (Tiendega, Tiendaghe, Teyendacha), and Hance (Hans) alias Canadagaia (Canadajaya, Candagaie, Kanachdegawa), to John Butler for 1,000 acres of land west of that of Cosby and Clark in Schoharie. Included with return of survey for John Butler of tract of 1,050 acres on Schoharie Kill.
Source: SEE 1769,09,08.
Comment:

Date: 1768,06,21
Description: Confirmation by Jacob Sternberger (Starnberg, Starnbergh) of sale to John Markell (Merckell; Marckell; Mirakle), yeoman, by Lambert Sternberger, April 7, 1761, of Lot 17 in Kniskerns (Kneescarns, Kniskorn, Knieskerk, Knieskirk, Kneiskerk) Town (Knisker Dorp), on the east side of Schoharie Creek, containing about 20 acres.
Source: N.Y.STATE LIBRARY, ALBANY, MANUSCRIPTS, SCHOHARIE COUNTY, PATENTEES, LAND RECORDS, DW10738.
Comment:

Date: 1768,07,01
Description: Return of survey for M. Salsbergh (Salsburg, Salsburgh) of land at Beaver Dam. Map included.
Source: N.Y.STATE ARCHIVES, ALBANY, N.Y.COL.MSS, INDORSED LAND PAPERS, 1643-1803, SERIES NO. A0272, DEPARTMENT OF STATE, APPLICATIONS FOR LAND GRANTS, VOL. 24, P. 139.
Comment: SEE 1770,01,12.

Date: 1768,07,16
Description: Return of survey for T. Eckerson and Cornelius Eckerson of two tracts of land containing 1,780 acres at what is now called Middleburgh. Map included.
Source: N.Y.STATE ARCHIVES, ALBANY, N.Y.COL.MSS, INDORSED LAND PAPERS, 1643-1803, SERIES NO. A0272, DEPARTMENT OF STATE, APPLICATIONS FOR LAND GRANTS, VOL. 24, P. 149.
Comment: SEE 1768,04,17; 1768,08,11; 1770,03,00.

Date: 1768,08,02
Description: Return of survey for Johannes Lawyer, Jacob Zimmer, Mosses (Moses) Ibbit and Jacob Enters and their associates for land "lying and being at Schohary (Schoharie)". Map included.
Source: N.Y.STATE ARCHIVES, ALBANY, N.Y.COL.MSS, INDORSED LAND PAPERS, 1643-1803, SERIES NO. A0272, DEPARTMENT OF STATE, APPLICATIONS FOR LAND GRANTS, VOL. 24, P. 154.
Comment: SEE 1768,12,01; 1768,12,29; 1785,00,00-1791,00,00; 1794,05,05.

Date: 1768,08,04
Description: Petition of Adam Vrooman (Vroman) with Mann, Swart, and Zeelie to buy land on the west side of Schoharie Kill from the Indians.
Source: N.Y.STATE ARCHIVES, ALBANY, N.Y.COL.MSS, INDORSED LAND PAPERS, 1643-1803, SERIES NO. A0272, DEPARTMENT OF STATE, APPLICATIONS FOR LAND GRANTS, VOL. 24, P. 158.
Comment:

Date: 1768,08,05
Description: Petition of Johannes Hanse (Hance) Becker and others for land east of Schoharie Kill.
Source: N.Y.STATE ARCHIVES, ALBANY, N.Y.COL.MSS, INDORSED LAND PAPERS, 1643-1803, SERIES NO. A0272, DEPARTMENT OF STATE, APPLICATIONS FOR LAND GRANTS, VOL. 24, P. 160.
Comment:

Date: 1768,08,08°
Description: Contemporary copy of William Johnson's account against the British Crown from 26 March-14 November 1768. On August 8, 1768, money was disbursed to a Schoharie Indian who lost the use of his leg in the service. On August 12, money was given for burial expenses of the chief and oldest sachem of "Scohwee" (Schoharie).
Source: SEE 1768,11,14.
Comment:

Date: 1768,08,11
Description: Patent to Thomas Eckerson and Cornelius Eckerson for two tracts of land, the first being for 1,680 acres and the second being for 100 acres.
Source: N.Y.STATE ARCHIVES, ALBANY, N.Y. LETTERS PATENT, 1664-1780, SERIES NO. 12590, BOOK 14, P. 283.
Comment: CALENDAR OF LAND PAPERS notes that the land is in Middleburgh. 1768,04,17; 1768,07,16; 1770,03,00.

Date: 1768,08,12°
Description: Contemporary copy of William Johnson's account against the British Crown from 26 March-14 November 1768. On August 8, 1768, money was disbursed to a Schoharie Indian who lost the use of his leg in the service. On August 12, money was given for burial expenses of the chief and oldest sachem of "Scohwee" (Schoharie).
Source: SEE 1768,11,14.
Comment:

Date: 1768,08,13
Description: Affidavit of John R. Bleeker concerning land of Johan Nicholl Mathias (Matice, Mattice) and Lawrence Lawyer on the southeast side of Schoharie river.
Source: N.Y.STATE ARCHIVES, ALBANY, N.Y.COL.MSS, INDORSED LAND PAPERS, 1643-1803, SERIES NO. A0272, DEPARTMENT OF STATE, APPLICATIONS FOR LAND GRANTS, VOL. 25, P. 002.
Comment: SEE 1766,10,03; 1766,10,18; 1767,04,04; 1768,00,00 (Map of land); 1768,08,23.

Date: 1768,08,23°
Description: John Glen attests that map and explanation of lands on Schoharie river laid out for J.N. Mathias (Matice, Mattice) and Lawrence Lawyer are correct.
Source: SEE 1768,00,00.
Comment: SEE 1766,10,03; 1766,10,18; 1767,04,04; 1768,08,13.

Date: 1768,09,09
Description: Petition of Jellis (Jelles) Fonda and others for land at Cobuskill (Cobleskill).
Source: N.Y.STATE ARCHIVES, ALBANY, N.Y.COL.MSS, INDORSED LAND PAPERS, 1643-1803, SERIES NO. A0272, DEPARTMENT OF STATE, APPLICATIONS FOR LAND GRANTS, VOL. 25, P. 019.
Comment:

Date: 1768,09,15-10,30
Description: Report of a Congress at Fort Stanwix. On 2 October, a number of Mohawks and Indians of Schoharie arrived at Fort Stanwix. An enumeration of Indians present on 30 October indicates that there were 36 Indians of Schoharie, 175 Indians of Onoquaga (Oquaga,Onoquoaga, Aquago, Aughquago), etc.
Source: THE PAPERS OF SIR WILLIAM JOHNSON. ED. BY JAMES SULLIVAN, ET AL. ALBANY: STATE UNIVERSITY OF NEW YORK, 14 VOLS., 1921-1965, 12: 0617-0629.
Comment:

Date: 1768,10,10°
Description: The will of Peter Vrooman (Vroman), dated 10 October 1768, mentions land acquired from the Indians, "now in Possession of the Indians..."
Source: SEE 1946,00,00.
Comment: SEE 1768,11,05 for specific wording that refers to land ceded to non-Indians upon which Native rights to occupation and use are retained.

Date: 1768,11,05
Description: Deed, executed at the Treaty of Fort Stanwix between the Six Nations and the English, determining the Boundary Line between English and Indian settlement. The deed states, "That the Lands occupied by the Mohocks [Mohawks] around their villages as well as by any other Nation affected by this our Cession may effectually remain to them and to their Posterity and that any engagements regarding Property which they may now be under may be prosecuted and our present Grants deemed valid on our parts with the several other humble requests contained in our said Speech."
Source: DOCUMENTS RELATIVE TO THE COLONIAL HISTORY OF THE STATE OF NEW YORK, ED. BY E.B. O'CALLAGHAN AND BERTHOLD FERNOW, 15 VOL. (ALBANY, N.Y.: WEED, PARSONS, AND CO., 1856-87), 8: 135-137.
Comment: N.B. Indian settlement at Schoharie was on the English side of the boundary established by the Treaty of Fort Stanwix, but was reserved to Indians settled there under the terms of the statement quoted above. SEE 1772,07,28-30. SEE 1768,11,18 for map of boundary line.

Date: 1768,11,08
Description: Return of survey for William Smith.
Source: N.Y.STATE ARCHIVES, ALBANY, N.Y.COL.MSS, INDORSED LAND PAPERS, 1643-1803, SERIES NO. A0272, DEPARTMENT OF STATE, APPLICATIONS FOR LAND GRANTS, VOL. 25, P. 026.
Comment: CALENDAR OF LAND PAPERS notes that the land is in Broome, Schoharie County. SEE 1768,04,29.

Date: 1768,11,13
Description: Henry Moore to William Johnson, mentioning that Mr. Lawyer has been inquiring twice about the Schoharie patent. Moore writes that he is waiting for Johnson's orders, before acting on the matter.
Source: THE PAPERS OF SIR WILLIAM JOHNSON. ED. BY JAMES SULLIVAN, ET AL. ALBANY: STATE UNIVERSITY OF NEW YORK, 14 VOLS., 1921-1965, 12: 0637-0638.
Comment: Manuscript is in N.Y. PUBLIC LIBRARY, NEW YORK, N.Y. SEE 1768,11,24; 1769,01,05; 1769,01,29; 1769,02,10.

Date: 1768,11,14
Description: Contemporary copy of William Johnson's account against the British Crown from 26 March-14 November 1768. On August 8, 1768, money was disbursed to a Schoharie Indian who lost the use of his leg in the service. On August 12, money was given for burial expenses of the chief and oldest sachem of "Scohwee" (Schoharie).
Source: THE PAPERS OF SIR WILLIAM JOHNSON. ED. BY JAMES SULLIVAN, ET AL. ALBANY: STATE UNIVERSITY OF NEW YORK, 14 VOLS., 1921-1965, 12: 0644-0649.
Comment: Manuscript is in WILLIAM L. CLEMENTS LIBRARY, ANN ARBOR, MICH., GAGE PAPERS, ENCLOSED IN GAGE'S WARRANT TO MORTIER, 6 DECEMBER 1768.

Date: 1768,11,18
Description: Contemporary copy of the map of the frontiers of the Northern Colonies with the boundary line established between Euroamericans and Indians at the Treaty at Fort Stanwix in November 1768.
Source: DOCUMENTS RELATIVE TO THE COLONIAL HISTORY OF THE STATE OF NEW YORK, 15 VOL. (ALBANY, N.Y.: WEED, PARSONS, AND CO., 1856-87), 8: between 136 & 137.
Comment: SEE 1768,11,05.

Date: 1768,11,21°
Description: Parcel of land at Schoharie is divided into two tracts, one for J.N. Matthias (Matice, Mattice) et al., and the other for L. Lawyer.
Source: SEE 1768,06,06.
Comment:

Date: 1768,11,24
Description: William Johnson to Goldsbrow Banyar. Johnson mentions that Mr. Lawyer of "Scohare" (Schoharie) is very anxious to obtain a patent for a tract of 30,000 acres in Schoharie, of which Johnson has a fourth part. Johnson encloses the remainder that he owes for his portion of the tract in this letter to Banyar.
Source: THE PAPERS OF SIR WILLIAM JOHNSON. ED. BY JAMES SULLIVAN, ET AL. ALBANY: STATE UNIVERSITY OF NEW YORK, 14 VOLS., 1921-1965, 12: 0656-0659.
Comment: Manuscript is in N.Y. HISTORICAL SOCIETY, NEW YORK, N.Y., BANYAR PAPERS. SEE 1768,11,13; 1769,01,05; 1769,01,29; 1760,02,10.

Date: 1768,11,24 (2)
Description: An Account of Expenses, including those paid for securing Lawyer's Tract at Schoharie.
Source: THE PAPERS OF SIR WILLIAM JOHNSON. ED. BY JAMES SULLIVAN, ET AL. ALBANY: STATE UNIVERSITY OF NEW YORK, 14 VOLS., 1921-1965, 12: 0659-0660.
Comment: Manuscript is in N.Y. HISTORICAL SOCIETY, NEW YORK, N.Y., BANYAR PAPERS. SEE 1768,11,13; 1769,01,05; 1769,01,29; 1769,02,10.

Date: 1768,12,01
Description: Petition of Johannes Lawyer, Jacob Zimmer, Moses Ibbit, Jacob Enters, and their associates for letters patent.
Source: N.Y.STATE ARCHIVES, ALBANY, N.Y.COL.MSS, INDORSED LAND PAPERS, 1643-1803, SERIES NO. A0272, DEPARTMENT OF STATE, APPLICATIONS FOR LAND GRANTS, VOL. 25, P. 030.
Comment: Their associates are listed as: J. Archer, A. Jeffreys, G. Tice, D. Jecocks, M. Hind, A. Clark, P. Miller, P. Young, P. Wadman(?), J. Irwin, J. Titchet, A. Van Sickler, M. Sopwith, L. Lawyer, H. Sidnigh (Sidney), T. Bowden, C. Markel, E. Bowler, C. Redigh, M. Markel, J. Bauch, Jr., J. Borst, D. Hosack, A. Starnberger, H. Weber, J. Wilkinson, J. Becker, P. Zimmer, G. Hawksford, G. Zimmer, P. Zeely, J. Swart, P. Snyder, Jr. SEE 1768,08,02; 1768,12,29.

Date: 1768,12,01 (2)
Description: Return of survey for Heeger (Heegar, Heger). Map included.
Source: N.Y.STATE ARCHIVES, ALBANY, N.Y.COL.MSS, INDORSED LAND PAPERS, 1643-1803, SERIES NO. A0272, DEPARTMENT OF STATE, APPLICATIONS FOR LAND GRANTS, VOL. 25, P. 031.
Comment: SEE 1766,10,03; 1766,10,18.

Date: 1768,12,01 (3)
Description: Return of survey for N. Mathias (Matice, Mattice)) of land in what is now called Middleburgh. Map included.
Source: N.Y.STATE ARCHIVES, ALBANY, N.Y.COL.MSS, INDORSED LAND PAPERS, 1643-1803, SERIES NO. A0272, DEPARTMENT OF STATE, APPLICATIONS FOR LAND GRANTS, VOL. 25, P. 032.
Comment:

Date: 1768,12,01 (4)
Description: Return of survey for Lawrence Lawyer of land in what is now Middleburgh, east of Schoharie Creek. Map included.
Source: N.Y.STATE ARCHIVES, ALBANY, N.Y.COL.MSS, INDORSED LAND PAPERS, 1643-1803, SERIES NO. A0272, DEPARTMENT OF STATE, APPLICATIONS FOR LAND GRANTS, VOL. 25, P. 033.
Comment:

Date: 1768,12,13
Description: Return of survey for S. Stringer. Map included.
Source: N.Y.STATE ARCHIVES, ALBANY, N.Y.COL.MSS, INDORSED LAND PAPERS, 1643-1803, SERIES NO. A0272, DEPARTMENT OF STATE, APPLICATIONS FOR LAND GRANTS, VOL. 25, P. 043.
Comment: CALENDAR OF LAND PAPERS notes that the land is in Broome, Schoharie County.

Date: 1768,12,13 (2)
Description: Patent for a tract of 200 acres east of Edward Clarke's grant.
Source: N.Y.STATE ARCHIVES, ALBANY, N.Y. MILITARY PATENTS, 1764-1775, SERIES NO. A0447, BOOK 2, P. 349.
Comment: Land is in the town of Fulton (?) or Broome, Schoharie County. Military grant.

Date: 1768,12,29
Description: Patent to Johannes Lawyer, Jacob Zimmer, Jacob Borst (Burst), Johannes Becker, and others for 36,600 acres of land, known as Lawyer and Zimmer's Patent.
Source: N.Y.STATE ARCHIVES, ALBANY, N.Y. LETTERS PATENT, 1664-1780, SERIES NO. 12590, BOOK 14, P. 305.
Comment: SEE 1768,08,02; 1768,12,01. CALENDAR OF LAND PAPERS notes that the land is in Middleburgh, Schoharie County.

Date: 1768,12,29 (2)
Description: Survey map of land of Johannes Lawyer, Jacob Zimmer, and associates.
Source: MIX'S CATALOG OF MAPS AND SURVEYS IN OFFFICES OF THE SECRETARY OF STATE, STATE ENGINEER AND SURVEYOR AND COMPTROLLER AND N.Y. STATE LIBRARY, 1859, REFERENCES THIS MAP, LISTING IT AS BEING IN THE OFFICES OF GENERAL SERVICES, NEW YORK STATE, MAP #58.
Comment:

Date: 1769,00,00
Description: A large, silver ceremonial pipe, with a silver chain attached, is engraved as follows: "To the Mohock Indians from the Nine Partners of the Tract near Schoharie. Granted in 1769".
Source: THE FRONTIERSMEN OF NEW YORK: SHOWING CUSTOMS OF THE INDIANS, VICISSITUDES OF THE PIONEER WHITE SETTLERS, AND BORDER STRIFE IN TWO WARS, BY JEPTHA SIMMS, ALBANY, NY: G.C. RIGGS, 1882-1883, 2 VOLS., 1: 41-43.
Comment: See also THE PICTORIAL FIELDBOOK OF THE WAR OF 1812 BY BENJAMIN LOSSING: A FACSIMILE OF THE 1869 EDITION, WITH A FORWARD BY JOHN T. CUNNINGHAM, (SOMERSWORTH: NEW HAMPSHIRE PUBLISHING COMPANY, 1976, ORIGINAL PUBLISHED BY HARPER AND BROTHERS IN 1868), P. 422. See 1769,02,08°; 1769,02,08-09. "Nine Partners" most commonly refers to the Great Nine Partners, Caleb Heathcoate and others, who acquired the Great Nine Partners Tract (1697) and the Little Nine Partners, Sampson Broughton and others, who acquired the Little Nine Partners Tract (1706), both in what is now Dutchess County, New York. It is unclear to whom it refers here.

Date: 1769,00,00 [ ]
Description: Map of the Stone Heap or John Bowen's Patent.
Source: MIX'S CATALOG OF MAPS AND SURVEYS IN OFFFICES OF THE SECRETARY OF STATE, STATE ENGINEER AND SURVEYOR AND COMPTROLLER AND N.Y. STATE LIBRARY, 1859, REFERENCES THIS MAP, LISTING IT AS BEING IN THE OFFICES OF THE N.Y. STATE DEPARTMENT OF TAXATION & FINANCE, MAP #38.
Comment: SEE 1769,02,08; n.d.; 1819,00,00;

Date: 1769,00,00 [ ] (2)
Description: Map of the Blenheim Patent.
Source: MIX'S CATALOG OF MAPS AND SURVEYS IN OFFFICES OF THE SECRETARY OF STATE, STATE ENGINEER AND SURVEYOR AND COMPTROLLER AND N.Y. STATE LIBRARY, 1859, REFERENCES THIS MAP, LISTING IT AS BEING IN THE OFFICES OF THE N.Y. STATE DEPARTMENT OF TAXATION & FINANCE, MAP #240.
Comment: Copy of one in possession of John Taylor. SEE 1769,11,28.

Date: 1769,00,00 [ ]°
Description: William Cockburn's account against Jelles Fonda, including charges for surveys. Two items on the account are for surveying land in Schoharie in 1769: for Joseph Bowen, land between Canajoharie and Schoharie on the west side of Schoharie Kill, and for Sheffer, Bouch, and Becker, land along the Schoharie River. Another item is for a resurvey of the old patent in 1770.
Source: SEE 1770,11,15.
Comment:

Date: 1769,01,05
Description: William Johnson to Goldsbrow Banyar. Johnson writes that he has learned from Sir Henry Moore that initial calculations about fees and amount of land for Lawyer's Patent at Schoharie were wrong. William Johnson owes additional money for his share of the land.
Source: THE PAPERS OF SIR WILLIAM JOHNSON. ED. BY JAMES SULLIVAN, ET AL. ALBANY: STATE UNIVERSITY OF NEW YORK, 14 VOLS., 1921-1965, 12: 0684-0686.
Comment: Manuscript in N.Y. HISTORICAL SOCIETY, NEW YORK, N.Y., BANYAR PAPERS. SEE 1768,11,13; 1768,11,24; 1769,01,29; 1769,02,10.

Date: 1769,01,20
Description: Patent to Samuel Stringer for a tract of 2,000 acres of land, west of the Manor of Rennsylaerwyck.
Source: N.Y.STATE ARCHIVES, ALBANY, N.Y. MILITARY PATENTS, 1764-1775, SERIES NO. A0447, BOOK 2, 336.
Comment: Military grant.

Date: 1769,01,20 (2)
Description: Patent to Walter McFarlance for 200 acres of land, north of that surveyed for Samuel Stringer.
Source: N.Y.STATE ARCHIVES, ALBANY, N.Y. MILITARY PATENTS, 1764-1775, SERIES NO. A0447, BOOK 2, P. 347.
Comment: Military grant.

Date: 1769,01,29
Description: William Johnson to Goldsrow Banyar. Johnson writes that he hopes that Lawyer's purchase is completed.
Source: THE PAPERS OF SIR WILLIAM JOHNSON. ED. BY JAMES SULLIVAN, ET AL. ALBANY: STATE UNIVERSITY OF NEW YORK, 14 VOLS., 1921-1965, 12: 0692.
Comment: Manuscript in N.Y. HISTORICAL SOCIETY, NEW YORK, N.Y., BANYAR PAPERS. SEE 1768,11,13; 1768,11,24; 1769,01,05; 1769,02,10.

Date: 1769,02,08°
Description: Indian deed dated 8 February 1969. The land ceded begins at "a heap of stones near the Scohare [Schoharie] path in the North of a Tract Surveyed for Lawyer and others and running southerly to the Cobus Kill [Cobleskill]". It then runs north and west along the patent of Fredrick Young and others, "so round by scohare [Schoharie] Creek or the patented Lands to the place of Beginning." It is estimated to be about 20,000 acres.
Source: SEE 1769,02,08-09.
Comment: Deed is from Hendrick alias Teyendacha (Tiendega; Tiendaghe; Tiendaga), Daniel alias Ochnowia (Aughnoura), Hans (Hance) alias Kanachdegawa (Canadagaia; Candagaie; Canadajaya), Johannes Schrine, Abraham alias Tyrohannea(?sp.) (Teahansera;Tyhoohanna; Tiyahasara; Tiyahassary; Tiyorhasara; Tyrohannea[?sp.]), and John alias Saquotohquohse (Saquotohquohese) to John Bowen, Bartholemew Pickle(?), Jacob Shook(?), John Davies, Hugh Crawford, Jeles Funda (Fonda), Michael Byrn (Byrne), Robert Adams, and Gilbert Tice. N.B., signature of Daniel on the deed, and marks of the other Indians. SEE 1769,03,21; 1770,09,15; 1770,11,15; 1771,09,21; 1769,00,00 [ ]; 1819,00,00; n.d. Are Bowen and the others what are referred to as the Nine Partners in 1769,00,00?

Date: 1769,02,08°
Description: Indian deed to land between the patent of Volkt Outhout and others on the west and the patented lands on the north, from there along patented lands to the head of the Delaware River and then bordering the purchase of Harper and others to the northern corner thereof, from there westerly to a branch of the Susquehanna and "round a patent granted to A. Bradt, thence to another patent of A. Bradt at Tewanendadon and along its bounds to the Susquehanna river or patented lands, Thence to the South East corner" of Volkt Outhout's land.
Source: SEE 1769,02,08-09.
Comment: Deed is from Hendick alias T____dacha (Teyendacha; Tiendega; Tiendaghe; Tiendaga), Daniel alias Ochnoura (Aughnoura), Hans (Hance) alias Kanachdegawa (Canadagaia; Candagaie; Canadajaya), Johannes Schrine, Abraham alias Tyhoohanna (Teahansera, Tiyahasara; Tiyahassary; Tiyorhasara; Tyrohannea[?sp.]), and John alias Saquotohquohese (Saquotohquohse) to Colonel John Butler, John Wetherhead (Weatherhead), Stephen Skinner, Alexander McKee, and their associates. Note the signature of Daniel on the deed, and the marks of the other Indians. SEE 1769,03,22.

Date: 1769,02,08-09
Description: Four Indian deeds, executed in the presence of N.Y. Colonial Governor Sir Henry Moore at Johnson Hall.
Source: N.Y.STATE ARCHIVES, ALBANY, N.Y.COL.MSS, INDORSED LAND PAPERS, 1643-1803, SERIES NO. A0272, DEPARTMENT OF STATE, APPLICATIONS FOR LAND GRANTS, VOL. 25, P. 057.
Comment: See 1769,02,08 and 1769,02,09 in this calendar for detailed description of the three deeds that pertain to the Schoharie River Valley. The fourth deed is to a tract of land north of the Mohawk River, west of the Hudson River.

Date: 1769,02,08-09 (2)
Description: Four Indian deeds, executed in the presence of N.Y. Colonial Governor Sir Henry Moore at Johnson Hall.
Source: N.Y.STATE ARCHIVES, ALBANY, INDIAN TREATIES & DEEDS, SERIES #448, VOL. 1, PP. 117-133+.
Comment: See 1769,02,08 and 1769,02,09 in this calendar for detailed description of the three deeds that pertain to the Schoharie River Valley. The fourth deed is to a tract of land north of the Mohawk River, west of the Hudson River. These are not the original deeds. They are contemporary copies.

Date: 1769,02,09°
Description: Indian deed. The land ceded begins at Adiga creek, runs along the line of purchase made by Samuel Wharton and others to the corner of George Croghan's purchase, and from there southwesterly to the "Forks of Teneaderah known by the name of Aghawey, Thence down the said river Teneaderah to its Confluence with the River Susquehanna, Thence up the said river Susquehanna" to where it begins.
Source: SEE 1769,02,08-09.
Comment: The deed is from Jacob, Petrus, Peter, and Adam, "Chiefs and Proprietors of the Country of the Aquago (Oquaga, Onoquaga) Indians, and Being and effectualy[sic] representing the whole Tribe of the Aquagoes" (note their marks on document) to Colonel Staats, Long Morris, Clotworth Upton, John Butler, and their associates. John Butler, interpreter. Woods, creeks, rivers, "Fishings, Fowlings, Huntings," etc. are all ceded with the land. The Indians received "consideration money" when the deed was executed. SEE 1769,06,20.

Date: 1769,02,10
Description: William Johnson to Goldsbrow Banyar, acknowledging receipt of account of fees paid for William Johnson's fourth part of Lawyer's purchase of land at Schoharie.
Source: THE PAPERS OF SIR WILLIAM JOHNSON. ED. BY JAMES SULLIVAN, ET AL. ALBANY: STATE UNIVERSITY OF NEW YORK, 14 VOLS., 1921-1965, 12: 0696-0697.
Comment: Manuscript is in N.Y. HISTORICAL SOCIETY, NEW YORK, N.Y., BANYAR PAPERS. SEE 1768,11,13; 1768,11,24; 1769,01,29.

Date: 1769,03,18
Description: Affidavit of John DePeyster (Mayor of Albany) about Indian deed for 1,000 acres of land at Tienderoga (Fort Hunter) given by the Mohawks to Albany City Corporation, and destroyed by one of the Indians at the request of Governor Cosby.
Source: N.Y.STATE ARCHIVES, ALBANY, N.Y.COL.MSS, INDORSED LAND PAPERS, 1643-1803, SERIES NO. A0272, DEPARTMENT OF STATE, APPLICATIONS FOR LAND GRANTS, VOL. 47, P. 014.
Comment: SEE 1783,09,25.

Date: 1769,03,21
Description: Petition of John Butler for land on Schoharie Creek
Source: N.Y.STATE ARCHIVES, ALBANY, N.Y.COL.MSS, INDORSED LAND PAPERS, 1643-1803, SERIES NO. A0272, DEPARTMENT OF STATE, APPLICATIONS FOR LAND GRANTS, VOL. 25, P. 088.
Comment:

Date: 1769,03,21 (2)
Description: Petition of Stephen Skinner and thirty-nine others for 40,000 acres of land ceded by the Indians in October 1768 previous to the Treaty of Fort Stanwix, being two tracts purchased from the Indians: one, south of the Mohawk River, the other on the east side of Schoharie Creek.
Source: N.Y.STATE ARCHIVES, ALBANY, N.Y.COL.MSS, INDORSED LAND PAPERS, 1643-1803, SERIES NO. A0272, DEPARTMENT OF STATE, APPLICATIONS FOR LAND GRANTS, VOL. 25, PP. 089, 090.
Comment: N.B. In CALENDAR OF LAND PAPERS this document is said to pertain to land on the EAST side of Schoharie Creek purchased from Oneidas. Land east of the Schoharie River is usually not considered to be Oneida land. The 39 associates of Stephen Skinner are: Mathew Cusing, Patrick McDavitt, Smith Ramago(?), Isaac Hiron(?), Richard Graham, Thomas Stewart, John Stewart, Charles Ramage(?), John Turner, Eleazer Miller, Jr., James Seagrove, Alexander McAlister, John Dunlop, George Traile, Wiilliam Campbell, James Bennet, John Morton, James Dunscomb, Alexander Forbes, John Shaw, James Sackett, Samuel Stevens, Richard Nassau Stephens, Edmond Carrol, William Barker, Thomas Lupton, John Lamb, Fredrick Carrol, Edward Smith, John Marshall, Francis Rofflen (?), John Lambart, George Brewerton, Jr., Robert McMinnomy(?), Marinus Willett, Thomas Ryon, Alexander McGinniss(?), Joseph Becke(?). See 1769,03,21 (2). See also n.d. for map of what is known as Skinner's Patent.

Date: 1769,03,21 (3)
Description: Petition of John Wetherhead (Weatherhead), John Tabor Kempe and thirty-eight others for 40,000 acres of land ceded by the Indians in October 1768, previous to the Treaty of Fort Stanwix (1768), being two tracts: one, south of Mohawk River, the other, on east side of Schoharie Creek.
Source: N.Y.STATE ARCHIVES, ALBANY, N.Y.COL.MSS, INDORSED LAND PAPERS, 1643-1803, SERIES NO. A0272, DEPARTMENT OF STATE, APPLICATIONS FOR LAND GRANTS, VOL. 25, P. 091.
Comment: SEE 1769,11,16; 1769,11,17. The 38 other petitioners are: Elizabeth Kempe, Philadelphia Kempe, Catharine Kempe, Jane Kempe, James Downes, Robert Watts, Catherine Morris, Willliam Proctor, Cardan Proctor, John Van Allen, John R. Bleeker, Allan McDougall, Henry Remsen, Thomas Fisher, Anthony Rutgers, Hermanus Rutgers, Joseph Allicocke, John Lamb, Grove Bend, John Lambert, Charles Nicolls, Jonathan Lawrence, Thomas Jones, Thomas Crab, Alexander Robertson, Paul Miller, Nicholas Bogert, Jacobus Van Antwerp, William Campbell, William Benson, Alexander McDougall, Philip John Livingston, Samuel Bayard, Robert Harper, Joseph Haviland, Patrick McDewit, Robert Adams, and James Phyn.

Date: 1769,03,21 (4)
Description: Petition of Alexander McKee and thirty-nine others for 40,000 acres of land, being two tracts: one, south of Mohawk River; the other, east of Schoharie Creek.
Source: N.Y.STATE ARCHIVES, ALBANY, N.Y.COL.MSS, INDORSED LAND PAPERS, 1643-1803, SERIES NO. A0272, DEPARTMENT OF STATE, APPLICATIONS FOR LAND GRANTS, VOL. 25, P. 092.
Comment: SEE 1769,02,08; 1769,03,22.

Date: 1769,03,21 (5)
Description: Petition of John Bowen, Bartholomew Pickle, Jacob Snook, John Davis, Hugh Crawford, Jelles Fonda, Michael Byrn (Byrne), Robert Adams, Gilbert Tice and others for a grant of 20,000 acres near Cobus Kill (Cobleskill).
Source: N.Y.STATE ARCHIVES, ALBANY, N.Y.COL.MSS, INDORSED LAND PAPERS, 1643-1803, SERIES NO. A0272, DEPARTMENT OF STATE, APPLICATIONS FOR LAND GRANTS, VOL. 25, P. 094, 095.
Comment: SEE 1769,02,08; 1770,09,15; 1770,11,15; 1771,09,21.

Date: 1769,03,22
Description: A list of the names of associates of Alexander McKee in his petition for a patent of 40,000 acres of land.
Source: N.Y.STATE ARCHIVES, ALBANY, N.Y.COL.MSS, INDORSED LAND PAPERS, 1643-1803, SERIES NO. A0272, DEPARTMENT OF STATE, APPLICATIONS FOR LAND GRANTS, VOL. 25, P. 093.
Comment: The endorsement notes that the patent is "to be granted to them on the 22d Day of March 1769". SEE 1769,02,08; 1769,03,21.

Date: 1769,03,26-10,07
Description: William Johnson's account against the British Crown. Reports disbursement on 24 May to Schoharie Indians.
Source: THE PAPERS OF SIR WILLIAM JOHNSON. ED. BY JAMES SULLIVAN, ET AL. ALBANY: STATE UNIVERSITY OF NEW YORK, 14 VOLS., 1921-1965, 12: 0758-0763.
Comment: Manuscript is in WILLIAM L. CLEMENTS LIBRARY, GAGE PAPERS, ENCLOSED IN GAGE TO ABRAHAM MORTIER, 14 DECEMBER 1769. N.B. This account notes disbursements in April and May for attending to, and burying, Indians stricken with smallpox. There is no specific indication that any of these were for Indians of Schoharie; but it may be worth noting that smallpox was going around at the time.

Date: 1769,04,17
Description: Petition of Adam Vrooman (Vroman) for patent for 1,000 acres of land on west side of Schoharie river.
Source: N.Y.STATE ARCHIVES, ALBANY, N.Y.COL.MSS, INDORSED LAND PAPERS, 1643-1803, SERIES NO. A0272, DEPARTMENT OF STATE, APPLICATIONS FOR LAND GRANTS, VOL. 25, P. 112.
Comment: SEE 1768,06,10; 1770,03,19.

Date: 1769,04,24
Description: Petition of J.H. Ten Eyck, A. Colder (Colden[?]), J. Bleeker, and G. Banyar for patent to two tracts of land on both sides of Schoharie Creek, containing 3,500 acres.
Source: N.Y.STATE ARCHIVES, ALBANY, N.Y.COL.MSS, INDORSED LAND PAPERS, 1643-1803, SERIES NO. A0272, DEPARTMENT OF STATE, APPLICATIONS FOR LAND GRANTS, VOL. 25, P. 117.
Comment:

Date: 1769,04,26
Description: N.Y. Provincial Council Minutes. Petition of Adam Vrooman (Vroman) for land on west side of Schoharie river is granted.
Source: N.Y.STATE ARCHIVES,ALBANY, N.Y.COUN.MIN., VOL. 29, P. 318.
Comment: SEE 1769,04,17.

Date: 1769,05,10
Description: Warrant to prepare letters patent to J.H. Ten Eyck, A. Colder (Colden[?]), J. Bleeker, and G. Banyar.
Source: N.Y.STATE ARCHIVES, ALBANY, N.Y.COL.MSS, INDORSED LAND PAPERS, 1643-1803, SERIES NO. A0272, DEPARTMENT OF STATE, APPLICATIONS FOR LAND GRANTS, VOL. 25, P. 118.
Comment:

Date: 1769,05,17
Description: William Johnson to John Bradstreet, about dispute over Hardenburgh Patent. Johnson writes that Dr. Shuckburgh with whom he has discussed the dispute, says that he was present in 1734 when "Chiefs of Scoharee [Schoharie] Seth & Hance Ury &ca Summoned the Esopus or Delawares to a Meeting & told them that if ever they attempted to Sell any Lands Westward of Catskill Hills they would destroy them, or in their own Words hunt them up like Deer." Johnson suggests that Bradstreet talk with Shuckburgh about the subject.
Source: THE PAPERS OF SIR WILLIAM JOHNSON. ED. BY JAMES SULLIVAN, ET AL. ALBANY: STATE UNIVERSITY OF NEW YORK, 14 VOLS., 1921-1965, 06: 0760-0762.
Comment: SEE 1734,00,00.

Date: 1769,05,22
Description: Petition of John Jones, John Bruce, and Wolf Camp for grant of land on a branch of Schoharie Kill. Map included. Also, certificate of English General Thomas Gage that the above men served in the English army (bounty lands).
Source: N.Y.STATE ARCHIVES, ALBANY, N.Y.COL.MSS, INDORSED LAND PAPERS, 1643-1803, SERIES NO. A0272, DEPARTMENT OF STATE, APPLICATIONS FOR LAND GRANTS, VOL. 25, P. 125.
Comment:

Date: 1769,05,24°
Description: William Johnson's account against the British Crown. Reports disbursement on 24 May to Schoharie Indians.
Source: SEE 1769,03,26-10,07.
Comment:

Date: 1769,05,30
Description: Patent to Goldsbrow Banyar and others to 3,000 acres of land. Known as Ten Eyck Patent.
Source: N.Y.STATE ARCHIVES, ALBANY, N.Y. LETTERS PATENT, 1664-1780, SERIES NO. 12590, BOOK 14, P. 379.
Comment:

Date: 1769,06,14°
Description: Indian deed to John Butler for 1,000 acres in Schoharie west of Clark and Cosby patents near Breakabeen.
Source: SEE 1769,09,08.
Comment:

Date: 1769,06,20
Description: Petition of ensign James Savage for a grant of 2,000 acres of land in the tract purchased for Upton, Morris, and Butler. Also included is a certificate of General Gage, dated 21 June 1769, that ensign James Savage served in the 76th regiment during the Seven Years War.
Source: N.Y.STATE ARCHIVES, ALBANY, N.Y.COL.MSS, INDORSED LAND PAPERS, 1643-1803, SERIES NO. A0272, DEPARTMENT OF STATE, APPLICATIONS FOR LAND GRANTS, VOL. 25, P. 138.
Comment: SEE 1969,02,09. Bounty lands.

Date: 1769,06,27
Description: Petition of M. Dies and R. Smith for 2,000 acres east of and adjacent to the tract of Ury Regtmyer (Rightmyer, Rightmeyer, Rightmeir).
Source: N.Y.STATE ARCHIVES, ALBANY, N.Y.COL.MSS, INDORSED LAND PAPERS, 1643-1803, SERIES NO. A0272, DEPARTMENT OF STATE, APPLICATIONS FOR LAND GRANTS, VOL. 25, P. 142.
Comment:

Date: 1769,06,29
Description: Return of survey for J.M. Scott, H.A. Francklin (Franklin), M.G. Vanbergen and associates for three tracts, one of which is in what is now called Middleburgh. Map included.
Source: N.Y.STATE ARCHIVES, ALBANY, N.Y.COL.MSS, INDORSED LAND PAPERS, 1643-1803, SERIES NO. A0272, DEPARTMENT OF STATE, APPLICATIONS FOR LAND GRANTS, VOL. 25, P. 143.
Comment: SEE 1806,00,00.

Date: 1769,07,17
Description: Petition of John Rightmeyer (Rightmaier, Rightmyer) for a grant of 500 acres of land on the east (?) side of the Mohawk creek. A map is also included, showing the Schohary river. A note on the map states, "This Plan discribeth [sic] the Two Tracts of Land Granted to Jurie (or George) Rightme [sic] Hendrik Wever [Weaver] and Others (in which Captain John Dies Deced [deceased] was Considerably Interested) and Lye about Twenty nine Miles from Hudsons river in the County of Albany. The Small Tract Containd within the Red lines, are the Lands pray for by the within Petition. . ."
Source: N.Y.STATE ARCHIVES, ALBANY, N.Y.COL.MSS, INDORSED LAND PAPERS, 1643-1803, SERIES NO. A0272, DEPARTMENT OF STATE, APPLICATIONS FOR LAND GRANTS, VOL. 25, P. 145.
Comment:

Date: 1769,09,08
Description: Return of survey for John Butler for tract on 1,050 acres on Schoharie Kill. Map included. Also, Indian deed, signed by Hendrick alias Tiendaga (Tiendega, Teyendacha, Tiendaghe), Abraham alias Tiyahassary (Teahansera, Tiyahasara, Tyorhannea[?], Tijorhasara), and Hance (Hans) alias Canadagaia (Canadajaya, Kanachdegawa), and dated 14 June 1768, to John Butler for 1,000 acres of land in Schoharie west of Clark and Cosby patent(s) (near Breakabeen, surveyed in 1739).
Source: N.Y.STATE ARCHIVES, ALBANY, N.Y.COL.MSS, INDORSED LAND PAPERS, 1643-1803, SERIES NO. A0272, DEPARTMENT OF STATE, APPLICATIONS FOR LAND GRANTS, VOL. 26, P. 005.
Comment: Deed is signed by Hendrick, Abraham, and Hans, who are identified as "belonging to the Mohawk Castle" (most probably, the Lower Mohawk Castle). Their marks are on the deed. SEE 1768,06,14; 1769,06,14.

Date: 1769,09,30
Description: Patent to Jacob Starnberger, George Zimmer, Jacob Zimmer, William Zimmer, and Petrus Zimmer for 8,000 acres of land at Schoharie. Known as Starnberger Patent.
Source: N.Y.STATE ARCHIVES, ALBANY, N.Y. LETTERS PATENT, 1664-1780, SERIES NO. 12590, BOOK 14, P. 413.
Comment: SEE 1753,06,06; 1754,06,06; 1761,10,02; 1765,09,17; 1766,07,07; 1769,09,20.

Date: 1769,10,02
Description: Petition of John Butler for 1,000 acres of land on the west side of Schoharie Kill.
Source: N.Y.STATE ARCHIVES, ALBANY, N.Y.COL.MSS, INDORSED LAND PAPERS, 1643-1803, SERIES NO. A0272, DEPARTMENT OF STATE, APPLICATIONS FOR LAND GRANTS, VOL. 26, P. 005.
Comment: SEE 1770,05,09.

Date: 1769,10,24
Description: Return of survey, and map, for Adam Vrooman (Vroman) of land on west side of Schoharie river and north of Stony Brook.
Source: N.Y.STATE ARCHIVES, ALBANY, N.Y.COL.MSS, INDORSED LAND PAPERS, 1643-1803, SERIES NO. A0272, DEPARTMENT OF STATE, APPLICATIONS FOR LAND GRANTS, VOL. 26, P. 017.
Comment:

Date: 1769,11,00
Description: Map of several lots of land at Schoharie congruent with a map and division made by Isaac Vrooman (Vroman) in 1753. The lowlands, etc. were also divided by Mr. Collins in 1729. The map was drawn at the request of Johannes Mirakle in the month of November 1769 per Will Cockburn.
Source: N.Y.STATE LIBRARY, ALBANY, MANUSCRIPTS, SCHOHARIE COUNTY, PATENTEES, MAPS, DW10738, MAP #5.
Comment:

Date: 1769,11,16
Description: Return of survey of Weatherhead (Wetherhead) and others of 40,000 acres of land on the west side of Schoharie Creek at what is now called Blenheim. Map included.
Source: N.Y.STATE ARCHIVES, ALBANY, N.Y.COL.MSS, INDORSED LAND PAPERS, 1643-1803, SERIES NO. A0272, DEPARTMENT OF STATE, APPLICATIONS FOR LAND GRANTS, VOL. 26, P. 029.
Comment: SEE 1769,03,21; 1769,11,17.

Date: 1769,11,17
Description: Petition for establishing the township of Blenheim, and for altering some of the names on the return survey of Weatherhead (Wetherhead) and others of 40,000 acres of land on the west side of Schoharie Creek at Blenheim.
Source: N.Y.STATE ARCHIVES, ALBANY, N.Y.COL.MSS, INDORSED LAND PAPERS, 1643-1803, SERIES NO. A0272, DEPARTMENT OF STATE, APPLICATIONS FOR LAND GRANTS, VOL. 26, P. 036.
Comment: SEE 1769,11,16.

Date: 1769,11,17 (2)
Description: Petition of P.J. Livingston and thirty-nine others for grant of 1,000 acres each on the east side of Schoharie Creek, and another tract on the west side of the creek. Map included.
Source: N.Y.STATE ARCHIVES, ALBANY, N.Y.COL.MSS, INDORSED LAND PAPERS, 1643-1803, SERIES NO. A0272, DEPARTMENT OF STATE, APPLICATIONS FOR LAND GRANTS, VOL. 26, P. 037.
Comment: SEE 1769,03,21.

Date: 1769,11,20°
Description: Date of original petition of William Annin and others for 1,000 acres of land on west side of Schoharie river.
Source: SEE 1770,03,27.
Comment:

Date: 1769,11,28
Description: Patent for 40,000 acres of land, known as the Blenheim Patent, to Samuel Bayard, Grove Bend, and others.
Source: N.Y.STATE ARCHIVES, ALBANY, N.Y. LETTERS PATENT, 1664-1780, SERIES NO. 12590, BOOK 14, P. 455.
Comment: SEE 1769,00,00 [ ] (2).

Date: 1769,12,16
Description: Henry Van Schaack to William Johnson. Van Schaack mentions that a petition will be circulated at Kinderhook. The people who sign it join with Albanians in requesting that Schoharie remain in Albany County.
Source: THE PAPERS OF SIR WILLIAM JOHNSON. ED. BY JAMES SULLIVAN, ET AL. ALBANY: STATE UNIVERSITY OF NEW YORK, 14 VOLS., 1921-1965, 07: 0302-0303.
Comment: Editor of THE PAPERS OF SIR WILLIAM JOHNSON. ED. BY JAMES SULLIVAN, ET AL. ALBANY: STATE UNIVERSITY OF NEW YORK, 14 VOLS., 1921-1965, notes that by act of 12 March 1772, Schoharie was left in Albany County. SEE THE COLONIAL LAWS OF NEW YORK, 5: 320.

Date: 1769,12,18
Description: Petition of R. Lowdon and others for a grant of 13,000 acres on the west side of Schoharie Creek adjacent to land of McKee and others.
Source: N.Y.STATE ARCHIVES, ALBANY, N.Y.COL.MSS, INDORSED LAND PAPERS, 1643-1803, SERIES NO. A0272, DEPARTMENT OF STATE, APPLICATIONS FOR LAND GRANTS, VOL. 26, P. 049.
Comment:

Date: 1769,12,20
Description: Petition of D. Campbell for a grant of 2,000 acres east of the Susquehanna River within the Indian purchase of Weatherhead (Wetherhead), Butler, Skinner, and McKee.
Source: N.Y.STATE ARCHIVES, ALBANY, N.Y.COL.MSS, INDORSED LAND PAPERS, 1643-1803, SERIES NO. A0272, DEPARTMENT OF STATE, APPLICATIONS FOR LAND GRANTS, VOL. 26, P. 053.
Comment:

Date: 177[ ],05,23
Description: Extract of Indian deed, dated 6 June 1764, to Lawyer, Borst, Foster, and Hiets (Heints), conveying land west of Schoharie. Extract was made on 23 May 177[ ].
Source: N.Y.STATE ARCHIVES, ALBANY, N.Y.COL.MSS, INDORSED LAND PAPERS, 1643-1803, SERIES NO. A0272, DEPARTMENT OF STATE, APPLICATIONS FOR LAND GRANTS, VOL. 17, P. 143.
Comment: SEE ALSO 1753,07,20; 1753,07,28; 1764,06,06.

Date: 1770,00,00
Description: James Collins's draft of land at Schoharie.
Source: THE PAPERS OF SIR WILLIAM JOHNSON. ED. BY JAMES SULLIVAN, ET AL. ALBANY: STATE UNIVERSITY OF NEW YORK, 14 VOLS., 1921-1965, 07: 0336 Insert After.
Comment: Enclosed in letter dated 9 Jan 1770. Map. .

Date: 1770,00,00 (2)
Description: Map for William Wood of 2,000 acres on the east side of the Schoharie River near Breakabean.
Source: MIX'S CATALOG OF MAPS AND SURVEYS IN OFFFICES OF THE SECRETARY OF STATE, STATE ENGINEER AND SURVEYOR AND COMPTROLLER AND N.Y. STATE LIBRARY, 1859, REFERENCES THIS MAP, LISTING IT AS BEING FROM THE COMMISSIONER OF FORFEITURES, MAP # 874.
Comment: SEE 1770,07,13.

Date: 1770,00,00°
Description: Map of Stephen Skinner's Patent.
Source: SEE n.d.
Comment:

Date: 1770,00,00°
Description: Map of Schoharie County showing various patents and other tracts; Lawyer and two miner; Stoneheap Patent; Morris and Coeyman; A. Van Cortlandt; M. Schuyler and others; Teneyck (Ten Eyck) and Bleecker; Johannis Lawyer and others; Wiefield and Clifford; Jonathan Brewer. Shows "Cockburn's line run about the year 1770 or 1771". Latest date on map is 1819.
Source: SEE n.d.
Comment:

Date: 1770,01,02
Description: Patent for 37,840 acres of land to John Morin (Morine) Scott and others.
Source: N.Y.STATE ARCHIVES, ALBANY, N.Y. LETTERS PATENT, 1664-1780, SERIES NO. 12590, BOOK 14, P. 492.
Comment: Known as Scott's Patent. SEE 1768,03,02; 1769,06,29; 1771,05,03; 1806,00,00; n.d.

Date: 1770,01,02 (2)
Description: Map of southern division of third tract of John Morin (Morine) Scott's land.
Source: MIX'S CATALOG OF MAPS AND SURVEYS IN OFFFICES OF THE SECRETARY OF STATE, STATE ENGINEER AND SURVEYOR AND COMPTROLLER AND N.Y. STATE LIBRARY, 1859, REFERENCES THIS MAP, LISTING IT AS BEING IN THE OFFICES OF THE N.Y. STATE DEPARTMENT OF TAXATION & FINANCE, MAP #225.
Comment: SEE 1768,03,02; 1769,06,29; 1771,05,03; 1806,00,00; n.d.

Date: 1770,01,02 (3)
Description: Patent to Gerardus G. Beeckman, Egbert Benson, Robert Benson, Joseph Blanchard, and Abroaham Bloodgood.
Source: N.Y.STATE ARCHIVES, ALBANY, N.Y. LETTERS PATENT, 1664-1780, SERIES NO. 12590, BOOK 14, P. 493.
Comment:

Date: 1770,01,03
Description: Petition of Dinston of Catskill that he and others purchased land adjoining Cosby's Manor from Oneidas.
Source: N.Y.STATE ARCHIVES, ALBANY, N.Y.COL.MSS, INDORSED LAND PAPERS, 1643-1803, SERIES NO. A0272, DEPARTMENT OF STATE, APPLICATIONS FOR LAND GRANTS, VOL. 26, P. 072.
Comment: N.B. The land of concern is EAST of Schoharie and was apparently under the control of ONEIDAS.

Date: 1770,01,05
Description: Petition of John Wefield and John Clifford, for a grant of 250 acres of land on the south side of the Mohawk River, and to the west of the township of Schenectady, and to the east of Schoharie. Also included are certificates that John Clifford and John Wefield served during the war (Seven Years War).
Source: N.Y.STATE ARCHIVES, ALBANY, N.Y.COL.MSS, INDORSED LAND PAPERS, 1643-1803, SERIES NO. A0272, DEPARTMENT OF STATE, APPLICATIONS FOR LAND GRANTS, VOL. 26, P. 077.
Comment: Bounty land.

Date: 1770,01,09
Description: James Collins to William Johnson, about land transactions at Schoharie. It concerns a certificate for Ackeson for a tract with Lawyer and associates and 100 acres on Stoney Creek.
Source: THE PAPERS OF SIR WILLIAM JOHNSON. ED. BY JAMES SULLIVAN, ET AL. ALBANY: STATE UNIVERSITY OF NEW YORK, 14 VOLS., 1921-1965, 07: 0337-0338.
Comment: Collin's encloses draft of land at Schoharie. SEE 1770.

Date: 1770,01,12
Description: Patent to a tract of 120 acres of land to Michael Salsbergh (Salsburgh, Salsburg).
Source: N.Y.STATE ARCHIVES, ALBANY, N.Y. LETTERS PATENT, 1664-1780, SERIES NO. 12590, BOOK 14, P. 501.
Comment: SEE 1768,07,01. The land is in Schoharie.

Date: 1770,01,15
Description: Patent to Stephen Skinner, Joseph Beck, James Bennett, and others for 40,000 acres of land. Known as Skinner's Patent.
Source: N.Y.STATE ARCHIVES, ALBANY, N.Y. LETTERS PATENT, 1664-1780, SERIES NO. 12590, BOOK 14, P. 508.
Comment: See n.d. for map of the patent. See also 1769,03,21 (2).

Date: 1770,02,02
Description: William Johnson to Barent Vrooman (Vroman), reporting that three Indians from Schoharie, with wampum from the "whole castle," declared that they "will by no means part with the Lands they now live on & improve." Johnson writes that they are very much alarmed at Vrooman's proposal to meet with them in private to encourage them to sell their land.
Source: THE PAPERS OF SIR WILLIAM JOHNSON. ED. BY JAMES SULLIVAN, ET AL. ALBANY: STATE UNIVERSITY OF NEW YORK, 14 VOLS., 1921-1965, 12: 0776-0777.
Comment:

Date: 1770,02,10
Description: James Phyn to William Johnson. In post script, Phyn notes that next spring he will know better what position he is in to purchase land at Scoharie and in the Northern Tract (i.e., north of Mohawk River).
Source: THE PAPERS OF SIR WILLIAM JOHNSON. ED. BY JAMES SULLIVAN, ET AL. ALBANY: STATE UNIVERSITY OF NEW YORK, 14 VOLS., 1921-1965, 07: 0381-0382.
Comment:

Date: 1770,03,00
Description: Certificate stating that Peter Schuyler and Robert Adams were present when Canajoharie Indians agreed to sell land on branch of river Adagegtinge ceded to William Johnson in Indian deed to land south and southwest of Schoharie, dated 24 August 1751. Deed is included.
Source: N.Y.STATE ARCHIVES, ALBANY, N.Y.COL.MSS, INDORSED LAND PAPERS, 1643-1803, SERIES NO. A0272, DEPARTMENT OF STATE, APPLICATIONS FOR LAND GRANTS, VOL. 26, P. 127.
Comment: SEE 1770,04,12; 1751,05,06; 1751,08,24.

Date: 1770,03,19
Description: Patent for 1,000 acres of land on the west side of Schoharie Creek to Adam Vrooman(Vroman).
Source: N.Y.STATE ARCHIVES, ALBANY, N.Y. LETTERS PATENT, 1664-1780, SERIES NO. 12590, BOOK 15, P. 098.
Comment: The land is in Middleburgh. SEE 1768,06,10; 1769,04,17.

Date: 1770,03,27
Description: Petition of William Annin, John Campbell, G. Brown, Jacob Starnbrough, Richard Cartwright, and James Willson for a grant of 1,000 acres each of land on west side of Schoharie river.
Source: N.Y.STATE ARCHIVES, ALBANY, N.Y.COL.MSS, INDORSED LAND PAPERS, 1643-1803, SERIES NO. A0272, DEPARTMENT OF STATE, APPLICATIONS FOR LAND GRANTS, VOL. 27, P. 002.
Comment:

Date: 1770,04,04
Description: Certificate to Peter Livingston, Willing (William[?]) Wood, Morrison and others to locate 6,000 acres on a tract on the east side of Schoharie creek.
Source: N.Y.STATE ARCHIVES, ALBANY, N.Y.COL.MSS, INDORSED LAND PAPERS, 1643-1803, SERIES NO. A0272, DEPARTMENT OF STATE, APPLICATIONS FOR LAND GRANTS, VOL. 27, P. 016.
Comment:

Date: 1770,04,10
Description: Caveat of J. Duane against grant for lands in Nine Partner tract.
Source: N.Y.STATE ARCHIVES, ALBANY, N.Y.COL.MSS, INDORSED LAND PAPERS, 1643-1803, SERIES NO. A0272, DEPARTMENT OF STATE, APPLICATIONS FOR LAND GRANTS, VOL. 27, P. 017.
Comment: SEE 1774,01,27.

Date: 1770,04,12
Description: Return of survey for Sir William Johnson and his associates of a tract of 26,000 acres of land on the south side of the Mohawk River, and on both sides of a brook called Adagughtingay (Adagegtinge). Map included.
Source: N.Y.STATE ARCHIVES, ALBANY, N.Y.COL.MSS, INDORSED LAND PAPERS, 1643-1803, SERIES NO. A0272, DEPARTMENT OF STATE, APPLICATIONS FOR LAND GRANTS, VOL. 27, P. 023.
Comment: SEE 1770,03,00. CALENDAR OF LAND PAPERS notes that this tract is in Davenport, Delaware County. It is south and southwest of Schoharie, as described in the deed to the land.

Date: 1770,04,17
Description: Lease from Johannes Lawyer and others to Gerhart Nicholas for land west of Schoharie.
Source: N.Y.STATE LIBRARY, ALBANY, MANUSCRIPTS, JOHANNES LAWYER AND OTHERS, MAPS AND DEEDS OF SCHOHARIE VALLEY, ACC. NO. SC16469, DEEDS AND LEASES #1; SEE ALSO J. LAWYER PAPERS, PI 16480.
Comment:

Date: 1770,04,26
Description: William Johnson to James DeLancey, about discussions of the county into which Schoharie will be placed in proposed re-drawing of county lines.
Source: THE PAPERS OF SIR WILLIAM JOHNSON. ED. BY JAMES SULLIVAN, ET AL. ALBANY: STATE UNIVERSITY OF NEW YORK, 14 VOLS., 1921-1965, 07: 0594-0595.
Comment: Enclosed with this document were Johnson's remarks upon a proposed Road Bill (THE PAPERS OF SIR WILLIAM JOHNSON. ED. BY JAMES SULLIVAN, ET AL. ALBANY: STATE UNIVERSITY OF NEW YORK, 14 VOLS., 1921-1965, 07: 0596), mentioning among other places South Schoharie and Brekabeen (Breakabeen, Breakabine). Johnson thinks that the bill promotes the land claims of the Manor of Rensselaer. His remarks were badly damaged by fire, and are not printed (only noted) in THE PAPERS OF SIR WILLIAM JOHNSON. ED. BY JAMES SULLIVAN, ET AL. ALBANY: STATE UNIVERSITY OF NEW YORK, 14 VOLS., 1921-1965,.

Date: 1770,05,08
Description: Patent issued to William Johnson for 26,000 acres south of the Mohawk River.
Source: N.Y.STATE ARCHIVES, ALBANY, N.Y. LETTERS PATENT, 1664-1780, SERIES NO. 12590, BOOK 15, P. 170.
Comment:

Date: 1770,05,09
Description: Petiton of T.T. Newland for a 2,000 acre grant west of Schoharie Creek, with agreement to locate there.
Source: N.Y.STATE ARCHIVES, ALBANY, N.Y.COL.MSS, INDORSED LAND PAPERS, 1643-1803, SERIES NO. A0272, DEPARTMENT OF STATE, APPLICATIONS FOR LAND GRANTS, VOL. 27, P. 041.
Comment:

Date: 1770,05,09 (2)
Description: N.Y. Provincial Council Minutes. Patents granted to Achilles Preston and associates for 37,000 acres adjoining Vrooman's (Vroman's); and Leonard Gansevoort's patent and Northampton patent to John Butler, and to Lieut. William Houghton, Royal artillery.
Source: N.Y.STATE ARCHIVES,ALBANY, N.Y.COUN.MIN., VOL. 29, P. 385.
Comment: SEE 1769,10,02 for information about Butler's patent. SEE 1769,02,08 for information about the land granted to Achilles Preston and associates.

Date: 1770,05,17
Description: Patent to Daniel Crean, William Whitefield, and Felix Dougherty for 1,000 acres of land, adjacent to Samuel Stringer's tract.
Source: N.Y.STATE ARCHIVES, ALBANY, N.Y. MILITARY PATENTS, 1764-1775, SERIES NO. A0447, BOOK 2, P. 420.
Comment: Military grant.

Date: 1770,05,25
Description: Return of survey of two tracts of land for W. Franklin (Francklin) and others. Map included.
Source: N.Y.STATE ARCHIVES, ALBANY, N.Y.COL.MSS, INDORSED LAND PAPERS, 1643-1803, SERIES NO. A0272, DEPARTMENT OF STATE, APPLICATIONS FOR LAND GRANTS, VOL. 27, P. 049.
Comment: CALENDAR OF LAND PAPERS notes that the land on the map is in Cobleskill and Summit, Schoharie County.

Date: 1770,05,26
Description: Patent to Geroge Croghan and others for tract of 12,000 acres on the south side of the Mohawk River.
Source: N.Y.STATE ARCHIVES, ALBANY, N.Y. DEEDS, SERIES NO. A0453, BOOK 38, PP. 481-482.
Comment: Recorded by the N.Y. Secretary of State February 3, 1814.

Date: 1770,06,18
Description: Abraham Cuyler to William Johnson, about his desire to purchase land at Schoharie from Johnson.
Source: THE PAPERS OF SIR WILLIAM JOHNSON. ED. BY JAMES SULLIVAN, ET AL. ALBANY: STATE UNIVERSITY OF NEW YORK, 14 VOLS., 1921-1965, 07: 0754.
Comment:

Date: 1770,06,20
Description: Patent for 6,000 acres and other lands to Walter Franklin and others. Known as Walter Franklin's Patent.
Source: N.Y.STATE ARCHIVES, ALBANY, N.Y. LETTERS PATENT, 1664-1780, SERIES NO. 12590, BOOK 15, P. 242.
Comment:

Date: 1770,06,28
Description: William Johnson to Goldsbrow Banyar, about a patent boundary of Carl Hansen or Adam Vrooman (Vroman) at Sacondaga. Johnson is worried that, with the foundation of other patents being sixty-two years old, some disputes might arise concerning them. He would like to have the issue clarified. Johnson asks about his two patents by Mr. Adems (Adams) and the survey of them. He has already settled several families on the tract and has cut a road to Schoharie.
Source: THE PAPERS OF SIR WILLIAM JOHNSON. ED. BY JAMES SULLIVAN, ET AL. ALBANY: STATE UNIVERSITY OF NEW YORK, 14 VOLS., 1921-1965, 12: 0828-0830.
Comment: Manuscript is in N.Y. HISTORICAL SOCIETY, NEW YORK, N.Y., BANYAR PAPERS.

Date: 1770,06,29
Description: Map of the second tract of the Belvedere Patent granted to George Groghan.
Source: N.Y.STATE LIBRARY, ALBANY, MANUSCRIPTS, JOHANNES LAWYER AND OTHERS, MAPS AND DEEDS OF SCHOHARIE VALLEY, ACC. NO. 16469, MAP # 5.
Comment:

Date: 1770,07,04
Description: Patent for a tract of 1,420 acres of land to Volkert Douw, Johan Nicholas Matthias (Matice, Mattice), and J.N. Matthias, Jr.
Source: N.Y.STATE ARCHIVES, ALBANY, N.Y. LETTERS PATENT, 1664-1780, SERIES NO. 12590, BOOK 15, P. 265.
Comment: The land is in Middleburgh.

Date: 1770,07,04 (2)
Description: Patent for a tract of 630 acres of land to Lawrence Lawyer.
Source: N.Y.STATE ARCHIVES, ALBANY, N.Y. LETTERS PATENT, 1664-1780, SERIES NO. 12590, BOOK 15, P. 265.
Comment: The land is in Middleburgh.

Date: 1770,07,11
Description: Return of survey for D. Buffington and R. Morrison of land west of that of Scott and Francklin (Franklin) and east of Schoharie Kill. Map included.
Source: N.Y.STATE ARCHIVES, ALBANY, N.Y.COL.MSS, INDORSED LAND PAPERS, 1643-1803, SERIES NO. A0272, DEPARTMENT OF STATE, APPLICATIONS FOR LAND GRANTS, VOL. 27, P. 072.
Comment: CALENDAR OF LAND PAPERS notes that the land is in Broome, Schoharie County.

Date: 1770,07,11 (2)
Description: Return of survey for William Wood of a tract of 2,000 acres of land west of a tract granted to John Morin Scott, Henry Andrew Franckin and others, and to the east of Schoharie Kill. A map is included.
Source: N.Y.STATE ARCHIVES, ALBANY, N.Y.COL.MSS, INDORSED LAND PAPERS, 1643-1803, SERIES NO. A0272, DEPARTMENT OF STATE, APPLICATIONS FOR LAND GRANTS, VOL. 27, P. 073.
Comment: SEE 1770,07,11 for return of survey of Buffington and Morrison land which also adjoins that of Scott, Franckin and others. CALENDAR OF LAND PAPERS notes that the land is in Fulton, Schoharie County. SEE 1770,07,13.

Date: 1770,07,13
Description: Patent to William Wood for a tract of 2,000 acres of land east of Schoharie Kill.
Source: N.Y.STATE ARCHIVES, ALBANY, N.Y. MILITARY PATENTS, 1764-1775, SERIES NO. A0447, BOOK 08, P. 092.
Comment: SEE 1770,07,11; 1770,00,00. Military grant.

Date: 1770,07,13 (2)
Description: Patent to David Buffington and Robert Morrison for a tract of 4,000 acres adjoining land granted to Ury Rightmeyer (Rightmyer, Rightmeir) and others.
Source: N.Y.STATE ARCHIVES, ALBANY, N.Y. MILITARY PATENTS, 1764-1775, SERIES NO. A0447, BOOK 2, P. 514.
Comment: CALENDAR OF LAND PAPERS notes that the land is in Gilboa, Schoharie County. Military grant.

Date: 1770,07,13 (3)
Description: Patent to William Wood for 2,000 acres of land.
Source: N.Y.STATE ARCHIVES, ALBANY, N.Y. LETTERS PATENT, 1664-1780, SERIES NO. 12590, BOOK 2, P. 512.
Comment: Military grant

Date: 1770,07,23
Description: Petition of J. Downes and others for land bounded by Blenheim.
Source: N.Y.STATE ARCHIVES, ALBANY, N.Y.COL.MSS, INDORSED LAND PAPERS, 1643-1803, SERIES NO. A0272, DEPARTMENT OF STATE, APPLICATIONS FOR LAND GRANTS, VOL. 27, P. 079.
Comment:

Date: 1770,07,23 (2)
Description: Return of survey for John Butler of a tract of 1,000 acres of land on both sides of Schoharie Kill. Map included.
Source: N.Y.STATE ARCHIVES, ALBANY, N.Y.COL.MSS, INDORSED LAND PAPERS, 1643-1803, SERIES NO. A0272, DEPARTMENT OF STATE, APPLICATIONS FOR LAND GRANTS, VOL. 27, P. 080.
Comment: CALENDAR OF LAND PAPERS notes that land is in Blenheim.

Date: 1770,07,27
Description: Warrant of survey to J. Downes.
Source: N.Y.STATE ARCHIVES, ALBANY, N.Y.COL.MSS, INDORSED LAND PAPERS, 1643-1803, SERIES NO. A0272, DEPARTMENT OF STATE, APPLICATIONS FOR LAND GRANTS, VOL. 27, P. 081.
Comment: SEE 1770,07,23. CALENDAR OF LAND PAPERS notes that land is in Blenheim.

Date: 1770,07,31
Description: Patent to William York and others for 100 acres of land seven miles northwest of Huntersfield on both sides of Oscalleghe (Oscallaghe, Oschaleghe, Otsgarrege, Otsgarege, Otsgarage, Aschalege, Cobleskill).
Source: N.Y.STATE ARCHIVES, ALBANY, N.Y. LETTERS PATENT, 1664-1780, SERIES NO. 12590, BOOK 10, P. 123.
Comment: SEE 1728,04,25.

Date: 1770,08,02
Description: William Johnson to Goldsbrow Banyar, about patent for tract of land lying between Schoharie and the Mohawk Village.
Source: THE PAPERS OF SIR WILLIAM JOHNSON. ED. BY JAMES SULLIVAN, ET AL. ALBANY: STATE UNIVERSITY OF NEW YORK, 14 VOLS., 1921-1965,: 12: 0835-0836.
Comment: Original is in N.Y. HISTORICAL SOCIETY, NEW YORK, N.Y., BANYAR PAPERS.

Date: 1770,09,01
Description: William Johnson to Goldsbrow Banyar, about patent for land lying between Schoharie and the Mohawk Village. A list of names to be inserted in the patent is enclosed, dated [1 Sept 1770].
Source: THE PAPERS OF SIR WILLIAM JOHNSON. ED. BY JAMES SULLIVAN, ET AL. ALBANY: STATE UNIVERSITY OF NEW YORK, 14 VOLS., 1921-1965, 12: 0853-0854.
Comment: Original is in N.Y. HISTORICAL SOCIETY, NEW YORK, N.Y., BANYAR PAPERS.

Date: 1770,09,01 (2)
Description: List of names to be inserted in patent for land between Schoharie and the Mohawk Village.
Source: THE PAPERS OF SIR WILLIAM JOHNSON. ED. BY JAMES SULLIVAN, ET AL. ALBANY: STATE UNIVERSITY OF NEW YORK, 14 VOLS., 1921-1965, 12: 0855.
Comment: Original is in N.Y. HISTORICAL SOCIETY, NEW YORK, N.Y., BANYAR PAPERS, ENCLOSED IN LETTER OF 1 SEPT 1770.

Date: 1770,09,04
Description: William Johnson to John Inglis. Schoharie is one of three Mohawk villages--Fort Hunter, Canajoharie, Schoharie. At Schoharie "there are not above 16 familys [families]."
Source: THE PAPERS OF SIR WILLIAM JOHNSON. ED. BY JAMES SULLIVAN, ET AL. ALBANY: STATE UNIVERSITY OF NEW YORK, 14 VOLS., 1921-1965, 07: 0875-0879.
Comment:

Date: 1770,09,15
Description: Patent to Michael Byrne, Cornelius Bowen, John Bowen, and others for 15,500 acres of land.
Source: N.Y.STATE ARCHIVES, ALBANY, N.Y. LETTERS PATENT, 1664-1780, SERIES NO. 12590, BOOK 15, P. 382.
Comment: Known as Bowen's Patent. CALENDAR OF LAND PAPERS notes that the land is in the towns of Cobleskill, Carlisle, Esperance, and Charleston in Montgomery and Schoharie Counties. SEE 1769,02,08; 1769,03,21; 1770,11,15; 1771,09,21.

Date: 1770,09,27
Description: Patent to Hendrick Heeger (Heegar, Heger), Jacob Myer, Adam Zee, and Johan Nicholas Becker for 900 acres of land.
Source: N.Y.STATE ARCHIVES, ALBANY, N.Y. LETTERS PATENT, 1664-1780, SERIES NO. 12590, BOOK 15, P. 391.
Comment: Known as the Heeger Tract. CALENDAR OF LAND PAPERS notes that the land is in the town of Fulton.

Date:	**1770,10,29**
Description:	Petition of John Abeel, Jr. and others for a grant of land west of Caterskill.
Source:	N.Y.STATE ARCHIVES, ALBANY, N.Y.COL.MSS, INDORSED LAND PAPERS, 1643-1803, SERIES NO. A0272, DEPARTMENT OF STATE, APPLICATIONS FOR LAND GRANTS, VOL. 27, P. 111.
Comment:	It is unclear how close this land is to the Schoharie River. SEE 1771,09,26.

Date:	**1770,11,05**
Description:	William Johnson to Goldsbrow Banyar, about tract between Schoharie and the Mohawks for which Johnson is seeking a patent for "a Number of Officers who served in my Department."
Source:	THE PAPERS OF SIR WILLIAM JOHNSON. ED. BY JAMES SULLIVAN, ET AL. ALBANY: STATE UNIVERSITY OF NEW YORK, 14 VOLS., 1921-1965, 12: 0874-0876.
Comment:	Original is in N.Y. HISTORICAL SOCIETY, NEW YORK, N.Y., BANYAR PAPERS. SEE 1774,01,27 for similar wording, i.e., "between Schoharie and the Mohawks". Does that document pertain to the same land as this manuscript?

Date:	**1770,11,09**
Description:	William Johnson to James DeLancey, mentioning briefly that the "principal Inhabitants" of Albany County "are more than ever unanimous" for "Leaving the Settlements of Scohare to Albany County." Inhabitants of Schoharie, however, seem rather indifferent about the matter.
Source:	THE PAPERS OF SIR WILLIAM JOHNSON. ED. BY JAMES SULLIVAN, ET AL. ALBANY: STATE UNIVERSITY OF NEW YORK, 14 VOLS., 1921-1965, 07: 0995-0996.
Comment:	SEE 1769,12,16.

Date:	**1770,11,15**
Description:	William Cockburn's account against Jelles Fonda, including charges for surveys. Two items on the account are for surveying land in Schoharie in 1769: for Joseph Bowen, land between Canajoharie and Schoharie on the west side of Schoharie Kill, and for Sheffer, Bouch, and Becker, land along the Schoharie River. Another item is for a resurvey of the old patent in 1770.
Source:	THE PAPERS OF SIR WILLIAM JOHNSON. ED. BY JAMES SULLIVAN, ET AL. ALBANY: STATE UNIVERSITY OF NEW YORK, 14 VOLS., 1921-1965, 07: 1002-1003.
Comment:	SEE 1731,07,12 for other information about Cockburn. See also n.d.; 1770,00,00.

Date:	**1770,12,19**
Description:	James Cusick to William Johnson, about a letter to the Magistrates of Schoharie concerning the widow Deniston.
Source:	THE PAPERS OF SIR WILLIAM JOHNSON. ED. BY JAMES SULLIVAN, ET AL. ALBANY: STATE UNIVERSITY OF NEW YORK, 14 VOLS., 1921-1965, 07: 1042.
Comment:	No details are given.

Date:	**1771,00,00°**
Description:	Map of Schoharie County showing various patents and other tracts; Lawyer and two others; Stoneheap Patent; Morris and Coeyman; A. Van Cortlandt; M. Schuyler and others; Teneyck (Ten Eyck) and Bleecker; Johannis Lawyer and others; Wiefield and Clifford; Jonathan Brewer. Shows "Cockburn's line run about the year 1770 or 1771". Latest date on map is 1819.
Source:	SEE n.d.
Comment:	SEE 1737,07,12; 1770,11,05 for more information about Cockburn.

Date:	**1771,02,02**
Description:	Petition of Simon McTavish on behalf of his father John for a grant of 2,000 acres east of Schoharie Kill.
Source:	N.Y.STATE ARCHIVES, ALBANY, N.Y.COL.MSS, INDORSED LAND PAPERS, 1643-1803, SERIES NO. A0272, DEPARTMENT OF STATE, APPLICATIONS FOR LAND GRANTS, VOL. 28, P. 045.
Comment:	

Date: 1771,02,28
Description: Letter from William Johnson to Arthur Lee, giving information about the Iroquois Indians.
Source: THE DOCUMENTARY HISTORY OF THE STATE OF NEW YORK, ED. E.B. O'CALLAGHAN, (ALBANY; WEED, PARSONS, AND CO., CHARLES VAN BENTHUYSEN, 1849-1851), QUARTO ED., 4: 430-437.
Comment:

Date: 1771,03,07
Description: Money obligation from Peter and Bartholomew Vrooman (Vroman) to Indians of Schoharie. The document states, "Know all men by these presents, that we, Bartholomew Vrooman and Peter Vrooman, both of Schoharie, in the county of Albany and Province of New York are firmly bound unto John, William, Seth, Mary, and Catharine all chiefs of the Schoharie Indians, in the sum of 800 pounds." The document is signed by Guy Johnson and John Butler.
Source: OLD STONE CHURCH AND FORTRESS, SCHOHARIE, N.Y., CATALOGUE AND HISTORICAL NOTES, 1933, DEED #648.
Comment:

Date: 1771,03,15
Description: Petition from Indians of Schoharie.
Source: THE PAPERS OF SIR WILLIAM JOHNSON. ED. BY JAMES SULLIVAN, ET AL. ALBANY: STATE UNIVERSITY OF NEW YORK, 14 VOLS., 1921-1965, 08: 0020-0022.
Comment: Twenty-four Indians of Schoharie protest sale of land to Vrooman (Vroman). They say it was made without their consent. Women are among them.

Date: 1771,03,23
Description: An Account of Expenses for Indian Affairs at Johnson Hall, from 26 September 1770-23 Mar 1771, against the British Crown. On 14 March 1771, a disbursement was made to a party of "Schoharees" who were at Johnson Hall with some Dutchmen "to Close a Bargain for their Lands at Scohare."
Source: THE PAPERS OF SIR WILLIAM JOHNSON. ED. BY JAMES SULLIVAN, ET AL. ALBANY: STATE UNIVERSITY OF NEW YORK, 14 VOLS., 1921-1965, 12: 0897-0903.
Comment: Manuscript is in WILLIAM L. CLEMENTS LIBRARY, ANN ARBOR, MICH., GAGE PAPERS, ENCLOSED IN GAGE TO ABRAHAM MORTIER, 10 APRIL 1771.

Date: 1771,05,03
Description: Map of Scott's Patent.
Source: MIX'S CATALOG OF MAPS AND SURVEYS IN OFFFICES OF THE SECRETARY OF STATE, STATE ENGINEER AND SURVEYOR AND COMPTROLLER AND N.Y. STATE LIBRARY, 1859, REFERENCES THIS MAP, LISTING IT AS BEING IN THE OFFICES OF GENERAL SERVICES, NEW YORK STATE, MAP #52.
Comment: SEE 1768,03,02; 1769,06,29; 1770,01,02; 1806,00,00; n.d.

Date: 1771,05,24
Description: Petition of B. Glazier for a grant of 3,000 acres of land south of Van Bergen's land.
Source: N.Y.STATE ARCHIVES, ALBANY, N.Y.COL.MSS, INDORSED LAND PAPERS, 1643-1803, SERIES NO. A0272, DEPARTMENT OF STATE, APPLICATIONS FOR LAND GRANTS, VOL. 29, P. 031.
Comment: Is this land near Upper Schoharie Creek and the Catskills? Glazier served in the army and was presenting this request as one for bounty land. SEE 1772,05,08 for another petition submitted by Glazier.

Date: 1771,07,04
Description: William to Johannes Lawyer, about patent near Schoharie in which the late British colonial governor, Sir Henry Moore, was involved.
Source: THE PAPERS OF SIR WILLIAM JOHNSON. ED. BY JAMES SULLIVAN, ET AL. ALBANY: STATE UNIVERSITY OF NEW YORK, 14 VOLS., 1921-1965, 08: 0175-0176.
Comment: SEE 1768,11,13; 1768,11,24; 1769,01,05; 1769,01,29; 1769,02,10; 1774,03,24.

Date: 1771,07,10
Description: Release of farm lot 380 in Duanesburgh (Duanesburg) to Hendrick Kniskern (Knisker; Knieskirk) of Schoharie by James Duane of New York City, proprietor of Duanesbergh (Duanesburg). Reservations prescribed by the patent are in effect.
Source: N.Y.STATE LIBRARY, ALBANY, MANUSCRIPTS, SCHOHARIE COUNTY, PATENTEES, LAND RECORDS, DW10738.
Comment:

Date: 1771,08,13
Description: Return of survey for John Butler and others for 37,000 acres of land on the west side of Schoharie Kill. Map included.
Source: N.Y.STATE ARCHIVES, ALBANY, N.Y.COL.MSS, INDORSED LAND PAPERS, 1643-1803, SERIES NO. A0272, DEPARTMENT OF STATE, APPLICATIONS FOR LAND GRANTS, VOL. 29, P. 131.
Comment: CALENDAR OF LAND PAPERS notes that the land is in Jefferson and Summit, Schoharie County.

Date: 1771,09,17
Description: Petition of Alexander White for a return of survey of land on the east side of Schoharie Kill on behalf of six private soldiers (bounty land).
Source: N.Y.STATE ARCHIVES, ALBANY, N.Y.COL.MSS, INDORSED LAND PAPERS, 1643-1803, SERIES NO. A0272, DEPARTMENT OF STATE, APPLICATIONS FOR LAND GRANTS, VOL. 29, P. 151.
Comment:

Date: 1771,09,21
Description: An indenture between John Johnson, Daniel Claus, Guy Johnson, Michael Byrne, Jelles Fonda, and Gilbert Tice on the one part and Robert Adems [Adams(?)] on the other for land on the west side of Schoharie Hill. Based on patent, dated 15 Sept 1770, granted to John Bowen and others.
Source: THE PAPERS OF SIR WILLIAM JOHNSON. ED. BY JAMES SULLIVAN, ET AL. ALBANY: STATE UNIVERSITY OF NEW YORK, 14 VOLS., 1921-1965, 08: 0266-0270.
Comment: Original is in N.Y. STATE LIBRARY, ALBANY. Very detailed. No mention of Indians, however. SEE 1769,02,08 (Deed from Indians); 1769,03,21; 1770,09,15.

Date: 1771,09,26
Description: Return of survey for Abeel. Map included.
Source: N.Y.STATE ARCHIVES, ALBANY, N.Y.COL.MSS, INDORSED LAND PAPERS, 1643-1803, SERIES NO. A0272, DEPARTMENT OF STATE, APPLICATIONS FOR LAND GRANTS, VOL. 30, P. 010.
Comment: SEE 1770,10,29.

Date: 1771,09,28
Description: Receipt to Messrs. Bartholomew and Peter Vrooman (Vroman) of Schoharie for the sum paid for a tract of lowland bought by them from the Schoharie Indians. William Johnson is to deliver the money to the Indians when they are assembled in council.
Source: THE PAPERS OF SIR WILLIAM JOHNSON. ED. BY JAMES SULLIVAN, ET AL. ALBANY: STATE UNIVERSITY OF NEW YORK, 14 VOLS., 1921-1965, 13: 0505.
Comment: Facsimile copy by Rufus Grider in N.Y. STATE LIBRARY, GRIDER SCRAPBOOKS, VOL. 8, P. 18. Original manuscript was owned by A.G. Richmond of Canajoharie in April 1888.

Date: 1771,09,28°
Description: Tracing of receipt for 400 pounds paid by Bartholomew and Peter Vrooman for tract bought of the "Schohare" (Schoharie) Indians, signed by Sir William Johnson, 28 September 1771.
Source: SEE 1887,00,00-1888,00,00 (26).
Comment: Rufus Grider Collection.

Date: 1771,10,12
Description: Johannes Lawyer to William Johnson. Lawyer reports that he is happy to hear that Johnson agrees with the choice of Mr. Stanburrough to divide patents belonging to them on both sides of the Schoharie river. Lawyer says that he is anxious that a new surveying instrument be used because "our patents are bounded Chiefly by patents of an older Date than ours."
Source: THE PAPERS OF SIR WILLIAM JOHNSON. ED. BY JAMES SULLIVAN, ET AL. ALBANY: STATE UNIVERSITY OF NEW YORK, 14 VOLS., 1921-1965, 08: 0291-0292.
Comment: Manuscript is in NEW YORK STATE LIBRARY.

Date: 1771,10,25
Description: Hugh Wallace to William Johnson. Johnson suggests the use of "Scohary" (Schoharie) Creek, "the Mowhack [sic] Branch of Delaware," as a boundary for new county.
Source: THE PAPERS OF SIR WILLIAM JOHNSON. ED. BY JAMES SULLIVAN, ET AL. ALBANY: STATE UNIVERSITY OF NEW YORK, 14 VOLS., 1921-1965, 08: 0300-0301.
Comment:

Date: 1771,12,04
Description: Patent to Samuel Bayard and others for three tracts of land containing 24,760 acres, 2,240 acres and 10,000 acres respectively.
Source: N.Y.STATE ARCHIVES, ALBANY, COLONIAL PATENTS 1638-1780, BOOK 16, P. 103.
Comment: Known as the Strasburgh Patent.

Date: 1772,01,20
Description: Petition of D. Campbell, Burnell and Godfrey for a tract of 2,000 acres on the north side of Cobus Kill (Cobleskill).
Source: N.Y.STATE ARCHIVES, ALBANY, N.Y.COL.MSS, INDORSED LAND PAPERS, 1643-1803, SERIES NO. A0272, DEPARTMENT OF STATE, APPLICATIONS FOR LAND GRANTS, VOL. 30, P. 085.
Comment:

Date: 1772,01,27
Description: Petition of Alexander White that 350 acres of land be granted.
Source: N.Y.STATE ARCHIVES, ALBANY, N.Y.COL.MSS, INDORSED LAND PAPERS, 1643-1803, SERIES NO. A0272, DEPARTMENT OF STATE, APPLICATIONS FOR LAND GRANTS, VOL. 30, P. 097.
Comment: SEE 1771,09,17.

Date: 1772,03,28
Description: Return of survey for D. McIntosh, T. Brown, and Alexander Leslie for 600 acres of land.
Source: N.Y.STATE ARCHIVES, ALBANY, N.Y.COL.MSS, INDORSED LAND PAPERS, 1643-1803, SERIES NO. A0272, DEPARTMENT OF STATE, APPLICATIONS FOR LAND GRANTS, VOL. 31, P. 067.
Comment: CALENDAR OF LAND PAPERS notes that the land adjoins Batavia and is in Windham, Greene County. How close is this to the mouth of the Schoharie River?

Date: 1772,05,08
Description: Hendrick Heger (Heegar, Heeger), Johannes Kniskern (Knisker, Knieskirk, Kneiskerk, Kneescarn), Jacob Schefer, Jr. and Jacob Siejer[?] to William Johnson, about lands of Nicholas Beeker (Becker) sold to two "old" Indian women.
Source: THE PAPERS OF SIR WILLIAM JOHNSON. ED. BY JAMES SULLIVAN, ET AL. ALBANY: STATE UNIVERSITY OF NEW YORK, 14 VOLS., 1921-1965, 08: 0466-0467.
Comment: SEE 1772,05,18.

Date: 1772,05,08 (2)
Description: Petition of B. Glazier for a grant of 3,000 acres of land on the west side of Schoharie Kill. The land is bounded on the south by that of Franklin, Butler, and others.
Source: N.Y.STATE ARCHIVES, ALBANY, N.Y.COL.MSS, INDORSED LAND PAPERS, 1643-1803, SERIES NO. A0272, DEPARTMENT OF STATE, APPLICATIONS FOR LAND GRANTS, VOL. 31, P. 126.
Comment: SEE 1772,07,28 for a return of survey of this land. SEE 1771,05,24 for another petition of Glazier for land.

Date: 1772,05,18
Description: Nicholas Becker to William Johnson, about lands at Schoharie sold by Becker to Indians.
Source: THE PAPERS OF SIR WILLIAM JOHNSON. ED. BY JAMES SULLIVAN, ET AL. ALBANY: STATE UNIVERSITY OF NEW YORK, 14 VOLS., 1921-1965, 08: 0488-0489.
Comment: SEE 1772,05,08

Date: 1772,07,28
Description: Return of survey for B. Glazer (Glazier) of 3,000 acres of land on the west side of Schoharie Kill. Map included.
Source: N.Y.STATE ARCHIVES, ALBANY, N.Y.COL.MSS, INDORSED LAND PAPERS, 1643-1803, SERIES NO. A0272, DEPARTMENT OF STATE, APPLICATIONS FOR LAND GRANTS, VOL. 32, P. 039.
Comment: SEE 1772,05,08. CALENDAR OF LAND PAPERS notes that this land is in Cobleskill. The map shows land of John Frederick Bauch and others, Walter Franklin and others, Johannes Lawyer and others, John Butler and others, and Michael Byrne and others.

Date: 1772,07,28-30
Description: Proceedings of the Mohawks with Sir William Johnson. Refers to the Treaty of Fort Stanwix, ". . . when we joined with the rest of the Confederacy in making a great cession of Territory to the King, we particulary expected [excepted] such parts as were in the neighborhood of our Villages."
Source: DOCUMENTS RELATIVE TO THE COLONIAL HISTORY OF THE STATE OF NEW YORK, ED. BY E.B. O'CALLAGHAN AND BERTHOLD FERNOW, 15 VOL. (ALBANY, N.Y.: WEED, PARSONS, AND CO., 1856-87), 8: 304-310.
Comment: The Indians of Canajoharie are making the complaints. There is no specific reference to Schoharie. Schoharie, like Canajoharie, however, was the site of Indian settlement falling on the English side of the boundary established at Fort Stanwix. SEE 1768,11,05.

Date: 1772,09,10
Description: Patent to Beamsly Glazier for 3,000 acres of land..
Source: N.Y.STATE ARCHIVES, ALBANY, N.Y. MILITARY PATENTS, 1764-1775, SERIES NO. A0447, BOOK 2, P. 704.
Comment: Military grant.

Date: 1772,10,00-1773,11,00
Description: A Journal of the Rev. Samuel Kirkland. In his entry for 9 March 1773, Kirkland mentions that Indians received religious instruction from a Dutch minister "in Schoharry [Schoharie]".
Source: THE JOURNALS OF SAMUEL KIRKLAND, ED. WALTER PILKINGTON, (CLINTON, N.Y.: HAMILTON COLLEGE, 1980), P. 81.
Comment: The editor has a footnote indicating that the minister may have been John Jacob Oehl (Oel, Ehlig, Ehle, Ehl).

Date: 1772,10,24
Description: Account against the British Crown, for 24 March-25 September 1772. On 19 April, money was disbursed to Josiah Swart of Schoharie. On 9 May, a disbursement was made for "sundry meetings held in settling a dispute of long standing between the People of Scohare [Schohary] & Indians of that Settlement concerning Land."
Source: THE PAPERS OF SIR WILLIAM JOHNSON. ED. BY JAMES SULLIVAN, ET AL. ALBANY: STATE UNIVERSITY OF NEW YORK, 14 VOLS., 1921-1965, 12: 0998-1004.
Comment: Manuscript is in WILLIAM L. CLEMENTS LIBRARY, ANN ARBOR, MICH., GAGE PAPERS, ENCLOSED IN GAGE TO THOMAS BARROW, 26 OCTOBER 1772.

Date: 1773,02,15
Description: Return of survey for William Smith and others of 20,000 acres of land. Map included.
Source: N.Y.STATE ARCHIVES, ALBANY, N.Y.COL.MSS, INDORSED LAND PAPERS, 1643-1803, SERIES NO. A0272, DEPARTMENT OF STATE, APPLICATIONS FOR LAND GRANTS, VOL. 33, P. 033.
Comment: CALENDAR OF LAND PAPERS notes that this land is in Cobleskill and Carlisle in Schoharie County, and Root in Montgomery County. SEE 1785,03,24. Map shows Indian trail to Fort Hunter and to Canajoharie.

Date: 1773,08,26
Description: A tracing of a document granting an application by Peter Vrooman (Vroman) to construct and maintain a swing gate on the division line between his property and that of John Vrooman in Schoharie.
Source: N.Y.STATE LIBARY, ALBANY, MANUSCRIPTS, RUFUS GRIDER COLLECTION (1886-1900), SC A974.7/FG84 [VAULT], VOL. 8, P. 140.
Comment: Rufus Grider traced the document in 1888. The original was in the possession of J.L. Earll at the time that Grider did the tracing.

Date: 1773,09,04
Description: Deed from Johannes and Lawrence Lawyer to Jacob Fredrick Lawyer for land in Waggoner's (Wagoner's) Patent.
Source: N.Y.STATE LIBRARY, ALBANY, MANUSCRIPTS, JOHANNES LAWYER AND OTHERS, MAPS AND DEEDS OF SCHOHARIE VALLEY, ACC. NO. SC16469, DEEDS AND LEASES #2.
Comment:

Date: 1773,11,14
Description: Allan MacDonell to William Johnson. MacDonnell mentions 18,000 acres of land at "Schoherry" (Schoharie) that are apparently available. He does not know the land, so does not have an opinion about it.
Source: THE PAPERS OF SIR WILLIAM JOHNSON. ED. BY JAMES SULLIVAN, ET AL. ALBANY: STATE UNIVERSITY OF NEW YORK, 14 VOLS., 1921-1965, 08: 0916-0917.
Comment:

Date: 1773,11,14 (2)
Description: Allan MacDonnell to William Johnson. In discussing settlement plans, MacDonnell briefly mentions "18,000 Acres adjoining to" Schoharie.
Source: THE PAPERS OF SIR WILLIAM JOHNSON. ED. BY JAMES SULLIVAN, ET AL. ALBANY: STATE UNIVERSITY OF NEW YORK, 14 VOLS., 1921-1965, 12: 1041-1042.
Comment: Printed in an article by W.L. Scott in CANADIAN CATHOLIC HISTORICAL ASSOCIATION REPORT 1934-1935, PP. 30-31.

Date: 1774,01,27
Description: Will of Sir William Johnson. Land of the "Nine Partner Patent" between Schoharie and the Mohawks, owned at one time by Gilbert Tice, is bequeathed to Daniel Claus.
Source: THE PAPERS OF SIR WILLIAM JOHNSON. ED. BY JAMES SULLIVAN, ET AL. ALBANY: STATE UNIVERSITY OF NEW YORK, 14 VOLS., 1921-1965, 12: 1062-1076.
Comment: Attested copy appears in N.Y. STATE COURT OF APPEALS, CLERK'S OFFICE, ALBANY, BOOK OF RECORD OF WILLS, VOL. 4. SEE 1770,04,10 for more information on the Nine Partner tract. SEE 1770,11,05 for similar wording, i.e., "between Schoharie and the Mohawks". Does that document pertain to the same land as this manuscript? N.B., A pipe was at Six Nations Reserve, at some points at least during the nineteenth and twentieth centuries, that reportedly has an inscription on it referring to the Nine Partner Patent.

Date: 1774,03,00
Description: George Mann to William Johnson, about land at Schoharie.
Source: THE PAPERS OF SIR WILLIAM JOHNSON. ED. BY JAMES SULLIVAN, ET AL. ALBANY: STATE UNIVERSITY OF NEW YORK, 14 VOLS., 1921-1965, 08: 1088-1089.
Comment: No information about Indians.

Date: 1774,03,24
Description: George Mann to William Johnson, about Lawyer's tract at Schoharie of which Johnson owns a share.
Source: THE PAPERS OF SIR WILLIAM JOHNSON. ED. BY JAMES SULLIVAN, ET AL. ALBANY: STATE UNIVERSITY OF NEW YORK, 14 VOLS., 1921-1965, 08: 1088-1089.
Comment: This letter is about disagreement concerning land divisions involving Lawyer, Zimmer, Johnson, Girtman, Swart, Snyder, Balk, Dietz and others, as well as Sidney and Houck. SEE 1768,11,13; 1768,11, 24; 1769,01,05; 1769,01,29; 1769,02,10.

Date: 1774,04,15-28
Description: William Johnson to the Corporation of Albany, about land. Mentions possible release of lands off Schoharie Creek at Tionnonderoge (Tienonderoge, Tienonderoga).
Source: THE PAPERS OF SIR WILLIAM JOHNSON. ED. BY JAMES SULLIVAN, ET AL. ALBANY: STATE UNIVERSITY OF NEW YORK, 14 VOLS., 1921-1965, 08: 1120-1121
Comment: Contains important details. Original draft is badly burned, however, so some key words are missing.

Date: 1774,06,11 [ ]
Description: Report of N.Y. Governor Tryon on the Province of New York. Answers to Questions No. 17 & 18 present information about the number and "strength" of the Indians. Of the Mohawks, it says that they are "the first in Rank of the Six Nation Condederacy tho' now . . . reduced to Two Villages on the Mohawk River and a few Families at Schoharie. The lower Mohawks are in Number about One Hundred and Eighty Five, and the Upper or those of Canajoharie Two Hundred and Twenty One making together Four Hundred and Six. . ." See Question No.13 & 14 for population of "Whites and Black".
Source: DOCUMENTS RELATIVE TO THE COLONIAL HISTORY OF THE STATE OF NEW YORK, ED. BY E.B. O'CALLAGHAN AND BERTHOLD FERNOW, 15 VOL. (ALBANY, N.Y.: WEED, PARSONS, AND CO., 1856-87), 8: 434-459.
Comment: Discusses boundaries of New York in answer to Question No. 2, making reference to the Five Nations in doing so. Gives English interpretation of 1701 treaty as cession of land by the Five Nations. Five Nations interpretation was that it did not cede the land in the sense of giving it up, but instead put the land under the protection of the British Crown. See end of answer to Question No. 3 for English attitude toward native land tenure. The report was included by Gov. Tryon in a letter to the English Earl of Dartmouth, dated 11 June 1774.

Date: 1774,08,04
Description: Patent to George Smart of 200 acres of land.
Source: N.Y.STATE ARCHIVES, ALBANY, N.Y. MILITARY PATENTS, 1764-1775, SERIES NO. A0447, BOOK 3, P. 8.
Comment: Military grant.

Date: 1774,08,04 (2)
Description: Patent to Charles Tate for 200 acres of land.
Source: N.Y.STATE ARCHIVES, ALBANY, N.Y. MILITARY PATENTS, 1764-1775, SERIES NO. A0447, BOOK 3, P. 6.
Comment: Military grant.

Date: 1774,11,12
Description: Petition of Blagg and Fanning for grant of land next to that of B. Glazier and Cockcroft.
Source: N.Y.STATE ARCHIVES, ALBANY, N.Y.COL.MSS, INDORSED LAND PAPERS, 1643-1803, SERIES NO. A0272, DEPARTMENT OF STATE, APPLICATIONS FOR LAND GRANTS, VOL. 34, P. 137.
Comment: For information about B. Glazier's land SEE 1772,05,08; 1771,05,24.

Date: 1775,02,10-16
Description: Proceedings of the Oneidas and Indians of Oughquaga (Oquaga) with English Colonel Guy Johnson. On 11 Feb., Adam of Oquaga reported, "That many years ago, Mr Schuyler the Presbyterian Minister at Scohare applied to them [Indians at Oquaga] for some lands at their village for Baptizing their Children, and other Religious services, which he had long neglected, and therefore they had resolved on taking the lands back; that some of their people were for, and others against it, . . ."
Source: DOCUMENTS RELATIVE TO THE COLONIAL HISTORY OF THE STATE OF NEW YORK, ED. BY E.B. O'CALLAGHAN AND BERTHOLD FERNOW, 15 VOL. (ALBANY, N.Y.: WEED, PARSONS, AND CO., 1856-87), 8: 549-555.
Comment: A letter from Aaron Crosby, a missionary for the Society for Propagating the Gospel among the Indians, was also presented. Crosby (Congregational) and Schuyler (Presbyterian) were involved in a theological controversy, centered on whether or not to baptize children. Crosby, a missionary at Oquaga, wrote, "Against the Church of England, have I spoken nothing, neither against the Church at Scohare." SEE 1757,05,02.

Date: 1775,03,27
Description: Patent to James Black and others for 100 acres of land.
Source: N.Y.STATE ARCHIVES, ALBANY, N.Y. MILITARY PATENTS, 1764-1775, SERIES NO. A0447, BOOK 3, P. 045.
Comment: Military grant.

Date: 1775,03,27 (2)
Description: Patent to John Craney for 200 acres of land.
Source: N.Y.STATE ARCHIVES, ALBANY, N.Y. MILITARY PATENTS, 1764-1775, SERIES NO. A0447, BOOK 3, P. 44.
Comment: Military grant.

Date: 1775,08,15-09,02
Description: Proceedings of the Six Nations with the Commissioners of the Twelve United Colonies.
Source: DOCUMENTS RELATIVE TO THE COLONIAL HISTORY OF THE STATE OF NEW YORK, ED. BY E.B. O'CALLAGHAN AND BERTHOLD FERNOW, 15 VOL. (ALBANY, N.Y.: WEED, PARSONS, AND CO., 1856-87), 8: 605-631.
Comment: Does not make specific reference to Indians of Schoharie. It is included in this compilation because it gives a good idea of the consternation of the Six Nations and the difficult choices facing them in deciding who-- Rebels or Loyalists--held the other end of the Covenant Chain.

Date: 1777,02,20 [ ]
Description: Proceedings of the Albany Committee of Correspondence. It is resolved "That an order be given on Mr. Henry Roseboom in favour of Mr. Adam Vrooman (Vroman) for twenty eight pounds of Lead, and some Flints for the use of the Indians in Schoharry District".
Source: ALBANY COMMITTEE OF CORRESPONDENCE, 1775-1777, VOL. I, (ALBANY, N.Y.: STATE UNIVERSITY OF NEW YORK, 1923).
Comment:

Date: 1777,07,09°
Description: Tracing of a certificate that a Cayuga Indian had been in the King's service, signed by Daniel Claus, 9 July 1777. Refers to Schoharie.
Source: SEE 1887,00,00-1888,00,00 (28).
Comment: Rufus Grider Collection.

Date: 1778,00,00°
Description: Tracing of Schoharie Lutheran church records regarding murders by Indians, 1778.
Source: SEE 1887,00,00-1888,00,00 (29).
Comment: Rufus Grider Collection.

Date: 1778,00,00°
Description: Tracing of a map of "Schohara" (Schoharie) by Captain William Gray, 1778.
Source: SEE 1887,00,00-1888,00,00 (35).
Comment: Rufus Grider Collection.

Date: 1778,09,10
Description: Letter from Colonel Guy Johnson to British Lord George Germain. Johnson reports, "...whilst another Division under Mr Brandt, the Indian Chief cutt [sic] off 294 Men near Schohare and destroyed the adjacent settlements with several Magazines from whence the Rebels have derived great recourses."
Source: DOCUMENTS RELATIVE TO THE COLONIAL HISTORY OF THE STATE OF NEW YORK, 15 VOL. (ALBANY, N.Y.: WEED, PARSONS, AND CO., 1856-87), 8: 751-752.
Comment:

Date: 1779,00,00°
Description: Water color reconstruction of the Upper Fort, Schoharie, as it appeared in 1779.
Source: SEE 1887,00,00-1888,00,00 (20).
Comment:

Date: 1779,01,01
Description: A detailed map of land patents in the "Province of New York." Schoharie region is included.
Source: A CHOROGRAPHICAL MAP OF THE PROVINCE OF NEW-YORK, IN NORTH AMERICA, DIVIDED INTO COUNTIES, MANORS, PATENTS AND TOWNSHIPS; ... COMPILED FROM ACTUAL SURVEYS DEPOSITED IN THE PATENT OFFICE AT NEW YORK ..., BY CLAUDE JOSEPH SAUTHIER. LONDON, ENGLAND: ENGRAVED AND PUBLISHED BY WILLIAM FADEN, JANUARY 1, 1779.
Comment: Scale of English Statute Miles is about 69 1/2 to a Degree.

Date: 1779,06,01°
Description: Copy of list on file in U. S. War Office of Indian names commissioned by Gen. Schuyler.
Source: SEE 1791,02,08.
Comment:

Date: 1779,11,26
Description: Release to Jacob Enders by Johannes Merckel (Markell; Merckell; Marckell; Mirakle) of a lot in Schoharie, on a south line between Lots 3 and 4 in the patent granted to Lewis Morris and Andres Coeman (Coeyman, Coeymans), being that lot upon which Enders' house and barn stand. The parties to the agreement are yeomen of Schoharie.
Source: N.Y.STATE LIBRARY, ALBANY, MANUSCRIPTS, SCHOHARIE COUNTY, PATENTEES, LAND RECORDS, DW10738.
Comment: For documents pertaining to the Morris and Coeyman Patent, see 1725,10,28 (3); 1726,04,30; 1726,04,30 (2); 1726,05,02; 1726,05,24; 1819,11,00 [ ].

Date: 1780,00,00°
Description: Original engraving of Sir John Johnson, woodcut of Joseph Brant, and watercolor copy of portrait of Cornplanter, leaders in the raid of 1780.
Source: SEE 1887,00,00-1888,00,00 (12).
Comment:

Date: 1780,04,10°
Description: Tracing of statement of Joseph Brant regarding his treatment of captives, 10 April 1780.
Source: SEE 1887,00,00-1888,00,00 (36).
Comment:

Date: 1780,10,17°
Description: Rufus Grider Collection. Pen and ink map of the route of Johnson's army in Schoharie Valley, 17 October 1780.
Source: SEE 1887,00,00-1888,00,00 (5).
Comment:

Date: 1781,00,00°
Description: Tracing of entry from Lutheran church records, Schoharie Village, 1781, relative to two murders by Indians at Dorlach.
Source: SEE 1887,00,00-1888,00,00 (27).
Comment: Rufus Grider Collection.

Date: 1783,09,25
Description: Return of Six Nations Indians and Confederates at Niagara. Forty-eight Indians of the Loyal Village are identified as Schoharie Indians. Of these, twelve are men, twenty-two are women and fourteen are children.
Source: PUBLIC ARCHIVES OF CANADA, OTTAWA, INDIAN RECORDS, RG10, SERIES 2, VOL. 15, P. 71.
Comment: Population data. Date may be 3 Sept 1783 instead.

Date: 1783,09,25 (2)
Description: Map of Albany Corporation lands at Fort Hunter and thereabouts.
Source: N.Y.STATE ARCHIVES, ALBANY, N.Y.COL.MSS, INDORSED LAND PAPERS, 1643-1803, SERIES NO. A0272, DEPARTMENT OF STATE, APPLICATIONS FOR LAND GRANTS, VOL. 47, P. 019.
Comment: SEE 1769,03,18.

Date: 1784,07,08°
Description: Bond to convey land to G. Marlatt.
Source: SEE 1786,10,16; 1789,03,19.
Comment:

Date: 1784,11,13
Description: Caveat of W. Harper against granting 2,000 acres of land on the west side of the Schoharie River.
Source: N.Y.STATE ARCHIVES, ALBANY, N.Y.COL.MSS, INDORSED LAND PAPERS, 1643-1803, SERIES NO. A0272, DEPARTMENT OF STATE, APPLICATIONS FOR LAND GRANTS, VOL. 37, P. 054.
Comment:

Date: 1784,12,18
Description: Deed from Jacob Sternberg (Sternbergh) to Johannes Lawyer for lot No. 35 in New Durlach, Montgomery County.
Source: N.Y.STATE LIBRARY, ALBANY, MANUSCRIPTS, JOHANNES LAWYER AND OTHERS, MAPS AND DEEDS OF SCHOHARIE VALLEY, ACC. NO. SC16469, DEEDS AND LEASES #3.
Comment:

Date: 1785,00,00
Description: Map of a hill and parcel of land on the east side of Schoharie Creek. Land of William Harper, near Fort Hunter.
Source: N.Y.STATE ARCHIVES, ALBANY, N.Y.COL.MSS, INDORSED LAND PAPERS, 1643-1803, SERIES NO. A0272, DEPARTMENT OF STATE, APPLICATIONS FOR LAND GRANTS, VOL. 46, P. 129.
Comment: SEE 1789,04,18.

Date: 1785,00,00 (2)
Description: Draft of a letter about the laying out of lands. The claim of Robert Lettice Hooper and associates under an Indian deed to Sir William Johnson is rejected, and their claim for 2,000 acres of land, under military right of John Morris is granted.
Source: N.Y.STATE ARCHIVES, ALBANY, N.Y.COL.MSS, INDORSED LAND PAPERS, 1643-1803, SERIES NO. A0272, DEPARTMENT OF STATE, APPLICATIONS FOR LAND GRANTS, VOL. 39, P. 092 (2 documents).
Comment:

Date: 1785,00,00 [ ]
Description: Names of patentees of three tracts between Schoharie and Canajoharie granted to Livingston and others, plus an abstract showing the tracts.
Source: N.Y.STATE ARCHIVES, ALBANY, N.Y.COL.MSS, INDORSED LAND PAPERS, 1643-1803, SERIES NO. A0272, DEPARTMENT OF STATE, APPLICATIONS FOR LAND GRANTS, VOL. 39, P. 076.
Comment:

Date: 1785,00,00-1791,00,00
Description: Schoharie and Coeyman's (Coeman) Field Book, containing manuscripts pertaining to the partition and division of Coeyman's Patent, i.e. land granted to Johannes Lawyer, Jacob Zimmer, and others.
Source: ALBANY COUNTY CLERK'S OFFICE, HALL OF RECORDS, ALBANY, N.Y., REAL PROPERTY RECORDS, FIELD BOOKS & SURVEYS, SCHOHARIE & COEYMAN'S FIELD BOOK (1785-1791), 1 VOLUME.
Comment: Manuscripts in the field book are arranged first by recording date, then by lot number. See 1766,10,03 (5); 1768,08,02; 1794,05,05.

Date: 1785,02,27
Description: Acknowledgement of John Win (Winn) of the sale of his house and land on the east side of Schoharie Creek to Gideon Marlatt.
Source: N.Y.STATE ARCHIVES, ALBANY, N.Y.COL.MSS, INDORSED LAND PAPERS, 1643-1803, SERIES NO. A0272, DEPARTMENT OF STATE, APPLICATIONS FOR LAND GRANTS, VOL. 46, P. 124.
Comment:

Date: 1785,03,08
Description: Peppercorn lease to John and Jacob Kniskern (Knisker, Knieskirk, Kneiskerk, Kneescarn) by Nicolas (Nicklas, Nicholas) and Abraham Sternberg (Starnberg; Starnburgh; Sternbergh) of two-thirds of lowland Lot 4 in Kniskerns Dorp (Knisker Dorp) at Schoharie in the patent granted to Coeman (Coeyman; Coeymans) and Marries (Morris), which lot lies on the left side of the Schoharie River and uppermost half of Littel (Little) Flatt (Flat, Flats); also two-thirds of 20 acres of undivided woodland adjoining. The parties to the agreement are yeomen of Schoharie.
Source: N.Y.STATE LIBRARY, ALBANY, MANUSCRIPTS, SCHOHARIE COUNTY, PATENTEES, LAND RECORDS, DW10738.
Comment: Little Flat is in Kniskerns Dorp (Kniskern Dorp, Knisker Dorp), see 1788,04,29; 1788,08,04. For documents pertaining to the Morris and Coeyman Patent, see 1725,10,28 (3); 1726,04,30; 1726,04,30 (2); 1726,05,02; 1726,05,24; [1819,11,00].

Date: 1785,03,24
Description: Return of survey for Peter Dubois and others for 20,000 acres of land.
Source: N.Y.STATE ARCHIVES, ALBANY, N.Y.COL.MSS, INDORSED LAND PAPERS, 1643-1803, SERIES NO. A0272, DEPARTMENT OF STATE, APPLICATIONS FOR LAND GRANTS, VOL. 39, P. 075.
Comment: CALENDAR OF LAND PAPERS describes the land as being in Carlisle and Sharon, Schoharie County, and Root in Montgomery County. SEE 1773,02,15.

Date: 1785,04,25
Description: Draft of a claim described in a copy of an Indian deed. Certified copy of the Indian deed, dated 3 October 1766. Council minutes concerning.
Source: N.Y.STATE ARCHIVES, ALBANY, N.Y.COL.MSS, INDORSED LAND PAPERS, 1643-1803, SERIES NO. A0272, DEPARTMENT OF STATE, APPLICATIONS FOR LAND GRANTS, VOL. 39, P. 102.
Comment: SEE 1766,10,03.

Date: 1785,05,02
Description: Claim of Isaac Levey's (Levy's) representatives, presented by Aaron Burr, to 13,000 acres of land.
Source: N.Y.STATE ARCHIVES, ALBANY, N.Y.COL.MSS, INDORSED LAND PAPERS, 1643-1803, SERIES NO. A0272, DEPARTMENT OF STATE, APPLICATIONS FOR LAND GRANTS, VOL. 56, P. 128.
Comment: SEE 1793,09,18; n.d.

Date: 1785,05,05
Description: Locations of land for officers and soldiers of Col. Willet's Corp.
Source: SEE 1789,11,24.
Comment: Bounty lands.

Date: 1785,09,00
Description: Affidavit of Jacob Seebar and Jacob Putnam that Putnam has owned his lands on the east side of Schoharie Creek since the Fall of 1780.
Source: N.Y.STATE ARCHIVES, ALBANY, N.Y.COL.MSS, INDORSED LAND PAPERS, 1643-1803, SERIES NO. A0272, DEPARTMENT OF STATE, APPLICATIONS FOR LAND GRANTS, VOL. 41, P. 027.
Comment:

Date: 1785,09,20
Description: Copy of a report of N. Y. Provincial Council Meeting, attended by the Lieutenant Governor of New York, James DeLancey and Council members, about a petition of Mathew Ferrall in behalf of himself and others for a license to purchase 130,000 acres of "a large tract of vacant land lying . . . south and southwest of Schohary (Schoharie)". The date of the Council Meeting is 13 March 1754. The document states that the Council advised that the license be granted. The copy is certified as being true on 19 and 20 Sept 1985.
Source: N.Y.STATE ARCHIVES, ALBANY, N.Y.COL.MSS, INDORSED LAND PAPERS, 1643-1803, SERIES NO. A0272, DEPARTMENT OF STATE, APPLICATIONS FOR LAND GRANTS, VOL. 39, P. 092.
Comment: This document states that on 2 Dec1736 the Committee of the N.Y. Provincial Council passed a regulation requiring "an actual survey in the presence of the Indians." It provides information about the process of land transactions. SEE 1751,06,12; 1752,11,21; 1754,03,01; 1754,03,05.

Date: 1785,09,27
Description: Certificate of N. Quackenboss (Quackenbush, (Queckenbush) and J. Van Epps that William Hall has had possession for 13 years of lands on the west side of Schoharie Creek.
Source: N.Y.STATE ARCHIVES, ALBANY, N.Y.COL.MSS, INDORSED LAND PAPERS, 1643-1803, SERIES NO. A0272, DEPARTMENT OF STATE, APPLICATIONS FOR LAND GRANTS, VOL. 41, P. 018.
Comment:

Date: 1785,09,27 (2)
Description: Certificate of N. Quackenboss (Quackenbush, Queckenbush) and J. Van Epps that Isaac D. Queckenbush had possession of disputed land from 1779 until 5 April 1784 when he sold the land to Samuel Weeks who now possesses it.
Source: N.Y.STATE ARCHIVES, ALBANY, N.Y.COL.MSS, INDORSED LAND PAPERS, 1643-1803, SERIES NO. A0272, DEPARTMENT OF STATE, APPLICATIONS FOR LAND GRANTS, VOL. 41, P. 019.
Comment:

Date: 1785,09,27 (3)
Description: Certificate of N. Quackenbush and J.C. Van Epps that Hermanus Mabee (Maybe) has possessed land on the west side of Schoharie Creek for 23 years.
Source: N.Y.STATE ARCHIVES, ALBANY, N.Y.COL.MSS, INDORSED LAND PAPERS, 1643-1803, SERIES NO. A0272, DEPARTMENT OF STATE, APPLICATIONS FOR LAND GRANTS, VOL. 41, P. 020.
Comment:

Date: 1785,09,27 (4)
Description: Certificate that Isaac Collier possessed his lands on the west side of Schoharie Creek from 1778 to 27 Sept 1785.
Source: N.Y.STATE ARCHIVES, ALBANY, N.Y.COL.MSS, INDORSED LAND PAPERS, 1643-1803, SERIES NO. A0272, DEPARTMENT OF STATE, APPLICATIONS FOR LAND GRANTS, VOL. 41, P. 021.
Comment:

Date: 1785,09,28
Description: Certificate that Nicholas A. Van Slyke possessed land on the west side of Schoharie Creek from 1781 until 28 Sept 1785.
Source: N.Y.STATE ARCHIVES, ALBANY, N.Y.COL.MSS, INDORSED LAND PAPERS, 1643-1803, SERIES NO. A0272, DEPARTMENT OF STATE, APPLICATIONS FOR LAND GRANTS, VOL. 41, P. 021.
Comment:

Date: 1785,09,28 (2)
Description: Certificate of Justices John Van Eps and Nicholas Quakenbush that G. Marlatt possessed a house and lands on the south side of the highway leading from Schoharie Creek west up to the Mohawk River from 1780 until the present.
Source: N.Y.STATE ARCHIVES, ALBANY, N.Y.COL.MSS, INDORSED LAND PAPERS, 1643-1803, SERIES NO. A0272, DEPARTMENT OF STATE, APPLICATIONS FOR LAND GRANTS, VOL. 46, P. 125.
Comment:

Date: 1785,10,01
Description: Petition of David Prym (Pruyn[?]) for a patent to two tracts of land on Schoharie Creek, 18 October 1766. Certified 1 October 1785.
Source: N.Y.STATE ARCHIVES, ALBANY, N.Y.COL.MSS, INDORSED LAND PAPERS, 1643-1803, SERIES NO. A0272, DEPARTMENT OF STATE, APPLICATIONS FOR LAND GRANTS, VOL. 39.
Comment: SEE 1766,10,03; 1766,10,18; 1767,08,29.

Date: 1785,10,11
Description: Memorial of A. Putnam and G. Newkirk about a claim on the east side of Schoharie Kill. Certificates and affidavits are included pertaining to that land and some along the highway from Schoharie Creek to the Mohawk. Four maps are also with this document.
Source: N.Y.STATE ARCHIVES, ALBANY, N.Y.COL.MSS, INDORSED LAND PAPERS, 1643-1803, SERIES NO. A0272, DEPARTMENT OF STATE, APPLICATIONS FOR LAND GRANTS, VOL. 39, P. 106.
Comment:

Date: 1785,11,12
Description: Map of a part of Schoharie County lying on the west side of Schoharie River in a patent called Kniskerns (Knisker, Knieskirk, Kneescarn, Kneiskerk) Dorpf (Dorp), by Johannes Lawyer, Jr., surveyor.
Source: N.Y.STATE LIBRARY, ALBANY, MANUSCRIPTS, SCHOHARIE COUNTY, PATENTEES, MAPS, DW10738, MAP #2.
Comment:

Date: 1785,11,22°
Description: Release to John and Jacob Kniskern (Knisker, Knieskirk, Kneescarn, Kneiskerk) by Jost Kniskern, according to an agreement for the partition of lands in the Old Schoharie and Kniskerns Dorpt (Kniskers Dorp) patents, made November 22, 1785.
Source: SEE 1786,01,07.
Comment:

Date: 1785,12,21
Description: Will of Johannes Becker of Schoharie.
Source: N.Y.STATE LIBRARY, ALBANY, MANUSCRIPTS, JOHANNES LAWYER AND OTHERS, MAPS AND DEEDS OF SCHOHARIE VALLEY, ACC. NO. 16469, WILL.
Comment:

Date: 1786,00,00
Description: Copies of locations of various tracts of land at the conjunction of the Mohawk and Schoharie Rivers.
Source: N.Y.STATE ARCHIVES, ALBANY, N.Y.COL.MSS, INDORSED LAND PAPERS, 1643-1803, SERIES NO. A0272, DEPARTMENT OF STATE, APPLICATIONS FOR LAND GRANTS, VOL. 41, P. 029.
Comment: Names mentioned are Adam Putnam, Morgan Lewis, Leonard Gansevoort, Frederick Cluet, Gerret C. Newkerk (Newkirk), Benjamin Newkerk, and William Harper (as agent for William Hall, Isaac Collier, Samuel Weeks, Gideon Marlat, Nicholas Pamslyck (?), Vincent Quaquenbush, and Harmanus Mabie [Maybe]). SEE n.d. for a map.

Date: 1786,00,00 (2)
Description: Skeleton map of lands on the Mohawk and Schoharie rivers.
Source: N.Y.STATE ARCHIVES, ALBANY, N.Y.COL.MSS, INDORSED LAND PAPERS, 1643-1803, SERIES NO. A0272, DEPARTMENT OF STATE, APPLICATIONS FOR LAND GRANTS, VOL. 41, P. 032.
Comment:

Date: 1786,00,00°
Description: Map of lands on the Mohawk and Schoharie rivers referred to in a copy of Adam Putnam's location of a tract of 400 acres of land in the county of Montgomery, bounded on the north by the road leading from Fort Hunter, filed 5 July 1785.
Source: SEE n.d.
Comment: SEE 1725,10,13 for warrant to a patent that is shown on this map. The map is filed in the N.Y.STATE ARCHIVES among papers dated 1786. Adam Putnam's location of a tract of 400 acres may be found in the N.Y.STATE ARCHIVES, ALBANY, N.Y.COL.MSS, INDORSED LAND PAPERS, 1643-1803, SERIES NO. A0272, DEPARTMENT OF STATE, APPLICATIONS FOR LAND GRANTS, VOL., P. 29.

Date: 1786,01,04
Description: Letter from the surveyor general to Gov. Clinton of New York concerning the location of vacant lands near Fort Hunter.
Source: N.Y.STATE ARCHIVES, ALBANY, N.Y.COL.MSS, INDORSED LAND PAPERS, 1643-1803, SERIES NO. A0272, DEPARTMENT OF STATE, APPLICATIONS FOR LAND GRANTS, VOL. 41, P. 017.
Comment:

Date: 1786,01,07
Description: Release to John and Jacob Kniskern (Knisker, Knieskirk, Kneiskerk, Kneescarn) by Jost Kniskern, according to an agreement for the partition of lands in the Old Schoharie and Kniskerns Dorpt (Dorp) patents, made November 22, 1785, being part of Lot 8 and part of Lot 9, two parcels of land called Cribelbush, and part of a swamp, and half of the parcel of land called Clasner's Weise, and woodland lots 2, 4, 6, and 8 in the Old Schoharie Patent granted to Myndert Schuyler.
Source: N.Y.STATE LIBRARY, ALBANY, MANUSCRIPTS, SCHOHARIE COUNTY, PATENTEES, LAND RECORDS, DW10738.
Comment: See 1794,05,06. For documents pertaining to Myndert Schuyler's patent, see 1714,00,00; 1714,05,08; 1714,11,03 (4); 1887,00,00-1888,00,00 (34); 1722,09,28.

Date: 1786,01,11
Description: Caveat of John Ten Broeck and Catharine (Catherine) Wray against granting land on the north side of Cobus Kill (Cobleskill).
Source: N.Y.STATE ARCHIVES, ALBANY, N.Y.COL.MSS, INDORSED LAND PAPERS, 1643-1803, SERIES NO. A0272, DEPARTMENT OF STATE, APPLICATIONS FOR LAND GRANTS, VOL. 41, P. 038.
Comment:

Date: 1786,01,26
Description: Certificate of location of 7,000 acres of land for John D. Gros.
Source: N.Y.STATE ARCHIVES, ALBANY, N.Y.COL.MSS, INDORSED LAND PAPERS, 1643-1803, SERIES NO. A0272, DEPARTMENT OF STATE, APPLICATIONS FOR LAND GRANTS, VOL. 41, P. 052.
Comment: CALENDAR OF LAND PAPERS notes that the land is in Carlisle, Sharon, Schoharie County and Root, Montgomery County.

Date: 1786,06,07
Description: Return of survey for Isaac Levy (Levey) of 4,333 acres of land on the east side of Schoharie Creek. Map included.
Source: N.Y.STATE ARCHIVES, ALBANY, N.Y.COL.MSS, INDORSED LAND PAPERS, 1643-1803, SERIES NO. A0272, DEPARTMENT OF STATE, APPLICATIONS FOR LAND GRANTS, VOL. 41, P. 107.
Comment: SEE 1785,05,02; 1786,06,07; 1786,06,28; n.d. CALENDAR OF LAND PAPERS notes that the land is in Middleburgh and Broome, Schoharie County.

Date: 1786,06,26
Description: Return of survey for Philip Livingston, Catherine Westerlo, Margaret Jones, Sarah Livingston and H. Livingston of a tract of 7,000 acres of land north of Cobus Kill (Cobleskill). Map included.
Source: N.Y.STATE ARCHIVES, ALBANY, N.Y.COL.MSS, INDORSED LAND PAPERS, 1643-1803, SERIES NO. A0272, DEPARTMENT OF STATE, APPLICATIONS FOR LAND GRANTS, VOL. 42, P. 112.
Comment:

Date: 1786,06,28
Description: Ackowledgement that S. Bayard paid for land to be granted to representatives of Isaac Levey (Levy).
Source: N.Y.STATE ARCHIVES, ALBANY, N.Y.COL.MSS, INDORSED LAND PAPERS, 1643-1803, SERIES NO. A0272, DEPARTMENT OF STATE, APPLICATIONS FOR LAND GRANTS, VOL. 56, P. 129.
Comment: SEE 1793,09,18; 1785,05,02; 1786,06,28; n.d.

Date: 1786,07,05
Description: Return of survey for David Prym (Pruyn[?]) of 150 acres on the west side of Schoharie Creek.
Source: N.Y.STATE ARCHIVES, ALBANY, N.Y.COL.MSS, INDORSED LAND PAPERS, 1643-1803, SERIES NO. A0272, DEPARTMENT OF STATE, APPLICATIONS FOR LAND GRANTS, VOL. 42, P. 121.
Comment: CALENDAR OF LAND PAPERS notes that the land is in Glen, Montgomery County.

Date: 1786,07,27
Description: Philip Livingston Survey.
Source: MIX'S CATALOG OF MAPS AND SURVEYS IN OFFFICES OF THE SECRETARY OF STATE, STATE ENGINEER AND SURVEYOR AND COMPTROLLER AND N.Y. STATE LIBRARY, 1859, REFERENCES THIS MAP, LISTING IT AS BEING IN THE OFFICE OF THE N.Y. SECRETARY OF STATE, FIELDBOOK # 24, SUBDIVISION C, P. 053.
Comment:

Date: 1786,07,27 (2)
Description: Survey map of Philip Livingston's land.
Source: MIX'S CATALOG OF MAPS AND SURVEYS IN OFFFICES OF THE SECRETARY OF STATE, STATE ENGINEER AND SURVEYOR AND COMPTROLLER AND N.Y. STATE LIBRARY, 1859, REFERENCES THIS MAP, LISTING IT AS BEING IN THE OFFICES OF GENERAL SERVICES, NEW YORK STATE, MAP #210.
Comment:

Date: 1786,10,13
Description: Affidavit of David Masters to William Hall.
Source: N.Y.STATE ARCHIVES, ALBANY, N.Y.COL.MSS, INDORSED LAND PAPERS, 1643-1803, SERIES NO. A0272, DEPARTMENT OF STATE, APPLICATIONS FOR LAND GRANTS, VOL. 41, P. 024.
Comment: SEE 1785,09,27; 1786,10,16.

Date: 1786,10,16
Description: Affidavit of Gerrit Newkirk about title to property of William Hall.
Source: N.Y.STATE ARCHIVES, ALBANY, N.Y.COL.MSS, INDORSED LAND PAPERS, 1643-1803, SERIES NO. A0272, DEPARTMENT OF STATE, APPLICATIONS FOR LAND GRANTS, VOL. 41, P. 023.
Comment: SEE 1785,09,27.

Date: 1786,10,16 (2)
Description: Affidavit of William Harper about land of Jacob Putnam on the east side of Schoharie Creek.
Source: N.Y.STATE ARCHIVES, ALBANY, N.Y.COL.MSS, INDORSED LAND PAPERS, 1643-1803, SERIES NO. A0272, DEPARTMENT OF STATE, APPLICATIONS FOR LAND GRANTS, VOL. 41, P. 028.
Comment:

Date: 1786,10,16 (3)
Description: Affidavit of John Winn that Van Slyke (Van Slyck), Isaac Collier, Gerrit C. Newkirk, S. Quackenbush (Quackenboss, Queckenbush), Samuel Weeks, William Hall, H. Mabee (Maybe), Adam Putnam, and Gideon Marlatt were friendly and loyal to the American cause during the Revolutionary War.
Source: N.Y.STATE ARCHIVES, ALBANY, N.Y.COL.MSS, INDORSED LAND PAPERS, 1643-1803, SERIES NO. A0272, DEPARTMENT OF STATE, APPLICATIONS FOR LAND GRANTS, VOL. 46, P. 124.
Comment: SEE 1789,01,00; 1789,01,31; 1789,03,19; 1789,04,14; 1789,04,16; 1789,04,18; 1789,04,23; 1787; 1789,09,23; 1789,09,25; 1789,09,27; 1789,09,29; 1789,10,09; 1785,02,27. Bounty lands.

Date: 1786,11,11
Description: Map of a patent granted August 14, 1761 to Johannes Lawyer, Jr. and others. Map made October 6, 1763; made over again November 11, 1786 by Johannes Lawyer, Jr. for his own use.
Source: N.Y.STATE LIBRARY, ALBANY, MANUSCRIPTS, JOHANNES LAWYER AND OTHERS, MAPS AND DEEDS OF SCHOHARIE VALLEY, ACC. NO. 16469, MAP #4.
Comment:

Date: 1787,05,07
Description: Statement of Peter Vroman (Vrooman) of Schoharie that he has secured commutation of quit rent and has settled with the State of New York for arrears due on 88 acres of land within the 3500 acre patent granted to Lewis Morris and others May 24, 1726.
Source: N.Y.STATE LIBRARY, ALBANY, MANUSCRIPTS, SCHOHARIE COUNTY, PATENTEES, LAND RECORDS, DW10738.
Comment: See 1725,10,28 (3); 1726,04,30; 1726,04,30 (2); 1726,05,02; 1726,05,24; 1819,11,00 [ ].

Date: 1787,09,29
Description: Affidavit of John Newkirk and Jacob Hall in favor of Gerrit C. Newkirk's title to land west of Schoharie Kill.
Source: N.Y.STATE ARCHIVES, ALBANY, N.Y.COL.MSS, INDORSED LAND PAPERS, 1643-1803, SERIES NO. A0272, DEPARTMENT OF STATE, APPLICATIONS FOR LAND GRANTS, VOL. 46, P. 105.
Comment: SEE 1786,10,16.

Date: 1787,09,29 (2)
Description: Affidavit of John McGraw and William Philips in favor of Gerrit Newkirk's title to land east of Schoharie Kill.
Source: N.Y.STATE ARCHIVES, ALBANY, N.Y.COL.MSS, INDORSED LAND PAPERS, 1643-1803, SERIES NO. A0272, DEPARTMENT OF STATE, APPLICATIONS FOR LAND GRANTS, VOL. 46, P. 107.
Comment: SEE 1786,10,16.

Date: 1788,01,12
Description: Petition of 28 Mohawk Indians to be reinstated with land and other property held before the revolutionary war, so that such can be leased or suitably disposed of before the Indians remove to other land.
Source: N.Y. HISTORICAL SOCIETY, NEW YORK, NEW YORK.
Comment: N.B. The list of Indian signers includes both the Christian and Indian names of the signers.

Date: 1788,02,20
Description: Certificate of location for Jeremiah Van Rensselaer of 1,500 acres of land.
Source: N.Y.STATE ARCHIVES, ALBANY, N.Y.COL.MSS, INDORSED LAND PAPERS, 1643-1803, SERIES NO. A0272, DEPARTMENT OF STATE, APPLICATIONS FOR LAND GRANTS, VOL. 45, P. 148.
Comment: CALENDAR OF LAND PAPERS notes that this land is in Carlisle, Schoharie County.

Date: 1788,02,20 (2)
Description: Certificate of location for Thomas Machin of 1,500 acres of land.
Source: N.Y.STATE ARCHIVES, ALBANY, N.Y.COL.MSS, INDORSED LAND PAPERS, 1643-1803, SERIES NO. A0272, DEPARTMENT OF STATE, APPLICATIONS FOR LAND GRANTS, VOL. 45, P. 150.
Comment:

Date: 1788,02,20 (3)
Description: Certificate of location for Henry Oothout of 919 acres of land.
Source: N.Y.STATE ARCHIVES, ALBANY, N.Y.COL.MSS, INDORSED LAND PAPERS, 1643-1803, SERIES NO. A0272, DEPARTMENT OF STATE, APPLICATIONS FOR LAND GRANTS, VOL. 45, P. 150.
Comment: CALENDAR OF LAND PAPERS notes that the land is in Carlisle, Schoharie County.

Date: 1788,04,29
Description: Release to John and Jacob Kniskern (Knisker, Knieskirk, Kneiskerk, Kneescarn) by David Sternbergh (Starnberg, Starnbergh, Sternberg) of nine acres, two rods lowland and thirteen acres, two rods woodland on the west bank of Schoharie River, on the uppermost side of the Little Flat in Kniskerns Dorp (Knisker Dorp), being those lands marked "J.K." on an included map of lowland lot 4, containing fourteen acres, three rods, and an adjoining woodland lot containing 20 acres. The parties to the agreement are yeoman of Schenectady.
Source: N.Y.STATE LIBRARY, ALBANY, MANUSCRIPTS, SCHOHARIE COUNTY, PATENTEES, LAND RECORDS, DW10738.
Comment:

Date: 1788,08,04
Description: Lease to Peter Enders, Jr. by David Sternbergh (Starnberg, Starnbergh, Sternberg) of Schoharie, for one year, of the lower end of lowland Lot 4 and of an adjoining piece of land in the Homestead woodland at Kniskern's Dorp (Knisker Dorp, Kniskern Dorp, Kniskerns Dorp) along the west side of the Schoharie River on the Little Flat, containing four acres, three rods and six acres, two rods respectively. The parties to the agreement are yeoman of Schoharie.
Source: N.Y.STATE LIBRARY, ALBANY, MANUSCRIPTS, SCHOHARIE COUNTY, PATENTEES, LAND RECORDS, DW10738.
Comment:

Date: 1789,00,00
Description: Affidavits about Jacob Seeber's claims of land near Fort Hunter on the west side of Schoharie Creek.
Source: N.Y.STATE ARCHIVES, ALBANY, N.Y.COL.MSS, INDORSED LAND PAPERS, 1643-1803, SERIES NO. A0272, DEPARTMENT OF STATE, APPLICATIONS FOR LAND GRANTS, VOL. 47, P. 052.
Comment:

Date: 1789,01,00
Description: Field book of locations made by William Harper for men who served with him in the late war. Concerns titles to lands around Fort Hunter.
Source: N.Y.STATE ARCHIVES, ALBANY, N.Y.COL.MSS, INDORSED LAND PAPERS, 1643-1803, SERIES NO. A0272, DEPARTMENT OF STATE, APPLICATIONS FOR LAND GRANTS, VOL. 46, P. 100.
Comment: SEE 1786,10,16.

Date: 1789,01,31
Description: Affidavit of William Quackenbush for Van Slyke (Van Slyck) title to lands on the west side of Schoharie Creek.
Source: N.Y.STATE ARCHIVES, ALBANY, N.Y.COL.MSS, INDORSED LAND PAPERS, 1643-1803, SERIES NO. A0272, DEPARTMENT OF STATE, APPLICATIONS FOR LAND GRANTS, VOL. 46, P. 101.
Comment: SEE 1786,10,16.

Date: 1789,01,31 (2)
Description: Affidavit of J. Garider in favor of Isaac Collier's title to land west of Schoharie Creek.
Source: N.Y.STATE ARCHIVES, ALBANY, N.Y.COL.MSS, INDORSED LAND PAPERS, 1643-1803, SERIES NO. A0272, DEPARTMENT OF STATE, APPLICATIONS FOR LAND GRANTS, VOL. 46, P. 103.
Comment: See 1785,09,27; 1786,10,16.

Date: 1789,01,31 (3)
Description: Affidavit of William Colon in favor of Samuel Week's title to land west of Schoharie.
Source: N.Y.STATE ARCHIVES, ALBANY, N.Y.COL.MSS, INDORSED LAND PAPERS, 1643-1803, SERIES NO. A0272, DEPARTMENT OF STATE, APPLICATIONS FOR LAND GRANTS, VOL. 56, P. 110.
Comment: SEE 1786,10,16; 1789,03,19.

Date: 1789,01,31 (4)
Description: Affidavit of Gerrit Putnam in favor of William Hall's title to land west of Schoharie Creek.
Source: N.Y.STATE ARCHIVES, ALBANY, N.Y.COL.MSS, INDORSED LAND PAPERS, 1643-1803, SERIES NO. A0272, DEPARTMENT OF STATE, APPLICATIONS FOR LAND GRANTS, VOL. 46, P. 112.
Comment: SEE 1786,10,16; 1789,03,19.

Date: 1789,01,31 (5)
Description: Affidavit of A. Quackenbush (Quackenboss, Queckenbush) in favor of H. Mabee's (Maybe's) title to land west of Schoharie Creek.
Source: N.Y.STATE ARCHIVES, ALBANY, N.Y.COL.MSS, INDORSED LAND PAPERS, 1643-1803, SERIES NO. A0272, DEPARTMENT OF STATE, APPLICATIONS FOR LAND GRANTS, VOL. 46, P. 115.
Comment: SEE 1786,10,16; 1789,03,19.

Date: 1789,01,31 (6)
Description: Affidavit of Jacob Colyer in favor of Gideon Marlatt's title to land west of Schoharie Creek.
Source: N.Y.STATE ARCHIVES, ALBANY, N.Y.COL.MSS, INDORSED LAND PAPERS, 1643-1803, SERIES NO. A0272, DEPARTMENT OF STATE, APPLICATIONS FOR LAND GRANTS, VOL. 46, P. 121.
Comment: SEE 1786,10,16; 1789,03,19.

Date: 1789,03,19
Description: Affidavit of N. Quackenbush (Quackenboss, Queckenbush) in favor of Samuel Week's title to land west of Schoharie.
Source: N.Y.STATE ARCHIVES, ALBANY, N.Y.COL.MSS, INDORSED LAND PAPERS, 1643-1803, SERIES NO. A0272, DEPARTMENT OF STATE, APPLICATIONS FOR LAND GRANTS, VOL. 46, P. 111.
Comment: SEE 1786,10,16; 1789,01,31.

Date: 1789,03,19 (2)
Description: Affidavit of A. Quackenbush (Quackenboss, Queckenbush) in favor of William Hall's title to land west of Schoharie Creek.
Source: N.Y.STATE ARCHIVES, ALBANY, N.Y.COL.MSS, INDORSED LAND PAPERS, 1643-1803, SERIES NO. A0272, DEPARTMENT OF STATE, APPLICATIONS FOR LAND GRANTS, VOL. 46, P. 113.
Comment: SEE 1786,10,16; 1789,01,31.

Date: 1789,03,19 (3)
Description: Affidavit of John Hall in favor of H. Mabee's title to land west of Schoharie Creek.
Source: N.Y.STATE ARCHIVES, ALBANY, N.Y.COL.MSS, INDORSED LAND PAPERS, 1643-1803, SERIES NO. A0272, DEPARTMENT OF STATE, APPLICATIONS FOR LAND GRANTS, VOL. 46, P. 114.
Comment: SEE 1786,10,16; 1789,01,31.

Date: 1789,03,19 (4)
Description: Affidavit of Samuel Week's that he witnessed bond, dated 8 July 1784, to convey land to G. Marlatt. Bond included.
Source: N.Y.STATE ARCHIVES, ALBANY, N.Y.COL.MSS, INDORSED LAND PAPERS, 1643-1803, SERIES NO. A0272, DEPARTMENT OF STATE, APPLICATIONS FOR LAND GRANTS, VOL. 46, P. 122.
Comment: SEE 1786,10,16; 1785,02,27.

Date: 1789,03,19 (5)
Description: Affidavit of Victor C. Putnam in favor of G. Marlatt's title to land west of Schoharie Creek.
Source: N.Y.STATE ARCHIVES, ALBANY, N.Y.COL.MSS, INDORSED LAND PAPERS, 1643-1803, SERIES NO. A0272, DEPARTMENT OF STATE, APPLICATIONS FOR LAND GRANTS, VOL. 46, P. 123.
Comment: SEE 1789,03,19; 1789,01,31.

Date: 1789,04,03
Description: Certificate of location for John Robinson of 900 acres of land west of Schoharie.
Source: N.Y.STATE ARCHIVES, ALBANY, N.Y.COL.MSS, INDORSED LAND PAPERS, 1643-1803, SERIES NO. A0272, DEPARTMENT OF STATE, APPLICATIONS FOR LAND GRANTS, VOL. 46, P. 092.
Comment: CALENDAR OF LAND PAPERS notes that the land is in Cobleskill.

Date: 1789,04,14
Description: Affidavit of M. Wood in favor of William Van Slyke's (Van Slyck's) land title.
Source: N.Y.STATE ARCHIVES, ALBANY, N.Y.COL.MSS, INDORSED LAND PAPERS, 1643-1803, SERIES NO. A0272, DEPARTMENT OF STATE, APPLICATIONS FOR LAND GRANTS, VOL. 46, P. 102.
Comment: SEE 1785,09,28; 1786,10,16.

Date: 1789,04,16
Description: Affidavit of William Putnam in favor of Adam Putnam's title to land.
Source: N.Y.STATE ARCHIVES, ALBANY, N.Y.COL.MSS, INDORSED LAND PAPERS, 1643-1803, SERIES NO. A0272, DEPARTMENT OF STATE, APPLICATIONS FOR LAND GRANTS, VOL. 46, P. 118.
Comment: SEE 1786,10,16; 1789,04,23; 1789,09,25.

Date: 1789,04,16 (2)
Description: Affidavit of J. Putnam in favor of Adam Putnam's title to land.
Source: N.Y.STATE ARCHIVES, ALBANY, N.Y.COL.MSS, INDORSED LAND PAPERS, 1643-1803, SERIES NO. A0272, DEPARTMENT OF STATE, APPLICATIONS FOR LAND GRANTS, VOL. 46, P. 119.
Comment: SEE 1786,10,16; 1789,04,23; 1789,09,25.

Date: 1789,04,18
Description: Affidavit of William Quackenbush in favor of S. Quackenbush's (Quackenboss's, Queckenbush's) title to land west of Schoharie.
Source: N.Y.STATE ARCHIVES, ALBANY, N.Y.COL.MSS, INDORSED LAND PAPERS, 1643-1803, SERIES NO. A0272, DEPARTMENT OF STATE, APPLICATIONS FOR LAND GRANTS, VOL. 46, P. 108.
Comment: SEE 1786,10,16; 1789,01,31.

Date: 1789,04,18 (2)
Description: Affidavit of William Colon in favor of William Harper's title to land on the east side of Schoharie Creek.
Source: N.Y.STATE ARCHIVES, ALBANY, N.Y.COL.MSS, INDORSED LAND PAPERS, 1643-1803, SERIES NO. A0272, DEPARTMENT OF STATE, APPLICATIONS FOR LAND GRANTS, VOL. 46, P. 128.
Comment: For map, SEE 1785,00,00.

Date: 1789,04,23
Description: Affidavit of Jacob Seeler in favor of Adam Putnam's title to land.
Source: N.Y.STATE ARCHIVES, ALBANY, N.Y.COL.MSS, INDORSED LAND PAPERS, 1643-1803, SERIES NO. A0272, DEPARTMENT OF STATE, APPLICATIONS FOR LAND GRANTS, VOL. 46, P. 116.
Comment: SEE 1786,10,16; 1789,04,16; 1789,09,25.

Date: 1789,04,23 (2)
Description: Affidavit of William Colon in favor of Adam Putnam's title to land on the west side of Schoharie Creek.
Source: N.Y.STATE ARCHIVES, ALBANY, N.Y.COL.MSS, INDORSED LAND PAPERS, 1643-1803, SERIES NO. A0272, DEPARTMENT OF STATE, APPLICATIONS FOR LAND GRANTS, VOL. 46, P. 116 OR 117.
Comment: SEE 1786,10,16; 1789,04,16; 1789,09,25.

Date: 1789,09,23
Description: Affidavit of Conrad Stone in favor of G. Newkirk's title to land east of Schoharie Creek.
Source: N.Y.STATE ARCHIVES, ALBANY, N.Y.COL.MSS, INDORSED LAND PAPERS, 1643-1803, SERIES NO. A0272, DEPARTMENT OF STATE, APPLICATIONS FOR LAND GRANTS, VOL. 46, P. 117.
Comment: SEE 1786,10,16; 1787,09,29; 1789,10,09.

Date: 1789,09,25
Description: Affidavit of J. Van Aken Jr. in favor of Adam Putnam's title to land.
Source: N.Y.STATE ARCHIVES, ALBANY, N.Y.COL.MSS, INDORSED LAND PAPERS, 1643-1803, SERIES NO. A0272, DEPARTMENT OF STATE, APPLICATIONS FOR LAND GRANTS, VOL. 46, P. 120.
Comment: SEE 1786,10,16; 1789,04,16; 1789,04,23.

Date: 1789,09,31
Description: Affidavit of Francis Pryme (Pruyn[?]) in favor of S. Quackenbush's (Quackenboos's, Queckenbush's) title to land west of Schoharie Creek.
Source: N.Y.STATE ARCHIVES, ALBANY, N.Y.COL.MSS, INDORSED LAND PAPERS, 1643-1803, SERIES NO. A0272, DEPARTMENT OF STATE, APPLICATIONS FOR LAND GRANTS, VOL. 46, P. 109.
Comment: SEE 1786,10,16; 1789,04,18.

Date: 1789,10,09
Description: Affidavit of John Newkirk in favor of Gerrit Newkirk's title to land on the east side of Schoharie Kill.
Source: N.Y.STATE ARCHIVES, ALBANY, N.Y.COL.MSS, INDORSED LAND PAPERS, 1643-1803, SERIES NO. A0272, DEPARTMENT OF STATE, APPLICATIONS FOR LAND GRANTS, VOL. 46, P. 105.
Comment: SEE 1786,10,16.

Date: 1789,11,24
Description: Locations of land for officers and soldiers of Col. Willet's Corp, 5 May 1785.
Source: N.Y.STATE ARCHIVES, ALBANY, N.Y.COL.MSS, INDORSED LAND PAPERS, 1643-1803, SERIES NO. A0272, DEPARTMENT OF STATE, APPLICATIONS FOR LAND GRANTS, VOL. 47, P. 170.
Comment: Bounty land.

Date: 1789,12,28
Description: Affidavit about John T. Vischer's claim to the title to land east of Schoharie Creek near Fort Hunter. Other affidavits are also included.
Source: N.Y.STATE ARCHIVES, ALBANY, N.Y.COL.MSS, INDORSED LAND PAPERS, 1643-1803, SERIES NO. A0272, DEPARTMENT OF STATE, APPLICATIONS FOR LAND GRANTS, VOL. 47, P. 124, 125.
Comment:

Date: 1789,12,28 (2)
Description: Return of survey for Cluet, Quackenbos(Quackenbush), Hall, Weeks, Collier, Van Slyke, Marlett (Marlatt), Newkirk, and Mabie (Maybe, Mabee) for 145 acres of land each on the west side of Schoharie Creek.
Source: N.Y.STATE ARCHIVES, ALBANY, N.Y.COL.MSS, INDORSED LAND PAPERS, 1643-1803, SERIES NO. A0272, DEPARTMENT OF STATE, APPLICATIONS FOR LAND GRANTS, VOL. 48, P. 059 or 060.
Comment: CALENDAR OF LAND PAPERS notes that the land is in the town of Glen. SEE 1790,03,02.

Date: 1789,12,30
Description: Caveat of John Van Aken against granting land on the east side of Schoharie to Charles Williams and others.
Source: N.Y.STATE ARCHIVES, ALBANY, N.Y.COL.MSS, INDORSED LAND PAPERS, 1643-1803, SERIES NO. A0272, DEPARTMENT OF STATE, APPLICATIONS FOR LAND GRANTS, VOL. 47, P. 125.
Comment:

Date: 1790,00,00
Description: Indexes to military claims filed in 1790.
Source: N.Y.STATE ARCHIVES, ALBANY, N.Y.COL.MSS, INDORSED LAND PAPERS, 1643-1803, SERIES NO. A0272, DEPARTMENT OF STATE, APPLICATIONS FOR LAND GRANTS, VOL. 48, P. 001-007.
Comment: Bounty lands.

Date: 1790,00,00 (2)
Description: Map of early patents on the south side of the Mohawk River by Simeon DeWitt.
Source: DOCUMENTS RELATIVE TO THE COLONIAL HISTORY OF THE STATE OF NEW YORK, ED. BY E.B. O'CALLAGHAN AND BERTHOLD FERNOW, 15 VOL. (ALBANY, N.Y.: WEED, PARSONS, AND CO., 1856-87), 1: BETWEEN 274 & 275.
Comment:

Date: 1790,00,00 [ ]
Description: List of persons (Indians and Euroamericans) not compensated for their services during the late war (American Revolution).
Source: N.Y.STATE ARCHIVES, ALBANY, N.Y.COL.MSS, INDORSED LAND PAPERS, 1643-1803, SERIES NO. A0272, DEPARTMENT OF STATE, APPLICATIONS FOR LAND GRANTS, VOL. 50, P. 029.
Comment: Bounty lands.

Date: 1790,00,00°
Description: Copy of a map of a tract of land near Schoharie granted to Walter Franklin and others, serveyed and laid into lots in 1790 by William Cockburn. Copy by grandson W. A. Cockburn.
Source: SEE n.d.
Comment:

Date: 1790,00,00°
Description: Printed map of the head waters of the Rivers Susquehanna and Delaware embracing the early patents on the south side of the Mohawk River from the original drawn about 1790 by Simeon DeWitt, surveyor general.
Source: SEE n.d.
Comment:

Date: 1790,00,00°
Description: Tracing of map of early patents on south side of Mohawk River, by Simeon DeWitt, 1790.
Source: SEE 1887,00,00-1888,00,00 (33).
Comment: Rufus Grider Collection.

Date: 1790,00,00°
Description: Rufus Grider Collection. Pen and ink tracing of map showing original patents south of the Mohawk River, about 1790, by Simeon DeWitt.
Source: SEE 1887,00,00-1888,00,00 (11).
Comment: From DOCUMENTS RELATIVE TO THE COLONIAL HISTORY OF NEW YORK..., 1: 421.

Date: 1790,00,00°
Description: List of persons (Indians and Euroamericans) not compensated for their services during the late war (American Revolution).
Source: SEE 1790,00,00 [ ].
Comment: Bounty lands.

Date: 1790,00,00°
Description: First Census of the United States Taken in the Year 1790, Schoharie Town (Schoharie Valley or Schoharie District of Albany County), printed in the Schoharie County Historical Review of Spring-Summer 1987.
Source: SEE 1987,00,00.
Comment:

Date: 1790,01,04
Description: Caveat by Jacob Seeber against Capt. John Vischer's claim to land on the east side of Schoharie Creek, near Fort Hunter.
Source: N.Y.STATE ARCHIVES, ALBANY, N.Y.COL.MSS, INDORSED LAND PAPERS, 1643-1803, SERIES NO. A0272, DEPARTMENT OF STATE, APPLICATIONS FOR LAND GRANTS, VOL. 48, P. 011.
Comment:

Date: 1790,01,20
Description: Claim of Christopher McGraw to 60 acres of bounty land on the east side of Schoharie Creek on the southeast corner of H. Barclay's tract.
Source: N.Y.STATE ARCHIVES, ALBANY, N.Y.COL.MSS, INDORSED LAND PAPERS, 1643-1803, SERIES NO. A0272, DEPARTMENT OF STATE, APPLICATIONS FOR LAND GRANTS, VOL. 48, P. 023.
Comment:

Date: 1790,03,01
Description: Return of survey for G. Newkirk and Adam Putnam of two tracts on the east side of Schoharie Creek, near Fort Hunter.
Source: N.Y.STATE ARCHIVES, ALBANY, N.Y.COL.MSS, INDORSED LAND PAPERS, 1643-1803, SERIES NO. A0272, DEPARTMENT OF STATE, APPLICATIONS FOR LAND GRANTS, VOL. 48, P. 058.
Comment:

Date: 1790,03,02
Description: Receipt pertaining to the Return of Survey of land for Cluet, Quackenbush (Quackenboss, Queckenbush), and others.
Source: N.Y.STATE ARCHIVES, ALBANY, N.Y.COL.MSS, INDORSED LAND PAPERS, 1643-1803, SERIES NO. A0272, DEPARTMENT OF STATE, APPLICATIONS FOR LAND GRANTS, VOL. 48, P. 060.
Comment: SEE 1789,12,28.

Date: 1790,06,22
Description: Certificate of the location of land for E.L. Nathan Fitch, consisting of 950 acres of the North Hardenbergh Patent on the West Bank of Schoharie Creek (called Eastkill).
Source: N.Y.STATE ARCHIVES, ALBANY, N.Y.COL.MSS, INDORSED LAND PAPERS, 1643-1803, SERIES NO. A0272, DEPARTMENT OF STATE, APPLICATIONS FOR LAND GRANTS, VOL. 48, P. 181.
Comment: CALENDAR OF LAND PAPERS notes that the land is in Hunter, Greene County.

Date: 1790,09,20
Description: Estimate of Sluman Wattles and Wittin Johnson of the expense of making a road from the Susquehanna River to "Schohary Flaats" (Schoharie Flats).
Source: N.Y.STATE ARCHIVES, ALBANY, N.Y.COL.MSS, INDORSED LAND PAPERS, 1643-1803, SERIES NO. A0272, DEPARTMENT OF STATE, APPLICATIONS FOR LAND GRANTS, VOL. 49, P. 101.
Comment:

Date: 1790,11,10
Description: Deed from Lawrence Lawyer and others to Commissioners in Partition of lands in Schoharie (Schoharie Patent): Lot 32 in first allotment, Lot 12 in second allotment, and Lot 11 in third allotment.
Source: ALBANY COUNTY CLERK'S OFFICE, ALBANY, N.Y., HALL OF RECORDS, DEEDS, F. BOOK __.
Comment:

Date: 1791,01,08
Description: Petition of certain Indians for bounty lands.
Source: N.Y.STATE ARCHIVES, ALBANY, N.Y.COL.MSS, INDORSED LAND PAPERS, 1643-1803, SERIES NO. A0272, DEPARTMENT OF STATE, APPLICATIONS FOR LAND GRANTS, VOL. 50, P. 027.
Comment:

Date: 1791,01,31
Description: Release to Jacob Kniskern (Knisker, Knieskirk, Kneescarn, Kneiskerk) by Johannes (John) Knies Kern owners in common of certain lands lying on the east and on the west side of the Schoharie River in Kniskern's Dorp (Knisker Dorp; Kniskern Dorp; Kniskerns Dorp), of all lowland, meadow ground and homestead woodland on the west side of the river, being that land where the new house and barn now stand; two pieces of land of three acres and nearly one rod, and of nearly six acres respectively excepted.
Source: N.Y.STATE LIBRARY, ALBANY, MANUSCRIPTS, SCHOHARIE COUNTY, PATENTEES, LAND RECORDS, DW10738.
Comment:

Date: 1791,02,08
Description: Copy of list on file in the U.S. War Office of Indian names commissioned by General Schuyler, 1 June 1779.
Source: N.Y.STATE ARCHIVES, ALBANY, N.Y.COL.MSS, INDORSED LAND PAPERS, 1643-1803, SERIES NO. A0272, DEPARTMENT OF STATE, APPLICATIONS FOR LAND GRANTS, VOL. 50, P. 028.
Comment:

Date: 1791,12,07
Description: Proposal of C. Petrie and J. Reghtmeyer (Rightmyer, Rightmeir, Rightmeyer) for 525 acres on the east side of Schoharie Creek adjoining Dice's (Die's) Manor.
Source: N.Y.STATE ARCHIVES, ALBANY, N.Y.COL.MSS, INDORSED LAND PAPERS, 1643-1803, SERIES NO. A0272, DEPARTMENT OF STATE, APPLICATIONS FOR LAND GRANTS, VOL. 52, P. 080.
Comment: SEE N.Y.STATE ARCHIVES, ALBANY, N.Y.COL.MSS, INDORSED LAND PAPERS, 1643-1803, SERIES NO. A0272, DEPARTMENT OF STATE, APPLICATIONS FOR LAND GRANTS, VOL. 51, P. 110 for document, dated 20 July 1791, that pertains to Dice's Manor.

Date: 1792,05,09
Description: Petition of Nicholas Kanatsogh, an Indian who served as a lieutenant in the United States service during the late war, for bounty lands.
Source: N.Y.STATE ARCHIVES, ALBANY, N.Y.COL.MSS, INDORSED LAND PAPERS, 1643-1803, SERIES NO. A0272, DEPARTMENT OF STATE, APPLICATIONS FOR LAND GRANTS, VOL. 53, P. 021.
Comment: Kanatsogh is an Oneida Indian, not from Schoharie.

Date: 1792,11,08
Description: Return of survey for William Harper of 32 1/2 acres of land on the east side of Schoharie Creek near Fort Hunter. Map included.
Source: N.Y.STATE ARCHIVES, ALBANY, N.Y.COL.MSS, INDORSED LAND PAPERS, 1643-1803, SERIES NO. A0272, DEPARTMENT OF STATE, APPLICATIONS FOR LAND GRANTS, VOL. 53, P. 133.
Comment:

Date: 1793,02,02
Description: Proposal of John Sanders for payment for 600 acres of land.
Source: N.Y.STATE ARCHIVES, ALBANY, N.Y.COL.MSS, INDORSED LAND PAPERS, 1643-1803, SERIES NO. A0272, DEPARTMENT OF STATE, APPLICATIONS FOR LAND GRANTS, VOL. 56, P. 087.
Comment: CALENDAR OF LAND PAPERS notes that the land is in Schoharie County.

Date: 1793,09,18
Description: Petition of Stephen Bayard for a grant of land to representatives of Isaac Levey (Levy) at Breekenbeen (Breakabeen, Breakabine, Breakaben, Brekabeen).
Source: N.Y.STATE ARCHIVES, ALBANY, N.Y.COL.MSS, INDORSED LAND PAPERS, 1643-1803, SERIES NO. A0272, DEPARTMENT OF STATE, APPLICATIONS FOR LAND GRANTS, VOL. 56, P. 127.
Comment: SEE 1785,05,02; 1786,06,07; 1786,06,28; n.d.

Date: 1794,04,01
Description: Deed to William Bleecker [Bleeker] for 20,000, being Lot 19 of Young's Patent from John H. Livingston and others.
Source: N.Y. STATE ARCHIVES, ALBANY, N.Y. DEEDS, SERIES A0453, BOOK 26, P. 96.
Comment: Recorded by the N.Y. Secretary of State August 5, 1794.

Date: 1794,05,05
Description: Peppercorn lease to Jacob Kniskern (Knisker, Knieskirk, Kneiskerk, Kneescarn) by Peter Enders, Jr. and Johannes Enders, for one year, of Lot 5 of the Second Allotment of a patent granted to Johannes Lawyer, Jacob Zimmer, and others on the west side of the Schoharie River at Schoharie, containing 330 acres, more or less.
Source: N.Y.STATE LIBRARY, ALBANY, MANUSCRIPTS, SCHOHARIE COUNTY, PATENTEES, LAND RECORDS, DW10738.
Comment: See 1766,10,03 (5); 1768,08,02; 1785,00,00-1791,00,00.

Date: 1794,05,06
Description: Deed to Peter Enders, Jr. and Johannes Enders by Jacob Knies Kern (Knisker, Kniskern, Kniskirn, Knieskirk, Kneescarn, Kneiskerk) for half of Lots 2, 4, 6, and 8 in Lot 135 on the east side of the Schoharie River in the Old Schoharie Patent granted to Myndert Schuyler and others, containing 88, 88, 67 and 69 acres, respectively, or 150 acres in all, more or less. The parties to the agreement are yeomen of Schoharie.
Source: N.Y.STATE LIBRARY, ALBANY, MANUSCRIPTS, SCHOHARIE COUNTY, PATENTEES, LAND RECORDS, DW10738.
Comment: See 1786,01,07. For documents pertaining to Myndert Schuyler's patent, see 1714,00,00; 1714,05,08; 1714,11,03 (4); 1887,00,00-1888,00,00 (34); 1722,09,28.

Date: 1794,05,10
Description: Deed to William Bleecker [Bleeker] for 20,000 acres of land, being Lots 2, 3 and 45 in Young's Patent.
Source: N.Y.STATE LIBRARY, ALBANY, N.Y. DEEDS, SERIES NO. A0453, BOOK 26, P. 2.
Comment: Recorded by the N.Y. Secretary of State May 30, 1794.

Date: 1794,07,31
Description: A letter from Gideon Hawley, missionary. Hawley visited Schoharie in 1753, and writes about his visit in detail.
Source: THE DOCUMENTARY HISTORY OF THE STATE OF NEW YORK, ED. E.B. O'CALLAGHAN, (ALBANY: WEED, PARSONS, AND CO., CHARLES VAN BENTHUYSEN, 1849-1851), QUARTO ED., 3: 1033-1046
Comment:

Date: 1794,07,31 (2)
Description: A letter from Gideon Hawley, missionary. Hawley visited Schoharie in 1753, and writes about his visit in detail.
Source: THE DOCUMENTARY HISTORY OF THE STATE OF NEW YORK, ED. E.B. O'CALLAGHAN, (ALBANY; WEED, PARSONS, AND CO., CHARLES VAN BENTHUYSEN, 1849-1851), 3: 625-634.
Comment:

Date: 1794,12,31
Description: Deed from Nicholas Lawyer to Jacob F. Lawyer for a tract of four and three-quarters acres of land, and one for twenty-two acres in Schoharie.
Source: ALBANY COUNTY CLERK'S OFFICE, ALBANY, N.Y., HALL OF RECORDS, DEEDS, BOOK 13, P. 549.
Comment:

Date: 1795,05,09
Description: Deed from Jacob Frederick Lawyer to Johannes Lawyer for land in Schoharie Patent.
Source: N.Y.STATE LIBRARY, ALBANY, MANUSCRIPTS, JOHANNES LAWYER AND OTHERS, MAPS AND DEEDS OF SCHOHARIE VALLEY, ACC. NO. SC16469, DEEDS AND LEASES #4; SEE ALSO J. LAWYER PAPERS, PI 16480.
Comment:

Date: 1795,08,03
Description: Deed from Moses Soule to Johannes Lawyer for land in Butler's Patent, Schoharie.
Source: N.Y.STATE LIBRARY, ALBANY, MANUSCRIPTS, JOHANNES LAWYER AND OTHERS, MAPS AND DEEDS OF SCHOHARIE VALLEY, ACC. NO. SC16469, DEEDS AND LEASES #5.
Comment:

Date: 1796,00,00
Description: Map of Schoharie County, sent by Martin Bellinger.
Source: MIX'S CATALOG OF MAPS AND SURVEYS IN OFFFICES OF THE SECRETARY OF STATE, STATE ENGINEER AND SURVEYOR AND COMPTROLLER AND N.Y. STATE LIBRARY, 1859, REFERENCES THIS MAP, LISTING IT AS BEING IN THE OFFICE OF THE N.Y. OFFICE OF SURVEYOR GENERAL, MAP # 363.
Comment:

Date: 1796,00,00(?) [ ]
Description: Map of Jeremiah Van Rensselaer's Patent.
Source: MIX'S CATALOG OF MAPS AND SURVEYS IN OFFFICES OF THE SECRETARY OF STATE, STATE ENGINEER AND SURVEYOR AND COMPTROLLER AND N.Y. STATE LIBRARY, 1859, REFERENCES THIS MAP, LISTING IT AS BEING IN THE OFFICES OF THE N.Y. STATE DEPARTMENT OF TAXATION & FINANCE, MAP #72.
Comment: SEE 1796,02,03.

Date: 1796,00,00°
Description: Rufus Grider Collection. Watercolor drawing of the First Lutheran Church, Schoharie Village, 1796.
Source: SEE 1887,00,00-1888,00,00 (2)
Comment:

Date: 1796,00,00°
Description: Map of Jeremiah Van Rensselaer's Patent.
Source: SEE 1796,00,00(?) [ ].
Comment: SEE 1796,02,03.

Date: 1796,02,03
Description: Certificate of location of 1,500 acre tract of land of Jeremiah Van Rensselaer. Map included.
Source: N.Y.STATE ARCHIVES, ALBANY, N.Y.COL.MSS, INDORSED LAND PAPERS, 1643-1803, SERIES NO. A0272, DEPARTMENT OF STATE, APPLICATIONS FOR LAND GRANTS, VOL. 60, P. 141.
Comment: CALENDAR OF LAND PAPERS notes that the land is in Gilboa and Conesville, Schoharie County. SEE [1796,00,00(?)].

Date: 1798,10,29
Description: Deed to Peter Enders, Jr. from Henry Houck (Hauck) and wife Elizabeth for lands in the town of Schoharie, being lowland Lot 7 commonly known as Shuttis's flatts, on the east side of the Schoharie River, containing nearly 41 acres; homestead Lot 7, containing 20 acres, more or less; and half of an undivided third of a tract on both sides of the Schoharie River lying between patents granted to Myndert Schuyler and others and to Lewis Morris, Jr. and others. The parties to the agreement are yeomen of Schoharie.
Source: N.Y.STATE LIBRARY, ALBANY, MANUSCRIPTS, SCHOHARIE COUNTY, PATENTEES, LAND RECORDS, DW10738.
Comment:

Date: 1800,04,10
Description: Petition of Joseph Desylva to grant land to Henry Schoomaker.
Source: N.Y.STATE ARCHIVES, ALBANY, N.Y.COL.MSS, INDORSED LAND PAPERS, 1643-1803, SERIES NO. A0272, DEPARTMENT OF STATE, APPLICATIONS FOR LAND GRANTS, VOL. 63, P. 158.
Comment: CALENDAR OF LAND PAPERS notes that the land is in Schoharie County.

Date: 1800,07,12
Description: Return of survey for Henry Schoomaker of 200 acres of land east of Dice's (Die's) Manor. Map included.
Source: N.Y.STATE ARCHIVES, ALBANY, N.Y.COL.MSS, INDORSED LAND PAPERS, 1643-1803, SERIES NO. A0272, DEPARTMENT OF STATE, APPLICATIONS FOR LAND GRANTS, VOL. 62, P. 174.
Comment: CALENDAR OF LAND PAPERS notes that the land is in Conesville, Schoharie County.

Date: 1802,00,00°
Description: Tracing of survey by Thomas Machin, 1802, of the Old Schoharie Patent granted to Myndert Schuyler.
Source: SEE 1887,00,00-1888,00,00 (34).
Comment: Rufus Grider Collection.

Date: 1805,06,00
Description: Map of the Town of Bristol, with notes on unappropriated lands adjoining Die's (Dice's) Manor.
Source: MIX'S CATALOG OF MAPS AND SURVEYS IN OFFFICES OF THE SECRETARY OF STATE, STATE ENGINEER AND SURVEYOR AND COMPTROLLER AND N.Y. STATE LIBRARY, 1859, REFERENCES THIS MAP, LISTING IT AS BEING IN THE OFFICE OF THE N.Y. SECRETARY OF STATE, FIELDBOOK #20, SUBDIVISION A, P. 001.
Comment:

Date: 1806,00,00
Description: Map of grant of land to John Morine (Morin) Scott. Run and marked out in 1806 at the request of proprietor John Livingston.
Source: MIX'S CATALOG OF MAPS AND SURVEYS IN OFFFICES OF THE SECRETARY OF STATE, STATE ENGINEER AND SURVEYOR AND COMPTROLLER AND N.Y. STATE LIBRARY, 1859, REFERENCES THIS MAP, LISTING IT AS BEING IN THE OFFICE OF THE N.Y. OFFICE OF SURVEYOR GENERAL, MAP #147A.
Comment: SEE 1769,06,29; 1770,01,02; 1771,05,03; n.d.

Date: 1806,11,14
Description: Deed from John Watts to David Elias Young for lots no. 2, 9, 19, 21, 42, 45, and 49 in Skinner's Patent, Schoharie County.
Source: N.Y.STATE LIBRARY, ALBANY, MANUSCRIPTS, JOHANNES LAWYER AND OTHERS, MAPS AND DEEDS OF SCHOHARIE VALLEY, ACC. NO. SC16469, DEEDS AND LEASES # 6.
Comment: SEE 1763,03,21 (2); 1822,10,07; n.d.

Date: 1807,00,00°
Description: Rufus Grider water color facsimile of illuminated family chart of John Lawyer, 1807.
Source: SEE 1887,00,00-1888,00,00 (16).
Comment:

Date: 1808,05,04
Description: Deed to Jacob Kniskern (Knisker, Knieskirk, Kneescarn, Kneiskerk, Kneskarn) by George Kneskarn (Kniskern, Knisker, Knieskirk, Kneescarn, Kneiskerk) for Lot 28 in a patent granted to Lewis Morris and others in the town of Schoharie, containing two acres, three rods and eight perches. The parties to the agreement are of the town of Schoharie.
Source: N.Y.STATE LIBRARY, ALBANY, MANUSCRIPTS, SCHOHARIE COUNTY, PATENTEES, LAND RECORDS, DW10738.
Comment: For documents pertaining to the Morris and Coeyman Patent, see 1725,10,28 (3); 1726,04,30; 1726,04,30 (2); 1726,05,02; 1726,05,24; 1819,11,00 [ ].

Date: 1808,07,28
Description: Map of Becker's Patent and Franklin's Patent.
Source: MIX'S CATALOG OF MAPS AND SURVEYS IN OFFFICES OF THE SECRETARY OF STATE, STATE ENGINEER AND SURVEYOR AND COMPTROLLER AND N.Y. STATE LIBRARY, 1859, REFERENCES THIS MAP, LISTING IT AS BEING IN THE OFFICES OF THE N.Y. STATE DEPARTMENT OF TAXATION & FINANCE, MAP #18.
Comment:

Date: 1810,00,00°
Description: Warrant issued 1810 by an Indian justice, Captain Hawdy; two local ball tickets, one 1817, on backs of playing cards, mail stage advertisement. Tracings.
Source: SEE 1887,00,00-1888,00,00 (13).
Comment: N.B. Captain Hawdy is identified as an Indian justice.

Date: 1814,05,00
Description: Copy of a map of a tract of land in the Schoharie River Valley containing 2,984 acres protracted from a scale of 10 chains to an inch in the month of June 1814 by Peter Mann.
Source: N.Y.STATE LIBRARY, ALBANY, MANUSCRIPTS, JOHANNES LAWYER AND OTHERS, MAPS AND DEEDS OF SCHOHARIE VALLEY, ACC. NO. 16469, MAP #8.
Comment: This document is said to be a "correct copy of the original map."

Date: 1814,06,25
Description: Deed of Release from Jacob F. Lawyer and others to Thomas Lawyer for lots no. 1, 3, 4, 8, 9, 10, and 18 in Butler's Patent.
Source: N.Y.STATE LIBRARY, ALBANY, MANUSCRIPTS, JOHANNES LAWYER AND OTHERS, MAPS AND DEEDS OF SCHOHARIE VALLEY, ACC. NO. SC16469, DEEDS AND LEASES #7.
Comment:

Date: 1814,06,25 (2)
Description: Deed from Jacob F. Lawyer and others to Philip Sternbergh (Sternberg), Jr. for land in Middleburgh, being lot no. 26 in Butler's Patent.
Source: N.Y.STATE LIBRARY, ALBANY, MANUSCRIPTS, JOHANNES LAWYER AND OTHERS, MAPS AND DEEDS OF SCHOHARIE VALLEY, ACC. NO. SC16469, DEEDS AND LEASES #8.
Comment:

Date: 1814,06,25 (3)
Description: Deed from Johannes I.J. Lawyer and others to Jacob F. Lawyer for lots no. 2, 5, 14, 15, 18, and 22 in Butler's Patent.
Source: N.Y.STATE LIBRARY, ALBANY, JOHANNES LAWYER AND OTHERS, MAPS AND DEEDS OF SCHOHARIE VALLEY, ACC. NO. SC16469, DEEDS AND LEASES #9.
Comment:

Date: 1814,10,18
Description: Return of the Six Nations residing at Grand River.
Source: PUBLIC ARCHIVES OF CANADA, OTTAWA, RG 10 (ONTARIO, MISCELLANEOUS LAND RECORDS, 1790-1893), VOL. 715.
Comment:

Date: 1815,04,13
Description: Deed to Jacob P. and Peter I. (J.[?]) Enders by Philip Dietz and wife Nancy for Lot 6 in Large Lot 133, Mynerds (Myndert) Skylers (Schuyler) patent, town of Schoharie, on the north side of the Crabskill, containing 65 12 acres. Parties to the agreement are of the town of Schoharie.
Source: N.Y.STATE LIBRARY, ALBANY, MANUSCRIPTS, SCHOHARIE COUNTY, PATENTEES, LAND RECORDS, DW10738.
Comment:

Date: 1815,05,31
Description: Deed to Peter Enders, Jr. by John (Johan, Johannes) Enders, Jr., Jacob Sidnich (Sidney), John Jost Sidney, Anna Margaret Sidney, and Caty E. Houck, Jr. for lands in Cortland's (Cortlandt) patent, town of Schoharie, being Lots 13, 14, 15, and 8 on the southeast side of Schoharie Creek, the northerly half of Lot 2, and fifteen acres, one rod out of the east part of Lot 23 on the northwest side of Schoharie Creek. The parties to the agreement are of the town of Schoharie.
Source: N.Y.STATE LIBRARY, ALBANY, MANUSCRIPTS, SCHOHARIE COUNTY, PATENTEES, LAND RECORDS, DW10738.
Comment:

Date: 1815,12,00
Description: Deed to Peter Enders, Jr., George Houck (Hauck), and Henry Houck, Jr. for land in Lot 135 Mynant (Myndert) Schuyler patent, town of Schoharie, being Lot 1 in the subdivision of Lot 6, containing 17 acres, Lot 1 in the subdivision of Lot 2, containing 17 3/10 acres, and Lot 4 in the subdivision of Lot 4, containing 26 4/10 acres. The parties to the agreement are of the town of Schoharie.
Source: N.Y.STATE LIBRARY, ALBANY, MANUSCRIPTS, SCHOHARIE COUNTY, PATENTEES, LAND RECORDS, DW10738.
Comment: SEE 1710,10,19; 1714,11,03. For subsequent divisions of the land, see 1722,09,28; and a series of documents in 1736 and 1737 in Vol. 12 of N.Y.STATE ARCHIVES, ALBANY, N.Y.COL.MSS, INDORSED LAND PAPERS, 1643-1803, SERIES NO. A0272, DEPARTMENT OF STATE, APPLICATIONS FOR LAND GRANTS. (They are listed in this calendar.) See also 1786,01,07; 1794,05,06.

Date: 1819,00,00 [ ]
Description: Map of patent granted in 1726 to Morris and Coeymans, resurveyed in November 1819 by Lawrence Vrooman and Tobias A. Stontenburgh. It shows old divided land laid out by Edward Collins in Knieskerns (Knisker, Knieskirk, Kneescarn, Knescarn, Kneiskerk) Dorp in 1729 and lots laid out by Isaac Vrooman in 1753. The map also shows the Schoharie Turnpike and Dorp Road.
Source: N.Y.STATE LIBRARY, ALBANY, MANUSCRIPTS, SCHOHARIE COUNTY, PATENTEES, MAPS, DW10738, MAP #4.
Comment: See 1725,10,28 (3); 1726,04,30; 1726,04,30 (2); 1726,05,02; 1726,05,24.

Date: 1819,00,00°
Description: Map of Schoharie County showing various patents and other tracts; Lawyer and two miners; Stoneheap Patent; Morris and Coeyman (Coeman); A. Van Cortlandt; M. Schuyler and others; Teneyck (Ten Eyck) and Bleecker; Johannis Lawyer and others; Wiefield and Clifford; Jonathan Brewer. Shows "Cockburn's line run about the year 1770 or 1771". Latest date on map is 1819.
Source: SEE n.d.
Comment:

Date: 1820,00,00 [ ]
Description: Transcription of an extract from a manuscript book of notes taken down by Christopher Pyrlaus between the Years 1742 and 1748 while in the country of the Five Nations. The extract was apparently copied by John Heckewelder. It appears to be in his handwriting (SEE 1820,03,04). Pyrlaus explains that the names of the founders of the League of the Iroquois have been passed down to their successors. He received his information from an Indian named Sganarady.
Source: AMERICAN PHILOSOPHICAL SOCIETY LIBRARY, PHILADELPHIA, PA., MANUSCRIPT, # 2275.
Comment: The transcription was probably done ca. 1820. SEE 1820,03,04.

Date: 1820,03,04
Description: Letter from John Heckewelder to Peter DuPonceau, explaining that he has been transcribing manuscripts, including those of Pyrlaus.
Source: AMERICAN PHILOSOPHICAL SOCIETY LIBRARY, PHILADELPHIA, PA., MANUSCRIPT, #666.
Comment: SEE n.d.

Date: 1822,10,07
Description: Deed from Elias Young to David Young for one half of lot no. 49 in the first allotment of Skinner's Patent in Cobleskill.
Source: N.Y.STATE LIBRARY, ALBANY, MANUSCRIPTS, JOHANNES LAWYER AND OTHERS, MAPS AND DEEDS OF SCHOHARIE VALLEY, ACC. NO. SC16469, DEEDS AND LEASES #10; SEE ALSO J. LAWYER PAPERS, PI 16480.
Comment: SEE 1763,03,21 (2); 1806,11,14; n.d.

Date: 1824,00,00
Description: Survey of the Town of Broome.
Source: MIX'S CATALOG OF MAPS AND SURVEYS IN OFFFICES OF THE SECRETARY OF STATE, STATE ENGINEER AND SURVEYOR AND COMPTROLLER AND N.Y. STATE LIBRARY, 1859, REFERENCES THIS MAP, LISTING IT AS BEING IN THE OFFICE OF THE N.Y. SECRETARY OF STATE, FIELDBOOK # 42, LOT #12, P. 108.
Comment:

Date: 1824,00,00 (2)
Description: Map of Subdivision #12. Map, that shows a bit of Schoharie County.
Source: MIX'S CATALOG OF MAPS AND SURVEYS IN OFFFICES OF THE SECRETARY OF STATE, STATE ENGINEER AND SURVEYOR AND COMPTROLLER AND N.Y. STATE LIBRARY, 1859, REFERENCES THIS MAP, LISTING IT AS BEING IN THE OFFICE OF THE N.Y. SECRETARY OF STATE, FIELDBOOK #42, P. 125.
Comment:

Date: 1828,00,00
Description: List of accounts for the Town of Schoharie, 1828, giving names of persons involved.
Source: N.Y.STATE LIBRARY, ALBANY, MANUSCRIPTS, 13159.
Comment:

Date: 1828,09,15-10,04
Description: Journal of the travels of Uriah Edwards from Canaan to the Counties of Cortland, Broome, Delaware, Schoharie, etc. in the State of New York.
Source: N.Y.STATE LIBRARY, ALBANY, MANUSCRIPTS, 16802.
Comment: The document is a bound manuscript, 28 pages long.

Date: 1830,09,13
Description: Exemplification of last will and testament of Peter Enders, Jr. by the Schoharie County Surrogate. Named as heirs are his wife Elizabeth, sons Jacob P. Enders, Peter I., daughters Catherine (wife of Joseph I. Borst) and Nancy (wife of Johan Enders).
Source: N.Y.STATE LIBRARY, ALBANY, MANUSCRIPTS, SCHOHARIE COUNTY, PATENTEES, LAND RECORDS, DW10738.
Comment:

Date: 1831,03,28
Description: Christian Harker's map of land conveyed to Henry L. Russell of Cobleskill in the county of Schoharie.
Source: N.Y.STATE LIBRARY, ALBANY, MANUSCRIPTS, JOHANNES LAWYER AND OTHERS, MAPS AND DEEDS OF SCHOHARIE VALLEY, ACC. NO. 16469, MAP #9.
Comment:

Date: 1837,09,14
Description: Deed of sale to Jacob P. Enders by George Taylor, Eve Taylor, and Elizabeth Houck (Hauck) for a tract of land in the town of Schoharie in Morris and Coeymans (Coeman; Coemans; Coeyman) Patent on the east side of Schoharie Creek, another tract on the south bank of Schoharie Creek, and a third piece beginning at the southwest corner of Lot 16 in Cortland Patent, being 11.6 acres.
Source: N.Y.STATE LIBRARY, ALBANY, MANUSCRIPTS, SCHOHARIE COUNTY, PATENTEES, LAND RECORDS, DW10738.
Comment: For documents pertaining to the Morris and Coeyman Patent, see 1725,10,28 (3); 1726,04,30; 1726,04,30 (2); 1726,05,02; 1726,05,24; 1819,11,00 [ ].

Date: 1844,00,00°
Description: Picture by Rufus Grider of Schoharie Village, 1844, copied from a woodcut.
Source: SEE 1887,00,00-1888,00,00 (18).
Comment:

Date: 1844,04,15
Description: Sheriff's (Henry Mann, Jr.) deed of sale to Jacob P. Enders of premises of David Bliven, namely a sawmill and lot in Sloansville; land at Schoharie bounded south and east by Schoharie Creek, north and west by lands of Schuyler Briggs; land at Schoharie bounded south by Schoharie Creek, west by lands at Widow Enders, north by the pond; land at Schoharie bounded north by lands lately owned by Benjamin B. Bliven east by patent line, south by pond, west by public highway.
Source: N.Y.STATE LIBRARY, ALBANY, MANUSCRIPTS, SCHOHARIE COUNTY, PATENTEES, LAND RECORDS, DW10738.
Comment:

Date: 1886,00,00
Description: Rufus Grider Collection. Original photograph of the Lower Fort.
Source: N.Y.STATE LIBARY, ALBANY, MANUSCRIPTS, RUFUS GRIDER COLLECTION (1886-1900), SC A974.7/FG84 [VAULT], VOL. 8, P. 015.
Comment:

Date: 1887,00,00-1888,00,00
Description: Rufus Grider Collection. Watercolor drawing of the First Lutheran Church, Schoharie Village, 1743.
Source: N.Y.STATE LIBARY, ALBANY, MANUSCRIPTS, RUFUS GRIDER COLLECTION (1886-1900), SC A974.7/FG84 [VAULT], VOL. 8, P. 002.
Comment:

Date: 1887,00,00-1888,00,00 (02)
Description: Rufus Grider Collection. Watercolor drawing of St. Paul's Lutheran Church, Schoharie Village, 1796.
Source: N.Y.STATE LIBARY, ALBANY, MANUSCRIPTS, RUFUS GRIDER COLLECTION (1886-1900), SC A974.7/FG84 [VAULT], VOL. 8, P. 003.
Comment:

Date: 1887,00,00-1888,00,00 (03)
Description: Rufus Grider Collection. Watercolor drawing of the restored appearance of the Lower Fort, Schoharie Valley, showing stockade and block houses.
Source: N.Y.STATE LIBARY, ALBANY, MANUSCRIPTS, RUFUS GRIDER COLLECTION (1886-1900), SC A974.7/FG84 [VAULT], VOL. 8, P. 008.
Comment:

Date: 1887,00,00-1888,00,00 (04)
Description: Rufus Grider Collection. Pen and ink drawing of the ground plan of the Lower Fort and surrounding territory.
Source: N.Y.STATE LIBARY, ALBANY, MANUSCRIPTS, RUFUS GRIDER COLLECTION (1886-1900), SC A974.7/FG84 [VAULT], VOL. 8, P. 009a.
Comment:

Date: 1887,00,00-1888,00,00 (05)
Description: Rufus Grider Collection. Pen and ink map of the route of Johnson's army in Schoharie Valley, 17 October 1780.
Source: N.Y.STATE LIBRARY, ALBANY, MANUSCRIPTS, RUFUS GRIDER COLLECTION (1886-1900), SC A974.7/FG84 [VAULT], VOL. 8, P. 009a.
Comment:

Date: 1887,00,00-1888,00,00 (06)
Description: Rufus Grider Collection. Watercolor drawing of slate stone lizard of Indian workmanship found in Schoharie Valley. Owned by H.F. Kingley when drawn by Grider.
Source: N.Y.STATE LIBRARY, ALBANY, MANUSCRIPTS, RUFUS GRIDER COLLECTION (1886-1900), SC A974.7/FG84 [VAULT], VOL. 8, P. 017.
Comment:

Date: 1887,00,00-1888,00,00 (07)
Description: Rufus Grider Collection. Watercolor drawing of three bone or horn Indian tools, found at Schoharie by F.L. Becker and drawn by Grider, 1887-1888.
Source: N.Y.STATE LIBRARY, ALBANY, MANUSCRIPTS, RUFUS GRIDER COLLECTION (1886-1900), SC A974.7/FG84 [VAULT], VOL. 8, P. 020.
Comment:

Date: 1887,00,00-1888,00,00 (08)
Description: Rufus Grider Collection. Watercolor drawings of five Indian stone artifacts found at Schoharie and owned by F.G. Mix when Grider drew them.
Source: N.Y.STATE LIBRARY, ALBANY, MANUSCRIPTS, RUFUS GRIDER COLLECTION (1886-1900), SC A974.7/FG84 [VAULT], VOL. 8, P. 025.
Comment:

Date: 1887,00,00-1888,00,00 (09)
Description: Rufus Grider Collection. Watercolor drawing of a view of the Schoharie River Valley showing the placement of the "New Fort" which the British planned to build but never erected. (Based on map of 1754-1755 showing a "Plan of the Indian Castel[sic]".)
Source: N.Y.STATE LIBRARY, ALBANY, MANUSCRIPTS, RUFUS GRIDER COLLECTION (1886-1900), SC A974.7/FG84 [VAULT], VOL. 8, P. 027.
Comment:

Date: 1887,00,00-1888,00,00 (10)
Description: Rufus Grider Collection. Map of the Schoharie River Valley showing "Plan of the Indian Castel[sic]" at Vrooman's (Vroman's) land about 1754-1755, and plan and elevation of the "New Fort" never erected. From original in the British Museum, London. Pen and ink tracing for which Grider paid $27.
Source: N.Y.STATE LIBRARY, ALBANY, MANUSCRIPTS, RUFUS GRIDER COLLECTION (1886-1900), SC A974.7/FG84 [VAULT], VOL. 8, P. 27a.
Comment: Notes in the Crown Collection publication of photographs of original maps in the British Museum give the date of the map as being ca. 1758. Size 11 in. x 10 in. SEE 1758,00,00 [ ]. The date of the map may be 1756 instead, however. SEE 1756,05,28.

Date: 1887,00,00-1888,00,00 (11)
Description: Rufus Grider Collection. Pen and ink tracing of map showing original patents south of the Mohawk River, about 1790, by Simeon DeWitt.
Source: N.Y.STATE LIBARY, ALBANY, MANUSCRIPTS, RUFUS GRIDER COLLECTION (1886-1900), SC A974.7/FG84 [VAULT], VOL. 8, P. 29a.
Comment: From DOCUMENTS RELATIVE TO THE COLONIAL HISTORY OF NEW YORK..., 1: 421.

Date: 1887,00,00-1888,00,00 (12)
Description: Original engraving of Sir John Johnson, woodcut of Joseph Brant and watercolor copy of portrait of Cornplanter, leaders in the raid of 1780.
Source: N.Y.STATE LIBARY, ALBANY, MANUSCRIPTS, RUFUS GRIDER COLLECTION (1886-1900), SC A974.7/FG84 [VAULT], VOL. 8, P. 36.
Comment:

Date: 1887,00,00-1888,00,00 (13)
Description: Warrant issued 1810 by an Indian justice, Captain Hawdy; two local ball tickets, one 1817, on backs of playing cards, mail stage advertisement. Tracings.
Source: N.Y.STATE LIBARY, ALBANY, MANUSCRIPTS, RUFUS GRIDER COLLECTION (1886-1900), SC A974.7/FG84 [VAULT], VOL. 8, P. 048.
Comment: N.B. Captain Hawdy is identified as an Indian justice.

Date: 1887,00,00-1888,00,00 (14)
Description: Remains of the ancient Weisersdorf buildings; key of the Middle Fort, owned by Mr. Sidney of Middleburgh. Water color.
Source: N.Y.STATE LIBARY, ALBANY, MANUSCRIPTS, RUFUS GRIDER COLLECTION (1886-1900), SC A974.7/FG84 [VAULT], VOL. 8, P. 049.
Comment:

Date: 1887,00,00-1888,00,00 (15)
Description: Water color of the Schoharie River from the Mountain Road, and another of an Indian pipe, two other Indian artifacts and bone handled fork owned by Dr. Swart, then by his son-in-law, William B. Murphy, grandson of Timothy Murphy.
Source: N.Y.STATE LIBARY, ALBANY, MANUSCRIPTS, RUFUS GRIDER COLLECTION (1886-1900), SC A974.7/FG84 [VAULT], VOL. 8, P. 063.
Comment:

Date: 1887,00,00-1888,00,00 (16)
Description: Water color facsimile of illuminated family chart of John Lawyer, 1807.
Source: N.Y.STATE LIBARY, ALBANY, MANUSCRIPTS, RUFUS GRIDER COLLECTION (1886-1900), SC A974.7/FG84 [VAULT], VOL. 8, P. 069a.
Comment:

Date: 1887,00,00-1888,00,00 (17)
Description: Water color of mound builder clay figure of a woman, and two other Indian artifacts.
Source: N.Y.STATE LIBARY, ALBANY, MANUSCRIPTS, RUFUS GRIDER COLLECTION (1886-1900), SC A974.7/FG84 [VAULT], VOL. 8, P. 070.
Comment:

Date: 1887,00,00-1888,00,00 (18)
Description: Picture of Schoharie Village, 1844, copied from a woodcut. Water color of Mount Onis-Ta-Gra-Wa. Pen and ink drawing of plan and sketch of Indian fort at Vrooman's land.
Source: N.Y.STATE LIBARY, ALBANY, MANUSCRIPTS, RUFUS GRIDER COLLECTION (1886-1900), SC A974.7/FG84 [VAULT], VOL. 8, P. 071.
Comment:

Date: 1887,00,00-1888,00,00 (19)
Description: Pen and ink drawing of the plan of the Upper Fort, Schoharie Valley.
Source: N.Y.STATE LIBARY, ALBANY, MANUSCRIPTS, RUFUS GRIDER COLLECTION (1886-1900), SC A974.7/FG84 [VAULT], VOL. 8, P. 079.
Comment:

Date: 1887,00,00-1888,00,00 (20)
Description: Water color reconstruction of the Upper Fort, Schoharie, as it appeared in 1779.
Source: N.Y.STATE LIBARY, ALBANY, MANUSCRIPTS, RUFUS GRIDER COLLECTION (1886-1900), SC A974.7/FG84 [VAULT], VOL. 8, P. 080.
Comment:

Date: 1887,00,00-1888,00,00 (21)
Description: Water color picture by Rufus Grider of scalps with Indian markings to show history of each.
Source: N.Y.STATE LIBARY, ALBANY, MANUSCRIPTS, RUFUS GRIDER COLLECTION (1886-1900), SC A974.7/FG84 [VAULT], VOL. 8, PP. 101-103.
Comment:

Date: 1887,00,00-1888,00,00 (22)
Description: Two engraved portraits of Joseph Brant.
Source: N.Y.STATE LIBARY, ALBANY, MANUSCRIPTS, RUFUS GRIDER COLLECTION (1886-1900), SC A974.7/FG84 [VAULT], VOL. 8, P. 105.
Comment:

Date: 1887,00,00-1888,00,00 (23)
Description: Engraved portraits of John Brant and Sir William Johnson.
Source: N.Y.STATE LIBARY, ALBANY, MANUSCRIPTS, RUFUS GRIDER COLLECTION (1886-1900), SC A974.7/FG84 [VAULT], VOL. 8, P. 106.
Comment:

Date: 1887,00,00-1888,00,00 (24)
Description: Engraved portrait of Red Jacket, woodcut of his home.
Source: N.Y.STATE LIBARY, ALBANY, MANUSCRIPTS, RUFUS GRIDER COLLECTION (1886-1900), SC A974.7/FG84 [VAULT], VOL. 8, P. 107.
Comment:

Date: 1887,00,00-1888,00,00 (25)
Description: Tracing of deed from Mohawks Indians to Walter Butler for 160,000 acres of land south of the Mohawk, 18 September 1733.
Source: N.Y.STATE LIBARY, ALBANY, MANUSCRIPTS, RUFUS GRIDER COLLECTION (1886-1900), SC A974.7/FG84 [VAULT], VOL. 8, P. 109a.
Comment: Traced from original in N.Y.STATE ARCHIVES, ALBANY, N.Y.COL.MSS, INDORSED LAND PAPERS, 1643-1803, SERIES NO. A0272, DEPARTMENT OF STATE, APPLICATIONS FOR LAND GRANTS, VOL. 11, P. 065. Cf. 1733,09,18; 1733,10,16. Note, difference in acreage given in desciptions of documents.

Date: 1887,00,00-1888,00,00 (26)
Description: Tracing of receipt for 400 pounds paid by Bartholomew and Peter Vrooman for tract bought of the "Scohare" (Schoharie) Indians, signed by Sir William Johnson, 28 September 1771.
Source: N.Y.STATE LIBRARY, ALBANY, MANUSCRIPTS, RUFUS GRIDER COLLECTION (1886-1900), SC A974.7/FG84 [VAULT], VOL. 8, P. 118.
Comment: Rufus Grider Collection. Original owned by A.J. Richmond when Grider did the tracing, 1887-1888. Included is a list of what Peter and Cornelius Vrooman "have & did and Delivered To the Indians". N.B. The high proportion spent on rum.

Date: 1887,00,00-1888,00,00 (27)
Description: Tracing of entry from Lutheran church records, Schoharie Village, 1781, relative to two murders by Indians at Dorlach.
Source: N.Y.STATE LIBARY, ALBANY, MANUSCRIPTS, RUFUS GRIDER COLLECTION (1886-1900), SC A974.7/FG84 [VAULT], VOL. 8, P. 118.
Comment: Rufus Grider Collection.

Date: 1887,00,00-1888,00,00 (28)
Description: Tracing of a certificate that a Cayuga Indian had been in the King's service, signed by Daniel Claus, 9 July 1777.
Source: N.Y.STATE LIBRARY, ALBANY, MANUSCRIPTS, RUFUS GRIDER COLLECTION (1886-1900), SC A974.7/FG84 [VAULT], VOL. 8, P. 123.
Comment: Rufus Grider Collection. Original was owned by George Danforth of Middleburgh when Grider did the tracing, 1887-1888.

Date: 1887,00,00-1888,00,00 (29)
Description: Tracing of Schoharie Lutheran church records regarding murders by Indians, 1778.
Source: N.Y.STATE LIBARY, ALBANY, MANUSCRIPTS, RUFUS GRIDER COLLECTION (1886-1900), SC A974.7/FG84 [VAULT], VOL. 8, P. 123.
Comment: Rufus Grider Collection.

Date: 1887,00,00-1888,00,00 (30)
Description: Tracing of an Indian deed to a group of Schoharie men for 4,000 acres of land in Schoharie Valley, 9 November 1752. Signed with Indian totems.
Source: N.Y.STATE LIBRARY, ALBANY, MANUSCRIPTS, RUFUS GRIDER COLLECTION (1886-1900), SC A974.7/FG84 [VAULT], VOL. 8, PP. 128-129.
Comment: Rufus Grider Collection. Traced by Grider from original in N.Y.STATE ARCHIVES, ALBANY, N.Y.COL.MSS, INDORSED LAND PAPERS, 1643-1803, SERIES NO. A0272, DEPARTMENT OF STATE, APPLICATIONS FOR LAND GRANTS, VOL. 15, P. 019. Date of original 1752,11,09; 1752,11,09 (2).

Date: 1887,00,00-1888,00,00 (31)
Description: Tracing of Indian deed signed with totems, for a tract of land in Schoharie Valley, 1729.
Source: N.Y.STATE LIBRARY, ALBANY, MANUSCRIPTS, RUFUS GRIDER COLLECTION (1886-1900), SC A974.7/FG84 [VAULT], VOL. 8, P. 128-129.
Comment: Rufus Grider Collection. Original traced by Grider from N.Y.STATE ARCHIVES, ALBANY, N.Y.COL.MSS, INDORSED LAND PAPERS, 1643-1803, SERIES NO. A0272, DEPARTMENT OF STATE, APPLICATIONS FOR LAND GRANTS, VOL. 10, P. 099. Date original, 1729,09,27.

Date: 1887,00,00-1888,00,00 (32)
Description: Tracing of an Indian deed, 1734.
Source: N.Y.STATE LIBRARY, ALBANY, MANUSCRIPTS, RUFUS GRIDER COLLECTION (1886-1900), SC A974.7/FG84 [VAULT], VOL. 8, P. 130.
Comment: Rufus Grider Collection. Traced by Grider for original in N.Y.STATE ARCHIVES, ALBANY, N.Y.COL.MSS., INDORSED LAND PAPERS, 1643-1803, SERIES NO. A0272, DEPARTMENT OF STATE, APPLICATIONS FOR LAND GRANTS, VOL. 11, P. 153. Date of original 1734, 12, 11.

Date: 1887,00,00-1888,00,00 (33)
Description: Tracing of map of early patents on south side of Mohawk River, by Simeon DeWitt, 1790.
Source: N.Y.STATE LIBARY, ALBANY, MANUSCRIPTS, RUFUS GRIDER COLLECTION (1886-1900), SC A974.7/FG84 [VAULT], VOL. 8, P. 131.
Comment: Rufus Grider Collection. Traced by Grider for DOCUMENTS RELATIVE TO THE COLONIAL HISTORY OF NEW YORK. . ., 1: 420.

Date: 1887,00,00-1888,00,00 (34)
Description: Tracing of survey by Thomas Machin, 1802, of the Old Schoharie Patent (1714) granted to Myndert Schuyler.
Source: N.Y.STATE LIBRARY, ALBANY, MANUSCRIPTS, RUFUS GRIDER COLLECTION (1886-1900), SC A974.7/FG84 [VAULT], VOL. 8, P. 138.
Comment: Rufus Grider Collection. Traced by Grider in 1887-1888 from original in possession of A.G. Richmond. SEE 1710,10,19; 1714,05,08; 1714,11,03. For subsequent divisions of the land, see a series of documents in 1736 and 1737 in Vol. 12 of N.Y.STATE ARCHIVES, ALBANY, N.Y.COL.MSS, INDORSED LAND PAPERS, 1643-1803, SERIES NO. A0272, DEPARTMENT OF STATE, APPLICATIONS FOR LAND GRANTS. (They are listed in this calendar.) See also 1786,01,07; 1794,05,06; 1815,12,00.

Date: 1887,00,00-1888,00,00 (35)
Description: Tracing of a map of Schohara (Schoharie) by Captain William Gray, 1778.
Source: N.Y.STATE LIBRARY, ALBANY, MANUSCRIPTS, RUFUS GRIDER COLLECTION (1886-1900), SC A974.7/FG84 [VAULT], VOL. 8, PP. 142-144.
Comment: Rufus Grider Collection. Traced by Grider from official New York State volume on the Sullivan Expedition.

Date: 1887,00,00-1888,00,00 (36)
Description: Tracing of statement of Joseph Brant regarding his treatment of captives, 10 April 1780.
Source: N.Y.STATE LIBRARY, ALBANY, MANUSCRIPTS, RUFUS GRIDER COLLECTION (1886-1900), SC A974.7/FG84 [VAULT], VOL. 8, P. 145.
Comment:

Date: 1887,00,00-1888,00,00 (37)
Description: Tracing of Indian deed for 260 acres in the Schoharie Valley to Adam Vrooman of Schenectady, 22 August 1711. Signed with totems.
Source: N.Y.STATE LIBRARY, ALBANY, MANUSCRIPTS, RUFUS GRIDER COLLECTION (1886-1900), SC A974.7/FG84 [VAULT], VOL. 8, P. 149.
Comment: Rufus Grider Collection. Traced by Grider, 1887-1888, from original in possession of A.G. Richmond.

Date: 1887,00,00-1888,00,00 (38)
Description: Tracing of Indian deed for 340 acres in the Schoharie Valley to Adam Vrooman of Schenectady, 30 April 1714. Signed with totems.
Source: N.Y.STATE LIBRARY, ALBANY, MANUSCRIPTS, RUFUS GRIDER COLLECTION (1886-1900), SC A974.7/FG84 [VAULT], VOL. 8, P. 150.
Comment: Rufus Grider Collection. Traced by Grider from original in possession of A.G. Richmond.

Date: 1887,00,00-1888,00,00 (39)
Description: Tracing of confirmation of purchases in 1711 and 1714 of land in the Schoharie Valley. Signed with totems, including that of Hendrick, 30 March 1726.
Source: N.Y.STATE LIBARY, ALBANY, MANUSCRIPTS, RUFUS GRIDER COLLECTION (1886-1900), SC A974.7/FG84 [VAULT], VOL. 8, PP. 151-152.
Comment: Rufus Grider Collection. Traced by Grider from original in possession of A.G. Richmond.

Date: 1887,00,00-1888,00,00 (40)
Description: Tracing of petition of the Schoharie Mohawks to the Governor of New York against the River Indians for stealing their lands, accompanied by a map of upper Schoharie Creek showing the location of the village of the Schoharie Indians and the 6,000 acres stolen from them by the River Indians and sold to Vincent Matthews in 1734.
Source: N.Y.STATE LIBARY, ALBANY, MANUSCRIPTS, RUFUS GRIDER COLLECTION (1886-1900), SC A974.7/FG84 [VAULT], VOL. 8, PP 154-155.
Comment: Rufus Grider Collection. Traced by Grider from original in N.Y.STATE ARCHIVES, ALBANY, N.Y.COL.MSS, INDORSED LAND PAPERS, 1643-1803, SERIES NO. A0272, DEPARTMENT OF STATE, APPLICATIONS FOR LAND GRANTS, VOL. 11, P. 106. Original is 1734,00,00 [ ].

Date: 1887,00,00-1888,00,00 (41)
Description: Tracing of a map made in 1731 of a grant of land in 1711 from Indians to Adam Vrooman and Martinus Van Slyck (Van Slyke).
Source: N.Y.STATE LIBARY, ALBANY, MANUSCRIPTS, RUFUS GRIDER COLLECTION (1886-1900), SC A974.7/FG84 [VAULT], VOL. 8, P. 156.
Comment: Rufus Grider Collection. Traced by Grider, 1887-1888, from a copy by Henry Cady of original in the Schoharie Court House.

Date: 1887,00,00-1888,00,00 (42)
Description: Tracing of "a map of the lands mentioned in the different releases" by William Cockburn. Latest date on map is 12 February 1731, but map is undated. Shows Vrooman lands.
Source: N.Y.STATE LIBARY, ALBANY, MANUSCRIPTS, RUFUS GRIDER COLLECTION (1886-1900), SC A974.7/FG84 [VAULT], VOL. 8, P. 156a.
Comment: Rufus Grider Collection. Traced by Grider, 1887-1888, from original in possession of A.G. Richmond. SEE 1731,07,12; 1770,11,15; n.d.; 1770,00,00. Referred to as the "Old Bowry" map.

Date: 1887,00,00-1888,00,00 (43)
Description: Undated early map of Schoharie showing lot numbers.
Source: N.Y.STATE LIBARY, ALBANY, MANUSCRIPTS, RUFUS GRIDER COLLECTION (1886-1900), SC A974.7/FG84 [VAULT], VOL. 8, P. 157.
Comment: Rufus Grider Collection. Traced by Grider, 1887-1888, from original in possession of A.G. Richmond.

Date: 1887,00,00-1888,00,00 (44)
Description: Tracing of map of the Indian reservation of 260 acres (later given by them to Adam Vrooman). The tracing is from an original manuscript, but the map is undated.
Source: N.Y.STATE LIBARY, ALBANY, MANUSCRIPTS, RUFUS GRIDER COLLECTION (1886-1900), SC A974.7/FG84 [VAULT], VOL. 8, P. 158.
Comment: Rufus Grider Collection. Traced by Grider, 1887-1888, from manuscript in possession of A.G. Richmond. SEE 1887,00,00-1888,00,00 (41).

Date: 1887,00,00-1888,00,00 (45)
Description: Tracing of a map showing the division of Fountain's Town or Brunnen Dorf, now Schoharie Village, copied from a map made in May 1753 by John Rutse Bleeker, Surveyor. There is a water color inset of the Lutheran parsonage.
Source: N.Y.STATE LIBARY, ALBANY, MANUSCRIPTS, RUFUS GRIDER COLLECTION (1886-1900), SC A974.7/FG84 [VAULT], VOL. 8, P. 141.
Comment:

Date: 1887,00,00-1888,00,00 (46)
Description: Tracing of a map showing lots and locations along the Schoharie River. A note on the map states, "This Division was made, 16 May Anno 1750".
Source: N.Y.STATE LIBRARY, ALBANY, MANUSCRIPTS, RUFUS GRIDER COLLECTION (1886-1900), SC A974.7/FG84 [VAULT], VOL. 8.
Comment: This is a tracing by Rufus Grider Rufus Grider done in 1887 from the original which was in the possession of Henry Cady of Schoharie at the time.

Date: 1896,10,07°
Description: Map of part of Schoharie County showing Enders Woods. Survey made for David Enders, October 7, 1896 by Walter Melius, engineer and surveyor. Map made in Albany, N.Y. October 13,1896.
Source: SEE 1896,10,13.
Comment:

Date: 1896,10,13
Description: Map of part of Schoharie County showing Enders Woods. Survey made for David Enders, October 7, 1896 by Walter Melius, engineer and surveyor. Map made in Albany, N.Y. October 13,1896.
Source: N.Y.STATE LIBRARY, ALBANY, MANUSCRIPTS, SCHOHARIE COUNTY, PATENTEES, MAPS, DW10738, MAP #6.
Comment:

Date: 1910,11,14
Description: An article in the Amsterdam Evening Recorder reports that a 22 August 1711 Indian deed to Adam Vrooman is to be sold at auction in New York City at Anderson's the following Thursday. The articles gives the text of the deed.
Source: AMSTERDAM EVENING RECORDER, AMSTERDAM, N.Y., 14 NOVEMBER 1910.
Comment:

Date: 1946,00,00
Description: The will of Peter Vrooman (Vroman), dated 10 October 1768, mentions land "now in Possession of the Indians. . ."
Source: JOSIAH B. VROOMAN: HIS ANCESTORS AND DESCENDANTS, BY LORA VROOMAN RANDALL AND FLORENCE VROOMAN HOUGHTON, (EL PASO, TX.: CAROL HERTZOG, PRINTER, 1946), PP. 184-187.
Comment:

Date: 1987,00,00
Description: First Census of the United States Taken in the Year 1790, Schoharie Town (Schoharie Valley or Schoharie District of Albany County), printed in the Schoharie County Historical Review of Spring-Summer 1987.
Source: SCHOHARIE COUNTY HISTORICAL REVIEW, (SCHOHARIE, N.Y.: SCHOHARIE COUNTY HISTORICAL SOCIETY), SPRING-SUMMER 1987, VOL. 51, NO. 1, PP. 24-27.
Comment:

Date:	**n.d**
Description:	Johannes Lawyer Papers.
Source:	N.Y.STATE LIBRARY, ALBANY, MANUSCRIPTS, PI 16480.
Comment:	These papers date from 1753 to 1822.

Date: **n.d.**
Description: Schoharie Land Records. Hendrick Matys (Mattice, Matice, Mattys).
Source: N.Y.STATE LIBRARY, ALBANY, MANUSCRIPTS, DW10738.
Comment:

Date: **n.d.**
Description: N.Y. Colonial Manuscripts. Letter from Isaac Vrooman (Vroman) to Alexander Colden giving an account of his surveys of land north of Otsguago (Otsquaga) Brook under licenses granted to Livingston and others.
Source: N.Y. STATE ARCHIVES, ALBANY, N.Y.COL.MSS., 1664-1776, VOL. 89, P. 144.
Comment: The document was destroyed by fire in 1911.

Date: **n.d.**
Description: Map of land east of the Schoharie River near Breakabean (Breakabeen). The land was surveyed in pursuance of a warrant of survey to Laurence (Lawrence) Vrooman (Vroman), surveyor, for the representative of Isaac Levy (Levey), deceased.
Source: MIX'S CATALOG OF MAPS AND SURVEYS IN OFFFICES OF THE SECRETARY OF STATE, STATE ENGINEER AND SURVEYOR AND COMPTROLLER AND N.Y. STATE LIBRARY, 1859, REFERENCES THIS MAP, LISTING IT AS BEING IN THE OFFICE OF THE N.Y. OFFICE OF SURVEYOR GENERAL, MAP. # 83.
Comment: SEE 1785,05,02; 1786,06,07; 1786,06,28; 1793,09,18.

Date: **n.d.**
Description: Map of Butler's Patent, Great Lot # 1 and Lot #4.
Source: MIX'S CATALOG OF MAPS AND SURVEYS IN OFFFICES OF THE SECRETARY OF STATE, STATE ENGINEER AND SURVEYOR AND COMPTROLLER AND N.Y. STATE LIBRARY, 1859, REFERENCES THIS MAP, LISTING IT AS BEING IN THE OFFICES OF THE N.Y. STATE DEPARTMENT OF TAXATION & FINANCE, MAP #100.
Comment: The land is in Fulton.

Date: **n.d.**
Description: Map of Otsquaga (Otsquago) Patent or Young and Livingston Patent.
Source: MIX'S CATALOG OF MAPS AND SURVEYS IN OFFFICES OF THE SECRETARY OF STATE, STATE ENGINEER AND SURVEYOR AND COMPTROLLER AND N.Y. STATE LIBRARY, 1859, REFERENCES THIS MAP, LISTING IT AS BEING IN THE OFFICES OF THE N.Y. STATE DEPARTMENT OF TAXATION & FINANCE, MAP #201.
Comment: SEE 1767,06,00.

Date: **n.d.**
Description: Map of north division of third tract of John Morine (Morin) Scott's land.
Source: MIX'S CATALOG OF MAPS AND SURVEYS IN OFFFICES OF THE SECRETARY OF STATE, STATE ENGINEER AND SURVEYOR AND COMPTROLLER AND N.Y. STATE LIBRARY, 1859, REFERENCES THIS MAP, LISTING IT AS BEING IN THE OFFICES OF THE N.Y. STATE DEPARTMENT OF TAXATION & FINANCE, MAP #219.
Comment: SEE 1769,06,29; 1770,01,02; 1771,05,03; 1806,00,00.

Date: n.d.
Description: Map of the east side of Schoharie Creek and west of the Manor of Rensselaer, including the lands of Heeger (Heegar, Heger), Rightmeyer (Rightmyer, Rightmeir, Reghtmeyer) and Buffington.
Source: MIX'S CATALOG OF MAPS AND SURVEYS IN OFFFICES OF THE SECRETARY OF STATE, STATE ENGINEER AND SURVEYOR AND COMPTROLLER AND N.Y. STATE LIBRARY, 1859, REFERENCES THIS MAP, LISTING IT AS BEING IN THE OFFICES OF THE N.Y. STATE DEPARTMENT OF TAXATION & FINANCE, MAP #106.
Comment: SEE 1770,07,13.

Date: n.d.
Description: Map of Stephen Skinner's Patent.
Source: MIX'S CATALOG OF MAPS AND SURVEYS IN OFFFICES OF THE SECRETARY OF STATE, STATE ENGINEER AND SURVEYOR AND COMPTROLLER AND N.Y. STATE LIBRARY, 1859, REFERENCES THIS MAP, LISTING IT AS BEING IN THE OFFICES OF THE N.Y. STATE DEPARTMENT OF TAXATION & FINANCE, MAP #28.
Comment: SEE 1763,03,21 (2); 1806,11,14; 1822,10,07.

Date: n.d.
Description: Map of second and third allotments of Skinner's Patent.
Source: MIX'S CATALOG OF MAPS AND SURVEYS IN OFFFICES OF THE SECRETARY OF STATE, STATE ENGINEER AND SURVEYOR AND COMPTROLLER AND N.Y. STATE LIBRARY, 1859, REFERENCES THIS MAP, LISTING IT AS BEING IN THE OFFICES OF THE N.Y. STATE DEPARTMENT OF TAXATION & FINANCE, MAP #194.
Comment: SEE 1763,03,21 (2); 1806,11,14; 1822,10,07.

Date: n.d.
Description: Map of land lying on both sides of Keyser's Kill.
Source: MIX'S CATALOG OF MAPS AND SURVEYS IN OFFFICES OF THE SECRETARY OF STATE, STATE ENGINEER AND SURVEYOR AND COMPTROLLER AND N.Y. STATE LIBRARY, 1859, REFERENCES THIS MAP, LISTING IT AS BEING IN THE OFFICES OF THE N.Y. STATE DEPARTMENT OF TAXATION & FINANCE, MAP #153.
Comment: The land is in Broome and Fulton.

Date: n.d.
Description: Map of Jacob Borst's land.
Source: MIX'S CATALOG OF MAPS AND SURVEYS IN OFFFICES OF THE SECRETARY OF STATE, STATE ENGINEER AND SURVEYOR AND COMPTROLLER AND N.Y. STATE LIBRARY, 1859, REFERENCES THIS MAP, LISTING IT AS BEING IN THE OFFICES OF THE N.Y. STATE DEPARTMENT OF TAXATION & FINANCE, MAP #206.
Comment:

Date: n.d.
Description: Map of Nettlefield granted to Lowden and others.
Source: N.Y.STATE LIBRARY, ALBANY, MANUSCRIPTS, JOHANNES LAWYER AND OTHERS, MAPS AND DEEDS OF SCHOHARIE VALLEY, ACC. NO. 16469, MAP #1.
Comment:

Date: n.d.
Description: Caveat on behalf of the City of Albany against granting 500 acres of land at Schaahtecoghe (Scaticoke) and 1,000 acres at Tionnondorage.
Source: N.Y.STATE ARCHIVES, ALBANY, N.Y.COL.MSS, INDORSED LAND PAPERS, 1643-1803, SERIES NO. A0272, DEPARTMENT OF STATE, APPLICATIONS FOR LAND GRANTS, VOL. 16, P. 60.
Comment: This manuscript is found in Vol. 16 of the Indorsed Land Papers, between documents dated June 15, 1761 and June 17, 1761.

Date: n.d.
Description: Copy of a map of a tract of land near Schoharie granted to Walter Franklin and others, surveyed and laid into lots in 1790 by William Cockburn. Copy by grandson W. A. Cockburn.
Source: N.Y.STATE LIBRARY, ALBANY, MANUSCRIPTS, JOHANNES LAWYER AND OTHERS, MAPS AND DEEDS OF SCHOHARIE VALLEY, ACC. NO. 16469, MAP #6.
Comment:

Date: n.d.
Description: Printed map of the head waters of the Rivers Susquehanna and Delaware embracing the early patents on the south side of the Mohawk River from the original drawn about 1790 by Simeon DeWitt, surveyor general.
Source: N.Y.STATE LIBRARY, ALBANY, MANUSCRIPTS, JOHANNES LAWYER AND OTHERS, MAPS AND DEEDS OF SCHOHARIE VALLEY, ACC. NO. 16469, MAP #7.
Comment:

Date: n.d.
Description: Map of Schoharie County showing various patents and other tracts; Lawyer and two miners; Stoneheap Patent; Morris and Coeyman; A. Van Cortlandt; M. Schuyler and others; Teneyck (Ten Eyck) and Bleecker; Johannis Lawyer and others; Wiefield and Clifford; Jonathan Brewer. Shows "Cockburn's line run about the year 1770 or 1771". Latest date on map is 1819.
Source: N.Y.STATE LIBRARY, ALBANY, MANUSCRIPTS, SCHOHARIE COUNTY, PATENTEES, MAPS, DW10738, MAP #1.
Comment:

Date: n.d.
Description: Map of a part of Schoharie County, showing lands of George Kniskern (Knisker, Knieskirk, Kneescarn, Knescarn, Kneiskerk), Henry Houck, Jacob P. Enders, Jacob Henry Smith, Christina Ann Smith, and Peter Enders.
Source: N.Y.STATE LIBRARY, ALBANY, MANUSCRIPTS, SCHOHARIE COUNTY, PATENTEES, MAPS, DW10738, MAP #3.
Comment:

Date: n.d.
Description: Map of lands on the Mohawk and Schoharie rivers referred to in a copy of Adam Putnam's location of a tract of 400 acres of land in the county of Montgomery, bounded on the north by the road leading from Fort Hunter, filed 5 July 1785.
Source: N.Y.STATE ARCHIVES, ALBANY, N.Y.COL.MSS, INDORSED LAND PAPERS, 1643-1803, SERIES NO. A0272, DEPARTMENT OF STATE, APPLICATIONS FOR LAND GRANTS, VOL. 41, P. 030.
Comment: SEE 1725,10,13 for warrant to a patent that is shown on this map. The map is filed in the N.Y.STATE ARCHIVES among papers dated 1786. Adam Putnam's location of a tract of 400 acres may be found in the N.Y.STATE ARCHIVES, ALBANY, N.Y.COL.MSS, INDORSED LAND PAPERS, 1643-1803, SERIES NO. A0272, DEPARTMENT OF STATE, APPLICATIONS FOR LAND GRANTS, VOL. 41, P. 29.

Date: n.d.
Description: Abstract of the land titles of William and Henry Cosby.
Source: N.Y. STATE ARCHIVES, ALBANY, N.Y.COL.MSS, INDORSED LAND PAPERS, 1643-1803, SERIES NO. A0272, DEPARTMENT OF STATE, APPLICATIONS FOR LAND GRANTS, VOL. 13, P. 015.
Comment:

Date: n.d.
Description: A description of sundry tracts of land granted to Henry Cosby, William Cosby, and others.
Source: N.Y. STATE ARCHIVES, ALBANY, N.Y.COL.MSS, INDORSED LAND PAPERS, 1643-1803, SERIES NO. A0272, DEPARTMENT OF STATE, APPLICATIONS FOR LAND GRANTS, VOL. 13, P. 013.
Comment:

Date: n.d.
Description: Map of Sir William Johnson's Patent on both sides of the Charlotte River.
Source: MIX'S CATALOG OF MAPS AND SURVEYS IN OFFFICES OF THE SECRETARY OF STATE, STATE ENGINEER AND SURVEYOR AND COMPTROLLER AND N.Y. STATE LIBRARY, 1859, REFERENCES THIS MAP, LISTING IT AS BEING IN THE OFFICES OF THE N.Y. STATE DEPARTMENT OF TAXATION & FINANCE, MAP #48.
Comment:

Date: n.d.
Description: Description of a survey of 300 acres of land southward of Schoharie. Surveyed for William York and Lewis York by Phillip Verplank.
Source: N.Y. STATE ARCHIVES, ALBANY, N.Y.COL.MSS, INDORSED LAND PAPERS, 1643-1803, SERIES NO. A0272, DEPARTMENT OF STATE, APPLICATIONS FOR LAND GRANTS, VOL. 09, P. 154.
Comment: This manuscript is in the Indorsed Land Papers with documents dated 1725. See 1725,11,02 (2).

Date: n.d.°
Description: Undated early map of Schoharie showing lot numbers.
Source: SEE 1887,00,00-1888,00,00 (43).
Comment: Rufus Grider Collection.

INDEX

The following is an index to the Calendar of Documents to facilitate use of the Calendar. Entries are cross-referenced for researchers. They provide suggestions for other entries under which to look for the appropriate documents. Personal names are complex; and those listed in the index should not be considered equivalent to distinct individuals. They are simply references to those names in the documents. The same individual may appear under one or more name; and surnames, and names of Native Americans—particularly Christian first names--may apply to more than one individual. The index may be used as an aid to research. Conclusions about identity should be based on study of the Calendar and the documents that it cites.

Abbit, Moses SEE ALSO Ibbit, Moses, 1766,10,03 (5)
Abeel, 1771,09,26
Abeel, John, Jr., 1770,10,29
Abercromby, James, 1757,09,16; 1757,10,21; 1757,12,27; 1757,12,27 (2); 1757,12,28; 1758,05,17; 1758,07,16
Abraham, 1732,05,09; 1736,08,13; 1766,10,03 (3); 1766,10,03 (5); 1768,06,10; 1768,06,11; 1768,06,14°; 1769,02,08°; 1769,09,08
Abraham alias Tiyorhasara (Tiyahasara, Teahansera, Tyrohannea[?], Tiyahassary), 1766,10,03 (3); 1768,06,10; 1768,06,11; 1768,06,14°; 1769,02,08°
Accounts, 1710,08,07°; 1710,08,09-21; 1722,09,28; 1744,04,16°; 1746,12,13-1747,11,07; 1747,04,29°; 1748,07,28; 1754,08,04; 1755,03,00-1756,10,00; 1755,05,24°; 1755,06,01°; 1756,11,00-1757,03,00; 1758,11,00-1759,12,00; 1761,09,25-1771,10,13; 1764,02,27 [ ]; 1766,04,30 [ ]°; 1766,09,28 [ ]°; 1766,12,02 [ ]°; 1767,04,24 [ ]°; 1768,08,08°; 1768,08,12°; 1768,11,14; 1768,11,24 (2); 1769,00,00 [ ]°; 1769,02,10; 1769,03,26-10,07; 1769,05,24°; 1770,11,15; 1770,11,15; 1772,10,24; 1828,00,00; n.d.
Ackerson, John SEE ALSO Eckerson, John, 1752,00,00 [ ]
Ackeson, 1762,03,10; 1770,01,09
Ackeson, Thomas, 1764,03,10
Adagegtinge (Adagughtingay) River (Brook/Creek), 1751,00,00°; 1770,03,00; 1770,04,12
Adam, 1732,05,09; 1756,02,27; 1757,05,01; 1764,02,01-04; 1769,02,09°; 1775,02,10-16
Adams (Adems), 1770,06,28
Adams, R., 1752,11,16
Adams (Adems), Robert, 1751,00,00°; 1769,02,08°; 1769,03,21 (3); 1769,03,21 (5); 1770,03,00; 1771,09,21
Adiga Creek, 1769,02,09°
Agarhetonthea, 1734,00,00 [ ]

Aghawey, 1769,02,09°
Agriculture, 1757,05,01
Albany, Corporation of, 1769,03,18; 1774,04,15-28; 1783,09,25 (2)
Albany County, 1769,12,16; 1770,11,09
Alcohol, 1715,07,09
Alexander, 1734,04,18
Alida, 1733,09,18
Allicocke, Joseph, 1769,03,21 (3)
Ana, 1744,09,02
Andone, 1744,09,02
Andrews, William, 1712,11,14-15; 1713,03,09; 1713,09,07
Anharissa, 1723,02,06
Annanias, 1732,05,09
Annin, William, 1769,11,20°; 1770,03,27
Anthony, 1723,02,12; 1732,05,09 1752,05,01; 1752,05,01 (2); 1752,11,09; 1754,06,06 (2); 1754,06,06 (4)
Antonios Nose, 1727,05,06
Archer, J., 1768,12,01
Aria, 1736,08,13
A[r]iadikha, 1732,05,09
Aries Creek, 1734,11,05; 1735,12,24; 1735,12,24 (2); 1737,08,02; 1754,11,01
Arondiak, 1734,04,18
Arrundias, 1729,09,27
Art, 1887,00,00-1888,00,00 (06)
Asarias (Asaras, Asurus, Assarus, Asarus, Asarius), 1733,09,18; 1735,12,24; 1735,12,24 (2); 1736,08,13
Aschelege Creek SEE Oscalleghe
Attrewaghti SEE ALSO Joseph, 1764,01,02-31
Auchmuty, Samuel, 1752,08,14; 1753,02,05
Aughnoura alias Daniel, 1766,10,03 (3); 1769,02,08°; 1769,02,08°
Aurey, Arey, 1733,09,18
Avery, Ann, 1753,02,05
Avery (Avory), John, 1731,06,03; 1735,02,15; 1735,02,15 (2); 1735,02,15 (3); 1735,06,10;

1735,06,10 (2); 1735,06,10 (3); 1735,06,10 (4); 1735,06,10 (5); 1737,07,26
Avigo, 1758,11,00-1759,12,00
Bagg, 1774,11,12
Bagley (Bagly), Daniel, 1737,07,26; 1737,10,12; 1737,10,25
Bagley (Bagly), Timothy, 1736,06,17; 1736,06,25°; 1736,06,25 (2); 1737,07,26; 1737,10,12; 1737,10,25; 1738,10,28; 1739,02,09
Balk, 1774,03,24
Banks, Josiah, 1766,07,02°; 1766,08,20
Banyar, 1753,04,14
Banyar, G., 1751,00,00 [ ]; 1751,00,00°; 1769,04,24; 1769,05,10
Banyar, Goldsbrow, 1751,05,06 (2); 1751,05,18; 1752,01,08; 1752,11,30 (2); 1752,12,06; 1753,04,14 (2); 1753,04,14 (3); 1755,09,24; 1766,09,22; 1767,04,27; 1767,07,28; 1768,11,24; 1769,01,05; 1769,02,10; 1769,05,30; 1770,06,28; 1770,08,02; 1770,09,01; 1770,11,05
Barclay, Henry, 1740,04,03; 1740,11,24; 1741,10,10; 1741,10,19; 1790,01,20
Barclay, Thomas, 1710,08,10°; 1710,09,26
Bard, Bernice, 1734,10,26
Bard, Peter, 1734,10,26
Barker, William, 1769,03,21 (2)
Barneger, Hans George (Hans Jury), 1728,02,00; 1728,04,25; 1730,07,31
Batavia, 1761,06,29
Bauch, J., Jr., 1768,12,01
Bauch, John Frederick, 1751,10,07; 1752,11,09; 1752,11,09 (2); 1752,11,30; 1752,11,30 (2); 1752,12,01; 1753,07,16; 1754,03,19; 1772,07,28
Bauch, William, 1742,10,02; 1743,11,02; 1744,04,14; 1744,04,17; 1744,09,02; 1750,12,14; 1751,03,22; 1752,09,18; 1752,09,18; 1752,10,04; 1752,10,04°; 1752,10,05; 1753,04,10; 1753,05,06; 1753,09,13; 1754,09,30; 1754,11,06; 1755,05,31
Bayard, 1766,10,18 (4); 1767,03,29
Bayard, Nicholas, 1694,05,14°; 1694,05,16°; 1695,09,28; 1695,12,12; 1695,12,12 (3); 1695,12,12°; 1698,05,31; 1699,05,19; 1709,05,27°; 1710,07,24; 1710,07,24 (2); 1710,10,19; 1714,05,08; 1714,06,03; 1722,09,26
Bayard, S., 1786,06,28
Bayard, Samuel, 1694,00,00°; 1713,05,27; 1713,05,27 (2); 1713,10,01; 1769,03,21 (3); 1769,11,28; 1771,12,04
Bayard, Stephen, 1744,05,18; 1751,10,00; 1793,09,18
Bayard's Grant, 1699,05,19; 1710,07,24; 1710,07,24 (2); 1714,05,08; 1714,06,03

Bear, 1710,08,22; 1733,09,18; 1733,09,18; 1766,10,03 (5)
Beaver Dam, 1768,07,01
Beck[e?], Joseph, 1769,03,21 (2); 1770,01,15
Becker (Beeker), 1759,02,10; 1769,00,00 [ ]°; 1770,11,15
Becker, Abraham, 1753,05,29
Becker, David, 1753,05,29; 1753,05,29 (2)
Becker, F. L., 1887,00,00-1888,00,00 (07)
Becker, J., 1768,12,01
Becker, Johan Nicholas, 1770,09,27
Becker (Beeker), Johannis (Johannes), 1750,11,29; 1752,09,18; 1754,09,30; 1755,02,28; 1755,05,02; 1755,06,02 (2); 1768,12,29; 1785,12,21
Becker, Johannis (Johannes), Jr., 1752,11,13 (3); 1752,11,16; 1753,05,06; 1753,05,19 (2); 1753,05,29; 1753,07,18; 1753,09,10 (2); 1754,03,19 (3)
Becker, Johannes Hanse (Hance), 1768,08,05
Becker, John, 1744,10,15; 1750,09,11; 1751,11,07; 1753,04,10
Becker, John Joost, 1765,02,27
Becker (Beeker), Nicholas, 1772,05,08; 1772,05,18
Becker's Patent, 1808,07,28
Beckford, Ballard, 1731,06,03; 1735,02,15; 1735,02,15 (2); 1735,02,15 (3); 1735,06,10; 1735,06,10 (2); 1735,06,10 (3); 1735,06,10 (4); 1735,06,10 (5); 1737,07,26
Beeckman, Gerardus G., 1770,01,02 (3)
Bellinger, Martin, 1796,00,00
Bend, Grove, 1769,03,21 (3); 1769,11,28
Bennet[t], James, 1769,03,21 (2); 1770,01,15
Benson, 1753,04,14
Benson, Egbert, 1770,01,02 (3)
Benson, John, 1752,11,30 (2); 1753,04,14 (3)
Benson, Robert, 1770,01,02 (3)
Benson, William, 1769,03,21 (3)
Berg (Bergh), Phillip, 1751,10,08; 1752,05,01; 1752,05,01 (2); 1752,06,24; 1752,08,01; 1753,02,06; 1753,07,16;
Bickerton, John, 1753,02,05
Black, James, 1775,03,27
Blanchard, Joseph, 1770,01,02 (3)
Bleecker, 1771,00,00°; 1819,00,00°; n.d.
Bleecker (Bleeker), William, 1794,04,01; 1794,05,10
Bleeker, 1734,04,18
Bleeker, J., 1769,04,24; 1769,05,10
Bleeker, John Rutse, 1753,05,00°; 1761,04,16; 1768,08,13; 1769,03,21 (3); 1887,00,00-1888,00,00 (45)
Blenheim, 1769,11,16; 1769,11,17; 1770,07,23; 1770,07,23 (2)

Blenheim Patent, 1769,00,00 [ ] (2); 1769,11,28
Blew Hills, 1734,00,00 [ ]; 1734,08,07; 1734,08,07 (2)
Bliven, Benjamin B., 1844,04,15
Bliven, David, 1844,04,15
Bloodgood, Abraham, 1770,01,02 (3)
Bobin, Isaac, 1723,11,13; 1728,07,13
Bogert, Nicholas, 1769,03,21 (3)
Bornheyer, William, 1761,08,14; 1763,10,06
Borst (Bourst, Burst), 1764,06,06°; 177[ ],05,23
Borst (Bourst, Burst), Catherine, 1830,09,13
Borst (Bourst, Burst), J., 1761,06,15; 1768,12,01
Borst (Bourst, Burst), Jacob, 1728,00,00 [ ]°; 1728,02,00; 1728,04,25; 1728,11,00(?) [ ]; 1729,11,00°; 1730,02,01-02; 1751,01,31; 1751,05,23; 1751,05,23 (2); 1751,06,10; 1751,09,18; 1751,10,05; 1752,01,08; 1752,02,21; 1752,11,13 (3); 1752,11,30 (2); 1753,07,28; 1754,06,06 (2); 1761,06,27; 1761,08,14; 1768,12,29, n.d.
Borst (Bourst, Burst), Jacob, Jr., 1753,07,20; 1753,07,28; 1763,10,06
Borst (Bourst, Burst), Joseph I., 1830,09,13
Borst (Bourst, Burst), Martin, 1728,00,00 [ ]°; 1728,11,00(?) [ ]; 1729,11,00°; 1730,02,01-02; 1729,11,00°; 1730,02,01-02
Borst-Keyser Tract, 1764,06,06
Bouch, 1769,00,00 [ ]°; 1770,11,15
Bouck Patent, 1766,10,03 (8)
Boundary Line, 1768,11,05; 1768,11,18
Bowden, T., 1768,12,01
Bowen, John, 1769,02,08°; 1769,03,21 (5); 1770,09,15; 1771,09,21
Bowen, Joseph, 1769,00,00 [ ]°; 1770,11,15
Bowen, Cornelius, 1770,09,15
Bowen's Patent, 1769,00,00 [ ]
Bowler, E., 1768,12,01
Bowman, Mathew, 1753,07,20; 1753,07,28
Bowman, Mathias, 1751,06,10; 1751,09,18; 1751,10,05
Brackan, John, 1768,03,25
Bradley, Richard, 1738,10,05; 1738,10,24°; 1739,04,12
Bradstreet, John, 1734,00,00°; 1769,05,17
Bradt (Bratt), Aron (Aaron, Arent), 1737,11,12; 1737,12,16; 1738,03,16 (2); 1738,04,10; 1739,04,10°; 1739,05,17 (3); 1769,02,08°
Bradt (Bratt), Dirck, 1755,02,05
Braine, Thomas, 1751,09,17
Brammatacha, 1726,02,26
Brandt SEE Brant, Joseph
Brant, 1733,09,18
Brant, Joseph, 1778,09,10; 1780,00,00°; 1780,04,10°; 1887,00,00-1888,00,00 (12); 1887,00,00-1888,00,00 (22); 1887,00,00-1888,00,00 (23); 1887,00,00-1888,00,00 (36)
Breakabeen (Breakabine), 1753,08,27; 1753,09,01; 1761,09,12; 1766,12,27 [ ]; 1766,12,27°; 1769,06,14°; 1769,09,08; 1770,04,26; 1793,09,18
Breakabeen (Breakabine) Creek, 1766,10,03; 1766,10,03 (2); 1767,12,14
Brewer, 1766,11,20
Brewer, Jonathan, 1770,00,00°; 1771,00,00°; 1819,00,00°; n.d.
Brewerton, George, Jr., 1769,03,21 (2)
Bridger, J., 1710,11,10
Briggs, Schuyler, 1844,04,15
Broughton, Sampsom, 1769,00,00
Brown, Andrew, 1686,00,00
Brown, David, 1763,11,05
Brown, G., 1770,03,27
Brown, T., 1772,03,28
Bruce, John, 1769,05,22
Brunnen Dorf (Fountain's Town), 1753,05,00°; 1887,00,00-1888,00,00 (45)
Buffington, David, 1770,07,11; 1770,07,11 (2); 1770,07,13 (2); n.d.
Burges, John, 1753,02,05
Burial, 1768,08,08°; 1768,08,12°
Burnell, 1772,01,20
Burnet, 1724,11,21; 1726,12,20; 1727,12,21; 1721,10,16; 1721,10,16 (2)
Burnet, William, Jr., 1726,02,25°; 1726,11,24°; 1727,02,25; 1726,11,24; 1727,05,06
Butler, 1735,06,27 [ ]; 1759,02,03-10; 1766,11,20 (2); 1769,06,20
Butler, John, 1759,02,10; 1761,09,25-1771,10,13; 1766,04,30 [ ]°; 1766,09,28 [ ]°; 1766,12,02 [ ]°; 1767,04,24 [ ]°; 1768,06,14°; 1769,02,08°; 1769,02,09°; 1769,03,21; 1769,06,14°; 1769,09,08; 1769,10,02; 1769,12,20; 1770,05,09 (2); 1770,07,23 (2); 1771,03,07; 1771,08,13; 1772,05,08 (2); 1772,07,28
Butler, Thomas, 1757,10,21
Butler, Walter, 1731,06,03; 1733,09,18; 1733,09,18°; 1733,10,16; 1733,10,16°; 1735,02,15; 1735,02,15 (2); 1735,02,15 (3); 1735,06,10; 1735,06,10 (2); 1735,06,10 (3); 1735,06,10 (4); 1735,06,10 (5); 1735,07,04; 1735,07,05; 1735,08,29 (2); 1735,10,11; 1735,12,24; 1736,06,10; 1736,06,12; 1736,06,26; 1737,07,26; 1737,07,28; 1737,11,12; 1738,03,31; 1738,03,31 (2); 1738,04,21; 1738,07,00 [ ]; 1738,10,20l 1738,10,28; 1739,04,12; 1739,05,17 (5); 1739,05,21°;

1750,12,14; 1751,09,17; 1752,08,14; 1753,02,05; 1887,00,00-1888,00,00 (25)
Butler's Patent, 1795,08,03; 1814,06,25; 1814,06,25 (2); 1814,06,25 (3); n.d.
Butler's Purchase, 1738,04,21
Byrne, 1766,10,18 (2); 1767,12,14; 1768,01,21
Byrne (Byrn), Michael, 1766,10,03; 1766,10,03 (2); 1768,01,22; 1768,03,25; 1768,03,25 (2); 1769,02,08°;1769,02,08°; 1769,03,21; 1769,03,21 (5); 1770,09,15; 1771,09,21; 1772,07,28
Byrne Patent, 1768,00,00 [ ]; 1768,01,21; 1768,03,25; 1768,03,25 (2)
Byrne Tract, 1767,07,28
Cady, Henry, 1750,05,16°; 1887,00,00-1888,00,00 (41); 1887,00,00-1888,00,00 (46)
Cajiguate, 1754,10,25
Calhoun (Colhoun), Alexander, 1739,02,09
Camp, Wolf, 1769,05,22
Campbell, D., 1769,12,20; 1772,01,20
Campbell, Daniel, 1768,03,25
Campbell, John, 1770,03,27
Campbell, William, 1769,03,21 (2); 1769,03,21 (3)
Canadagaia (Canadagaya; alias Hance), 1766,10,03 (3); 1768,06,10; 1768,06,11; 1768,06,14°; 1769,02,08°; 1769,02,08°; 1769,09,08
Candagaia (Candagaie; Kanachdegawa; Candagaie; Canadajaya) alias Hance the Wilt (Hans), 1754,10,25; 1766,10,03 (3); 1768,06,10; 1768,06,11; 1768,06,14°; 1769,02,08°; 1769,09,08
Canajoharie (Conjohare; Connajagara), 1723,03,04; 1725,10,28; 1734,04,18; 1738,10,05; 1738,10,24°; 1751,00,00°; 1751,05,08; 1754,07,27; 1763,10,04-17; 1766,05,19; 1766,09,05-19 [ ]; 1769,00,00 [ ]°; 1770,03,00; 1770,09,04; 1770,11,15; 1771,09,28; 1772,07,28-30; 1773,02,15; 1774,06,11 [ ]; 1785,00,00 [ ]
Canajosery, Johannes, 1754,04,27
Cankeskoha, 1761,12,23
Canoes, 1751,00,00 [ ]; 1751,00,00°; 1751,05,06
Captives, 1753,09,02; 1757,05,24; 1757,06,26-30; 1764,02,28; 1764,03,12; 1780,04,10°; 1887,00,00-1888,00,00 (36)
Carrol, Edmond, 1769,03,21 (2)
Carrol, Frederick, 1769,03,21 (2)
Cartwright, Richard, 1770,03,27
Carvik, 1733,10,16
Castle(s) (Village), 1713,09,07; 1714,05,03; 1734,00,00 [ ]; 1752,11,09; 1754,00,00-1755,00,00°; 1754,10,25; 1754,10,25 (2); 1754,11,01; 1756,00,00°; 1757,09,28; 1757,12,27; 1758,00,00 [ ]; 1758,00,00 [ ] (2); 1766,10,03 (3); 1768,06,11; 1769,09,08; 1770,02,02; 1754,00,00-1755,00,00°; 1887,00,00-1888,00,00; 1887,00,00-1888,00,00 (10) (09)
Castleman, Christian, 1728,00,00 [ ]°; 1728,11,00(?) [ ]; 1729,11,00°; 1730,02,01-02
Catarinet, 1733,09,18
Catharine, 1771,03,07
Catherine, 1752,11,09; 1754,06,06; 1754,06,06 (4); 1766,05,24-27; 1766,05,24-27
Cathrina, 1744,09,02; 1752,11,09
Catrine, 1733,09,18
Catskill (Cattskill, Katskill, Kattskill), 1734,00,00 [ ]; 1734,00,00°; 1734,08,07; 1734,08,07 (2); 1734,10,03 (3); 1734,10,05; 1734,10,12; 1734,12,11; 1734,12,11 (2); 1735,04,03; 1737,12,06; 1757,09,15-20; 1757,09,16; 1761,06,29; 1761,12,23; 1764,03,05-23; 1768,03,02; 1769,05,17; 1770,01,03; 1771,05,24
Caughnawaga, 1746,07,07
Cayuga, 1722,07,091757,09,15-20; 1777,07,09°; 1887,00,00-1888,00,00 (28)
Census, 1713,09,07; 1720,11,01; 1760,08,05; 1763,11,18; 1763,11,18 [ ]; 1774,06,11 [ ]; 1783,09,25; 1790,00,00°; 1987,00,00
Chain, 1769,00,00
Chan_anguina, 1734,00,00 [ ]
Charlotte Creek (River), 1751,00,00 [ ]; n.d.
Chawtickagnack (Chawtickignank, Chawtiekignack) Creek, 1734,00,00 [ ]; 1734,08,07; 1734,08,07 (2); 1734,10,05; 1734,10,12
Chenochquatha, 1731,07,13
Cherokee, 1757,09,15-20
Cherry Valley, 1761,01,28; 1763,11,07-24; 1763,12,07; 1763,12,23; 1763,12,25; 1764,01,27; 1764,02,01-04; 1764,02,21; 1764,02,28; 1764,04,22
Chief(s), 1722,07,09; 1734,00,00 [ ]; 1734,00,00°; 1752,11,09; 1756,03,05-05,26; 1757,01,15-25; 1757,02,20-04,01; 1757,05,24; 1758,11,18-12,04; 1763,10,04-17; 1764,01,02-31; 1764,02,01-04; 1766,05,24-27; 1766,10,03 (3); 1766,10,03 (5); 1768,08,08°; 1768,08,12°; 1768,11,14; 1769,02,09°; 1769,05,17; 1771,03,07; 1778,09,10
Chief Women, 1766,05,24-27
Children, 1710,10,03; 1756,03,05-05,26; 1758,11,18-12,04; 1759,02,11-23; 1764,01,02-31; 1764,02,01-04; 1775,02,10-16; 1783,09,25
Chriss, Hans, 1766,10,03 (5)
Chugnut, 1763,10,04-17
Cinajacqua, 1742,08,30

Clans SEE ALSO Kinship, 1710,08,22;
 1722,07,091723,02,12; 1732,05,09; 1733,09,18;
 1751,08,24; 1757,05,27-06,07; 1766,10,03 (3)
Clark, A., 1768,12,01
Clark (Clarke) and Cosby Patent, 1769,06,14°;
 1769,09,08
Clarke (Clark), 1738,08,30; 1768,06,14°;
 1769,06,14°
Clarke, Edward, 1738,09,06; 1738,09,25;
 1738,10,20; 1739,05,17 (4); 1739,05,17 [ ];
 1739,06,28 [ ]; 1739,07,07; 1739,08,25;
 1739,08,29' 1744,04,17; 1750,12,14; 1752,00,00 [
 ] (2); 1753,09,01; 1753,10,26; 1754,05,01;
 1768,12,13 (2)
Clarke (Clark), George, 1711,05,30' 1711,05,30 (2);
 1717,06,15; 1722,09,28; 1723,11,13; 1726,07,20;
 1734,05,30; 1734,07,15; 1734,11,11 ; 1734,11,21
Clasner's Weise, 1786,01,07
Claus, Daniel, 1760,10,00; 1771,09,21; 1774,01,27;
 1777,07,09°; 1887,00,00-1888,00,00 (28)
Claus (Classen), Lawrence, 1715,02,25
Clifford, John, 1770,00,00°; 1770,01,05;
 1819,00,00°; n.d.
Clinton, George, 1746,12,13-1747,11,07;
 1747,04,29°; 1748,07,28; 1750,05,22
Cluet, Frederick, 1786,00,00; 1789,12,28 (2);
 1790,03,02
Cniskernsdorp SEE Kniskern Dorp
Cobleskill (Cobellskill, Cobus Kill) Creek SEE
 ALSO Oscalleghe, 1727,05,06; 1752,11,09 (2);
 1752,11,13; 1752,11,13 (2); 1752,11,13 (2);
 1752,11,16; 1752,11,30; 1753,05,19 (2);
 1753,07,16; 1753,07,18; 1753,09,10 (2);
 1764,06,06; 1767,06,00; 1769,02,08°; 1769,03,21
 (5); 1772,01,20; 1786,01,11; 1786,06,26
Cockburn, W. A., 1790,00,00°; n.d.
Cockburn, William, 1731,02,12°; 1731,07,12;
 1769,00,00 [ ]°; 1769,11,00; 1770,11,15;
 1770,11,15; 1771,00,00°; 1790,00,00°;
 1887,00,00-1888,00,00 (42); n.d.1887,00,00-
 1888,00,00 (42)
Cockburn's Line, 1770,00,00°; 1771,00,00°;
 1819,00,00°; n.d.1887,00,00-1888,00,00 (42)
Cockcroft, 1774,11,12
Coeyman, 1726,04,30
Coeymans (Coeyman, Coeiman, Coeman), Adries,
 1724,08,06; 1724,09,04°; 1725,10,28 (3);
 1725,11,02 (3); 1725,11,04; 1725,11,04 (2);
 1726,05,24; 1726,05,24; 1726,05,24°;
 1729,00,00°; 1729,10,21; 1737,05,04; 1752,05,01;
 1753,00,00°; 1756,11,00; 1770,00,00°;
 1771,00,00°; 1779,11,26; 1785,03,08; 1808,05,04;
 1819,00,00 [ ]; 1819,00,00°; 1837,09,14, n.d.
Coeymans Field Book, 1785,00,00-1791,00,00
Coeymans Patent, 1760,04,05; 1785,00,00-
 1791,00,00
Colden, 1734,04,18
Colden, Alexander, 1753,09,01; 1753,09,07°;
 1761,01,28; 1769,04,24; 1769,05,10; n.d.
Colden, Cadwallader, 1725,10,04; 1726 (?) [ ];
 1734,04,18; 1738,10,05; 1738,10,24°; 1739,05,17
 (5); 1739,05,21°; 1752,05,01; 1752,11,09;
 1752,11,09 (2); 1752,11,16; 1752,12,06;
 1753,09,01; 1753,09,07°; 1763,12,07; 1763,12,19;
 1764,01,27; 1764,04,22
Colden, Cadwallader, Jr., 1753,05,19; 1753,05,19
 (2); 1753,05,19 (3); 1754,06,06 (2); 1754,06,06
 (4); 1754,06,06 (5)
Collier, Isaac, 1785,09,27 (4); 1786,00,00;
 1786,10,16 (3); 1789,01,31 (2); 1789,12,28 (2)
Collins, 1769,11,00
Collins, Edward, 1726,05,24°; 1728,11,07;
 1729,00,00°; 1731,06,03; 1734,10,03 (2);
 1735,06,27 [ ]; 1739,06,15; 1753,00,00°;
 1819,00,00 [ ]
Collins, James, 1770,00,00; 1770,01,09
Colon, William, 1789,01,31 (3); 1789,04,18 (2);
 1789,04,23 (2)
Colyer, Jacob, 1789,01,31 (6)
Condolence, 1755,09,24; 1757,01,15-25; 1757,02,20-
 04,01; 1757,05,24; 1760,06,29-1761,07,03
Cooper, Thomas, 1734,10,26
Corksill, Thomas, 1734,10,26
Cornelius (Cornelus), 1723,02,12; 1736,08,13'
 1754,10,25
Cornplanter, 1780,00,00°; 1887,00,00-1888,00,00
 (12)
Cornwell, John, 1729,09,03; 1730,02,01-02
Corporation of Albany SEE Albany, Corporation of
Corry, 1737,09,26
Corry, Catherine, 1737,10,12; 1737,10,25
Corry (Correy), William, 1734,11,05; 1737,08,02;
 1737,10,12; 1737,10,25; 1737,11,19; 1754,10,25;
 1754,10,25 (2); 1754,11,01
Corrysbush, 1763,12,08
Cortlandt Patent SEE ALSO Van Cortlandt,
 1815,05,31; 1837,09,14
Cosby, 1734,04,18; 1768,06,14°; 1769,03,18
Cosby, Alexander, 1729,11,00°; 1738,02,09;
 1738,06,22
Cosby, Henry, 1734,10,26; 1734,11,12; 1734,12,11
 (2); 1735,04,03; 1735,06,10 (5); 1739,01,04, n.d.
Cosby, Philip, 1738,02,09; 1738,06,22

Cosby, William, 1734,10,26; 1734,11,12; 1737,10,12; 1737,10,25; 1738,02,09; 1739,01,04; n.d.
Cosby, William, Jr., 1734,10,26; 1734,12,11; 1734,12,11 (2); 1735,04,03; 1735,08,29
Cosby's Manor, 1770,01,03
Cosby Patent, 1769,06,14°; 1769,09,08
County, 1720,00,00-1792,00,00; 1724,11,21; 1727,12,21; 1769,12,16; 1770,00,00°; 1770,04,26; 1770,11,09; 1771,00,00°; 1771,10,25; 1796,00,00; 1819,00,00°; n.d.
Crab, Thomas, 1769,03,21 (3)
Crane, Josiah, 1753,02,05
Craney, John, 1775,03,27 (2)
Crawford, Hugh, 1769,02,08°; 1769,03,21 (5)
Cregier, Jennike, 1731,07,13
Cribelbush, 1786,01,07
Crisler (Crissler, Greslaer, Greslar, Kreisler), Jeronimus (Heronimus, Hieronimus), 1742,07,14; 1742,10,02 (2); 1742,10,13; 1743,06,21; 1744,04,17; 1744,09,02; 1750,11,29; 1750,12,14; 1751,05,23; 1751,06,10; 1751,09,18; 1751,10,05; 1752,00,00 [ ] (2); 1752,10,04
Crisler (Grelaer), Marie Margarieta, 1751,10,05
Crisler, Phillip, 1728,00,00 [ ]°; 1728,11,00(?) [ ]; 1729,11,00°; 1730,02,01-02
Croghan, George, 1769,02,09°; 1770,05,26; 1757,12,28
Cropsy, Hendrick, 1753,02,05
Crosby, Aaron, 1775,02,10-16
Crosby, William, 1736,06,17; 1736,06,25°
Crown Point, 1747,06,16; 1757,06,26-30; 1757,10,21; 1758,07,16
Cusick, James, 1770,12,19
Cusing, Mathew, 1769,03,21 (2)
Cuyler, Abraham, 1710,07,19°; 1714,05,28; 1714,05,28 (2); 1770,06,18
Dagnatagonghe (Dagnatagunoke, 1723,02,06
Danagerane, 1723,02,06
Daniel, 1766,10,03 (3); 1769,02,08°; 1769,02,08°; 1766,10,03 (5);
Daniel alias Aughnoura, 1766,10,03 (3); 1769,02,08°; 1769,02,08°
David, 1756,03,05-05,26; 1757,01,15-25; 1757,05,24; 1758,11,00-1759,12,00; 1763,12,05-22
Davies, John, 1769,02,08°
Davis, John, 1769,03,21 (5)
Debo__?)__, 1767,06,00
DeGarydonde (Dagarytunteey), 1723,02,06
Deed, 1701,07,19°; 1711,08,22; 1714,04,13; 1714,04,30°; 1714,05,28; 1714,05,28 (2); 1717,06,15; 1722,07,09; 1723,02,06; 1723,02,12; 1723,05,10; 1723,11,13; 1724,09,21; 1726,02,26; 1726,07,20; 1726,09,14; 1729,09,27; 1730,09,29 (2); 1732,05,09; 1733,09,18; 1733,09,18°; 1733,10,16; 1733,10,16°; 1734,04,18; 1734,07,09; 1734,08,07; 1734,08,07 (2); 1734,12,11; 1734,12,11 (2); 1735,12,24; 1735,12,24 (2); 1736,08,13; 1738,04,10; 1738,09,06; 1738,10,20; 1739,04,10°; 1739,05,17 (3); 1740,11,24; 1742,08,30; 1744,04,14; 1744,04,17; 1744,09,02; 1751,00,00°; 1751,05,06 (2); 1751,05,23; 1751,05,23 (2); 1751,08,24; 1751,08,24°; 1752,05,01; 1752,05,01 (2); 1752,10,04; 1752,11,09; 1752,11,09 (2); 1753,04,00; 1753,05,06; 1753,05,19; 1753,05,19 (2); 1753,05,19 (3); 1753,10,18°; b1753,10,26; 1754,04,27; 1754,06,06; 1754,06,06 (2); 1754,06,06 (3); 1754,06,06 (4); 1754,06,06 (5); 1754,06,06 (6); 1754,06,06 (7); 1754,10,25; 1754,10,25 (2); 1761,12,23; 1763,00,00; 1763,10,06; 1763,11,05; 1764,06,06; 1764,06,06°; 1765,09,22; 1766,09,26; 1766,10,03; 1766,10,03 (3); 1766,10,03 (4); 1766,10,03 (5); 1766,10,03 (6); 1766,10,03 (7); 1766,10,03 (8); 1766,10,03 (9); 1768,06,10; 1768,06,10 (2); 1768,06,11; 1768,06,14°; 1768,11,05; 1769,02,08°; 1769,02,08°; 1769,02,08-09; 1769,02,08-09 (2); 1769,02,09°; 1769,03,18; 1769,06,14°; 1769,09,08; 177[ ],05,23; 1770,03,00; 1770,04,12; 1770,04,17; 1770,05,26; 1771,03,07; 1771,09,21; 1773,09,04; 1784,12,18; 1785,00,00 (2); 1785,04,25; 1790,11,10; 1794,04,01; bb1794,05,06; 1794,05,10; 1794,12,31; 1795,05,09; 1795,08,03; 1798,10,29; 1806,11,14; 1808,05,04; 1814,05,00; 1814,06,25; 1814,06,25 (2); 1814,06,25 (3); 1815,04,13; 1815,05,31; 1815,12,00; 1822,10,07; 1837,09,14; 1844,04,15; 1887,00,00-1888,00,00 (25); 1887,00,00-1888,00,00 (30); 1887,00,00-1888,00,00 (31); 1887,00,00-1888,00,00 (32); 1887,00,00-1888,00,00 (37); 1887,00,00-1888,00,00 (38); 1910,11,14
DeLancey, James, 1735,12,24 (2); 1754,03,13°; 1754,11,01; 1755,06,02; 1755,06,02 (3); 1770,04,26; 1770,11,09; 1785,09,20
Delaware, 1734,00,00°; 1763,10,04-17; 1763,12,05-22; 1764,02,01-04; 1764,02,21; 1769,05,17
Dellemont, John, 1737,11,12
Dellius, Domine, 1699,05,19
Deniston, 1770,12,19
Denton, Daniel, 1734,00,00 [ ]; 1734,08,07; 1734,10,03; 1734,10,05; 1734,10,12

DePeyster, John, 1736,04,14; 1736,05,13; 1737,05,04; 1737,06,16°; 1737,10,15; 1738,08,30; 1750,12,14; 1769,03,18
DeQuayne, 1757,10,21
Desylva, Joseph, 1800,04,10
Dewighnidage, Gidion (Gideon), 1740,11,24
DeWitt, Simeon, 1790,00,00 (2); 1790,00,00°; 1790,00,00°; 1790,00,00°; 1887,00,00-1888,00,00 (11); 1887,00,00-1888,00,00 (33); n.d.
Dick, William, 1731,06,03
Dies, John, 1753,09,01; 1753,09,07°; 1769,07,17
Dies, M., 1769,06,27
Dies (Dice's) Manor, 1791,12,07; 1800,07,12; 1805,06,00
Dietz, 1774,03,24
Dietz, Philip, 1815,04,13
Dinston, 1770,01,03
Divisions, 1756,03,05-05,26; 1756,05,21°
Donachqua, 1723,02,06; 1723,06,27
Dongan, Thomas, 1686,00,00
Douw, Volkert P., 1767,07,06; 1768,06,06; 1770,07,04
Dove-Gatt, 1763,00,00
Downes, J., 1770,07,23; 1770,07,27
Downes, James, 1769,03,21 (3)
Drummond, Evan, 1728,11,07
Duane, J[ames], 1766,00,00 [ ]; 1766,05,17; 1766,08,25; 1767,05,11; 1770,04,10; 1771,07,10
Dubois, Peter, 1785,03,24
Dunbar, Jeremiah, 1739,05,17 (5); 1739,05,21°
Dunbar, John, 1714,05,03
Duncan, John, 1763,12,08; 1765,09,30
Dunlop, John, 1769,03,21 (2)
Dunlop, Samuel, 1763,12,25
Dunning, Michael, 1734,00,00 [ ]; 1734,08,07 (2); 1734,10,03; 1734,10,05; 1734,10,12
Dunscomb, James, 1769,03,21 (2)
DuPonceau, Peter, 1820,03,04
Dutch, 1734,04,18; 1763,00,00; 1771,03,23; 1772,10,00-1773,11,00
Dutch Reform Church, 1730,00,00-1752,03,19
Dyer, John, 1737,10,12; 1737,10,25
Earll, J. L., 1773,08,26
Eastkill, 1790,06,22
Eckerson, Cornelius, 1768,07,16; 1768,08,11
Eckerson, Johannes (Johannis), 1744,10,15; 1750,09,11; 1750,11,29; 1751,11,07; 1753,04,10; 1754,09,30; 1755,02,28; 1755,06,02 (2)
Eckerson, John SEE ALSO Ackerson, John, 1742,10,02 (2)
Eckerson, T., 1755,06,02 (2); 1768,04,17
Eckerson, Teunis, 1753,05,06

Eckerson (Eskeson), Thomas, 1752,10,05; 1753,05,29; 1753,05,29 (2); 1753,09,13; 1754,09,30; 1755,02,28; 1768,06,10; 1768,07,16; 1768,08,11
Edwards, Uriah, 1828,09,15-10,04
Ehle, SEE Oehl, 1731,06,24; 1731,09,25; 1732,05,09; 1732,09,15
Eliza, 1732,05,09
Ellwood, 1754,08,04
Enders, [Widow], 1844,04,15
Enders, David, 1896,10,07°; 1896,10,13
Enders, Elizabeth, 1830,09,13
Enders, Jacob SEE ALSO Enters, Jacob, 1762,03,20; 1779,11,26; 1815,04,13
Enders, Jacob P., 1830,09,13; 1837,09,14; 1844,04,15; n.d.
Enders, Johannes (John, Johan), 1794,05,05; 1794,05,06; 1830,09,13
Enders, John (Johan, Johannes), Jr., 1815,05,31
Enders, Nancy, 1830,09,13
Enders, Peter I. (J.?), 1815,04,13; 1830,09,13; 1896,10,13
Enders, Peter, Jr., 1788,08,04; 1794,05,05; 1794,05,06; 1798,10,29; 1815,05,31; 1815,12,00; 1830,09,13
Enders Woods, 1896,10,07°; 1896,10,13
English, William, 1737,10,12; 1737,10,25; 1739,02,09
Enter(s), Jacob SEE ALSO Ender, Jacob, 1766,10,03 (5); 1768,08,02; 1768,12,01
Esopus, 1734,00,00°; 1769,05,17
Estaghrogon (Estagrogan), 1736,08,13; 1737,11,12 (2)
Eutus, Bardrom, 1733,03,26
Factions, 1756,03,05-05,26; 1756,05,21°
Falls, 1734,00,00 [ ]
Famine, 1757,05,04-12; 1758,12,05-09
Fanning, 1774,11,12
Fee Simple, 1710,10,19
Fees, 1714,09,05; 1714,11,03 (3); 1725,10,13; 1726,05,24°; 1744,04,16°; 1769,01,05; 1769,02,10; 1768,11,24 (2); 1771,09,28; 1771,09,28°; 1887,00,00-1888,00,00 (26)
Felton, John, 1734,12,11 (2)
Ferrall, Mathew, 1751,06,12; 1752,11,16; 1752,11,21; 1754,03,01; 1754,03,01 (2); 1754,03,05; 1754,03,13°; 1785,09,20
Firewood, 1710,08,22; 1711,08,22
Fisher, Johannes Harmense, 1716,02,14
Fisher, Thomas, 1769,03,21 (3)
Fitch, E. L. Nathan, 1790,06,22

Five Nations, 1701,07,19°; 1710,08,07-21;
  1710,08,09-21; 1710,08,10°; 1710,08,15;
  1710,09,26; 1710,10,03 [ ]; 1722,07,09;
  1726,09,14; 1742,00,00-1748,00,00 [ ]°;
  1750,05,22; 1757,09,15-20; 1774,06,11 [ ];
  1820,00,00 [ ]
Fonda, D., 1752,11,16
Fonda, Dow, 1739,02,09
Fonda, J., 1752,11,16
Fonda (Funda), Jelles, 1758,12,09; 1758,12,16-18;
  1760,10,00; 1768,09,09; 1769,00,00 [ ]°;
  1769,02,08°; 1769,03,21 (5); 1770,11,15;
  1771,09,21
Forbes, Alexander, 1769,03,21 (2)
Forster (Foster), 1764,06,06°; 177[ ],05,23
Forster (Foster), George, 1753,07,20; 1753,07,28
Fort SEE ALSO Lower Fort; Middle Fort; Upper
  Fort, 1754,00,00-1755,00,00°; 1756,00,00°;
  1756,03,05-05,26; 1756,04,22; 1758,00,00 [ ];
  1758,00,00 [ ] (2); 1764,02,01-04; 1887,00,00-
  1888,00,00 (04); 1887,00,00-1888,00,00 (18)
Fort Hunter, 1713,09,07; 1716,02,14; 1721,10,16 (2);
  1723,06,20 (3); 1734,05,30 (2); 1734,10,26;
  1735,02,15; 1735,02,15 (2); 1735,02,15 (3);
  1735,02,15 (4); 1735,12,24; 1735,12,24 (2);
  1737,10,12; 1737,11,12 (2); 1741,10,10;
  1754,10,25; 1763,11,18; 1769,03,18; 1770,09,04;
  1773,02,15; 1783,09,25 (2); 1785,00,00;
  1786,00,00°; 1786,01,04; 1789,00,00; 1789,01,00;
  1789,12,28; 1790,01,04; 1790,03,01; 1792,11,08,
  n.d.
Fort Johnson, 1756,07,00; 1757,01,15-25;
  1757,02,20-04,01; 1757,05,02; 1757,05,24;
  1757,05,27-06,07; 1757,06,26-30; 1757,07,18-31;
  1757,08,23-29; 1757,09,15-20; 1758,06,21-07,01;
  1758,11,18-12,04; 1759,02,03-10; 1759,02,11-23;
  1714,08,26 (4); 1714,08,26°; 1714,09,05;
  1714,11,03; 1714,11,03 (4); 1714,11,03 (5);
  1722,09,28; 1723,02,06°; 1723,03,07; 1723,06,20
  (2); 1723,06,28; 1725,02,10; 1725,09,29;
  1725,10,13; 1725,10,28 (2); 1725,11,02;
  1725,11,04; 1726,02,04; 1726,02,10°;
  1726,02,25°; 1726,03,10; 1726,04,16; 1726,05,24;
  1726,05,24°; 1726,07,20; 1726,10,21;
  1726,11,24°; 1727,02,25; 1726,11,24; 1728,02,00;
  1729,00,00°; 1729,10,21; 1729,11,00°;
  1730,02,01-02; 1730,02,10; 1730,07,30;
  1730,07,31; 1730,09,29; 1733,10,16; 1734,00,00°;
  1734,04,18; 1734,05,30; 1734,05,30 (2);
  1734,07,15; 1734,10,03; 1734,10,03 (3);
  1734,10,12; 1734,11,05; 1734,11,11; 1734,11,21;
  1735,02,15; 1735,02,15 (2); 1735,02,15 (3);
  1735,06,10; 1735,06,10 (2); 1735,06,10 (3);
  1735,06,10 (4); 1735,06,10 (5); 1735,09,10°;
  1735,10,07; 1736,05,13; 1736,06,26; 1737,05,04;
  1737,06,16°; 1737,07,26; 1737,08,02; 1737,10,15;
  1737,10,25; 1737,11,12; 1737,11,12 (2);
  1738,04,21; 1738,05,05°; 1738,08,30; 1738,10,05;
  1738,10,24°; 1738,10,28; 1739,04,12; 1739,05,17
  (3); 1739,05,17 [ ]; 1739,06,15; 1739,08,01;
  1739,08,08 (2); 1739,08,25; 1739,08,29;
  1740,07,26; 1742,10,13; 1743,07,14; 1744,04,16°;
  1744,04,17; 1751,04,03; 1751,05,18; 1751,06,10;
  1751,10,05; 1751,10,08; 1752,00,00 [ ];
  1752,00,00 [ ] (2); 1752,01,08; 1752,02,21;
  1752,05,07; 1752,05,25; 1752,06,24 (2);
  1752,08,14; 1752,10,05; 1752,11,13; 1752,11,13
  (3); 1752,11,16; 1752,11,30; 1752,12,01;
  1752,12,06; 1753,00,00°; 1753,02,06; 1753,02,19;
  1753,04,10; 1753,04,14 (3); 1753,05,06;
  1753,05,29 (2); 1753,06,06; 1753,07,16;
  1753,07,18; 1753,07,18 (2); 1753,07,20;
  1753,07,28; 1753,08,27; 1753,08,31; 1753,09,01;
  1753,09,10; 1753,09,13; 1753,10,26; 1754,03,01
  (3); 1754,03,19; 1754,03,19 (2); 1754,03,19 (3);
  1754,05,06; 1754,07,27; 1754,09,30; 1754,10,25;
  1754,10,25 (2); 1754,11,01; 1754,11,06;
  1755,02,05; 1755,02,28; 1755,05,02; 1755,05,31;
  1755,06,02 (2); 1760,04,05; 1761,01,28;
  1761,06,15; 1761,08,14; 1761,08,14°; 1761,09,17;
  1762,07,16; 1762,09,20; 1763,05,19; 1763,10,06;
  1763,10,06°; 1763,11,05; 1765,02,27; 1765,10,11;
  1766,10,03 (6); 1766,10,03 (8); 1766.03.12;
  1767,04,27; 1767,07,28; 1768,00,00 [ ];
  1768,00,00°; 1768,01,21; 1768,03,25; 1768,03,25
  (2); 1768,04,17; 1768,08,11; 1768,11,13;
  1768,11,24; 1768,12,01; 1768,12,13 (2);
  1768,12,29; 1769,00,00 [ ]; 1769,00,00 [ ] (2);
  1769,00,00°; 1769,01,05; 1769,01,20; 1769,01,20
  (2); 1769,02,08°; 1769,03,21 (2); 1769,03,22;
  1769,04,17; 1769,04,24; 1769,05,10; 1769,05,17;
  1769,05,30; 1769,06,14°; 1769,09,08; 1769,09,30;
  1769,11,28; 1770,00,00; 1770,00,00°; 1770,01,02;
  1770,01,02 (3); 1770,01,12; 1770,01,15;
  1770,03,19; 1770,05,08; 1770,05,09 (2);
  1770,05,17; 1770,06,20; 1770,06,28; 1770,06,29;
  1770,07,04; 1770,07,04 (2); 1770,07,13;
  1770,07,13 (2); 1770,07,13 (3); 1770,07,31;
  1770,08,02; 1770,09,01; 1770,09,01 (2);
  1770,09,15; 1770,09,27; 1770,11,05; 1770,11,15;
  1771,00,00°; 1771,05,03; 1771,07,04; 1771,07,10;
  1771,09,21; 1771,10,12; 1771,12,04; 1772,09,10;
  1773,09,04; 1774,01,27; 1774,08,04; 1774,08,04
  (2); 1775,03,27; 1775,03,27 (2); 1779,01,01;

1779,11,26; 1785,00,00 [ ]; 1785,00,00-
1791,00,00; 1785,00,00°; 1785,03,08; 1785,10,01;
1785,11,12; 1785,11,22°; 1786,00,00°;
1786,01,07; 1786,11,11; 1787,05,07; 1790,00,00
(2); 1790,00,00°; 1790,06,22; 1790,11,10;
1794,04,01; 1794,05,05; 1794,05,06; 1794,05,10;
1795,05,09; 1795,08,03; 1796,00,00(?) [ ];
1796,00,00°; 1798,10,29; 1802,00,00°;
1806,11,14; 1808,05,04; 1808,07,28; 1814,06,25;
1814,06,25 (2); 1814,06,25 (3); 1815,04,13;
1815,05,31; 1815,12,00; 1819,00,00 [ ];
1819,00,00°; 1822,10,07; 1837,09,14; 1844,04,15;
1887,00,00-1888,00,00 (11); 1887,00,00-
1888,00,00 (33); 1887,00,00-1888,00,00 (34); n.d.
Fort Stanwix, 1768,09,15-10,30; 1768,11,05;
1768,11,18; 1769,03,21 (2); 1769,03,21 (3);
1772,07,28-30
Foster, 1764,06,06°
Fountain's Land (Town) SEE Brunnen Dorf,
1753,05,00°; 1887,00,00-1888,00,00 (45)
Fox (Foxes, Fauxes) Creek, 1714,11,11; 1714,11,11
(2); 1737,05,04; 1750,02,04; 1751,02,04;
1752,11,13; 1753,06,06
Franck[l]in, Henry Andrew, 1769,06,29; 1770,07,11
(2)
Franklin (Francklin), 1770,07,11; 1772,05,08 (2)
Franklin (Francklin), Walter, 1770,05,25;
1770,06,20; 1772,07,28; 1790,00,00°; n.d.
Franklin's Patent SEE ALSO Walter Franklin Patent,
1808,07,28
Frazer, John, 1768,03,25
Frazer, William, 1768,03,25
Freeman, Thomas, 1735,09,10°; 1735,10,07
French, 1698,05,31; 1738,08,30; 1755,09,24;
1757,06,26-30; 1757,09,15-20; 1757,09,28;
1757,10,19; 1757,10,21; 1758,06,21-07,01
Fry, 1761,09,25-1771,10,13
Furgerg, 1744,04,17
Gage, [General], 1763,12,23; 1769,06,20
Gage, Thomas, 1767,05,11; 1769,05,22
Gansevoort, Leonard, 1786,00,00; 1770,05,09 (2)
Garider, J., 1789,01,31 (2)
Garlick (Garlach), John (Johann) Christian,
1716,02,10; 1723,02,12; 1728,08,28
Garlick (Garlach), Elias, 1728,08,28
Garlick land, 1723,08,00-09,00
Garrison, 1756,04,03
Gataraga Hill, 1734,12,11; 1734,12,11 (2)
George, 1734,12,11
Germain, George, 1778,09,10

Germans, 1720,00,00; 1720,11,01; 1734,04,18;
1751,00,00 [ ]; 1751,00,00°; 1751,05,06;
1758,11,18-12,04; 1759,02,10
Gideon, 1732,05,09; 1733,09,18; 1735,12,24;
1735,12,24 (2)
Gillam, J., 1739,08,08
Girtman, 1774,03,24
Glazier, B[eamsley], 1771,05,24; 1772,05,08 (2);
1772,07,28; 1772,09,10; 1774,11,12
Glen, Abraham, 1733,11,03
Glen, Jacob, 1733,11,03; 1735,12,24 (2); 1752,08,14;
1753,02,05; 1754,10,25; 1754,10,25 (2)
Glen, John, 1753,02,05; 1768,00,00; 1768,08,23°
Godfrey, 1772,01,20
Goelet, Isaac, 1753,10,26; 1754,01,11; 1754,05,01
Graham, Agustin, 1710,09,01 (2)
Graham, Agustin, 1737,12,06
Graham, Richard, 1769,03,21 (2)
Grand River (Six Nations), 1774,01,27; 1814,10,18
Gray, William, 1778,00,00°; 1887,00,00-1888,00,00
(35)
Greslaer, SEE Crisler,
Grider, Rufus, 1711,00,00°; 1711,08,22°;
1714,00,00°; 1714,04,30°; 1726,03,30°;
1731,00,00°; 1731,02,12°; 1731,07,12;
1733,09,18°; 1733,10,16°; 1743,00,00°;
1750,05,16°; 1754,00,00-1755,00,00°;
1756,00,00°; 1758,00,00 [ ]; 1758,00,00 [ ] (2);
1758,00,00°; 1771,09,28; 1771,09,28°;
1773,08,26; 1777,07,09°; 1778,00,00°;
1780,10,17°; 1781,00,00°; 1790,00,00°;
1796,00,00°; 1802,00,00°; 1807,00,00°;
1844,00,00°; 1886,00,00; 1887,00,00-1888,00,00;
1887,00,00-1888,00,00 (02); 1887,00,00-
1888,00,00 (03); 1887,00,00-1888,00,00 (04);
1887,00,00-1888,00,00 (05); 1887,00,00-
1888,00,00 (06); 1887,00,00-1888,00,00 (07);
1887,00,00-1888,00,00 (08); 1887,00,00-
1888,00,00 (09); 1887,00,00-1888,00,00 (10);
1887,00,00-1888,00,00 (11); 1887,00,00-
1888,00,00 (21); 1887,00,00-1888,00,00 (26);
1887,00,00-1888,00,00 (27); 1887,00,00-
1888,00,00 (28); 1887,00,00-1888,00,00 (29);
1887,00,00-1888,00,00 (30); 1887,00,00-
1888,00,00 (31); 1887,00,00-1888,00,00 (32);
1887,00,00-1888,00,00 (33); 1887,00,00-
1888,00,00 (34); 1887,00,00-1888,00,00 (35);
1887,00,00-1888,00,00 (37); 1887,00,00-
1888,00,00 (38); 1887,00,00-1888,00,00 (39);
1887,00,00-1888,00,00 (40); 1887,00,00-
1888,00,00 (41); 1887,00,00-1888,00,00 (42);
1887,00,00-1888,00,00 (43); 1887,00,00-

1888,00,00 (44); 1887,00,00-1888,00,00 (46); n.d.°
Groesbeck, Stevanus, 1714,05,03
Gros, John D., 1786,01,26
Guerin, Elizabeth, 1734,10,26; 1735,02,15 (3); 1735,06,10; 1735,08,29 (2)
Guerin, Menard (Maynard), 1734,10,26; 1735,02,15 (3); 1735,06,10; 1735,08,29 (2)
Hagadorn, Direck (Dirck), 1752,09,18
Hall, 1789,12,28 (2)
Hall, Jacob, 1787,09,29
Hall, John, 1789,03,19 (3)
Hall, William, 1785,09,27; 1786,00,00; 1786,10,13; 1786,10,16; 1786,10,16 (3); 1789,01,31 (4); 1789,03,19 (2)
Hance alias Canadagaia (Canadagaya), 1766,10,03 (3); 1768,06,10; 1768,06,11; 1768,06,14°; 1769,02,08°; 1769,02,08°; 1769,09,08
Hance (Hans) the Wilt (Wild) SEE ALSO Canadagaia, 1754,10,25
Handedick, 1733,09,18
Hanlon, Andrew, 1768,03,25
Hans, 1752,05,01 (2)
Hans (Hance, Seth's Hans), 1757,05,27-06,07
Hans (Hance) alias Canadagaia, 1766,10,03 (3); 1768,06,10; 1768,06,11; 1768,06,14°; 1769,02,08°; 1769,02,08°; 1769,09,08
Hans Chriss SEE Chris, Hans
Hans (Hance) Ury (Jury) SEE Ury, Hans
Hanse, Henrick, 1699,05,19; 1735,06,27 [ ];
Hansen, Carl, 1770,06,28
Hansen, Hans, 1735,06,27 [ ]
Hansen, Hendrick, 1735,06,27 [ ]
Hansen, John, 1764,01,20; 1764,02,01
Hanson (Hansen, Honsan), 1764,03,12; 1764,03,10; 1764,03,12
Hanson, Edward SEE ALSO Harrison, Edward, 1734,10,26
Hanson, Phillis SEE ALSO Harrison, Phillis, 1734,10,26
Hardenberg (Hardenburgh) Patent, 1734,00,00°; 1763,11,05; 1769,05,17; 1790,06,22
Hardy (Governor), 1754,08,04
Hardy, Charles, 1755,09,00
Hare, William, 1764,02,21; 1764,02,28
Harker, Christian, 1831,03,28
Harper, 1769,02,08°
Harper, Robert, 1769,03,21 (3)
Harper, William, 1784,11,13; 1785,00,00; 1786,00,00; 1786,10,16 (2); 1789,01,00; 1789,04,18 (2); 1792,11,08

Harrison, Edward, 1735,02,15 (4); 1735,06,10 (3); 1735,10,11
Harrison, F., 1725,11,04 (2)
Harrison, Morley, 1753,02,05
Harrison, Phillis (Phillas), 1735,02,15 (4); 1735,06,10 (3); 1735,10,11
Haskell (Haskoll), John, 1728,07,13
Hauck, SEE ALSO Houck,
Hauck (Houck), Elizabeth, 1798,10,29; 1837,09,14
Hauck (Houck), George, 1815,12,00
Hauck (Houck), Hendrick, 1733,03,26; 1762,03,20
Hauck (Houck), Henry, 1798,10,29; n.d.
Hauck (Houck), Henry, Jr., 1815,12,00
Haviland, Joseph, 1769,03,21 (3)
Hawdy, 1810,00,00°; 1887,00,00-1888,00,00 (13)
Hawksford, G., 1768,12,01
Hawley, Gideon, 1753,00,00°; 1794,07,31; 1794,07,31 (2)
Heath, Samuel, 1729,09,03; 1737,10,12; 1737,10,25
Heathcoate, Caleb, 1769,00,00
Heckewelder, John, 1742,00,00-1748,00,00 [ ] °; 1820,00,00 [ ]; 1820,03,04
Heegar (Heeger; Heger), Hendrick, 1766,10,03 (6); 1766,10,18 (2); 1768,12,01 (2); 1770,09,27; 1772,05,08; n.d.
Heegar Tract, 1770,09,27
Heints, 1762,07,16; 1764,06,06°; 177[ ],05,23
Heints (Hiets), Reinhart, 1753,07,20; 1753,07,28
Heints, William, 1763,05,19
Henderson, James, 1731,06,03; 1735,02,15; 1735,02,15 (2); 1735,02,15 (3); 1735,06,10; 1735,06,10 (2); 1735,06,10 (3); 1735,06,10 (4); 1735,06,10 (5); 1737,07,26; 1739,05,17 (4); 1739,05,17 [ ] (2); 1739,08,08 (2); 1753,08,31
Hendrick, 1710,09,26; 1726,03,30°; 1732,05,09; 1733,09,18; 1734,04,18; 1751,05,08; 1754,07,27; 1768,06,10; 1768,06,11; 1768,06,14°; 1769,02,08°; 1769,09,08; 1887,00,00-1888,00,00 (39)
Hendrick alias Tiendaghe (Tiendega, Tiendaga, Teyendacha), 1768,06,10; 1768,06,11; 1768,06,14°; 1769,02,08°
Henry, 1698,05,31
Hens, Hendrick, 1751,06,10; 1751,09,18; 1751,10,05
Hind, M., 1768,12,01
Hiron[?], Isaac, 1769,03,21 (2)
Holland, Edward, 1753,03,11
Holton, John, 1734,11,12; 1735,04,03
Hooper, Robert Lettice, 1765,09,22; 1785,00,00 (2)
Home, Charles, 1731,06,03; 1735,02,15; 1735,02,15 (2); 1735,02,15 (3); 1735,06,10; 1735,06,10 (2);

1735,06,10 (3); 1735,06,10 (4); 1735,06,10 (5); 1737,07,26
Horsmanden, 1738,05,05°; 1739,05,17 [ ]; 1739,05,21°; 1739,06,28 [ ]
Hosack, D., 1768,12,01
Houck, SEE ALSO Hauck, 1774,03,24
Houck, Caty E., Jr., 1815,05,31
Houses (Native Dwellings), 1734,00,00 [ ]; 1751,00,00 [ ]; 1751,00,00°; 1751,05,06; 1763,00,00
Hudson River, 1710,10,03; 1710,10,03 [ ]; 1710,10,03°; 1710,11,10; 1726 (?) [ ]; 1734,00,00 [ ]; 1734,00,00°; 1734,08,07; 1734,08,07 (2); 1734,10,03; 1734,10,03 (2); 1734,10,03 (3); 1734,12,11; 1734,12,11 (2); 1761,06,29; 1769,02,08-09; 1769,02,08-09 (2)
Huit, Catharine, 1737,10,12; 1737,10,25
Huit, Sarah (Sara), 1737,10,12; 1737,10,25
Hunter, Robert, 1710,07,24; 1710,07,24 (2); 1710,08,07-21; 1710,08,09-21; 1710,08,07°; 1710,08,10°; 1710,08,15; 1710,08,22; 1710,09,26; 1710,10,03; 1710,10,03 [ ]; 1712,10,31; 1713,05,11; 1713,07,18; 1713,09,07; 1715,06,09; 1715,07,09; 1718,07,07; 1720,07,26; 1721,08,29; 1721,10,16 (2)
Huntersfield, 1726,04,30; 1726,04,30 (2); 1726,05,24; 1728,04,25; 1730,07,31; 1732,09,25; 1734,11,21; 1738,04,10; 1738,05,05°; 1739,04,10°; 1739,05,17 (3); 1755,02,28; 1760,09,09; 1768,00,00; 1770,07,31
Hunters Land, 1755,02,28
Hunting, 1757,05,04-12; 1757,09,28; 1758,12,05-09; 1769,05,17
Huser(?sp.), B., 1761,06,15
Ibbit, Moses SEE ALSO Abbit, Moses, 1768,03,25; 1768,08,02; 1768,12,01
Inglis, John, 1770,09,04
Ingoldsby, George, 1731,06,03; 1737,07,26; 1737,07,28; 1739,02,09
Interpreters, 1715,07,09; 1752,05,01; 1752,11,09; 1754,06,06 (4); 1769,02,09°
Irwin, Joseph, 1768,03,25; 1768,12,01; 1770,05,09 (2); 1768,12,01
Jacob, 1738,10,20; 1753,05,19; 1753,05,19 (3); 1754,04,27; 1769,02,09°
Jan, 1723,02,12
Janaentadego SEE ALSO Juneontago (Ianoentago), 1742,07,14
Jaromme, 1733,09,18
Jecocks, D., 1768,12,01
Jeffreys, A., 1768,12,01
Jeux's Creek, 1725,10,28 (3)

Johannes (Johannis), 1723,02,12; 1732,05,09; 1733,09,18; 1733,09,18; 1735,12,24 (2); 1738,04,10
Johannes Canajosery, 1738,04,10
Johannes de Wilt, 1733,09,18
Johannes Schrine, 1769,02,08°
John, 1744,09,02; 1746,07,07; 1746,07,07; 1755,05,24°; 1771,03,07
John alias Saquotohquohse (Saquotohquohese), 1769,02,08°
Johnson, Guy, 1771,03,07; 1771,09,21; 1775,02,10-16; 1778,09,10
Johnson, John, 1771,09,21; 1780,00,00°; 1887,00,00-1888,00,00 (12)
Johnson, Warren, 1760,06,29-1761,07,03
Johnson, William, 1734,00,00°; 1746,07,07; 1746,07,28; 1746,12,13-1747,11,07; 1747,04,29°; 1747,06,16; 1748,02,04; 1748,07,28; 1750,05,22; 1751,00,00 [ ]; 1751,00,00°; 1751,05,06; 1751,05,06 (2); 1751,05,08; 1751,05,18; 1751,08,24; 1751,08,24°; 1754,03,05; 1754,08,04; 1755,03,00-1756,10,00; 1755,05,24°; 1755,06,01°; 1755,06,02; 1755,06,02 (3); 1755,09,24; 1756,03,05-05,26; 1756,04,03; 1756,04,22; 1756,05,28; 1756,05,28 (2); 1756,05,28 (3); 1757,01,15-25; 1757,02,20-04,01; 1757,05,04-12; 1757,05,24; 1757,07,18-31; 1757,08,01-21; 1757,08,23-29; 1757,09,15-20; 1757,09,16; 1757,09,28; 1757,10,19; 1757,10,21; 1757,12,27; 1757,12,27 (2); 1757,12,28; 1758,05,17; 1758,06,21-07,01; 1758,07,16; 1758,11,00-1759,12,00; 1758,11,18-12,04; 1758,12,09; 1758,12,16-18; 1759,02,11-23; 1760,06,29-1761,07,03; 1760,10,00; 1761,01,28; 1761,01,28 (2); 1763,11,07-24; 1763,12,05-22; 1763,12,07; 1763,12,08; 1763,12,19; 1763,12,23; 1763,12,25; 1764,01,02-31; 1764,01,15; 1764,01,20; 1764,01,27; 1764,02,01; 1764,02,21; 1764,02,27 [ ]; 1764,02,27°; 1764,02,28; 1764,03,05-23; 1764,03,10; 1764,03,12; 1764,04,22; 1765,09,22; 1765,09,30; 1766,05,24-27; 1766,09,22; 1766,12,27 [ ]; 1766,12,27°; 1767,03,29; 1767,04,08; 1767,04,27; 1767,07,28; 1768,01,09; 1768,01,22; 1768,02,18; 1768,06,08-28; 1768,11,13; 1768,11,14; 1768,11,24; 1769,01,05; 1769,01,29; 1769,02,10; 1769,03,26-10,07; 1769,05,17; 1769,12,16; 1770,01,09; 1770,02,02; 1770,02,10; 1770,03,00; 1770,04,12; 1770,04,26; 1770,05,08; 1770,06,18; 1770,06,28; 1770,08,02; 1770,09,01; 1770,09,04; 1770,11,05; 1770,11,09; 1770,12,19; 1771,02,28; 1771,09,28; 1771,09,28°; 1771,10,12; 1771,10,25; 1772,05,08;

1772,05,18; 1772,07,28-30; 1773,11,14;
1773,11,14 (2); 1774,01,27; 1774,03,00;
1774,03,24; 1774,04,15-28; 1785,00,00 (2);
1887,00,00-1888,00,00 (23); 1887,00,00-
1888,00,00 (26); n.d.
Johnson, Wittin, 1790,09,20
Johnston, John, 1764,02,21; 1764,02,28
Jones, John, 1769,05,22
Jones, Margaret, 1786,06,26
Jones, Thomas, 1769,11,28
Joseph, 1698,05,31; 1734,12,11; 1734,12,11 (2);
1735,12,24; 1735,12,24 (2); 1738,10,20;
1751,05,23 (2); 1752,05,01; 1752,05,01 (2);
1752,05,01 (2); 1754,04,27; 1754,06,06 (2);
1754,06,06 (4)
Joseph alias Attrewaghti, 1764,01,02-31
Joseph, Jr., 1754,04,27
Jttegarehontie (Ittegarehontie), 1742,08,30
Juneontago (Ianoentago) SEE ALSO Janaentadego,
1742,08,30
Jutrachcogte (Iutrachcogte), 1742,08,30; 1742,10,13
Kadarode (Kadarode, Kadarrode), 1693,07,22;
1705,06,28
Kadasede, 1731,07,13
Kahosetthare River, 1734,12,11; 1734,12,11 (2)
Kahyawgahrorun, an Onondaga, 1722,07,09
Kanatsogh, Nicholas, 1792,05,09
Kaneigarah, a Seneca, 1722,07,09
Kanjearegore, 1695,09,28
Keedsienoo, Onekeedsienos, 1710,07,19°;
1714,05,28; 1714,05,28 (2); 1714,05,28 (2)
Keiser, Barent, 1751,06,10; 1751,09,18; 1751,10,05
Kempe, Catharine, 1769,03,21 (3)
Kempe, Elizabeth, 1769,03,21 (3)
Kempe, Jane, 1769,03,21 (3)
Kempe, John Tabor, 1769,03,21 (3)
Kempe, Philadelphia, 1769,03,21 (3)
Kennedy, Archibald, 1726,02,25°; 1726,11,24°;
1727,02,25; 1726,11,24; 1727,05,06
Kennedy, Archibald, Jr., 1731,06,03
Keyser's Kill, n.d.
King of England, 1701,07,19°; 1726,09,14;
1735,12,24 (2); 1763,10,07°; 1768,04,29
Kingley, H. F., 1887,00,00-1888,00,00 (06)
Kingsfield, Manor of, 1695,12,12 (2); 1695,12,12 (3)
Kinship SEE ALSO Clans, 1723,02,12; 1733,09,18;
1744,04,14; 1766,10,03 (3)
Kirkland, Samuel, 1772,10,00-1773,11,00
Kniskern (Knisker, Kneescarn, Kniskorn, Knieskerk,
Knieskerk, Knieskirk), 1726,05,24°; 1729,00,00°;
1730,10,29; 1733,03,26; 1752,05,07; 1752,12,01
Kniskern (Kneskarn), George, 1808,05,04; n.d.

Kniskern, Hendrick, 1766,09,26; 1771,07,10
Kniskern (Knies Kern), Jacob, 1785,03,08;
1785,11,22°; 1786,01,07; 1788,04,29; 1791,01,31;
1794,05,05; 1794,05,06; 1808,05,04
Kniskern (Knies Kern), Johannes (Johannis),
1751,10,07; 1752,11,09; 1752,11,09 (2);
1752,11,30; 1752,12,01; 1753,07,16; 1772,05,08;
1791,01,31
Kniskern, John Peter, 1729,05,30; 1729,07,05°;
1729,09,27; 1729,10,21; 1729,10,29°; 1730,09,28;
1730,09,29
Kniskern, John, 1785,11,22°; 1786,01,07; 1788,04,29
Kniskern, Jost, 1766,09,26; 1785,11,22°
Kniskern Dorp (Cniskernsdorp, Knisker Dorp,
Knieskirkdorp, Knickskerksdorf)1726,05,24°;
1729,00,00°; 1733,03,26; 1752,05,07;
1753,00,00°; 1754,12,05; 1761,04,07°;
1762,03,20; 1766,09,26; 1768,06,21; 1785,03,08;
1785,11,12; 1785,11,22°; 1786,01,07; 1788,04,29;
1788,08,04; 1791,01,31; 1819,00,00 [ ]
Kreisler, SEE Crisler,
La Force, 1757,10,21
Lamb, John, 1769,03,21 (2)' 1769,03,21 (3)
Lambert (Lambart), John, 1769,03,21 (2); 1769,11,28
Land, Complaints about/Legitimacy of Transactions,
1698,05,31; 1699,05,19; 1721,10,16; 1722,09,26;
1734,00,00 [ ]; 1744,04,14; 1751,05,08;
1752,09,18; 1755,09,00; 1761,01,28; 1766,08,13-
30; 1767,04,09; 1769,03,18; 1771,03,15;
1772,10,24; 1774,03,24; 1775,02,10-16;
1887,00,00-1888,00,00 (25)
Land, Procedures Regarding, 1722,09,26;
1736,12,02° ; 1739,05,17 (5); 1739,05,21°;
1752,05,01; 1785,09,20
Lansing (Lansingh), Jacob, 1738,10,05; 1738,10,24°
Lansing (Lansingh), Johannes, 1734,10,03 (3)
Lansing (Lansingh), John, 1753,10,26; 1754,01,11;
1754,05,01
Lansing (Lansingh), Leendert, 1739,02,09
Lawrence (Lourence, Lowrence, Lowrance,
Laurence), 1732,05,09; 1734,12,11; 1734,12,11
(2); 1736,08,13; 1738,10,20; 1744,09,02;
1751,05,23; 1751,05,23 (2); 1752,11,09;
1753,05,19; 1753,05,19 (3); 1754,04,27;
1754,06,06 (2); 1754,06,06 (4); 1766,05,24-27
Lawrence, Jonathan, 1769,11,28
Lawyer, 1752,09,18; 1757,12,28; 1764,06,06°;
1766,10,18 (6); 1768,11,13; 1768,11,24;
1769,01,29; 1769,02,08°; 1769,02,10; 177[
],05,23; 1770,01,09; 1774,03,24
Lawyer, Frederick, 1750,12,14
Lawyer, Hannis, 1767,04,09

Lawyer, Hans (Hance), 1758,11,18-12,04
Lawyer, Jacob Frederick, 1723,02,06°; 1723,03,07; 1723,03,09; 1723,03,09; 1723,06,20 (2); 1723,06,27; 1723,06,28; 1742,10,02; 1743,11,02; 1744,04,14; 1744,04,16°; 1744,04,17; 1744,09,02; 1751,03,22; 1752,00,00 [ ] (2); 1752,09,18; 1752,10,04; 1752,10,04°; 1752,10,05; 1753,09,13; 1754,09,30; 1754,11,06; 1755,05,31; 1773,09,04; 1794,12,31; 1795,05,09; 1814,06,25; 1814,06,25 (2); 1814,06,25 (3); n.d.1887,00,00-1888,00,00 (16)
Lawyer, Johannes, 1736,04,14; 1736,05,13; 1737,05,04; 1737,06,16°;1737,10,15; 1744,04,17; 1750,12,14; 1752,05,01; 1752,05,01 (2); 1752,06,24; 1752,08,01; 1753,02,06; 1753,02,06; 1755,09,00; 1761,06,15; 1763,10,06; 1766,06,14; 1766,08,13-30; 1766,10,03 (5); 1766,10,18 (5); 1767,04,08; 1768,08,02; 1768,12,01; 1768,12,29; 1768,12,29 (2); 1770,00,00°; 1770,04,17; 1771,00,00°; 1771,07,04; 1771,10,12; 1772,07,28; 1784,12,18; 1785,00,00-1791,00,00; 1794,05,05; 1795,05,09; 1795,08,03; 1819,00,00°, n.d.
Lawyer, Johannes I. J., 1814,06,25 (3)
Lawyer, Johannis (Johannes), Jr., 1725,04,03; 1742,10,02 (2); 1752,00,00 [ ]; 1753,07,20; 1753,07,28; 1754,06,06; 1754,06,06 (2); 1754,06,06 (3); 1761,06,27; 1761,08,14°; 1763,10,06°; 1767,04,27; 1785,11,12; 1786,11,11
Lawyer, John, 1728,00,00 [ ]°; 1728,11,00(?) [ ]; 1729,11,00°; 1730,02,01-02; 1751,10,08; 1761,09,25-1771,10,13; 1766,12,02 [ ]°; 1807,00,00°; 1887,00,00-1888,00,00 (16)
Lawyer, Lawrence, 1752,11,13 (2); 1752,11,16; 1766,10,03 (3); 1766,11,03°; 1767,04,04°; 1768,00,00; 1768,08,13; 1768,08,23°; 1768,11,21°; 1768,12,01; 1768,12,01 (4); 1770,07,04 (2); 1773,09,04; 1790,11,10
Lawyer, Nicholas, 1794,12,31
Lawyer, Thomas, 1814,06,25
Lawyer and DePeyster Grant, 1750,12,14
Lawyer and York Patent, 1736,06,26
Lawyer and Zimmer Patent, 1768,12,29
Lawyer Patent, 1736,06,26; 1753,02,06; 1763,10,06; 1769,01,05
Lawyer Tract, 1768,02,18; 1768,11,24 (2); 1770,00,00°; 1771,00,00°; 1774,03,24; 1819,00,00°; n.d.1887,00,00-1888,00,00 (16)
Lease, 1753,03,11; 1766.03.12; 1785,03,08; 1794,05,05
Lee, Arthur, 1771,02,28
Leslie, Alexander, 1772,03,28

Levey (Levy), Isaac, 1785,05,02; 1786,06,07; 1786,06,28; 1793,09,18; n.d.
Lewis, Morgan, 1786,00,00
License, to purchase land, 1714,04,10; 1714,04,10 (3); 1714,04,10 (3); 1714,05,03; 1714,08,01; 1716,02,10; 1721,10,16 (2); 1723,03,04; 1724,04,08; 1725,10,28 (3); 1725,11,02 (3); 1728,08,28; 1729,05,30; 1735,07,04; 1737,12,06; 1740,04,03; 1742,07,14; 1742,10,02; 1742,10,02 (2); 1743,11,02; 1744,05,11; 1744,05,18; 1744,10,15; 1750,02,04; 1750,09,11; 1750,11,29; 1750,12,14; 1751,00,00 [ ]; 1751,00,00°; 1751,01,31; 1751,02,04; 1751,04,03; 1751,06,12; 1752,11,13; 1752,11,13 (2); 1752,11,13 (3); 1752,11,16; 1752,11,21; 1753,06,06; 1753,07,20; 1753,07,28; 1753,08,27; 1753,09,01; 1754,03,01; 1754,03,01 (2); 1754,03,13°; 1754,09,30; 1760,04,05;1760,12,31; 1761,06,29; 1762,03,10; 1785,09,20; n.d.
Lindsay (Lindesay), John, 1731,06,03; 1735,02,15 (3); 1735,06,10; 1735,06,10 (2); 1735,06,10 (3); 1735,06,10 (4); 1735,06,10 (5); 1737,07,26; 1735,02,15; 1735,02,15 (2); 1735,02,15 (3); 1735,06,10; 1735,06,10 (2); 1735,06,10 (3); 1735,06,10 (4); 1735,06,10 (5); 1737,07,26
Literacy, 1766,10,03 (3); 1768,06,11; 1769,02,08°
Little Flat (at Kniskerdorp), 1785,03,08; 1788,04,29; 1788,08,04
Livingston, 1767,06,00; 1785,00,00 [ ], n.d.
Livingston, H., 1786,06,26
Livingston, John, 1806,00,00
Livingston, John H., 1794,04,01
Livingston, Peter, 1769,11,17 (2)
Livingston, Philip, 1728,07,13; 1731,05,20; 1739,05,17 (4); 1739,05,17 [ ] (2); 1786,06,26; 1786,07,27; 1786,07,27 (2)
Livingston, Philip John, 1769,03,21 (3); 1769,11,17 (2)
Livingston, Robert, 1717,06,15; 1722,09,28; 1726,02,25°; 1726,03,10; 1736,05,13; 1737,10,15
Livingston, Robert, Jr., 1714,11,03; 1714,11,03 (2); 1726,02,25°; 1726,11,24°; 1727,02,25; 1726,11,24; 1727,05,06
Livingston, Sarah, 1786,06,26
Livingston Indian Records, 1710,00,00 (2);
Livingston's Tract, 1726,02,25°
Lodge, Abraham, 1729,09,03
Lott, Abraham, Jr., 1753,10,26; 1754,01,11; 1754,05,01
Lowdon, n.d.
Lowdon, R., 1769,12,18

185

Lower Fort SEE ALSO Fort, 1886,00,00; 1887,00,00-1888,00,00 (03); 1887,00,00-1888,00,00 (04)
Lower Mohawk Village, 1693,07,22; 1735,12,24; 1754,10,25; 1754,10,25 (2); 1754,11,01; 1758,06,21-07,01; 1763,10,04-17; 1774,06,11 [ ]
Lukyes, 1723,02,12
Lupton, Thomas, 1769,03,21 (2)
Lutheran, 1743,00,00°; 1753,05,00°; 1778,00,00°; 1781,00,00°; 1796,00,00°; 1887,00,00-1888,00,00; 1887,00,00-1888,00,00 (02); 1887,00,00-1888,00,00 (27); 1887,00,00-1888,00,00 (29); 1887,00,00-1888,00,00 (45)
Lydius, John H., 1747,06,16
Lydius, Nicholas Jacobus, 1751,04,03
Lyne, James, 1739,02,09
Mabee (Mabee; Maybe; Mebee; Mebie), 1789,12,28 (2)
Mabee (Mabee; Maybe; Mebee; Mebie), Hermanus, 1785,09,27 (3); 1786,00,00; 1786,10,16 (3); 1789,01,31 (5); 1789,03,19 (3)
Mabee (Mabee; Maybe; Mebee; Mebie), John Pieterson (Peterse; Pieterse), 1693,07,22. 1702,11,20; 1703,04,28; 1705,06,28; 1705,07,20; 1720,06,03; 1724,09,21; 1725,01,00 [ ]; 1725,01,25; 1725,09,29; 1725,09,29; 1725,10,04; 1725,10,13; 1754,10,25; 1754,10,25 (2)
Mabee (Mabee; Maybe; Mebee; Mebie), Peter, 1725,10,14; 1726,04,16
MacDon[n]ell, Allen, 1773,11,14; 1773,11,14 (2)
MacFarlance, 1769,01,20 (2)
Machin, Thomas, 1714,00,00°; 1788,02,20 (2); 1802,00,00°; 1887,00,00-1888,00,00 (34)
Mahicans, 1734,00,00 [ ]; 1734,00,00°; 1734,10,03; 1757,05,01; 1757,05,04-12; 1757,09,15-20; 1757,09,16; 1758,03,11-14; 1758,07,02-11; 1760,09,13; 1760,10,00; 1764,03,05-23
Malcom, Alexander, 1739,02,09
Mann,1768,08,04
Mann, George, 1774,03,00; 1774,03,24
Mann, Henry, Jr., 1844,04,15
Mann, Peter, 1814,05,00
Manorial Grants, 1726 (?) [ ]
Manture (Monture), Mitchell, 1783,09,25
Map, 1726 (?) [ ]; 1726,05,24°; 1729,00,00°; 1731,00,00°; 1731,02,12°; 1731,07,12; 1734,00,00 [ ]; 1736,06,17; 1736,06,25°; 1750,05,16°; 1753,00,00°; 1753,02,05; 1753,04,00; 1753,04,14; 1753,04,14 (2); 1753,05,00°; 1753,05,06; 1754,00,00-1755,00,00°; 1756,00,00°; 1758,00,00 [ ]; 1758,00,00 [ ] (2); 1758,00,00°; 1758,11,18-12,04; 1761,08,14°; 1762,09,25; 1763,10,06°; 1765,09,17; 1766,11,20; 1767,00,00 (2); 1767,06,00; 1767,08,29; 1768,00,00; 1768,00,00 [ ]; 1768,07,01; 1768,07,16; 1768,08,02; 1768,08,13; 1768,08,23°; 1768,08,23°; 1768,11,05; 1768,11,18; 1768,12,01 (2); 1768,12,01 (3); 1768,12,01 (4); 1768,12,13; 1768,12,29 (2); 1769,00,00 [ ]; 1769,00,00 [ ] (2); 1769,03,21 (2); 1769,05,22; 1769,06,29; 1769,07,17; 1769,09,08; 1769,10,24; 1769,11,00; 1769,11,16; 1769,11,17 (2); 1770,00,00; 1770,00,00 (2); 1770,00,00°; 1770,00,00°; 1770,01,02 (2); 1770,01,15' 1770,04,12; 1770,04,17; 1770,05,25; 1770,06,29; 1770,07,11; 1770,07,11 (2); 1770,07,23 (2); 1771,00,00°; 1771,05,03; 1771,08,13; 1771,09,26; 1772,07,28; 1773,02,15; 1778,00,00°; 1779,01,01; 1780,10,17°; 1783,09,25 (2); 1785,00,00; 1785,10,11; 1785,11,12; 1786,00,00; 1786,00,00 (2); 1786,00,00°; 1786,06,07; 1786,06,26; 1786,07,27 (2); 1786,11,11; 1788,04,29; 1789,04,18 (2); 1790,00,00 (2); 1790,00,00°; 1790,00,00°; 1790,00,00°; 1790,00,00°; 1792,11,08; 1796,00,00; 1796,00,00(?) [ ]; 1796,00,00°; 1796,02,03; 1800,07,12; 1805,06,00; 1806,00,00; 1808,07,28; 1814,05,00; 1819,00,00 [ ]; 1819,00,00°; 1824,00,00 (2); 1831,03,28; 1887,00,00-1888,00,00 (05); 1887,00,00-1888,00,00 (09); 1887,00,00-1888,00,00 (10); 1887,00,00-1888,00,00 (11); 1887,00,00-1888,00,00 (33); 1887,00,00-1888,00,00 (35); 1887,00,00-1888,00,00 (40); 1887,00,00-1888,00,00 (41); 1887,00,00-1888,00,00 (42); 1887,00,00-1888,00,00 (44)1887,00,00-1888,00,00 (43); 1887,00,00-1888,00,00 (45); 1887,00,00-1888,00,00 (46); 1896,10,07°; 1896,10,13; n.d.
Marckell (Merckell, Mirakle), Johannes (John), 1754,12,05; 1761,04,07°; 1768,06,21; 1779,11,26
Margate, 1733,09,18
Margritta, 1744,09,02
Maria, 1733,09,18; 1744,09,02; 1752,11,09
Markel, M., 1768,12,01
Marks SEE ALSO Totems, 1737,10,12; 1887,00,00-1888,00,00 (21)
Marks (Signatory), 1711,08,22; 1714,04,13; 1714,04,30°; 1722,07,09; 1723,02,06; 1723,02,12; 1723,05,10; 1726,03,30°; 1729,09,27; 1732,05,09; 1733,09,18; 1734,00,00 [ ]; 1734,04,18; 1734,12,11; 1734,12,11 (2); 1735,12,24; 1735,12,24 (2); 1736,08,13;1738,04,10; 1738,10,20; 1740,11,24; 1742,08,30; 1744,04,14;

1744,09,02; 1751,05,23 (2); 1751,08,24;
1752,05,01; 1752,05,01 (2); 1751,10,05;
1752,11,09; 1753,05,19; 1753,05,19 (2);
1753,05,19 (3); 1754,04,27; 1754,06,06;
1754,06,06 (2); 1754,06,06 (4); 1754,10,25;
1761,12,23; 1766,10,03 (3); 1766,10,03 (5);
1768,06,10; 1768,06,11; 1769,02,08°;
1769,02,09°; 1769,09,08; 1887,00,00-1888,00,00
(30); 1887,00,00-1888,00,00 (31); 1887,00,00-
1888,00,00 (37) ; 1887,00,00-1888,00,00 (38);
1887,00,00-1888,00,00 (39)
Marlatt (Marlett), G[ideon], 1784,07,08°;
1785,02,27; 1785,09,28 (2); 1786,10,16 (3);
1789,01,31 (6); 1789,03,19 (4); 1789,03,19 (5);
1789,12,28 (2)
Marshall, John, 1769,03,21 (2)
Mary, 1733,09,18; 1734,12,11; 1734,12,11 (2);
1738,10,20; 1771,03,07
Masters, David, 1786,10,13
Material Culture, 1753,00,00°; 1757,05,01;
1760,06,29-1761,07,03; 1764,01,02-31;
1794,07,31; 1794,07,31 (2); 1887,00,00-
1888,00,00 (06); 1887,00,00-1888,00,00 (07);
1887,00,00-1888,00,00 (08); 1887,00,00-
1888,00,00 (15); 1887,00,00-1888,00,00 (17)
Matrilineality, 1766,05,24-27
Matthews, Vincent, 1729,09,03; 1734,00,00 [ ];
1734,10,03; 1734,10,05; 1734,10,12; 1887,00,00-
1888,00,00 (40)
Mattice (Matice, Mattys), 1766,10,18 (6)
Mattice (Matice, Mattys), Coenradt, 1754,07,27
Mattice (Matice, Mattys, Matys), n.d.
Mattice (Mattys), Johan Joost, 1754,11,06
Mattice (Matice, Matthias), J[ohn] (Johan)
N[icholas], 1766,10,03°; 1766,11,03°;
1767,04,04°; 1768,06,06; 1768,08,13;
1768,08,23°; 1768,11,21°; 1770,07,04
Mattice (Matice, Mattys), Nicholas, 1754,11,06;
1755,09,00; 1766,10,03 (3); 1768,00,00;
1768,12,01 (3)
Maybe, SEE Mabee
McIntire, William, 1768,03,25
McAlister, Alexander, 1769,03,21 (2)
McDavitt (McDewitt}, Patrick, 1769,03,21 (2);
1769,03,21 (3)
McDougall, Allan, 1769,03,21 (3)
McDougall, Alexander, 1769,03,21 (3)
McGinnis[?], Alexander, 1769,03,21 (2)
McGraw, Christopher, 1790,01,20
McGraw, John, 1787,09,29 (2)
McIntosh, D., 1772,03,28
McKean, Robert, 1764,01,15

McKee, Alexander, 1769,02,08°; 1769,03,21 (4);
1769,03,22; 1769,12,18; 1769,12,20' 1769,12,18;
1769,12,20
McMinnomy[?], Robert, 1769,03,21 (2)
McTavish, John, 1771,02,02
McTavish, Simon, 1771,02,02
Mebie, SEE Mabee
Melius, Walter, 1896,10,07°; 1896,10,13
Merkell, Jacob, 1777,02,20 [ ]
Messengers, 1755,09,24
Meyer, John, 1753,08,31
Michum, John, 1768,03,25
Middle Fort SEE ALSO Fort, 1887,00,00-
1888,00,00 (14)
Middleburgh, 1725,02,10; 1726,02,10°; 1734,11,21;
1753,04,10; 1753,05,06; 1753,05,29; 1753,05,29
(2); 1754,00,00; 1754,09,30; 1755,02,28;
1755,06,02 (2); 1768,07,16; 1768,08,11;
1768,12,01 (3); 1768,12,01 (4); 1768,12,29;
1769,06,29; 1770,03,19; 1770,07,04; 1770,07,04
(2); 1786,06,07; 1814,06,25 (2); 1887,00,00-
1888,00,00 (14); 1887,00,00-1888,00,00 (28)
Militia, 1750,05,22; 1757,10,21; 1764,02,01;
1768,01,09
Military Grant, 1765,09,22; 1768,12,13 (2);
1769,01,20; 1769,01,20 (2); 1769,05,22;
1769,06,20; 1770,01,05; 1770,05,17; 1770,07,13;
1770,07,13 (2); 1770,07,13 (3); 1770,11,05;
1772,09,10; 1771,09,17; 1774,08,04; 1774,08,04
(2); 1775,03,27; 1775,03,27 (2); 1785,00,00 (2);
1785,05,05; 1786,10,16 (3); 1789,11,24;
1790,00,00; 1791,01,08; 1792,05,09
Mill Creek, 1754,09,30
Miller, Eleazer, Jr., 1769,03,21 (2)
Miller, Frederick, 1752,11,16
Miller, J., 1752,11,16
Miller, P., 1768,12,01
Miller, Paul, 1769,03,21 (3)
Mills, Elizabeth, 1737,10,25
Miln, 1735,06,27 [ ]
Miln, John, 1739,04,12; 1739,05,17 (5); 1739,05,21°
Minerals, 1734,12,11 (2); 1735,12,24 (2); 1738,10,20
Mine Patent, 1743,07,14
Mines, 1734,12,11 (2); 1735,12,24 (2); 1738,10,20;
1766,05,24-27
Mirakle, SEE Marckell,
Missions, Christian, 1710,08,10°; 1710,09,26;
1712,11,14-15; 1713,03,09; 1713,09,07;
1730,00,00-1752,03,19; 1731,06,24; 1731,09,25;
1732,05,09; 1732,09,15; 1743,00,00°; 1748,02,04;
1753,00,00°; 1753,05,00°; 1757,05,02;
1772,10,00-1773,11,00; 1775,02,10-16;

1778,00,00°; 1781,00,00°; 1794,07,31;
1794,07,31 (2); 1796,00,00°; 1887,00,00-1888,00,00; 1887,00,00-1888,00,00 (02)
Mitchel, William, 1753,02,05
Mix, F. G., 1887,00,00-1888,00,00 (08)
Mohawk (Mohaques), 1693,07,22; 1698,05,31; 1699,05,19; 1710,07,16; 1710,07,20; 1710,08,22; 1710,09,26; 1712,11,14-15; 1713,03,09; 1713,09,07; 1714,05,03; 1715,02,25; 1721,10,16; 1721,10,16 (2); 1722,07,09; 1723,02,12; 1724,04,08; 1731,05,20; 1731,06,03; 1731,06,24; 1732,05,09; 1732,09,15; 1733,09,18; 1733,09,18°; 1733,10,16°; 1734,00,00 [ ]; 1734,11,12; 1735,12,24; 1735,12,24 (2); 1748,02,04; 1750,08,25-10,13; 1753,09,02; 1754,08,04; 1754,10,25; 1754,10,25 (2); 1754,11,01; 1755,09,00; 1758,05,17; 1758,06,21-07,01; 1758,07,16; 1760,09,13; 1760,10,00; 1763,10,04-17; 1763,11,18; 1763,11,18 [ ]; 1766,05,19; 1766,08,13-30; 1766,09,05-19 [ ]; 1766,10,03 (3); 1767,04,09; 1768,06,11; 1768,09,15-10,30; 1768,11,05; 1769,03,18; 1769,09,08; 1770,08,02; 1770,09,01; 1770,09,01 (2); 1770,09,04; 1770,11,05; 1772,07,28-30; 1772,10,00-1773,11,00; 1774,01,27; 1774,06,11 [ ]; 1887,00,00-1888,00,00 (25); 1887,00,00-1888,00,00 (40)
Mohawk Castle, 1714,05,03; 1734,00,00 [ ]; 1754,10,25; 1754,10,25 (2); 1754,11,01; 1766,10,03 (3); 1768,06,11; 1769,09,08
Montgomery (Montgomerie), John, 1730,09,29 (2)
Montour, Henry, 1764,02,21; 1764,02,28
Monture, Mitchell SEE Manture, 1783,09,25
Moor (Moore), Phillip, 1728,00,00 [ ]°; 1728,02,00; 1728,04,25; 1728,11,00(?) [ ]; 1729,11,00°; 1730,02,01-02
Moore, Augustine, 1753,08,31
Moore, Henry, 1766,05,19; 1768,01,09; 1768,01,22; 1768,02,18; 1768,06,08-28; 1768,11,13; 1769,01,05; 1769,02,08-09; 1769,02,08-09 (2); 1771,07,04
Moore, Lewis, Jr. SEE ALSO Morris, Lewis, Jr., 1726,04,30
Morris, 1726,05,24°; 1729,00,00°; 1753,00,00°; 1769,06,20; 1808,05,04
Morris, Catherine, 1769,03,21 (3)
Morris, Frederick, 1737,07,26; 1739,02,09
Morris, John, 1765,09,22; 1785,00,00 (2)
Morris (Moriss), Lewis, 1723,06,20 (3); 1726,05,24°; 1752,05,01; 1752,05,25; 1787,05,07
Morris (Moriss), Lewis, Jr. SEE ALSO Moore, Lewis, Jr., 1724,08,06; 1724,09,04°; 1725,10,28

(3); 1725,11,02; 1725,11,02 (3); 1725,11,04; 1725,11,04 (2); 1726,04,30; 1726,04,30 (2); 1726,05,24; 1729,10,21; 1737,05,04; 1756,11,00; 1798,10,29
Morris, Long, 1769,02,09°
Morris, Richard, 1761,12,01
Morris and Coeyman Patent, 1726,05,24; 1726,05,24°; 1729,00,00°; 1729,10,21; 1751,10,08; 1753,00,00°; 1770,00,00°; 1771,00,00°; 1779,11,26; 1785,03,08; 1819,00,00 [ ]; 1819,00,00°; 1837,09,14; n.d.
Morris Patent, 1726,07,20
Morrison, 1770,04,04
Morrison, Robert, 1770,07,11; 1770,07,11 (2); 1770,07,13 (2)
Morton, John, 1769,03,21 (2)
Moses, 1732,05,09
Mountain Road, 1887,00,00-1888,00,00 (15)
Myer, Jacob, 1770,09,27
Murder, 1778,00,00°; 1781,00,00°; 1887,00,00-1888,00,00 (27); 1887,00,00-1888,00,00 (29)
Murphy, Timothy, 1887,00,00-1888,00,00 (15)
Murphy, William B., 1887,00,00-1888,00,00 (15)
Names, 1710,10,03; 1723,05,10; 1723,06,21; 1730,00,00-1752,03,19; 1732,05,09; 1733,11,03; 1734,10,26; 1742,00,00-1748,00,00 [ ] °; 1742,00,00-1748,00,00 [ ] °; 1751,05,06; 1751,05,23; 1752,11,09; 1760,09,13; 1760,10,00; 1760,10,00; 1761,01,28; 1769,03,22; 1769,11,17; 1770,09,01; 1770,09,01 (2); 1779,06,01°; 1785,00,00 [ ]; 1786,00,00; 1788,01,12; 1791,02,08; 1820,00,00 [ ]; 1828,00,00
Nanticoke, 1758,07,02-11
Naval Stores, 1710,11,10; 1711,05,30; 1711,05,30 (2)
Nascusaque (?sp), 1723,02,12
Nelson, Pashal, 1735,12,24 (2)
Netstograkaarawe Caghsoone Creek, 1710,07,19°; 1714,05,28; 1714,05,28 (2); 1714,05,28 (2)
Nettlefield, n.d.
New Durlach, 1753,04,00; 1784,12,18
Newburgh, Orange County, 1708,05,10
Newkirk, 1789,12,28 (2)
Newkirk (Newkerk), Benjamin, 1786,00,00
Newkirk, Gerrit C., 1785,10,11; 1786,00,00; 1786,10,16; 1786,10,16 (3); 1787,09,29; 1787,09,29 (2); 1789,09,23; 1789,10,09; 1790,03,01
Newkirk, John, 1787,09,29; 1789,10,09
Nicholas (Nicholaes), 1732,05,09; 1766,05,24-27
Nicholas, Gerhart, 1770,04,17
Nicholas Kanatsogh, 1792,05,09

Nicholls, Andrew, 1728,11,07
Nicholls, Richard, 1739,02,09
Nickus, 1754,07,27
Nicoll, Benjamin, 1750,02,04; 1751,02,04
Nicolls, Charles, 1769,03,21 (3)
Nicolls, Richard, 1737,07,26
Nine Partner Patent, 1769,00,00; 1769,02,08°; 1770,04,10; 1774,01,27
Nishogkampewine, 1761,12,23
Odaseatah, an Oneida, 1722,07,09
Oehl (Oel, Ehlig, Ehl, Ehle), John Jacob, 1772,10,00-1773,11,00
Ogilvie, William, 1753,02,05
Ogshontau(?)., 1766,10,03 (8)
Old Bowry Map, 1731,02,12°; 1731,07,12; 1887,00,00-1888,00,00 (42)
Ona'Ogh'da'gey SEE ALSO Onaughduagey, 1751,05,06
Onaughduagey SEE ALSO Ona'Ogh'da'gey, 1751,00,00 [ ]
Onawedake, 1734,07,09
Oneida, 1722,07,09; 1751,05,08; 1756,04,22; 1756,05,28; 1756,05,28 (2); 1756,05,28 (3); 1757,09,15-20; 1758,12,05-09; 1764,03,05-23; 1766,05,19; 1769,03,21 (2); 1770,01,03; 1775,02,10-16; 1792,05,09
O'Neil (Oneil), Charles, 1737,10,12; 1737,10,25; 1739,02,09
Onentadego, 1742,07,14
Oneyagine, 1744,04,17
Onichanorum, 1732,05,09
Onistagrawa (Onitstagrawae, Onitstaehragarawe), 1710,08,22; 1714,04,09; 1714,04,10; 1714,04,10 (2); 1714,07,12; 1714,08,23°; 1714,08,26; 1714,08,26 (2); 1714,08,26°; 1714,09,05; 1726,04,17°; 1887,00,00-1888,00,00 (18)
Onondaga, 1722,07,09; 1750,08,25-10,13; 1751,05,06; 1756,04,22; 1756,05,28; 1756,05,28 (2); 1756,05,28 (3); 1887,00,00-1888,00,00 (41)
Onondaga Council, 1757,05,02
Onuntadass (Onuntadasha, Onuntadashe, Onuntadagka) Hill(s), 1751,01,31; 1751,05,23; 1751,05,23 (2); 1751,06,10; 1751,09,18
Oothout (Outhout), Henry, 1788,02,20 (3)
Oothout (Outhout), Volkert, 1740,07,26; 1769,02,08°
Oquaga (Onoquaga, Aquaga, Aughquaga), 1755,09,24; 1756,02,27; 1756,04,22; 1757,02,20-04,01; 1757,05,01; 1757,05,02; 1757,07,18-31; 1757,09,28; 1757,12,28; 1758,05,17; 1758,07,02-11; 1763,10,04-17; 1763,11,07-24; 1764,02,01-04; 1764,04,24-05,11 [ ]; 1768,09,15-10,30; 1769,02,09°; 1775,02,10-16

Oquarady, 1729,09,27
Ore, 1734,12,11 (2); 1735,12,24 (2)
Oriskany, 1766,05,19
Oscalleghe (Otsgarage, Aschalege, Oscallaghe, Oschaleghe, Otsgarrege, Cobleskill) Creek; SEE ALSO Cobleskill Creek, 1728,04,25; 1730,07,31; 1751,05,23; 1751,05,23 (2); 1751,09,18; 1751,10,07; 1752,11,09; 1752,11,09 (2); 1752,11,30; 1753,05,19 (2); 1753,07,16; 1753,07,18; 1753,09,10 (2); 1754,06,06 (2); 1754,06,06; 1764,06,06; 1770,07,31
Otsiningo, 1758,07,02-11
Otsquage (Otqshage), 1722,03,09; 1723,03,04; 1723,05,10; 1724,01,20; 1725,04,03; 1738,10,05
Outhout, Volkt SEE Oothout, Volkert
Palatines, 1708,05,10; 1709,12,05; 1710,09,01 (2); 1710,10,03; 1710,10,03 [ ]; 1710,11,10; 1711,05,30; 1711,05,30 (2); 1712,10,31; 1713,05,11; 1713,07,18; 1715,02,28; 1715,06,09; 1715,07,09; 1718,07,07; 1720,00,00; 1720,07,26; 1720,08,02; 1720,09,06; 1720,11,01; 1721,08,29; 1721,09,02-09; 1721,09,09; 1721,10,16 (2); 1722,07,09; 1723,02,12; 1723,03,04; 1723,05,10; 1723,08,00-09,00; 1724,01,20; 1724,04,08; 1725,04,03; 1725,10,28; 1725,11,00(?) [ ]; 1725,11,02 (2); 1726,02,04 (2)
Pamslyck, Nicholas, 1786,00,00
Panenamet, 1761,12,23
Patent, 1695,12,12 (3); 1698,10,19; 1702,11,20; 1705,06,28; 1705,07,20; 1706,03,12; 1710,10,19; 1714,00,00°; 1714,04,09; 1714,07,12; 1714,08,06°; 1714,08,23°; 1714,08,26; 1714,08,26 (3); 1714,08,26 (4); 1714,08,26°; 1714,09,05; 1714,11,03; 1714,11,03 (4); 1714,11,03 (5); 1722,09,28; 1723,02,06°; 1723,03,07; 1723,06,20 (2); 1723,06,28; 1725,02,10; 1725,09,29; 1725,10,13; 1725,10,28 (2); 1725,11,02; 1725,11,04; 1726,02,04; 1726,02,10°; 1726,02,25°; 1726,03,10; 1726,04,16; 1726,05,24; 1726,05,24°; 1726,07,20; 1726,10,21; 1726,11,24°; 1727,02,25; 1726,11,24; 1728,02,00; 1729,00,00°; 1729,10,21; 1729,11,00°; 1730,02,01-02; 1730,02,10; 1730,07,30; 1730,07,31; 1730,09,29; 1733,10,16; 1734,00,00°; 1734,04,18; 1734,05,30; 1734,05,30 (2); 1734,07,15; 1734,10,03; 1734,10,03 (3); 1734,10,12; 1734,11,05; 1734,11,11; 1734,11,21; 1735,02,15; 1735,02,15 (2); 1735,02,15 (3); 1735,06,10; 1735,06,10 (2); 1735,06,10 (3); 1735,06,10 (4); 1735,06,10 (5); 1735,09,10°; 1735,10,07; 1736,05,13; 1736,06,26; 1737,05,04; 1737,06,16°; 1737,07,26; 1737,08,02; 1737,10,15;

1737,10,25; 1737,11,12; 1737,11,12 (2);
1738,04,21; 1738,05,05°; 1738,08,30; 1738,10,05;
1738,10,24°; 1738,10,28; 1739,04,12; 1739,05,17
(3); 1739,05,17 [ ]; 1739,06,15; 1739,08,01;
1739,08,08 (2); 1739,08,25; 1739,08,29;
1740,07,26; 1742,10,13; 1743,07,14; 1744,04,16°;
1744,04,17; 1751,04,03; 1751,05,18; 1751,06,10;
1751,10,05; 1751,10,08; 1752,00,00 [ ];
1752,00,00 [ ] (2); 1752,01,08; 1752,02,21;
1752,05,07; 1752,05,25; 1752,06,24 (2);
1752,08,14; 1752,10,05; 1752,11,13; 1752,11,13
(3); 1752,11,16; 1752,11,30; 1752,12,01;
1752,12,06; 1753,00,00°; 1753,02,06; 1753,02,19;
1753,04,10; 1753,04,14 (3); 1753,05,06;
1753,05,29 (2); 1753,06,06; 1753,07,16;
1753,07,18; 1753,07,18 (2); 1753,07,20;
1753,07,28; 1753,08,27; 1753,08,31; 1753,09,01;
1753,09,10; 1753,09,13; 1753,10,26; 1754,03,01
(3); 1754,03,19; 1754,03,19 (2); 1754,03,19 (3);
1754,05,06; 1754,07,27; 1754,09,30; 1754,10,25;
1754,10,25 (2); 1754,11,01; 1754,11,06;
1755,02,05; 1755,02,28; 1755,05,02; 1755,05,31;
1755,06,02 (2); 1760,04,05; 1761,01,28;
1761,06,15; 1761,08,14; 1761,08,14°; 1761,09,17;
1762,07,16; 1762,09,20; 1763,05,19; 1763,10,06;
1763,10,06°; 1763,11,05; 1765,02,27; 1765,10,11;
1766,10,03 (6); 1766,10,03 (8); 1766.03.12;
1767,04,27; 1767,07,28; 1768,00,00 [ ];
1768,00,00°; 1768,01,21; 1768,03,25; 1768,03,25
(2); 1768,04,17; 1768,08,11; 1768,11,13;
1768,11,24; 1768,12,01; 1768,12,13 (2);
1768,12,29; 1769,00,00 [ ]; 1769,00,00 [ ] (2);
1769,00,00°; 1769,01,05; 1769,01,20; 1769,01,20
(2); 1769,02,08°; 1769,03,21 (2); 1769,03,22;
1769,04,17; 1769,04,24; 1769,05,10; 1769,05,17;
1769,05,30; 1769,06,14°; 1769,09,08; 1769,09,30;
1769,11,28; 1770,00,00; 1770,00,00°; 1770,01,02;
1770,01,02 (3); 1770,01,12; 1770,01,15;
1770,03,19; 1770,05,08; 1770,05,09 (2);
1770,05,17; 1770,06,20; 1770,06,28; 1770,06,29
1770,07,04; 1770,07,04 (2); 1770,07,13;
1770,07,13 (2); 1770,07,13 (3); 1770,07,31;
1770,08,02; 1770,09,01; 1770,09,01 (2);
1770,09,15; 1770,09,27; 1770,11,05; 1770,11,15;
1771,00,00°; 1771,05,03; 1771,07,04; 1771,07,10;
1771,09,21; 1771,10,12; 1771,12,04; 1772,09,10;
1773,09,04; 1774,01,27; 1774,08,04; 1774,08,04
(2); 1775,03,27; 1775,03,27 (2); 1779,01,01;
1779,11,26; 1785,00,00 [ ]; 1785,00,00-
1791,00,00; 1785,00,00°; 1785,03,08; 1785,10,01;
1785,11,12; 1785,11,22°; 1786,00,00°;
1786,01,07; 1786,11,11; 1787,05,07; 1790,00,00
(2); 1790,00,00°; 1790,06,22; 1790,11,10;
1794,04,01; 1794,05,05; 1794,05,06; 1794,05,10;
1795,05,09; 1795,08,03; 1796,00,00(?) [ ];
1796,00,00°; 1798,10,29; 1802,00,00°;
1806,11,14; 1808,05,04; 1808,07,28; 1814,06,25;
1814,06,25 (2); 1814,06,25 (3); 1815,04,13;
1815,05,31; 1815,12,00; 1819,00,00 [ ];
1819,00,00°; 1822,10,07; 1837,09,14; 1844,04,15;
1887,00,00-1888,00,00 (11); 1887,00,00-
1888,00,00 (33); 1887,00,00-1888,00,00 (34); n.d.

Paulus, 1754,07,27
Pellenger, Jurian, 1728,00,00 [ ]°; 1728,11,00(?) [ ]
Peter, 1769,02,09°
Petrie, C., 1791,12,07
Petrus, 1733,09,18; 1769,02,09°
Philips, Wiliam, 1768,03,25; 1787,09,29 (2)
Phillips, Benjamin, 1768,03,25
Phyn, James, 1769,03,21 (3); 1770,02,10
Pickle(?), Bartholemew, 1769,02,08°; 1769,03,21 (5)
Pipe, 1769,00,00; 1774,01,27; 1887,00,00-
  1888,00,00 (15)
Popple, William, 1713,05,11; 1720,07,26
Population, 1713,09,07; 1720,11,01; 1760,08,05;
  1763,11,18; 1763,11,18 [ ]; 1770,09,04;
  1774,06,11 [ ];1783,09,25; 1790,00,00°;
  1987,00,00
Pottman, 1754,08,04
Preston, Achilles, 1768,03,25; 1770,05,09 (2)
Proclamation of 1763, 1768,04,29
Proctor, Carden, 1769,03,21 (3)
Proctor, William, 1769,03,21 (3)
Propagation of the Gospel in Foreign Parts,
  1710,08,10°; 1710,09,26; 1713,03,09; 1713,09,07;
  1710,08,10°
Proprietors, 1720,06,03; 1721,08,29; 1721,10,16 (2);
  1728,02,00; 1734,12,11 (2); 1735,12,24 (2);
  1737,05,04; 1737,06,16°; 1738,03,16; 1738,09,25;
  1751,04,03; 1752,05,01 (2); 1752,11,09;
  1752,11,21; 1753,08,27; 1753,10,26; 1765,09,17;
  1769,02,09°; 1771,07,10; 1806,00,00
Provoost, David, 1727,02,25; 1726,11,24; 1727,05,06
Provoost, Delia, 1727,02,25; 1726,11,24; 1727,05,06
Pruyn (Prym), 1766,10,03 (4); 1766,10,18 (3);
  1767,08,29
Pruyn (Prym), David, 1785,10,01; 1786,07,05
Pruyn (Prym), Francis, 1789,09,31
Pruyn, Johannes S[amuel], 1754,04,27; 1755,02,05
Putnam, A., 1785,10,11
Putnam, Adam, 1786,00,00; 1786,00,00°; 1786,10,16
  (3); 1789,04,16; 1789,04,16 (2); 1789,04,23;
  1789,04,23 (2); 1789,09,25; 1790,03,01; n.d.
Putnam, Gerrit, 1789,01,31 (4)

Putnam, J., 1789,04,16 (2)
Putnam, Jacob, 1785,09,00; 1786,10,16 (2)
Putnam, Victor C., 1789,03,19 (5)
Putnam, William, 1789,04,16
Pyrlaeus, Christopher, 1742,00,00-1748,00,00 [ ] °;
   1820,00,00 [ ]; 1820,03,04
Quackenboss (Quackenbush; Queckenbush),
   1789,12,28 (2); 1790,03,02
Quackenboss (Quackenbush; Queckenbush), N.,
   1785,09,27; 1785,09,27 (2); 1785,09,27 (3);
   1789,03,19
Quackenbush, A., 1789,01,31 (5); 1789,03,19 (2)
Quackenbush, S., 1786,10,16 (3); 1789,04,18;
   1789,09,31
Quackenbush (Quaquenbush), Vincent, 1786,00,00
Quackenbush, William, 1789,01,31; 1789,04,18
Quarries, 1738,10,20
Queckenbush, Isaac D., 1785,09,27 (2)
Queen of England, 1714,04,10
Ramage[?], Charles, 1769,03,21 (2)
Ramago[?], Smith, 1769,03,21 (2)
Rebecca, 1733,09,18
Red Jacket, 1887,00,00-1888,00,00 (24)
Redigh, C., 1768,12,01
Reikert, Lodowig, 1752,09,18
Remsen, Henry, 1769,03,21 (3)
Rensselaerwyck (Renselaerwick), 1736,09,23;
   1760,04,05; 1769,01,20; 1770,04,26; n.d.
Richmond, A. G., 1726,03,30°; 1731,02,12°;
   1771,09,28; 1887,00,00-1888,00,00 (26);
   1887,00,00-1888,00,00 (34); 1887,00,00-
   1888,00,00 (37); 1887,00,00-1888,00,00 (38);
   1887,00,00-1888,00,00 (39); 1887,00,00-
   1888,00,00 (42); 1887,00,00-1888,00,00 (43);
   1887,00,00-1888,00,00 (44)
Rightmyer (Rightmeyer, Rightmeir), n.d.
Rightmyer (Rightmeyer, Rightmeir), Anna Maria,
   1752,11,09; 1754,06,06 (4)
Rightmyer (Rightmeyer, Rightmeir), Conradt
   (Conrad), 1738,10,05; 1738,10,24°
Rightmyer (Rightmeyer, Rightmeir), J., 1791,12,07
Rightmyer (Rightmeyer, Rightmeir), John,
   1768,06,11; 1769,07,17
Rightmyer (Rightmeyer, Rightmeir), Maria,
   1752,05,01
Rightmyer (Regtmyer, Rightmeyer, Rightmeir), Ury
   (Jurie, George), 1753,08,27; 1753,09,01;
   1753,09,07°; 1753,10,18°; 1753,10,26;
   1754,01,11; 1754,03,01 (3); 1754,05,01;
   1754,05,06; 1769,06,27; 1769,07,17; 1770,07,13
   (2)

River Indians, 1710,08,07-21; 1734,00,00 [ ];
   1734,10,03; 1747,06,16; 1756,03,05-05,26;
   1757,05,01; 1757,05,04-12; 1757,09,15-20;
   1757,09,16; 1760,09,13; 1760,10,00; 1887,00,00-
   1888,00,00 (40)
Roach, Ed, 1768,03,25
Roads/Paths/Highways, 1712,10,31; 1720,00,00-
   1792,00,00; 1724,11,21; 1726,05,24°; 1726,12,20;
   1727,12,21; 1728,04,25; 1729,00,00°; 1737,10,12;
   1751,00,00 [ ]; 1751,00,00°; 1751,05,06;
   1752,08,01; 1753,00,00°; 1753,03,11; 1756,07,00;
   1763,12,08; 1769,02,08°; 1770,04,26; 1770,06,28;
   1785,09,28 (2); 1785,10,11; 1786,00,00°;
   1790,09,20; 1819,00,00 [ ]; 1844,04,15
Robertston, Alexander, 1769,03,21 (3)
Robinson, John, 1789,04,03
Rofflen[?], Francis, 1769,03,21 (2)
Roll Call of Chiefs, 1722,07,09; 1742,00,00-
   1748,00,00 [ ] °
Romers, Peter Willemse, 1710,10,03
Roode, 1693,07,22
Roseboom, Henry, 1777,02,20 [ ]
Roseboom, John Garret, 1751,04,03
Rupert, France, 1755,06,02; 1755,06,02 (3);
   1766,10,03; 1766,10,03 (2); 1768,03,25;
   1768,03,25 (2)
Runnion, Jonathan, 1768,03,25
Russell, Henry L., 1831,03,28
Rutgers, Anthony, 1769,03,21 (3)
Rutgers, Hermanus, 1769,03,21 (3)
Ryan, Thomas, 1769,03,21 (2)
Sachem(s), 1693,07,22; 1723,02,12; 1734,00,00 [ ];
   1734,00,00°; 1752,11,09; 1755,06,01°;
   1755,06,02; 1755,06,02 (3); 1757,01,15-25;
   1757,02,20-04,01; 1757,05,24; 1768,11,14
Sackett, James, 1769,03,21 (2)
Salisbury (Salsbury), Francis, 1753,10,26;
   1754,05,01
Salm Creek, 1766,10,03 (7)
Salsburgh (Salsbergh, Salsburg), Michael,
   1768,07,01; 1770,01,12
Sanders, John, 1793,02,02
Santford, Helena, 1727,02,25; 1726,11,24;
   1727,05,06
Saquotohquohse (Saquotohquohese), John SEE
   ALSO John, 1769,02,08°
Sarrah, 1733,09,18
Satergusqua, 1723,02,06
Sauldsberry, F.1762,01,16
Savage, James, 1769,06,20
Scalps, 1746,07,07; 1764,02,28; 1764,03,12;
   1757,05,24; 1887,00,00-1888,00,00 (21)

Scanewisse SEE ALSO Sonewesie, Skenewasey, 1742,08,30
Schaahtecoghe (Scaticoke), 1761,06,00 [ ]°; n.d.
Schafer, Hendrick, Jr., 1752,11,13 (3); 1753,07,18; 1753,09,10 (2)
Schafer, Jacob, 1752,11,13 (3); 1753,07,18; 1753,09,10 (2)
Schafer, Johannis, Jr., 1752,11,13 (3); 1753,07,18; 1753,09,10 (2)
Schefer, Jacob, Jr., 1772,05,08
Schefs, Johannes Wilhelm, 1720,11,01
Schemerhorn, Reyer, 1699,05,19
Schenectady, 1710,07,16; 1711,08,22; 1712,10,31; 1714,04,13; 1714,04,30°; 1733,09,18; 1733,10,16; 1735,10,07; 1736,09,23; 1737,11,12; 1739,01,04; 1739,04,12; 1770,01,05; 1788,04,29; 1887,00,00-1888,00,00 (37); 1887,00,00-1888,00,00 (38)
Schever, John, 1765,02,27
Schoharie, Native American Village, 1710,08,22; 1714,04,09; 1714,04,10; 1714,04,10 (2); 1754,00,00-1755,00,00°; 1755,09,24; 1756,00,00°; 1758,00,00 [ ]; 1758,00,00 [ ] (2); 1758,00,00°; 1763,10,04-17; 1763,11,18; 1764,04,24-05,11 [ ]; 1768,00,00; 1768,11,05; 1794,07,31; 1794,07,31 (2); 1887,00,00-1888,00,00 (09); 1887,00,00-1888,00,00 (10); 1887,00,00-1888,00,00 (40); 1887,00,00-1888,00,00 (44)
Schoharie John, 1755,05,24°
Schoharie Tract, 1768,01,09; 1768,01,09
Schrine, Johannes, 1769,02,08°
Schuyler, Gen., 1779,06,01°; 1791,02,08
Schuyler, Abraham, 1715,02,25
Schuyler, Arent, 1698,05,31; 1699,05,19
Schuyler, David, 1731,05,20; 1734,07,09
Schuyler, John, 1714,11,03; 1714,11,03 (2); 1714,11,03 (3); 1717,06,15; 1722,09,28 ; 1733,11,03
Schuyler, Myndert, 1714,00,00°; 1714,05,08; 1714,06,03; 1714,11,03; 1714,11,03 (2); 1714,11,03 (4); 1714,11,03 (5); 1717,06,15; 1717,06,15°; 1717,06,15°; 1722,09,28; 1723,02,06; 1723,02,06°; 1723,03,07; 1736,05,13; 1737,05,04; 1737,06,16°; 1737,10,15; 1744,04,17; 1751,10,08; 1752,00,00 [ ] (2)p; 1752,05,25; 1753,08,31; 1755,02,28; 1760,04,05; 1760,09,09; 1768,00,00; 1770,00,00°; 1771,00,00°; 1786,01,07; 1794,05,06; 1798,10,29; 1802,00,00°; 1815,04,13; 1815,12,00; 1819,00,00°; 1887,00,00-1888,00,00 (34); n.d.
Schuyler, Peter, 1751,00,00°; 1770,03,00

Schuyler, Philip, 1717,06,15°; 1722,09,28; 1724,08,06; 1724,09,04°; 1733,11,03
Schuyler, The Reverand Mr., 1748,02,04; 1757,05,02; 1775,02,10-16
Scott, 1768,03,02; 1770,07,11
Scott, John Morin (Morine), 1769,06,29; 1770,01,02; 1770,01,02 (2); 1770,07,11 (2); 1806,00,00; n.d.; 1806,00,00
Scott, Marianne, 1735,06,27 [ ]
Scott's Patent, 1770,01,02; 1771,05,03
Scurlock, Thomas, 1739,04,12; 1739,05,17 (5); 1739,05,21°
Seagrove, James, 1769,03,21 (2)
Seals (on Documents), 1733,09,18; 1752,05,01; 1752,05,01 (2); 1768,06,10
Seebar (Seeber), Jacob, 1785,09,00; 1789,00,00; 1790,01,04
Seeler, Jacob, 1789,04,23
Sejehowane, John, 1740,11,24
Seneca, 1722,07,09; 1756,04,22; 1756,05,28; 1756,05,28 (2); 1756,05,28 (3); 1757,09,15-20; 1764,02,01-04
Seth, 1732,05,09; 1733,09,18; 1734,00,00 [ ]; 1734,12,11; 1734,12,11 (2); 1735,12,24; 1736,08,13; 1738,04,10; 1738,10,20; 1751,05,08; 1751,05,23; 1751,05,23 (2); 1752,05,01; 1752,11,09; 1753,05,19; 1753,05,19 (3); 1754,04,27; 1754,06,06 (2); 1754,06,06 (4); 1755,06,01°; 1755,06,02; 1755,06,02 (3); 1756,03,05-05,26; 1757,01,15-25; 1757,02,20-04,01; 1757,05,24; 1758,11,18-12,04; 1769,05,17; 1771,03,07
Seth, Jr., 1754,04,27
Seth, the Younger, 1753,05,19; 1753,05,19 (3)
Seth's Hans (Hance), 1757,05,27-06,07
Sganarady, 1742,00,00-1748,00,00 [ ] °
Shaw, John, 1769,03,21 (2)
Shawnee, 1763,10,04-17
Sheffer, 1769,00,00 [ ]°; 1770,11,15
Shepokass, 1761,12,23
Shirley, William, 1756,04,03; 1756,04,22
Shook, Jacob SEE ALSO Snook, Jacob, 1769,02,08°
Schoomaker, Henry, 1800,04,10; 1800,07,12
Shrine, Johannes, 1769,02,08°
Shuckburgh,1769,05,17
Shuckburgh, Richard, 1739,02,09; 1746,07,07; 1746,07,28; 1754,10,25; 1754,10,25 (2); 1754,11,01
Shuttis's Flats, 1798,10,29
Sidney, 1774,03,24
Sidnich (Sydney?), David, 1815,05,31
Sidnigh (Sidney?), H., 1768,12,01

Sieber, Jacob, 1772,05,08
Sillye, Peter, 1742,10,02 (2)
Six Nations, 1722,09,26; 1752,11,21; 1754,03,01;
    1754,03,05; 1757,02,20-04,01; 1757,09,28;
    1758,05,17; 1763,11,18 [ ]; 1768,11,05;
    1774,01,27; 1775,08,15-09,02; 1783,09,25;
    1814,10,18
Skenewasey SEE ALSO Scanewisse, Sonewesie,
    1751,00,00 [ ]; 1751,00,00°; 1751,05,06
Skinner, Stephen, 1769,12,20; 1769,03,21 (2);
    1770,00,00°; 1770,01,15
Skinner's Patent, 1769,03,21 (2); 1770,00,00°;
    1770,01,15; 1806,11,14; 1822,10,07; n,d,
Smallpox, 1769,03,26-10,07
Smart, George, 1774,08,04
Smith, Christina Ann, n.d.
Smith, David, 1767,02,02
Smith, Edward, 1769,03,21 (2)
Smith, Jacob Henry, n.d.
Smith, R., 1769,06,27
Smith, William, 1768,04,29; 1768,11,08; 1773,02,15
Snowshoes, 1759,02,10; 1764,02,01; 1759,02,10;
    1764,02,01
Snook, Jacob SEE ALSO Shook, Jacob, 1769,03,21
    (5)
Snyder,1774,03,24
Snyder, P., Jr., 1768,12,01
Society for the Propagation of the Gospel,
    1710,08,10°; 1710,09,26; 1713,03,09; 1713,09,07;
    1775,02,10-16
Sonewesie SEE ALSO Scanewisse, Skenewasey,
    1751,05,08
Sopwith, M., 1768,12,01
Soule, Moses, 1795,08,03
Sounistiowan, 1729,09,27
Speaker, 1710,08,22; 1756,02,27; 1757,05,02;
    1764,02,01-04; 1710,08,22
Sporhnheyer, William Ernst, 1763,05,19
Spornheyer, 1762,07,16; 1762,09,25
Staats, 1769,02,09°
Staats, Samuel, 1714,11,11; 1714,11,11 (2);
    1717,06,15; 1724,08,06; 1724,09,04°
Stanburrough, 1771,10,12
Starmbergh, 1757,10,19
Starnberg, Adam, 1753,07,18 (2); 1753,09,10;
    1754,03,19 (2)
Starnberg (Starnbergh; Starnbrough), Jacob SEE
    ALSO Starnberger, Jacob, 1752,05,07;
    1761,10,02; 1770,03,27; 1784,12,18
Starnberg (Starenbergh, Starnbergh), Lambertus
    (Lambartus), 1752,11,13; 1752,11,16; 1753,05,19;
    1753,05,19 (3); 1753,07,18 (2); 1753,09,10;
    1754,03,19 (2); 1754,12,05
Starnberger, 1762,09,20; 1766,07,07
Starnberger, A., 1768,12,01
Starnberger, Abraham, 1785,03,08
Starnberger, Jacob SEE ALSO Starnberg, Jacob,
    1753,06,06; 1754,06,06 (4); 1754,06,06 (7);
    1765,02,27; 1765,09,17; 1768,06,21; 1769,09,30
Starnberger, Lambert SEE ALSO Starnberg,
    Lambertus, 1761,04,07°
Starnberger Patent, 1769,09,30
Stephens, Richard Nassau, 1769,03,21 (2)
Stephenson (Stevenson), James, 1731,06,03;
    1735,02,15; 1735,02,15 (2); 1735,02,15 (3);
    1735,06,10; 1735,06,10 (2); 1735,06,10 (3);
    1735,06,10 (4); 1735,06,10 (5); 1737,07,26
Sternberg, Abraham, 1785,03,08
Sternberg, Jacob SEE Starnberg, Jacob
Sternberg, Nicholas, 1785,03,08
Sternberg, Philip, 1814,06,25 (2)
Sternbergh, David, 1788,04,29; 1788,08,04
Stevens (Stephens), Arent, 1738,03,16; 1739,02,09;
    1751,05,08; 1752,11,16
Stevens, Samuel, 1769,03,21 (2)
Stewart, John, 1769,03,21 (2)
Stewart, Thomas, 1769,03,21 (2)
Stillwater (Still Water), 1746,07,07
Stonaraby, 1761,01,28
Stone, Conrad, 1789,09,23
Stone Creek, 1738,10,20; 1744,04,17; 1752,00,00 [ ]
    (2)
Stone Heap, 1769,00,00 [ ]; 1769,02,08°
Stoneheap Patent, 1770,00,00°
Stontenburgh, Tobias A., 1726,05,24°; 1729,00,00°;
    1753,00,00°; 1819,00,00 [ ]
Stony Brook, 1769,10,24
Stony Creek, 1714,06,12; 1766,10,03; 1766,10,03
    (2); 1767,12,14; 1768,06,10; 1768,06,10 (2)
Strasburgh Patent, 1771,12,04
Stringer, Samuel, 1768,12,13; 1769,01,20;
    1769,01,20 (2)
Stringer's Tract, 1770,05,17
Stuert (Stewart), Robert, 1751,06,10; 1751,09,18;
    1751,10,05
Subsistence, 1710,08,22; 1757,05,04-12
Sullivan Expedition, 1887,00,00-1888,00,00 (35)
Survey, 1710,07,13; 1710,07,20; 1710,07,24;
    1710,07,24 (2); 1714,00,00°; 1720,06,03;
    1722,09,26; 1723,06,20; 1725,00,00°; 1725,10,04;
    1726,04,17°; 1726,04,30; 1726,05,24°;
    1726,10,17; 1726,10,21; 1729,00,00°; 1730,10,29;
    1736,06,17; 1736,12,02°; 1737,10,12; 1738,03,31;

1738,03,31 (2); 1739,05,17 (5); 1750,09,11; 1751,05,23; 1752,05,01; 1752,11,09; 1752,11,21; 1753,00,00°; 1753,05,00°; 1753,09,01; 1753,09,07°; 1753,09,10; 1754,06,06 (2); 1754,06,06 (4); 1754,06,06 (5); 1761,01,28; 1761,04,16; 1761,12,23; 1765,09,22; 1766,11,03°; 1767,06,00; 1768,03,25 (2); 1768,12,29 (2); 1769,01,20 (2); 1769,02,08°; 1769,09,08; 1770,06,28; 1770,11,15; 1771,10,12; 1786,07,27; 1786,07,27 (2); 1790,00,00°; 1802,00,00°; 1819,00,00 [ ]; 1824,00,00; 1887,00,00-1888,00,00 (34); 1887,00,00-1888,00,00 (45); 1896,10,07°; 1896,10,13; n.d.

Survey, Cost of, 1710,09,01 (2)' 1769,00,00 [ ]°; 1770,11,15

Survey, Description of, 1725,11,00(?) [ ]; 1728,04,25; 1729,10,29°; 1730,09,28; 1734,05,30; 1734,10,05; 1734,10,26; 1736,04,14

Survey, Return of, 1726,02,25°; 1726,11,24°; 1727,02,25; 1726,11,24; 1738,03,31; 1738,06,22; 1739,07,07; 1741,10,10; 1743,06,21; 1751,09,17; 1751,09,18; 1752,08,01; 1752,09,22; 1752,11,30 (2); 1753,02,05; 1753,07,16; 1753,09,10; 1753,09,10 (2); 1754,05,01; 1761,06,27; 1761,08,24; 1761,09,00; 1762,09,25; 1765,09,17; 1766,11,20; 1766,11,20 (2); 1767,08,29; 1767,12,14; 1768,06,14°; 1768,07,01; 1768,07,16; 1768,08,02; 1768,11,08; 1768,11,08;1768,12,01 (3); 1768,12,01 (4); 1768,12,13; 1769,06,29; 1769,09,08; 1769,10,24; 1769,11,16; 1769,11,17; 1770,04,12; 1770,05,25; 1770,07,11; 1770,07,11 (2); 1770,07,23 (2); 1771,08,13; 1771,09,17; 1771,09,26; 1772,03,28; 1772,05,08 (2); 1772,07,28; 1773,02,15; 1785,03,24; 1785,09,20; 1786,06,07; 1786,06,26; 1786,07,05; 1789,12,28 (2); 1790,03,01; 1790,03,02; 1792,11,08; 1800,07,12

Survey, Warrant for/of/to, 1714,04,09; 1714,04,10 (2); 1714,06,03; 1723,03,09; 1723,06,20 (2); 1724,08,06; 1724,09,04°; 1725,01,25; 1725,09,29; 1725,10,28 (2); 1725,11,02 (2); 1726,05,02; 1738,03,31 (2); 1756,11,00; 1770,07,27' n.d.

Surveyor, 1710,07,24 (2); 1710,09,01 (2); 1725,00,00°; 1725,11,00(?) [ ]; 1725,09,29; 1725,11,00(?) [ ]; 1728,04,25; 1753,05,00°; 1753,09,01; 1753,09,07°; 1761,04,16; 1765,09,22; 1766,11,03°; 1769,00,00 [ ]°; 1770,11,15; 1785,11,12; 1786,01,04; 1790,00,00°; 1887,00,00-1888,00,00 (45); 1896,10,07°; 1896,10,13; n.d.

Susquehanna, 1757,09,28; 1758,11,00-1759,12,00; 1769,02,08°; 1769,02,09°; 1769,12,20; 1790,00,00°; 1790,09,20; n.d.

Swart, 1757,10,19; 1768,08,04; 1774,03,24; 1887,00,00-1888,00,00 (15)

Swart, J., 1768,12,01

Swart, Josiah, 1761,09,12; 1772,10,24

Swart, Josaias (Joseyas), 1742,08,30; 1742,10,13; 1743,06,21; 1764,03,12

Swart, Wouter, 1736,08,13; 1737,11,12 (2)

Sylvestor (Silvestor), Francis, 1737,10,12

Symon, 1732,05,09

Syms, Lancaster, Jr., 1727,05,06

Tagquatainigo, 1743,06,21

Tamphampamet, 1761,12,23

Targioris, 1732,05,09

Tate, Charles, 1774,08,04 (2)

Taylor, Edward, 1753,10,26; 1754,01,11; 1754,05,01

Taylor, Eve, 1837,09,14

Taylor, George, 1837,09,14

Taylor, John, 1769,00,00 [ ] (2)

Teaondaroge (Teatontaloga), 1695,09,28

Ten Broeck, John, 1786,01,11

Teneaderah, 1769,02,09°

Ten Eyck, 1760,09,09; 1770,00,00°; 1771,00,00°; 1819,00,00°; n.d.

Ten Eyck, Barent, 1751,06,10; 1751,09,18; 1751,10,05; 1769,03,21 (2)

Ten Eyck, J., 1761,07,08; 1761,08,24

Ten Eyck, Jacob, 1760,12,31; 1761,04,16

Ten Eyck, Jacob C., 1751,06,10; 1751,09,18; 1751,10,05

Ten Eyck, Jacob Hendrick, 1761,09,17; 1769,04,24; 1769,05,10

Ten Eyck Patent, 1761,09,17; 1769,05,30

Thom, 1734,04,18

Thomas, 1733,09,18; 1735,12,24; 1735,12,24 (2); 1736,08,13

Tice, Gilbert, 1768,03,25; 1768,12,01; 1769,02,08°; 1769,03,21 (5); 1771,09,21; 1774,01,27

Ticonderoga, 1758,06,21-07,01; 1758,07,16; 1759,02,11-23

Tiendaghe (Tiendega, Tiendaga, Teyendacha) SEE ALSO Hendrick, 1768,06,10; 1768,06,11; 1768,06,14°; 1769,02,08°

Tikjerere (Tekjerere), Esras, 1740,11,24

Tionderogoes (Trindorogoes, Tiondorogua, Tienonderoge, Tienonderoga, Tionnondorage; Tionnonderoga) Creek, 1693,07,22; 1702,11,20; 1703,04,28; 1705,06,28; 1720,06,03; 1724,09,21; 1725,01,00 [ ]; 1725,01,25; 1725,10,04; 1725,10,13; 1725,10,14; 1737,10,12; 1739,01,04;

1739,04,12; 1754,10,25; 1754,10,25 (2); 1754,11,01; 1761,06,00 [ ]° ; 1774,04,15-28
Titchet, J., 1768,12,01
Title, 1710,10,03 [ ]
Tiyorhasara (Tiyahasara, Teahansera, Tyrohannea[?], Tiyahassary) alias Abraham, 1766,10,03 (3); 1768,06,10; 1768,06,11; 1768,06,14°; 1769,02,08°
Todd, Robert, 1739,02,09
To-gri-hed-en-tis, 1763,00,00
Totems SEE ALSO Marks/Signatory, 1711,08,22; 1714,04,13; 1714,04,30°; 1722,07,09; 1723,02,06; 1723,02,12; 1723,05,10; 1726,03,30°; 1732,05,09; 1751,08,24; 1752,05,01; 1887,00,00-1888,00,00 (30); 1887,00,00-1888,00,00 (31); 1887,00,00-1888,00,00 (37) ; 1887,00,00-1888,00,00 (38); 1887,00,00-1888,00,00 (39)
Trade, 1756,02,27
Traile, George, 1769,03,21 (2)
Treaties, 1715,07,09; 1754,08,06; 1768,11,05; 1768,11,18; 1769,03,21 (2); 1769,03,21 (3); 1772,07,28-30; 1774,06,11 [ ]
Truax, Abraham, 1733,11,03; 1738,03,16; 1739,02,09
Tryon,1774,06,11 [ ]
Turner, John, 1769,03,21 (2)
Turtle, 1710,08,22; 1733,09,18; 1738,04,10; 1757,05,27-06,07; 1766,10,03 (3); 1766,10,03 (4)
Tuscarora, 1758,07,02-11
Umphry (Umphrey), James, Jr., 1761,06,29; 1761,12,23
Unanimity, 1757,01,15-25
Upper Fort SEE ALSO Fort, 1887,00,00-1888,00,00 (19); 1887,00,00-1888,00,00 (20)
Upton, Clotworth, 1769,02,09°; 1769,06,20
Ury (Jury, Jurie, Yury, Yurry), Hans (Hanse, Johan), 1738,04,10; 1738,10,20; 1744,04,14; 1752,05,01; 1752,11,09; 1753,05,19; 1753,05,19 (3); 1769,05,17
Van Aken, J., Jr., 1789,09,25
Van Aken, John, 1789,12,30
Van Allen, John, 1769,03,21 (3)
Van Antwerp, Jacobus, 1769,03,21 (3)
Vanbergen, Garret, 1754,05,01
Vanbergens, 1753,08,27; 1753,09,01
Van Bergen, Garet, 1753,10,26
Van Bergen, Martin Garetse, 1737,12,06; 1761,06,29; 1761,12,23; 1762,01,16; 1769,06,29
Van Bergen, Pieter, 1722,09,28
Van Bergen, William, 1761,06,29; 1761,12,23
Van Bergen's Land, 1771,05,24

Van Brugh (Van Burgh Vonbrugh), Peter, 1714,11,03; 1714,11,03 (2); 1732,09,25; 1736,05,13; 1737,05,04; 1737,06,16°; 1737,10,15; 1744,04,17; 1752,00,00 [ ] (2); 1768,00,00
Van Cortlandt, A., 1752,06,24 (2); 1770,00,00°; 1771,00,00°; 1819,00,00°; n.d.
Van Cortlandt, Augustus, 1752,05,25; 1752,09,22; 1753,02,19; 1753,03,11
Van Cortlandt Patent SEE Cortlandt Patent
Van Dam, Rip (Van Damet), 1714,11,11; 1714,11,11 (2); 1717,06,15; 1717,06,15°; 1722,09,28; 1724,08,06; 1724,09,04°; 1725,11,02 (3)
Vander Heyden, David, 1764,01,20; 1764,02,27 [ ]
Van Driessen, Petrus, 1731,06,24; 1731,09,25; 1732,05,09; 1732,09,15
Van Dyck, Jacob, 1753,09,13
Van Dyck, Jacobus, 1754,11,01
Van Dyck, John, 1753,05,29; 1753,09,13
Van Epps (Eps), J. C., 1785,09,27; 1785,09,27 (2); 1785,09,27 (3)
Van Eps (Epps), John, 1785,09,28 (2)
Van Eps (Epps), John Baptist, 1754,06,06 (3); 1754,06,06 (4); 1754,06,06 (6); 1785,09,28 (2)
Van Eps (Epps), John Baptist, Jr., 1739,02,09
Van Horne, Abraham, 1738,10,05; 1738,10,24°
Van Patten (Van Patton), Arent, 1737,11,12
Van Rensselaer (Van Renselaer), Henry, Jr., 1738,03,16
Van Rensselaer (Van Renselaer), Jeremiah, 1788,02,20; 1796,00,00(?) [ ]; 1796,00,00°; 1796,02,03
Van Rensselaer (Van Renselaer), John Baptist, 1744,05,11
Van Rensselaer (Van Renselaer), Stephen, 1758,11,18-12,04
Van Schaack, Henry, 1769,12,16
Van Sconover (Schoonhoven), Dirck B., 1754,04,27; 1755,02,05
Van Sicker, A., 1768,12,01
Van Slyke, 1786,10,16 (3); 1789,01,31; 1789,12,28 (2)
Van Slyke (Van Slyck), Albert, 1748,02,04
Van Slyke (Van Slyck), Cornelius, 1728,11,07
Van Slyke (Van Slyck), Martinus, 1711,00,00°; 1731,00,00°; 1887,00,00-1888,00,00 (41)
Van Slyke (Van Slyck), Nicholas A., 1785,09,28
Van Slyke (Van Slyck), William, 1789,04,14
Van Veghton, Volkert, 1738,04,10; 1738,05,05°; 1739,05,17 (3)
Van Wy[ ]k, Catherine, 1727,02,25; 1726,11,24; 1727,05,06
Vaughn, 1766,10,18

Vedder (Veder), Lucas, 1766,10,03; 1766,10,03 (2); 1768,03,25; 1768,03,25 (2)
Verbergh, 1726,12,20
Vergerau, Peter, 1766,12,27 [ ]; 1766,12,27°; 1766,12,27°
Verplank, Phillip, 1725,00,00°; 1725,11,00(?) [ ]; 1728,04,25; n.d.
Vischer, John T., 1789,12,28; 1790,01,04
Vroneger, Anna, 1733,03,26
Vrooman (Vroman; Vrouman), 1758,07,02-11; 1768,06,08-28; 1771,03,15
Vrooman (Vroman; Vrouman), Adam, 1708,08,05; 1711,00,00°; 1711,08,22; 1713,07,01; 1714,04,09; 1714,04,10; 1714,04,10 (2); 1714,04,10 (3); 1714,04,13; 1714,04,30°; 1714,06,12; 1714,07,12; 1714,08,01; 1714,08,06°; 1714,08,23°; 1714,08,26; 1714,08,26 (2); 1714,08,26 (3); 1714,08,26 (4); 1714,08,26°; 1714,09,05; 1714,09,05; 1715,06,09; 1715,07,09; 1722,07,09; 1723,02,06; 1723,02,06°; 1723,03,07; 1725,10,28 (2); 1725,11,00(?) [ ]; 1725,11,02; 1725,11,02 (2); 1726,02,03; 1726,02,04; 1726,02,04 (2); 1726,02,26; 1726,04,17°; 1726,10,17; 1726,10,21; 1731,00,00°; 1750,12,14; 1768,06,10; 1768,08,04; 1769,04,17; 1769,04,26; 1769,10,24; 1770,03,19; 1770,06,28; 1777,02,20 [ ]; 1887,00,00-1888,00,00 (37); 1887,00,00-1888,00,00 (38); 1887,00,00-1888,00,00 (41); 1887,00,00-1888,00,00 (44); 1910,11,14
Vrooman (Vroman; Vrouman), B., 1752,11,16
Vrooman (Vroman; Vrouman), Barent, 1742,10,13; 1743,06,21; 1743,07,14; 1763,12,05-22; 1770,02,02
Vrooman (Vroman; Vrouman), Bartholomew, 1742,08,30l; 1742,10,13; 1743,06,21; 1743,07,12; 1743,07,14; 1771,03,07; 1771,09,28; 1771,09,28°; 1887,00,00-1888,00,00 (26)
Vrooman, Cornelius, 1887,00,00-1888,00,00 (26
Vrooman (Vroman; Vrouman), Grietje, 1715,02,25; 1735,07,04; 1735,07,05
Vrooman (Vroman; Vrouman), Hendrick, 1738,03,16 (2)
Vrooman (Vroman; Vrouman), Isaac, 1726,05,24°; 1729,00,00°; 1753,00,00°; 1769,11,00; 1819,00,00 [ ]; n.d.
Vrooman (Vroman; Vrouman), Lawrence, 1726,05,24°; 1729,00,00°; 1753,00,00°; 1819,00,00 [ ]; n.d.
Vrooman (Vroman; Vrouman), Martinis, 1742,10,13; 1743,06,21; 1743,07,14
Vrooman (Vroman; Vrouman), Peter, 1726,02,26; 1726,05,24°; 1752,05,01; 1768,10,10°; 1771,03,07; 1771,09,28; 1771,09,28°; 1773,08,26; 1787,05,07; 1887,00,00-1888,00,00 (26); 1946,00,00
Vrooman (Vroman; Vrouman), Wouter (Wooter), 1731,02,12°; 1731,07,12; 1736,09,23
Vrooman (Vroman; Vrouman) Land, 1731,02,12°; 1731,07,12; 1754,00,00-1755,00,00°; 1758,00,00°; 1763,00,00; 1770,05,09 (2); 1887,00,00-1888,00,00 (10); 1887,00,00-1888,00,00 (18); 1887,00,00-1888,00,00 (42)
Wadman(?), P, 1768,12,01
Waggoner (Wagoner), Peter, 1722,03,09; 1723,03,04; 1725,04,03
Waggoner's Patent, 1773,09,04
Wallace, Hugh, 1771,10,25
Walter Franklin Patent, 1770,06,20
Wampum, 1757,05,04-12; 1757,05,24; 1757,08,01-21; 1760,06,29-1761,07,03
Wanner, Michael, 1751,10,07; 1752,11,09; 1752,11,09 (2); 1752,11,30; 1752,12,01; 1753,07,16
Warfare, 1698,05,31; 1746,12,13-1747,11,07; 1747,04,29°; 1748,07,28; 1757,05,24; 1757,05,27-06,07; 1757,09,28; 1758,05,30; 1760,08,05; 1764,03,10; 1790,00,00 [ ]; 1790,00,00°; 1791,02,08; 1887,00,00-1888,00,00 (05); 1887,00,00-1888,00,00 (36)
Warrel, Joseph, 1731,06,03; 1735,02,15; 1735,02,15 (2); 1735,02,15 (3); 1735,06,10; 1735,06,10 (2); 1735,06,10 (3); 1735,06,10 (4); 1735,06,10 (5); 1737,07,26
Wary, 1733,09,18
Wattles, Sluman, 1790,09,20
Watts, John, 1806,11,14
Watts, Robert, 1770,07,27
Weaver, Hendrick, 1753,06,06; 1753,08,27; 1753,09,01; 1753,09,07°; 1753,10,18°; 1753,10,26; 1754,01,11; 1754,05,01; 1754,06,06 (4); 1754,06,06 (4); 1769,07,17
Webb, 1753,04,14
Webb, Joseph, Jr., 1752,11,30 (2)
Weber, J., 1768,12,01
Weeks, Samuel, 1785,09,27 (2); 1786,00,00; 1786,10,16 (3); 1789,01,31 (3); 1789,03,19; 1789,03,19 (4); 1789,12,28 (2)
Weiser, 1720,11,01
Weiser, Conrad, 1750,08,25-10,13; 1753,09,02
Weiser, John C., Jr., 1722,03,09; 1722,07,09; 1723,03,04; 1723,05,10; 1724,01,20; 1725,04,03
Weiser (Visger, Wizer, Wyser), John Conrad, 1715,02,25; 1715,02,28; 1715,06,09; 1715,07,09; 1718,07,07

Weisersdorf, 1887,00,00-1888,00,00 (14)
Wemp, Hendrick, 1738,03,16
Wemp, John, 1728,11,07; 1736,08,13; 1737,11,12; 1737,11,12 (2); 1737,12,16
Wemp's Land, 1741,10,10
Wemple, Hendrick, 1761,09,25-1771,10,13; 1766,09,28 [ ]°
Wendell, Evert, 1710,07,19°;
Wendell, Harmanus, 1710,07,19°; 1714,05,28;
Westerlo, Catherine, 1786,06,26
Wharton, Samuel, 1769,02,09°
Whetherhead (Weatherhead), John, 1769,02,08°; 1769,03,21 (3); 1769,11,16; 1769,11,17; 1769,12,20
White, Alexander, 1771,09,17; 1772,01,27
White, John, 1734,10,26
Wiefield, 1770,00,00°; 1770,01,05; 1819,00,00°; n.d.
Wildman (Wileman), 1714,11,03; 1714,11,03 (2)
Wilkinson, J., 1768,12,01
Willem, 1732,05,09
Willet, 1785,05,05
Willett, Marinus, 1769,03,21 (2)
William, 1771,03,07
Williams, 1735,06,27 [ ]
Williams, Charles, 1734,10,26; 1735,02,15 (2); 1735,06,10 (4); 1789,12,30
Williams, Thomas, 1734,10,03 (2)
Williams Tract, 1735,06,10 (3); 1735,06,10 (4)
Willmot, Anne, 1734,05,30 (2); 1734,10,26; 1735,02,15; 1735,06,10 (2); 1735,08,29 (3)
Wilson, James, 1770,03,27
Windecker (Vindeker), Hartman, 1724,04,08
Winne (Win), John, 1760,04,05; 1785,02,27; 1786,10,16 (3)
Winne, William, 1760,04,05
Wistray, 1733,09,18
Wolf, 1710,08,22; 1733,09,18; 1766,10,03 (3); 1766,10,03 (5)
Women, 1733,09,18; 1734,12,11; 1738,10,20; 1744,04,14; 1744,09,02; 1752,11,09; 1753,09,02; 1754,06,06; 1756,03,05-05,26; 1758,07,02-11; 1758,11,18-12,04; 1759,02,11-23; 1764,01,02-31; 1766,05,24-27; 1771,03,15; 1772,05,08; 1783,09,25; 1887,00,00-1888,00,00 (17)
Wood, M., 1789,04,14
Wood, William, 1770,00,00 (2); 1770,04,04; 1770,07,11 (2); 1770,07,13; 1770,07,13 (3)
Wraxall, Peter, 1710,00,00; 1714,05,28
Wray, Catharine, 1786,01,11
Wyngaard, Luykas Johannis (Johannes), 1751,04,03
Yacomine, 1733,09,18
Yagoughsitawawanie, 1731,07,13
Yeats (Yates), 1761,09,25-1771,10,13
York, 1736,06,26; 1752,09,18
York, Lewis, 1725,00,00°; 1725,02,10; 1725,10,28 (2); 1725,11,00(?) [ ]; 1725,11,02; 1725,11,02 (2); 1726,02,03; 1726,02,04; 1726,02,04 (2); 1726,02,10°; 1730,02,10; 1730,07,30; 1730,07,31; n.d.1770,07,31
York, Nicholas, 1723,02,06; 1723,02,06°; 1723,03,07; 1723,03,09; 1723,06,20; 1723,06,20 (2); 1723,06,27; 1723,06,28; 1728,08,28; 1742,10,02 (2); 1744,04,16°; 1744,09,02; 1750,12,14; 1752,00,00 [ ]; 1752,09,18; 1752,10,05; 1753,09,13; 1754,11,06; 1755,05,31
York, William, 1723,02,06; 1723,02,06°; 1723,03,07; 1723,03,09; 1723,06,00; 1723,06,20; 1723,06,20 (2); 1723,06,27; 1723,06,28; 1725,00,00°; 1725,02,10; 1725,10,28; 1725,10,28 (2); 1725,11,00(?) [ ]; 1725,11,02; 1725,11,02 (2); 1726,02,03; 1726,02,04 1726,02,04 (2); 1726,02,10°; 1728,00,00 [ ]°; 1728,02,00; 1728,04,25; 1728,08,28; 1728,11,00(?) [ ]; 1730,02,10; 1752,10,05; 1770,07,31; n.d.1770,07,31
York Patent, 1766,10,03 (6); 1766,10,03 (8)
Young, 1767,06,00
Young, David, 1822,10,07
Young, David Elias, 1806,11,14
Young, Elias, 1822,10,07
Young, F[rederick], 1761,09,00; 1769,02,08°
Young, J., 1752,11,16
Young, P., 1768,12,01
Young and Livingston Patent, 1822,10,07
Young Men, 1757,02,20-04,01; 1764,02,01-04
Young's Patent, 1765,10,11; 1794,04,01; 1794,05,10
Zee, Adam, 1770,09,27
Zeelie, SEE ALSO Zielle, 1768,08,04
Zeely, P. SEE ALSO Zeelie; Zielle, 1768,12,01
Zehe, Adam, 1751,06,10; 1751,09,18; 1751,10,05; 1752,02,21
Zehe, Christian, 1751,10,07; 1752,11,09; 1752,11,09 (2); 1752,11,30; 1752,12,01; 1753,07,16; 1754,03,19
Zehe, Johannis (Johannes), 1751,10,07; 1752,11,09; 1752,11,09 (2); 1752,11,30; 1752,12,01; 1753,07,16; 1754,03,19
Zenger, John Peter, 1728,02,00; 1728,04,25; 1730,07,31
Zielle, Adam SEE ALSO Zeelie; Zeely, 1762,03,10
Ziellie, Annatie U. (V.) SEE ALSO Zeelie; Zeely, 1753,05,29; 1753,05,29 (2)
Ziellie, Peter U. SEE ALSO Zeelie; Zeely, 1753,05,29

Zimmer, 1774,03,24
Zimmer (Zemer), George, 1753,06,06; 1754,06,06 (4); 1754,06,06 (5); 1754,06,06 (6); 1765,02,27; 1765,09,17; 1768,12,01; 1769,09,30
Zimmer, Jacob, 1753,06,06; 1754,06,06 (4); 1754,06,06 (7); 1765,02,27; 1766,06,14; 1766,10,03 (5); 1768,08,02; 1768,12,01; 1768,12,29; 1768,12,29 (2); 1785,00,00-1791,00,00; 1794,05,05
Zimmer, Petrus, 1765,02,27; 1768,12,01; 1769,09,30
Zimmer, William, 1769,09,30

www.ingramcontent.com/pod-product-compliance
Lightning Source LLC
Chambersburg PA
CBHW081841230426
43669CB00018B/2778